Human conflict in Shakespeare

S. C. BOORMAN

Human Conflict in Shakespeare

Routledge and Kegan Paul

LONDON AND NEW YORK

First published in 1987 by
Routledge & Kegan Paul Ltd
11 New Fetter Lane, London EC4P 4EE

Published in the USA by
Routledge & Kegan Paul Inc.
in association with Methuen Inc.
29 West 35th Street, New York, NY 10001

Set in 10 on 12 pt Sabon
by Inforum Ltd, Portsmouth
and printed in Great Britain
by T.J. Press (Padstow) Ltd
Padstow, Cornwall

Library of Congress Cataloging in Publication Data

Boorman, S. C. (Stanley C.)
    Human conflict in Shakespeare.

    Bibliography: p.
    Includes indexes.
    1. Shakespeare, William, 1564–1616—Characters.
2. Interpersonal conflict in literature. 3. Characters
and characteristics in literature.   I. Title.
PR2989.B66   1987   822.3'3   87–4668
ISBN 0–7102–1164–3

British Library CIP Data also available

1

Contents

Introduction		vii
Part 1	Forms of human conflict	1
	(a) Soul–body	1
	(b) Immortal–mortal	2
	(c) Greatness–littleness	3
	(d) Freedom–fate	5
	(e) Reason–unreason (control of self—lack of control)	5
	(f) Reason–love (man and woman)	12
	(g) Reason–fantasy	16
	(h) Private man–public man	18
	(i) Order–disorder	24
	(j) Justice–mercy	26
Part 2	(a) Human conflict in early English drama	29
	(b) Human conflict in plays of Shakespeare's contemporaries	43
Part 3	Human conflict in Shakespeare	67
	Introduction	67
	Comedies	69
	English History plays	100
	Classical plays	113
	Tragedies R+J sechon.	138
	Retrospect	252
	The last plays	257
Appendix 1	Marlow's *Doctor Faustus*	271
Appendix 2	Comedy and tragedy in drama	281
Notes		285
Indexes		
1	Elizabethan (non-dramatic) references	311
2	Shakespeare's plays: (a) titles (b) characters	314
3	Non-Shakespearean plays: titles	319
4	General	321

Introduction

Human beings, by the very fact of being human, have always known the pressures within themselves of conflicting impulses, purposes and needs. This complex of personal inner forces I shall denote throughout this book by the term 'human conflict', as in my title, and by other equivalent terms such as '(human) tension', '(human) discord' and so on. In every case, according to the context, I shall be referring, either to this intrinsic quality of our nature which makes us inevitably and deeply aware of the incongruity between the urges within that nature, and so subject to major personal tensions, or to the subsequent effort which we may feel forced to make to find some relief from these tensions. Sometimes the stress within us will be extreme, and our attempts to ease it will be full of pain and even desperation; sometimes the incongruity will be less urgent and disruptive, and we can then accept it, even happily. As any study of them shows, the Elizabethans, like earlier and later people, knew such inner struggles, and expressed them and their results in many ways; therefore their human conflict forms a common ground upon which we today can meet them, and understand both themselves and their outward expression of that conflict.

Believing as I do that there is now a special need to assert anew what I would call the true human approach to the understanding and appreciation of Shakespeare's dramatic works (as of all literature), I seek in this book to show the effects of the human conflict known to Shakespeare and to his audience upon his plays as conceived and as performed; to do this in proper depth, I have considered it essential, also, to give some preliminary indications of the same inner tensions at work in earlier English drama, and in plays by Shakespeare's contemporaries.

Such tensions lie at the root of creative writing. This writing, interpretative rather than merely descriptive, can be seen as the result of the writer's urge to express to other human beings, directly or indirectly, and by means of verbal skills, his or her awareness of the business of living and of dying, as the writer experiences or conceives that awareness. Creative writing is therefore essentially concerned with human conflict, its trials, its delights and its demands, and as this conflict is known to every individual and so to all mankind, in the past as in the present, such writing can achieve that combination of the universal and the particular, the universal in the particular, which evokes both its immediate and its lasting significance for the reader. The conscious techniques or intuitive choices of verbal usages (often an infinitely various mixture of both) which are intended to convey the purpose or desire of the writer, may produce what can be called 'formations of language' that are in harmony with deep-seated perceptions of the human spirit, and therefore in themselves may give the reader or hearer a special satisfaction. But this so-called 'aesthetic' pleasure, and its techniques, cannot be fully experienced or considered in isolation, for it is a quality of the means by which the conscious or subconscious aims of the writer are expressed, just as the special nature of a great violinist's performance exists only in relation to the creative need or purpose of the composer of the music performed — what finally matters is the successful communication of that creative need or purpose.

These considerations, while of importance for understanding creative writing generally, are of especial importance for understanding dramatic writing, creative writing designed primarily to be conveyed in speech and action on a stage. Since personal discord is a matter of tensions (pleasant or unpleasant) in and between human beings, and of the effects of such tensions on individuals and on their fellows, and since drama, from its recorded beginnings, has been basically devoted to the direct portrayal or suggestion of the encounters of human life, offering its audience a physical and verbal microcosm of Man's existence, it is not surprising that drama should have shown itself particularly well fitted to give its audience the strongest and most immediate impression of human stress, the fullest sense of the sadness and delight, the terror and the beauty, of being alive. In this process, the actors are representatives of the audience (which exists both as individuals and as a unified body), and also living exponents of the dramatist's awareness of Man's struggles, expressed in the play for the audience to recognise and share with him. Thus the dramatist's text, words-in-combination conceived within the special added dimension of physical interpretation upon a stage, often creates a unique vitality and impact working both inside and outside the spectator, and this in turn leads him or her to a complex experience which will be noted more than once in the course of this work (see, for example pp. 68–9 below).

⌈In Shakespeare's plays, especially, human conflict is shown at work in character-in-situation, and can be shown fully only in this way; in drama (as in all other forms of creative writing, as in life itself) the human presence can never appear in isolation from its circumstances and setting. Every major character in a Shakespeare play starts its stage life in a primary situation, which includes other characters; this character's original nature and situation are postulated, as it were, by the dramatist early in the play; thereafter, the character's 'given' nature, with its accompanying forms of inner pressure, is presented by Shakespeare as modifying his situation; the situation thus modified is in turn shown to affect the working of his human discord – and so on, in an often complex process, a 'chain reaction' to which I shall frequently refer in Part 3.⌋ However, Shakespeare's plots and characters usually seem to be decided by a borrowed story, sometimes known (at least in outline) to his audience, and cannot easily be altered by him. But, as I shall show, his chief attention seems to be increasingly directed to the dramatic potentialities of inner struggle as portrayed in the 'chain reaction'. So he must have seen such potentialities implicit within the story that he wished to use, and known that they could be made to provide much of the dramatic interest of his play. Having selected his story, his creative dramatic powers are then used chiefly to convince his audience that the main shape and outcome of the once apparently predetermined story, as modified, are the natural and probable, even inevitable, results of human stress as he shows it working within the play. To examine this process is my chief purpose in Part 3, as also to show that sometimes it does not happen completely; for example, the first half of *Measure for Measure* suggests and portrays complexities of human stress which are then virtually ignored in the plot-manipulation and contrived ending of the second half (see pp. 91–100 below).

Shakespeare's use of Man's incongruities for comedy or for tragedy, or for significant mixtures of both, varies with each play, as Part 3 will show in some detail. This section will also show that every form of such incongruities in his drama, as in life, can produce anything from comedy to tragedy, according to the circumstances in which it operates and the dramatist's ways of presenting its effects, and that this becomes apparent only if the plays are constantly considered in relation to other plays in the canon rather than in isolation; an instance is the variety of comic and serious dramatic results of the reason–unreason conflict of the concept of 'honour' as seen in Coriolanus, Troilus, Parolles and Falstaff in their plays. Thus Part 3 will also demonstrate that this examination of Shakespeare's awareness and use of personal discords offers a way of seeing his dramatic work as a whole, despite the many differences between plays which have so often tended to fragment Shakespearean criticism.

In Part 1 I have described only certain major forms of human stress of which Elizabethans and their predecessors were especially conscious in their own natures and lives. This necessarily brief account is intended to supply reference-points to which the reader, whether at my prompting or not, can relate the more particular manifestations of such forms, and connected forms, shown in the plays discussed in Parts 2 and 3.

Parts 2(a) and (b) are obviously not meant to be a complete or detailed history and analysis of English drama before and during the age of Shakespeare. They are, however, designed to describe, with numerous examples, the ways in which English play-makers, from the beginnings of English drama, showed themselves conscious of the essentially dramatic quality of the joys and conflicts of Man's nature, and used them, both implicitly and explicitly, as the natural inspiration and material of their drama. Thus Parts 1 and 2 show, however briefly, the basic forms of human conflict, and the long and continuous tradition of the dramatic use of such forms, and related forms, so that we may see the setting for Shakespeare's use of them, and thus understand his plays more deeply and truly in a larger human and artistic context.

In Part 3 I come to the main purpose of this work, to describe in detail how these waring impulses, and their effects on people and their lives, are embodied and displayed at work in the plays of Shakespeare. There we shall find, in addition, an old but here especially effective use of what may be called 'social conflicts',[1] where the results of human conflicts within and between individuals take on a wider significance; often the society in which these individuals live and strive upon the stage is itself shown by Shakespeare to be affected by forms of this collective incongruity which members of the audience can recognise as relevant to their own social experience. But I must stress the fact that such forms of social human incongruity (matters, for example, of disorder–order or public man–private man) are always presented dramatically by

Introduction

Shakespeare through personal struggles, on which the primary emphasis is placed. Indeed, his special gifts of perception and deep understanding of these struggles and their effects are the source of his unique quality as a dramatist, and they will be seen to be active throughout his plays, affecting his technical methods and media, his conception of his characters and their acts and relationships, and finally his creation of human truth in the theatre and of the total effect of each play upon his audiences and still today upon us. I must make it clear that I do not suggest that Shakespeare ever wrote a play consciously in order to show the workings of human conflict as such; I am writing of the real Shakespeare-the-dramatist who was always chiefly (but not exclusively) concerned with effective presentation of dramatic entertainment for his audience, not of that Shakespeare who sometimes seems to be created mainly to furnish support for academic theories. But I do assert, and show, that Shakespeare, like earlier and contemporary dramatists, certainly sought to represent the nature of human beings active within a dramatic story, for the delighted and/or uneasy but interested recognition by the audience that this nature was inescapably their own. Thus, inevitably, the warfare of our nature and its results are of the essence of his drama; to appreciate this is to understand the greatness of so much of his work, and its relevance and importance to his age and our own.

⌐Therefore the basis of my treatment of Shakespeare's plays in Part 3 is the conviction that he is always seeking to make his characters behave as human beings might well behave in the contrived situations in which he first places them, and that in fact he increasingly shows those situations themselves changing under the pressures of the characters. It is thus necessary to accept the living quality of those characters, however selective or extraordinary it may be, their human reality which all audiences instinctively recognise, and which makes them dramatically effective in their particular situations⌐ After a critic has accepted this as his essential primary approach, he is then of course at liberty to see the characters also as symbols, metaphors, archetypes or what you will, and in addition, perhaps, to consider the plays in which they appear as akin to philosophical or metaphysical or linguistic analogies. Where the likelihood of such interpretations is related to evidence of the thoughts and feelings, the general outlook on life, of the Elizabethans, they can add much to our grasp of the plays; otherwise, they throw light (sometimes a very curious light) mainly upon the critic or his society. This may certainly be valuable in itself, but for the understanding and appreciation of

Shakespeare's plays no critic's personality, no personal or social preoccupation, is by itself important, no matter how novel or interesting it may be.

I hope that this book may also remind modern producers and their actors of the human values of Shakespeare's plays, and so encourage them to seek, above all, to convey fully to their audiences that insight into the truths of our human nature which constitutes the abiding importance of these plays. Today critics and stage-folk alike seem greatly exercised by what they feel to be the 'gap' between Shakespeare's plays and his modern audience; it appears to be taken for granted that the modern conception of drama is far from the Elizabethan conception. So there arises the dangerous assumption that every play by Shakespeare must, in production, be 're-interpreted' to a modern audience. Such 're-interpretation' frequently appears to involve using the Elizabethan text largely as a basis for alterations, and modifying the nature of the story and the characters, thus radically altering the plain significance of the play. The result is that modern audiences are often offered a performance which, however much it may cater for presumed modern taste, and however profitable it may be in box-office terms, is a long way from what Shakespeare actually provided. This assumption that we no longer feel that interest in the tensions of human nature which for Elizabethans produced the main attraction of the plays, is in fact entirely false; it is surely obvious that our age, more even than the Elizabethan, is deeply, sometimes anxiously, concerned about the fundamental complexities of human nature and the business of living in a world that, like Shakespeare's, is at once beautiful, amusing and threatening. The present work may serve to show that to allow Shakespeare's plays to display such fundamental complexities in action on the stage is to remind modern audiences, vividly and movingly, that they too know and share them, and to give them that special experience, born of mingled pleasure and disturbance, which is the gift of all good drama. In short, I would insist that a scrupulous, sincere and reasonably humble attempt to understand the nature of the plays as they exist, followed by a feeling and intelligent effort to present that understanding directly in words and action on the stage, will certainly show that there is no essential 'gap' between Shakespeare's plays and a modern audience. Indeed, it may even show that financial success does at times reward professional wisdom and integrity.

The vital thing remains to be said. This work is the product of many years of study and of thinking and feeling, not only about Shakespeare's plays and their background, but about life in general. It has evolved slowly, and in the process has given me great pleasure, unaffected by those periods of personal frustration, doubt and irritation which always (I am told) disturb the domestic harmony of an author. That it has reached its present form, however imperfect, without any such difficulty, is due entirely to the unfailing patience, encouragement and sympathetic understanding of my wife, and it is therefore to her that it must most justly, and most gratefully, be dedicated.

PART ONE

Forms of human conflict

(a) Soul–body

Our analysis of the forms of human conflict as they existed in the
consciousness of Elizabethans must begin with the religious tradition
into which they were born. Although even non-religious man has his
inevitable sense of his personal inner struggles, the Christian religion
is primarily concerned with this as the essence of the human condition, and it was religion that lay at the root of the Elizabethans'
awareness of it. The basic teaching of the Church was that Man[1] was
an uneasy combination of soul and body; the body was not to be
considered as a mere regrettable clog fastened upon the spiritual part
of Man (although the Puritans came very near to this view); it could
be seen as a necessary accompaniment to the soul, presenting in its
incongruity a challenge to Man in his daily life. All the traditional
teaching of the Church on this matter stressed the difference between
the soul and the body. The new and growing humanism which the ←
age also inherited accepted this difference, the Church's view that in
the soul was goodness and the hope of salvation, and in the body the
impermanent yet possibly fatal source of weakness and evil. A
forceful description of this form of Man's dichotomy is a passage
from Erasmus's *Enchiridion* written at the beginning of the sixteenth
century (but here as translated into English in 1534):

> A Man is than[then] a certayn monstrous
> beest compact togyder of partes, two or thre
> of great dyuersite. Of a soule, as of a certeyne
> goodly thynge: and of a body, as it were a brute
> or dombe beest. For certeynly, we so greatly
> excell not al other kyndes of brute beestes
> in perfytnes of body but that we in al his
> natural gyftes, are founde to them inferyours:
> as concernyng ye soule veryly, we be so
> receyuable of ye diuyne nature: that we may

1

surmount aboue the nature of angels and be
vnyt[united], knyt, and made one with god. Yf
thy body had not ben added to the[thee] thou
haddest ben a celestial or godly thyng. Yf this
mynde had not ben graffed in the[thee] playnly
thou haddest ben a brute beest. These two natures
bytwene them self so diuerse: that excellent
werkman had coupled togyder with blessed
concorde. But the serpent the enemy of peace,
put them asonder agayn with vnhappy discorde:
so yt now they neyther can be seperate, without
very great turment and payn neyther lyue ioyned
togyder, without continual warre.[2]

At the end of the Elizabethan period a very popular preacher is
making the same point:

> So man is created by God, *tanquam medius
> inter angelum & brutu*, a middling betweene an
> Angell, and a brute; being a good deale better
> then a beast, and a little[q] lower then an Angell.
> Hauing in respect of his body, something of a
> bruit, being sensuall and mortall; and in respect
> of his soule, something of an Angell, as being
> intellectuall and immortall[3]

q Psalm 8.5.

(b) Immortal–mortal

Thus Elizabethan man saw himself, to begin with, as a mixture of
soul and body, and so capable of being at once far more than mere
Man, and far less. With the awareness of this basic disparity was
joined the more immediate, everyday knowledge (reinforced by
religion) that the body would one day die. Indeed, considering
Elizabethan living conditions, the prevalence of the plague, the
scarcity of food in the 1590s and 1600s, and the still medieval state
of Elizabethan medicine, every Elizabethan must have been acutely
conscious of death as a close companion in his daily life. Yet, like
Man in every age, he held death at bay in the recesses of his mind, and
usually lived as if he were immortal. So Thomas Nashe wrote in
1593:

> We see great men dye, strong men dye,

2

wittie[clever] men dye, fooles dye, rich
Merchants, poor Artificers, Plowmen,
Gentlemen, high men, low men, wearish[sickly] men,
grosse men, and the fairest complexioned
[most healthy] men die, yet we perswade
our selues wee shall neuer dye. Or if we
do not so perswade our selues, why prepare
wee not to dye? Why doe wee raigne as Gods
on the earth, that are to bee eaten with
wormes?[4]

(c) Greatness–littleness

So an Elizabethan felt himself to be the meeting-place, the battleground, of the incongruities of soul and body, immortality and
mortality. At times he could see himself as a unique miracle of
ennobled clay; as a preacher said in a sermon in the early 1600s:

Who can sufficiently expresse or wonder
enough at the excellencie of man, so little a
creature made but of the dust? That he
by contemplation should soare vp to the
skies, and be able to discourse of the
motions, aspects, and effects of the
celestiall orbe; that he should ride vpon the
Seas, and search, and passe ouer the liquid
floods; that he should vendicate[claim] both
earth and sea vnto his profit, and domineere
ouer the beasts, and know the nature of all the
creatures; that he should contriue the Arts
and Sciences to a methode, and being absent
to speak to men farre distant by letters
written, that he should in this mortalitie
seeke after immortalitie, and haue a seate
prepared for him in heauen, after life ended
here on earth . . . No tongue is able to express[5]

Here speaks an age that, for a moment, can look with amazement
and pride at the new developments in both intellectual and physical
exploration of its world, a world growing daily more extended and
more various. Yet always behind this remains the thought of the
other dimension of Man, the once wholly divine creature brought by

→ the Fall within the reach of impermanence and sin. Sir George More in 1597 expresses the more specifically religious view of this conflict:

> double is the nature of man, and a perfect
> man is a double man in him selfe, one without,
> and another within: without[outside] his body
> is man, and within his minde, so as there is
> both an outward, and an inward man, and both
> in one, if that one have the perfection of a
> man. . . . (Man) being considered in his beginning,
> and after his ende truly as he is, by an auntient
> Father, is sayed to be, *Semen immundum, cibus*
> *vermium, post hominem vermis, post vermen faetor et horror.*
> Vncleane seed, wormes meate, after a man a worme,
> (after a worme) an ill sauor and a horror. Which
> two natures in man, as they were found to differ,
> so were they by name distinguished even at the
> first; the first earthly man being of the
> Hebrewes called *Adam*, as *homo tanquam ex humo*
> (man inasmuch as from earth), and the other
> heauenly of the Chaldeans *Enoch*, which signifieth
> true man[6] Ambros de Isa et anima.

Bernard Meditau

An ordinary Elizabethan may not have fully appreciated the authority of the Church Fathers, St Bernard and St Ambrose, to whom More is appealing, but certainly he felt within him the two natures of which the passage speaks, and with that realisation, the extent of his inner discord as a human being. He would have accepted as a truism that he was a soul and a body, each pulling him in an opposite direction; he would have feared death, and yet hoped that death was not the end; he would have aspired to great and memorable achievements in this life (the Elizabethan age was an age of ambition), and yet have been constantly aware of his littleness and impermanence as a mere sinful creature. Sir John Davies summed up the feeling thus:

> I know my bodie's of so frail a kind,
> As force without, feavers within can kill;
> I know the heavenly nature of my minde,
> But 'tis corrupted both in wit and will:
>
> I know my *Soule* hath power to know all things,
> Yet she is blind and ignorant in all;

I know I am one of Nature's little kings,
Yet to the least and vilest things am thrall.

I know my life's a pain and but a span,
I know my *Sense* is mockt with every thing:
And to conclude, I know my selfe a MAN,
Which is a *proud*, and yet a *wretched* thing.[7]

(d) Freedom–fate

The 'De Contemptu Mundi' tradition,[8] still part of course of Elizabethan religious teaching, probably did not persuade many healthy
persons to reject the attractions of being alive, any more than it
finally convinced Claudio in *Measure for Measure*, but it certainly
formed part of a much more widely accepted view which recognised
the mutability of life (of which Spenser wrote), the variations of
success and failure so often impossible to foresee or guard against,
and apparently dependent on blind chance. Of course, in religious
teaching there was no acceptance of 'blind chance', of the Wheel of
Fortune by which men rose to fame only to sink to failure; everything
existed within the total being of God, and formed his knowledge of
the course of Man's destiny. But within God's knowledge, in which
past, present and future were the eternal 'now', Man had for all
practical purposes been given free will, and in any case, however
much philosophy and theology might debate the meaning of 'free
will', an Elizabethan, like ourselves today, 'knew' that he had a
power to choose among the many possible paths presented by his
daily life. Here, then, was another form of conflict: he was convinced
of his freedom to choose, but still, he secretly admitted, there always
existed the possibility that chance would render this free will a highly
ambiguous blessing from God. By his very nature he was forced to
act, and wished to act, as a free agent, while yet suspecting, very
often, that he was by no means free.

(e) Reason–unreason (control of self—lack of control)

So far we have been considering forms of human incongruity arising
largely from a generally accepted religious view of life, but these were
only a part of the total stress which an Elizabethan experienced.
Indeed, the primary 'soul–body' incongruity which we have examined had wider and more disturbing implications than those

5

which we have so far seen. The Christian religion, beginning with the teaching of its Founder, had always emphasised the 'soul–body' incongruity of Man in terms of its practical consequences for everyday life on this earth; in these terms, the soul represented the gift of 'higher reason' which God had given Man to control, day by day, the non-rational impulses and desires of his physical body. Thus the practical guidance of Elizabethan religion was centred upon Man as a mixed creature in whom, by his inborn nature, reason and un-reason, the mind (when it served the soul) and the body, were always at variance, as Thomas Rogers, a Protestant rector, wrote in 1576:

> Hereof is man called *Mikpokosμos* a little
> worlde: because that with euerie thing created
> of God, he hath some affinitie. By which it is
> euident that he which throughly would know him
> selfe, must aswell knowe his boddie, as
> his minde. The boddie to put him in minde of
> his slauerie: the mind of his soueraigntie.
> The bodie of his misery, the minde of his
> felicitie. The bodie of his mortalitie, the
> mind of his eternitie. For by the one we
> participate the nature of beastes, by the
> other of Angels[9]

The Elizabethans saw clearly that this was not merely a philosophi-cal matter; serious writers and those supplying popular entertain-ment were equally ready to point out that the conflict of reason and unreason was a vital part of existence, and that the outcome of it determined the success or failure of a man's life. In 1603 an earnest (but anonymous) religious writer warned:

> Passions or perturbations, are vyolent
> motions which (vnlesse restrained) carrye
> the Soule headlong into many mischiefes. The
> groundes that they proceede from are false
> opinions, which perswade vs otherwise of
> things than they are in deed. And these false
> oppinions are alwayes accompanied with these
> foure thinges, immoderate desire, vnbridled
> ioy, immeasurable griefe, and extreame feare,
> which do carry the soule hither and thither,
> and in the ende so subdue the reasonable power

thereof, as they make it servile and obedient
vnto the sensuall appetite of the wil.[10]

Some forty years before, a compiler of popular tales had given King
Edward this comment in the same moral tradition:

> Knowe ye therefore, that I deeme him onely
> to be happy that by Reason can rule his wyttes, not
> suffering hym selfe to be caried into vayne
> desires: in whiche pointe wee do differ from
> beastes, who being lead onely by naturall
> order, doe indifferently [at random] runne
> headlong, whether [whither] their appetite
> doth guide them: but we with the measure of
> Reason ought to moderate our doinges with
> such prouidence, as without straying we may
> choose the right way of equitie and justice.[11]

⌐An awareness of this struggle of reason and unreason can be seen ⟵
in the Elizabethan tendency to dwell on the battle in Man between
'wit' (intelligence) and 'will' (impulse, desire), which gave much
scope for the witty handling of the anomalies of Man's situation.⌐The
first part of Nicholas Breton's *The Wil of Wit, Wits Will, or Wils
Wit, chuse you whether* (1599) gives a neat and typically ingenious
display of the incongruity, the strife, between these two sides of
Man's nature, with first an account of how Wit is constantly
opposed and frustrated by Will, and then Will's parallel claim to be
indispensable to Wit, yet scorned and mistreated by him. As we shall
see later, what was essentially a serious form of personal strife for
Elizabethans could often be seen by them as part of the inescapable
irony of human existence, and so as a subject for comedy.

The importance attached by religion to the struggle in Man
between reason and unreason was reinforced by that other great
moral influence on Elizabethan opinion, classical moral philosophy,
and especially the teaching of Cicero in the *De Officiis* and of
Aristotle's *Nicomachean Ethics*. The former work had been first
published in an English translation (by R. Whytinton) in 1534, and
another translation, by N. Grimalde, became an Elizabethan 'best-
seller', passing through eight editions from 1553 to 1600; a Latin
text did not appear in England until 1579. The *Nicomachean Ethics*
had appeared in England in a Latin translation as early as 1479, and
again, in a different Latin translation, in 1581, and had been

paraphrased in English, from an Italian version, in an edition of 1547. Thus the moral teaching of these two philosophers was available to English readers throughout the greater part of the sixteenth century. This 'moral philosophy' was also within the reach of many who were not learned: the Elizabethan fondness for 'sentences', pithy comments (preferably with great names attached) which could be used in conversation or argument, gave rise to a number of popular anthologies of moral sayings, mainly drawn, or purporting to be drawn, from a variety of classical and medieval thinkers, including especially Plato, Cicero and Aristotle. An exceptionally popular example of these collections was William Baldwin's *A treatise of morall phylosophie, contayning the sayinges of the wyse*; it was first published in 1547, and enlarged first by Baldwin and then by Thomas Paulfreyman, and went through fifteen editions by 1610.

The approach to moral questions of Cicero's *De Officiis*, in particular, well suited the increasing contemporary interest in the whole question of what moral standards best fitted a man to take a worthy part in the social life of his time. The emphasis, here, was becoming more social than religious, and was associated of course with the Elizabethan concern with the personal qualities which enabled a man to fill a position of authority.[12] Cicero had approached his subject, the responsibilities or duties of the good man, from the point of view of man living in society, and serving his society; for him, there is little importance, in this respect, in purely private virtues or in living divorced from one's kind. The essence of such a good man, for Cicero, is that he is a reasonable man, a man able to follow the rational ways of achieving the balanced just and worthy life. Whytinton, the earlier translator of Cicero's *De Officiis*, stresses the importance of reason, and links it to God's purpose, in his 'exhortacyon' to his readers:

> And for as moche as the excellente prince of
> phylosophers [Cicero] lefte in wrytynge this
> notable sentence. Every man naturally desyreth
> to have knowledge, which sentence me seemeth
> that he spake not without diuyne inspyracion.
> For god hath gyuen us not onely a body commen
> and indyfferent to us almoste with rude beestes
> but also a soule endued with reson[,] whiche
> soule is not ferre dyfferent fro the nature of
> aungell: for by reason we perceyue[,] understande

8

and remembre[,] which ornament of reason amonge
all creatures here mortall onely is gyue to man.[13]

  N. Grimalde's Dedication of his translation of the *De Officiis* to
the Bishop of Ely, Thomas Goodrich, and his preliminary Address to
the Reader, together indicate clearly the nature of the Elizabethan
interest in the work. To the Lord Chancellor Bishop, Grimalde
writes of 'the greatest and most profitable part of philosophie, which
is concerning maners', and then describes Cicero's work as 'a mater
conteining the holle trade, how to liue among men dyscreetly, and
honestly: and so rightly pointing out the pathway to all vertue: as
none can be righter, onely Scripture excepted'. It is significant that he
joins Cicero's teaching to that of the Scriptures as the truest guidance
for right living in his age; on the next page of this Dedication he
defines what the Elizabethans considered the important features of
this right living:

> either in priuate life, to attein quietnesse,
> and contentation, or in office-bearing, to winne
> fame, & honour: or in euery estate, both
> to auoide disorder, and enormity, and also
> to kepe a right rule, and commendable
> behauiour: this boke plainly is the mirrour
> of wisdome, the fortres of iustice, the master
> of manlines, the schoole of temperance, the
> iewel of comlines.

In his Address to the Reader, Grimalde again asserts the importance
of reason, as the controller of unreason, in procuring the good life in
this world:

> In us the best work is, to use our selues well,
> and worthely: who in the order of naturall things
> are of the best, and worthyest kinde. For what is
> ther, that can use it self: onlesse it be enfourmed
> wyth reason: and understanding?.

This recognition of the struggle between reason and unreason in the
make-up of Man, a fundamental conflict within human nature for
the Elizabethans (as indeed for later ages up to our own) is developed
a little later in a way that relates it, not just to the individual, but
more widely, to the conception of authority in Elizabethan society.
As Grimalde says:

> For in this world here beneath, are thre kindes
> of liuing wights: wherof somme haue nomore, but
> lyfe, as plantes, herbes, and trees, growing out
> of the grounde: somme haue not onely life, but
> senses also: as sheepe, oxen & other beastes:
> the third comprehendeth both these: & ouer life,
> and senses, hath the souerain ruler, Reason.

That is, Man's physical life is of two sorts, the living kind and the living plus feeling kind, together with a third kind in which these two are under the control of reason: it then follows that this control of reason marks the highest form of human existence:

> For like as god gouerneth thinges manyfolde,
> moueable, and fallying away, being himselfe but
> one, unremoouable, and euer during[lasting]: so
> reason within us ought to rule raging lusts, and
> rash motions of the mind, and the other unworthier,
> and weaker partes: being it selfe stedfaste, sage,
> principal, and strongly established.

Following the three-fold nature of life, and the comparison of the power of reason to God's divine control of this transitory world, there is an easy step to the assumption that the members of society itself should occupy positions corresponding to the forms of life and the superiority of reason:

> So shall the meanest sorte, lyke the vitall
> parcell in man, bee occupied aboute the moste
> seruile, and needfull workes: men of middle
> degree, like the sensiue[sensuous] soule, shall
> attend to affaires, and sciences more liberall:
> the nobilitie in the common gouernment, like
> reason in the nature of man, shall rule al the
> multitude.[14]

Thus Grimalde accepts the insistence on the importance of reason that runs throughout the *De Officiis*, and develops the social implications in a way more Elizabethan than Ciceronian. Certainly the association of reason and authority, the interpretation in this respect of individual man's struggle between reason and unreason in terms of the state, is a typical and important Elizabethan view, as we shall see later; some fifty years after Grimalde, a preacher in a sermon at Faversham in Kent can be found expressing a similar conception:

God hath giuen a man reason to be as a
Prince to rule him,[15] it being ruled by the
line of his Lawe: the supreame faculties of
the soule, be the Peeres or Nobles: the senses
are the guard and attendants: the outward part
are as the Commons: and our Sins, & sinfull
Affections[passions, feelings], are traitours,
rebells, and as factions and infectious persons,
which disturbe the peace of the Common-wealth,
and being desperate and irreconciliable enimies
vnto the State, doe striue to dismount the Prince
from her Throne, and vtterly to ruinate and
subuert the kingdome, which God by his holy
spirit hath begun to plant within vs.[16]

Aristotle's *Nicomachean Ethics* is also concerned mainly with
Man's best nature and behaviour in his society (the work prepares
for and leads on to his *Politics*). Throughout it runs the same view as
Cicero's, that reason is what distinguishes Man from beasts, and that
Man can by reason examine and order himself and his human
environment: Aristotle adds his personal conviction that Man can
through rational thought and choice make himself what he sees as
the balanced, 'great-souled' man, carefully poised between excesses
of many kinds. John Wilkinson's version of 1547 (the only known
Elizabethan version in English) is significantly entitled *The Ethiques
of Aristotle, that is to saye, preceptes of good behauioure and
perfighte honestie[worthiness]*. He does not translate the full detail
of Aristotle's work, but seeks only to produce an outline in which the
ethical guidance of the original is summarised in brief chapters of
moral comment. It is in fact, as the title suggests, a book of precepts
based on Aristotle, of a kind popular with Elizabethans, like Baldwin's 'Treatise' of the same date. But it keeps close enough to its
source to convey Aristotle's main ethical views, and especially his
emphasis on the power and importance of reason. For example,
towards the end of Aristotle's Book 1, Wilkinson paraphrases quite
closely as follows:

The Solle of man hath thre powers, one is
called ye lyfe vegitable: in ye whiche man is
partener with trees & with plantes: The second
power, is the life sensible[of feeling] in the
whiche man is partener with beastes, for why[,]

11

al beastes haue lifes sensible. The third,
is called solle reasonable, by the whiche a man
differeth from all other thinges, for there
is none reasonable but man. And this power
reasonable is sometyme in act, and sometime in
power [*in posse*], from whence the Beatitude is
whan it is in acte and not whan it is in power.[17]

Elizabethan man, then, through his own instinctive awareness of himself and from the consistent admonitions and teachings of his age, knew himself to be the battleground of these primary forms of incongruity, the tensions between soul and body, immortality and mortality, free will and fate, reason and unreason. They were of the essence of his human nature, the bases of his life as a man in a human world. Indeed, while in one sense Elizabethan man (like man today) had to make the best of them, in another sense they could be seen as the best of Man. I doubt whether he derived much consolation from the latter view in his times of personal stress, but religious teaching of course offered the comfort that Man's struggle with his human contradictions was part of God's plan for him, and that without struggle there could be no worthwhile success and ultimate goodness. As Thomas Rogers puts it succinctly in 1576:

And therefore except there bee passions and
perturbations in man, there is no place for
vertue. Euen as there is no victorie, where as
there is no aduersary . . .[18]

But ordinary Elizabethans were more often and more deeply concerned with the daily problems, the recurrent successes and failures, of life in their world, and it was here that the conflicts of reason and unreason were of immediate force. Every day the Elizabethan, like Man today and in every age, must have been aware that living in the world demands the constant making of rational judgements, but that these judgements are never purely rational, for they are affected always, to some degree at least, by irrational forces beyond the complete control of reason; that, indeed, completely rational judgements (if such were possible) would mark a man as divorced from humanity, perhaps less than human.[19]

(f) Reason–love (man and woman)

The strife of reason and unreason entered, of course, into many of the most personal, important and inescapable of an Elizabethan's daily concerns, and of these, obviously, the perennial and constant concern was with women. The religious teaching of the age, at its most anti-feminist, saw Woman as representing the irrational defeat by passion through which Mankind had suffered the Fall: as a rector said in a sermon in 1599:

> We know that the first follie that euer was wrought by
> mankinde, was wrought by a woman: and therefore women
> sithence are evermore accursed more then man, their bodies
> weaker, their stomacks ['guts'] tenderer, their paines greater;
> their liues more slauish, and their mindes more seruile.[20]

But this was by no means a general attitude to women: the more reasonable and practical point of view was that of, for example, William Averell, a London schoolmaster, in 1584:

> [concerning the treatment of a wife] . . . she was
> not made of the head nor of the foote [of Adam],
> but of the ryb and side of man, which sheweth,
> that as she may not be a mystresse, so must she
> be no maide, as no soueraigne, so no seruant,
> but an equall companion, and a friendly fellow
> [partner], to participate with thee of euery
> fortune.[21]

Our Elizabethan man, however willingly he might accept this role for Woman as wife, still had to cope with his inner discords as a man in relation to women. His sexual desire (that 'lust' which so many moralists considered the fatal enemy of reason, and hence the way by which a man could sink to the level of beasts) might drive him to use women solely for physical satisfaction, which was of course to reduce women, too, to the rank of beasts; but the popular tradition of the 'romantic' love-story, and the Petrarchan love-sonnet fashion of the later sixteenth century, stressed love rather than passion as the bond and attraction between the sexes, and love implied the man's devotion to the woman, not physical exploitation by him. Moreover, we must remember that love was considered to be as remote from reason as lust – both love and lust were seen as characteristically irrational. Thus an Elizabethan found himself in the midst of some most urgent and unavoidable dilemmas, subject to the conflicting pressures of reason and lust, reason and love, and lust and love. Of all Man's inner conflicts, these were the most complex, most directly and widely affecting everyday life in the Elizabethan world. They were of great force, and as likely to produce tragedy as comedy; they were a matter of common and unfailing interest to all Elizabethans, women as well as men.

In its simplest form, this personal struggle could be felt as a plain contrast between what may be called the 'worldly' view of love and the 'romantic' view (and this contrast has persisted to our day); the paradoxes of Man's dilemma fitted nicely into the old tradition of the 'witty' debate (continuing as an academic exercise), in which a proposition could be stated from diametrically opposite viewpoints; to show the conflicting responses to a woman struggling within the divided being of a man 'in love' could be ironically entertaining. Thus in George Pettie's popular collection of stories, Curiatus (after being repulsed by Horatia) soliloquises about her, first in cynical, worldly terms:

> Again if a man, making love in way of
> marriage, do but so much as touch one of these
> tender pieces, they crie 'fie, away, away', but
> let one that is married, or one that meaneth not
> marriage, dally with them, why they are as
> loose of their lips and free of their flesh
> as may be.

And then in the most romantic vein:

> But ah! blasphemous beast that I am!
> to cast such devilish doubts of her honesty,
> whose very countenance containeth continency
> in it, whose visage seems to be without vice,
> and looks without lust [etc].[22]

The Elizabethans, then, men and women, were fully aware of this basic form of the conflict of forces which split a man between a worldly-wise idea of himself as faced with a necessary evil called 'Woman', and an idealistic and romantic belief in Woman as the cause and inspiration of the finest emotions, the adornment and enrichment of life. But the matter was more involved than this simple contrast suggests: if Woman represented unreason, the attraction towards the irrational desires of the beast, her very remoteness from reason could give her, in Man's eyes, a special and even awesome quality, and so love could take on something of a supernatural force, an essential basis for that 'love-worship' which marks the Elizabethan romance tradition, as expressed by Pettie:

> [Reasons can be found for everything in Nature]. . . .
> But of love it is so far without the compass of
> reason and bounds of nature, that there can no
> reason, no cause, no conjecture be given of
> it; neither what it is, working such divers
> effects, neither wherever it is, proceeding of
> so diverse causes, neither whence it will, being
> never satisfied. Therefore no earthly thing but
> some supernal [divine] power sure it is.[23]

Thus love between Man and Woman was a state wherein the man was divided between the rational and the irrational, and the woman felt herself to be both the feared temptress and the adored partner. Elizabethan man, particularly, saw himself at one level as a soul linked to a body through the lusts of which a woman could destroy the soul, and also as a creature of finer feeling through which a woman could raise him, past mere lust, to a spiritual unity which had been described and celebrated since the days of Plato.[24] Such love as this, like the love of and for God, was based on faith, not reason; so Man had to accept the anomaly that, while reason must be chosen before unreason in so much of life, if that life was to be good, in love unreason was the essence of the glory. Yet the Elizabethans, of course, still married often for money or other practical reasons. We can appreciate why Elizabethan story, poetry and drama used love as a constant ingredient, as it is used today; because its complexities were known, in some measure, to everyone, but also because the forms of human incongruity it contained were fertile in possibilities of constant tension in comedy or tragedy, or both, of many kinds.

From the incongruities inherent in desire and love inevitably arose the possibility of the accompanying incongruity of jealousy, of a situation where a man could hate a woman because he loved her so much. For if the greatest love arose despite reason, was as much a matter of faith as religious belief, the conviction that love had been betrayed equally needed no rational basis; by transcending reason true love could be achieved, but by deserting reason a man could be dragged down to the bestiality of lust, or its equivalent, the bestiality of jealousy. For an Elizabethan, a man in love was beyond reason;

one admired and envied the lover, perhaps, but waited to laugh if and when reason finally returned to him; but a jealous man was a man who had lost his reason and still believed himself rational – he was a mad man, and as such could be comic or tragic, according to the nature and results of his madness.

(g) Reason–fantasy

In connection with this warfare of reason and unreason (faith, love), we should consider a parallel which is equally inherent in the nature of all men, then or now. Like ourselves, Elizabethan man, while accepting the importance of reason, was perversely unwilling to let it completely rule his life; fantasy, the holiday from reason, had a strong appeal for Elizabethans, whether in the form of everyday folk-tales, or in the literary shape of the vast make-believe world of Sidney's *Arcadia*, the moral pattern of tales of *The Faerie Queen*, and the slighter playfulness of Lyly's *Endymion*. The secret of popular fantasy is that it must never completely lose touch with reality, for to enjoy it one must retain a sense, no matter how slight, of the mundane world; otherwise, how can one feel oneself to be in the fantasy, and so enjoy it to the full as a relief from that mundane world? At its best, fantasy is a transfiguration of the ordinary, not a substitute for it; thereby it resolves both sides of the incongruity, and combines reason and unreason in a third dimension refreshingly different from either, and without conflict.

The existence of fantasy was another proof, if proof were needed, that no human being could be wholly confined within the bounds of reason and still remain human. Erasmus in *The Praise of Folly*, that great network of irony interwoven with humanist feeling, expressed the situation well:

> How euer in this poinct the *Archestoike*
> *Seneca* strongly againsaieth me, who in no
> wyse will a wyseman shoulde haue any maner
> affection [emotion] in hym. But whan he taketh
> that away, he leaueth man, no man, but
> rather a newfounde god without bodily
> sence, such as neuer was, nor euer shal
> be. Yea, to speake plainlier, he dooeth
> naught els than fourme a stone image of a
> man, without fealyng, or any maner inclinacion
> perteinyng to a man in deede.[25]

What could Elizabethan man do in this dilemma? He could refuse to take seriously his human stresses; he could find a comic side to his irrationalities and, placing them outside himself, laugh at drunkenness, lechery, cowardice, anger, covetousness and so on in the world around him: prose writers, poets and dramatists of the period (like the writers of earlier 'moral drama') gave him many opportunities to do so. But he might accept the gravity of his divided state, and with the help of religion strive to master his passions by reason (although, of course, his fellows might continue to find relief by laughing at his efforts). He could also confront the dangers of the irrational by enjoying the portrayal of other men's failure to control it; here again the drama and stories of the period helped him. There were modes of escape in accepting the contemporary attitudes to 'the wicked', to usurers or witches, for example: one might know oneself to be greedy, but at least one was superior to that enemy of society, a usurer; one might have rebellious passions, even forget reason and act like a beast at times, but one was far better than those wretched witches (uncomfortably ordinary in their origins) who, it was generally accepted, had taken the fatal step of trying to gain power or possessions by seeking the Devil's help.[26] No doubt the average Elizabethans adopted any or all of these expedients to escape, for a time at least, from the awareness of being torn between reason and unreason, soul and body, control and licence; being human beings and not Erasmus's 'stone image', they continued to live a life of mixed reason and folly among their similarly inconsistent companions. Add to such forms of conflict those others which we have touched on, the sense of being at once potentially god-like and potentially beast-like, of being immortal and yet all too mortal, of being wonderful in aspiration and feeble in achievement, and we can understand the truth of what a wise man wrote in 1597:

> Yea, oftentimes such odds there is betweene
> a man and him selfe, as not the same but an other
> then him selfe he seemeth to be, for he is both
> simple, and subtill, both gentle, and cruell, both
> hardy[bold], and fearfull, both dull, and quicke,
> both swift, and slow: subtill to deceaue an other,
> and simple to auoide his owne danger, cruell where
> he hateth, and gentle to those he loueth, hardy
> against a naked faynt harted enemie, and fearefull
> against an armed resolued aduersarie, swift to
> reuenge, and slow to forgiue, dull in learning

17

the best things, and quicke in apprehending the
worst. So he is most vnlike to him selfe, and
like affected to all the rest, yea sondry more
affections[feelings, passions] he hath then all
the rest besides. . . . The Leopard is not so
changeable in the spots of his skinne, as man
is variable in the affections of his minde.[27]

(h) Private man–public man

So far we have seen how his human incongruity as an individual
affected an Elizabethan, and it should be stressed that the various
forms of it were to be found in Elizabethans, male or female, of every
social level; they were the qualities of a common humanity.

But in a society as closely-knit as that of Elizabethan England (and
of course one must think especially of Elizabethan London), the
similar attitudes, hopes, fears and perplexities produced by this inner
personal struggle in individuals inevitably coalesced into wider
social attitudes. When we turn to these social attitudes, we must
think more, although not exclusively, of the better educated Elizabethan, the man more personally concerned in the nature of social
patterns and pressures. Such a man would have been more consciously and keenly aware of his human dichotomy and its effects on
his life in society; he would have had a more thoughtful, more
philosophic realisation (as Cicero had had) of the importance of
individual awareness of self to the stability and soundness of his
society. So our more thoughtful Elizabethan would have had to face
a further problem of personal attitude and behaviour as he entered
his public career as clergyman, lawyer, statesman or magistrate, or
even merely contemplated in his study the general state of his
country. If a private person failed to handle his problems successfully, the result was the collapse of his own life, a personal human
tragedy with, of course, universal implications for Mankind. But a
private person taking a position of any great responsibility to his
country, or even to his local community, became at once a public
person, and failure to sustain the stresses of his own nature might
have disastrous public consequences.[28] Both Aristotle and Cicero
had taught that every man wielding power in the state must be
controlled by his reason, and they pointed to history to show what
calamities happened to the realm when this was not so.

So, in the sixteenth century in England, both before and especially
after the accession of Elizabeth, there was widespread interest in this
private man–public man problem. Sir Thomas Elyot's *The Boke
named the Gouernour* (first published in 1531, and running through
at least seven more editions by 1580) was well-known to literate
Elizabethans, and gives good examples of contemporary attitudes to
this matter. The second and third books of the work are largely
indebted to the views of Cicero and Aristotle, with their emphasis on
the necessary rule of reason, and deal directly with the qualities
required by those who have the responsibilities of authority. Elyot
refers to the ruler's special situation as 'private man' and 'public
man':

> It is to be noted that to hym that is a
> gouernoure of a publike weale belongeth a double
> gouernaunce, that is to saye, an interior or
> inwarde gouernaunce, and an exterior or outwarde
> gouernaunce. The first is of his affectes [feelings]
> and passions, which do inhabite within his soule,
> and be subiectes to reason. The seconde is of
> his children, his seruauntes, and other subiectes
> to his authoritie.[29]

A preacher made the similar point in 1580:

> Besides this, we must also vnderstand, that
> as Princes are publique persons in respect of
> their gouernement of whole nations committed
> to their charge, so also before the Lord, they
> are priuate persons, to be called to account,
> not only for such things as they do in their
> publique gouernement, but also for such
> offences as they commit priuatly, as the sonnes
> of Adam.[30]

Thus the conflict of the private man is reinforced by the pressures on
the public man, the private stresses writ large, and the dangers are
greater. As Elyot warns:

> For moste harde and greuous iugement shall
> be on them that haue rule ouer other. To the
> poure man mercy is graunted, but the great

19

> men shall suffre great tourmentes. . . . The
> stronger or of more mighte is the persone,
> the stronger payne is to hym imminent.[31]

A further responsibility arises, he says, from the 'private' life of the 'public' man:

> They [rulers] shal also consider that by their
> pre-eminence they sitte, as it were on a piller
> on the toppe of a mountaine, where all the
> people do beholde them, not only in their open
> affaires, but also in their secret passetimes,
> priuie daliaunce, or other improfitable or
> wanton conditions.[32]

The point is still being made at the end of the century, in another context:

> the world is come to this passe nowe a daies,
> that we liue more by examples, then by good
> Lawes and preceptes: this saying was neuer more
> verified then in our time, *Regis ad exemplum, totus
> componitur orbis*.[33] The whole world is giuen
> to followe the example of those that are aboue them in
> authoritie.[34]

The Elizabethan interest in the human problems of the ruler is also shown in the well-known *A Mirror for Magistrates* which appeared in at least six editions from 1559 to 1610 (with later reprints): between these dates the number of historical figures presented grew from nineteen to ninety-eight. The purpose of the work, as explained by William Baldwin, the first editor,[35] was to display the lives and difficulties of past rulers and lords (mainly English) so as to give warning examples of how great men could be destroyed by personal vices together with the vagaries of fortune; the lessons were directed to all subjects as well as to rulers, and thus associated the dangers of discord within the private man with those, more widespread and terrible in their effects, in the public man. In his introduction, Baldwin, after quoting Plato: 'Well is that realme gouerned, in which the ambicious desyer not to beare office', proceeds:

> where the ambicious seeke no office, there
> is no doubt, offices are duly ministered: and
> where offices are duly ministred, it can not be

20

chosen but [it is inevitable] the people are
good, whereof must nedes folow a good common
weale. For if the officers be good, the people
can not be yll. Thus the goodness or badnes of
any realme lyeth in the goodness or badnes of
the rulers.[36]

Later, in his Address to the Reader, he makes the wider moral
purpose of the work quite clear:

[This work] might be as a myrrour for al men
as well noble as others, to shewe the slippery
deceytes of the wauering lady [Fortune], and the
due rewarde of all kinde of vices.[37]

So *A Mirror for Magistrates* stresses the importance of goodness, the
control of vices, for the man in authority and for the common man
living under that authority, and also recognises the power of Fortune, a sense of which, as we have seen, is part of the Elizabethan's
awareness of his mixed quality.

This concern with the flaws of personal character which can cause
trouble to all men, in authority or not, is closely linked, of course, to
the question of what makes a man fit to exercise power. Elyot's
second and third sections are concerned with this problem, and the
qualities of the good 'Gouernour' are discussed along the lines laid
down by Cicero's *De Officiis* and, especially, Aristotle's *Nicomachean Ethics*. The former is more concerned with the necessary
'virtue' (proceeding from control by reason) of the man taking a
responsible part in the affairs of his society; the latter puts more
emphasis on the ideal character of a ruler: Elyot follows Aristotle
closely in his analysis of the qualities required by a ruler, although in
fact he quotes far more often from Cicero on particular points. The
general result is that, from his two main sources and, one should add,
from his own experience of state affairs, Elyot offers a thesis in which
the self-control of the private man's passions by his reason is held to
be the obvious need, and is extended into the field of public service.
Indeed, the pattern of his work, with the first Book devoted to the
upbringing and education of the upper-class boy, a 'private' person
destined for 'public' life, shows this clearly. Elyot translates 'the
versis of Claudiane, the noble poet, whiche he wrate to Theodosius
and Honorius, emperours of Rome', as precepts which, he says,
should be hung up in the bedchamber of a noble man. The second of
the four stanzas gives the essence of the teaching of *The Gouernour*:

> Thou shalt be demed than worthy for to raigne,
> Whanne of thy selfe thou wynnest the maistry.
> Euil custome bringeth vertue in disdaine,
> Licence superfluous persuadeth moche foly;
> In to moche pleasure set nat felicitie,
> If lust or anger do thy mynde assaile,
> Subdue occasion [the cause], and thou shalte
>   sone preuaile.[38]

In effect, this advice was equally applicable to the 'private man', as we have seen, although of course the role and importance of the 'public man' gave it greater, wider importance. Even a private man had to take some part in the world around him, and his fitness for that minor role depended on his power to master unreason with reason.

The demands made upon the public man were, in moral terms, heavy, and (as the 'Mirror for Magistrates' tradition showed) in political terms dangerous. It was an Elizabethan commonplace that the life of a king was harder than the people realised. As Henry Howard (himself later Earl of Northampton, and a prominent politician under James I) wrote in 1593:

> And they that are aduaunced to the tipe of
> honour by the grace of times, and Princes,
> vnder and in whome they liue, are ouerwhelmed
> and oppressed, with so many bleeding cares, as
> more in number by a multitude, haue lamented
> with salte teares that euer they were borne to
> weare a crowne, then delighted with secure
> content in the glory of theyr Empire.[39]

And the Bishop of Rochester, in a sermon preached in 1606:

> some *Kings* haue auowed it, if Men knew
> the hazzards annexed to a *Crowne*, they would
> not stoope to take it vp, if it lay vpon the
> grounde.[40]

In passing, I would point out that the contrast between the quiet life of the 'private man' and the disturbed life of the 'public man' is also expressed in Elizabethan times in the 'debate' concerning the relative advantages and disadvantages of private life and public life. Although the convention dates back to classical times,[41] it had a special interest for an age like the Elizabethan, when the country magnate was being more and more drawn into the central state organisation in London, and when he himself was showing an increasing desire to share in the central power. An interesting expression of contemporary attitudes is an anonymous work of 1579 called *Cyuile and uncyuile life; a discourse where is disputed, what order of life best beseemeth a gentleman (etc)*. The book is in the form of a conversation between Vincent, a country gentleman, and Valentine, a Court gentleman, and it reads like government propaganda. Although Vincent has his fair share of the argument, there is much emphasis on Valentine's view that a country gentleman should not vegetate on his estates, should have tenant-farmers rather than farm himself, and should keep a smaller establishment, and the work ends with a summary of the greater advantages, for a gentleman, of living in town, which means London and the Court. On the other hand, there were many traditional celebrations of the peace and simple goodness of country life as contrasted with the cares and vices of Court life, of which Barnabe Googe's poem *To M. Henrye Cobham, of the most blessed state of lyfe*[42] is a characteristic example.

The fact was that, on the merely human level of life in this world, forgetting (as we human beings so often, so naturally forget) the spiritual dimension of his existence, Elizabethan man could see in worldly importance, in playing a special part in society, a practical way of rising above his own insignificance. Contemporary records show clearly that to be merely a justice of the peace, even a churchwarden, gave a man a kind of local social immortality denied to the common man.[43] At a higher national level, lords and kings, even if remembered only for their evils or failures, were alive in history or legend long after the worthy and devoted village schoolmaster had been forgotten: life has always been like that. It is not surprising, therefore, seeing that both play-makers and play-goers in Elizabethan times shared a common interest in 'fame', 'immortality', of this sort, that a large part of the most popular drama of the period (including Shakespeare's) was about the struggle for social importance, for kingship or other power. Sometimes the most appealing thing was the display of failure in this struggle, or, as a further development, of the littleness and evils of success. For the Elizabethan was often pleased, as we are, to believe that the battle for worldly triumph may bring 'fame', but rarely happiness, and the Church would so often bring the ordinary Elizabethan back to the contradictions of his human nature by proclaiming the futility of earthly glory. A nice example of such contradictions even at papal level is the fact that Pope Innocent III (1161–1217), noted for his worldly political ambitions for the Church, nevertheless wrote a powerful description of the littleness of Man and all worldly things This work, *De Contemptu Mundi, sive de Miseria Humanae Conditionis* (Concerning contempt of the world, or concerning the misery of the human condition), was still available in English translation in Elizabethan times.[44]

(i) Order–disorder

We have seen how the pressures of Man's conflicts worked outwards from the life of the individual to affect some of the most important social attitudes of the time. One of these, and one vital for an understanding of the Elizabethans, was the general attitude to the common people. We can go below the contemporary political and social conditions which helped to shape this attitude, to a deeper human level. Let us begin with another passage from Erasmus's *Enchiridion*; soon after the passage quoted at the beginning of section (a), occurs the following:

> In man reason beareth ye rowme of a kyng.
> Thou mayst accompt for the chefe lordes certeyn
> affections [feelings], and them of the body: but
> yet not all thinges so beastly. . . . But suche
> affections or passyons which be very greatly
> disagreyng from the decrees of reason and which
> be cast downe, and must bow euen to the vylenes
> of brute beestes: thynke and reken those, to be
> as it were the most raskal and vile sort of ye
> commune people. Of which kynde and sort be
> lechery, ryot, enuy, and such like diseases
> [troubles] which al without excepcion, must be
> kept vnder with prison and punyshment, as vyle
> and bonde seruauntes, that they may rendre to
> their mayster, their taske and worke appoynted
> to them, yf they can: but yf not, at the least yt
> they may do no harme.

> (loc. cit., 62–3)

Thus the unreason which in religious thinking represented the constant danger to Man's Christian life on earth, his hope of salvation, could also be seen in social, political terms. In a recent work, Penry Williams recognises this connection between religious views of Man and the state's attitude to the role of government in Elizabethan times:

> The emphasis put by religious reformers
> upon the iniquity of man demanded in response
> an acceptance of strong government. . . . Unless
> man's sinful nature were curbed by the painful
> bridle of government, chaos would ensue.
> The teachings of religion were reinforced,
> from about 1540, by fears of invasion and civil
> war. . . . There was always the danger that, if
> the government's vigilance slackened, the whole
> social order would be overthrown by that 'many-
> headed monster', the common people of England.[45]

I would agree that the Elizabethan fear of the mob went even deeper than 'fears of invasion and civil war'; it is clear that many thinking Elizabethans (and not only those among the upper classes, or in positions of power) had learnt to recognise the dangers of their 'human incongruity' in their own personal lives, to regard the control by reason as the good and safe way of life: so they feared disorder, irrational licence, in themselves, and, being human, feared it even more in those around them, whose unthinking passions they saw as a threat to all, socially and nationally. The distrust of the mob is an Elizabethan commonplace.[46]

The major official religious and political expression of this fear of national disorder is of course to be found in the 'Homilies' (*Certayne sermons, or homilies . . .*), which were first published by authority in 1547 (Book 1) and 1563 (Book 2); both Books were constantly republished up to 1640, and long after, even in the nineteenth century.[47] These Homilies were ordered to be read out in every church, in order, one on each Sunday of the year (unless there was another sermon), and as Sunday church-going was compulsory, they formed a widespread and consistent influence upon the religious, moral and social outlook of the majority of Elizabethans, a channel for the government's fears and warnings concerning the behaviour of the people, an attempt to control the nation's political views and social outlook.[48]

The Homilies all emphasise the danger to the state, and to the individual citizen, of human disorder in its various forms, and always in religious and political terms – the two are synonymous. Homily X especially, an outstanding example of Elizabethan rhetorical prose, should be read in its entirety by anyone who wishes to understand one of the strongest preconceptions of so many Elizabethan writers and their audience concerning social order. An established and unquestionable pattern of order, it asserts, runs from the Almighty down through the hierarchy of his angels to the physical framework of Creation, in which the order of rulers and subjects gives each man (in himself an ordered creation of body and soul) his assured place in society:

> Euery degree of people in their vocation,
> calling, and office, hath appointed to them,
> their duetie and order. Some are in high
> degree, some in lowe, some Kinges and princes,
> some inferiours and subiectes, priestes, and
> laye men, Maysters and Seruauntes, Fathers and
> children, husbandes, and wiues, riche and poore,
> and euery one haue neede of other, so that in all
> thinges is to be lauded and praysed the goodlye
> order of God, without the whiche, no house, no
> Citie, no common wealth can continue and indure,
> or last. For where there is no right order, there
> reigneth all abuse, carnall libertie, enormitie,
> sinne, and Babilonicall confusion.[49]

> (Homily x, near beginning)

It is the natural sinfulness of Man which threatens the stability of this 'right order'. The personal struggles of the individual are seen as linked to society, itself conceived as a human unit with its own struggles. Thus not only is Man subject always to personal conflicts within himself, but the results of these conflicts, good or bad, affect the wider conflicts within the body of the state. We shall see later that Shakespeare shows in his plays, always for the delight and concern of his audience, the nature and results of both forms of conflict, personal and social, setting the personal within the social with various degrees of emphasis on one or the other.

(j) Justice–mercy

Given, then, this Elizabethan consciousness of the dangers presented by the irrationality of the mass of men, and of the necessity for stable order in society, we are led to consider, next, a related Elizabethan concern regarding the control of the law, the symbol of order, over lawlessness and disorder. Once again we must start from the inner tensions felt by the individual Elizabethan.

At the root of his human awareness, as we have seen, is his conception of himself as, hopefully, a religious being. As such, he is committed to belief in the importance of God's word as expressed in the Bible. The Old Testament is the story of the workings of God the giver of the Law, and that Law is one of clearly-defined and rigid justice between God and Man. The New Testament, however, shows the New Dispensation by which love transcends the logic of justice: Christ died to save, through love, those sinners whom strict justice would condemn; indeed, through the teaching of Christ shines the startling and strange message that the greater the sin, the greater the need for love and mercy. So our Elizabethan, brought up in the general teaching of the Church, found himself in the thick of incompatibilities: logically he was a fallen creature, born in original sin, and therefore liable to suffer the inevitable, just results of sinfulness: reason was to be regarded as the only means of controlling his irrational, beast-like desires. On the other hand, his ministers assured him (with differing emphases, it is true) that the logic of his damnation could be swept aside by heartfelt repentance and, above all, faith in God's mercy through the love of Christ for sinners, and in this there was no human reason: Christ's passionate love for Man, culminating in his self-sacrifice on the cross, was beyond Man's rational understanding. Faith alone could resolve this dilemma of Man as both guilty and forgiven, and faith is above and beyond reason.[50] The Church has always debated this problem, and 'solved' it within the higher technicalities of theological, scholastic argument, but for the average Elizabethan, as for many ordinary Christians today, it was a part of his human condition that, at best, must be recognised and, by some means or other, resolved.

When such an Elizabethan moved from these 'private' perplexities to the exercise, as a 'public' figure, of the power of the law of the land, inevitably reservations had to be made, religious beliefs had to be adapted and modified. The law had to be seen as strictly logical in its workings, and the age was convinced of the danger of illogical mercy, the unfortunate intrusion of love into the process of law. Here again, a Homily gives the official, rational view; Homily VI (Book 1) in the second part of 'The Sermon of Charitie [loving kindness]' points out:

For declaration wherof you shall understande,
that charitie hath two offices, thone[the one]
contrary to the other, and yet both necessary to
be used upon men of contrarie sorte and disposition.
The one office of charitie is, to cherish
good and harmles men . . . the other office of
charitie is to rebuke, correct and punishe vice,
without regarde of persons, and is to be used
agaynst them onely, that be euill men, and
malefactors or euill doers. And that it is
aswell the office of charitie to rebuke,
punishe, and correct them that be euill, as
it is to cherish and rewarde them that be
good and harmles.[51]

This justice–mercy form of human incongruity (the rationality of legal and political logic at odds with the human irrational impulse towards love and forgiveness) was obviously a constant and dramatic force in the Elizabethan world, as it continues to be in our world. This tension could arise at any time, in any human relationship where respect for the law was incompatible with pity for the law-breaker. Here was a conflict which was allied to the problem of order and disorder, which linked 'private life' and 'public life' throughout society, and which was an epitome of the worldly consequences of the divided nature of Man.

These are the main forms of Man's inner warfare, his human conflict, of which Shakespeare and his contemporaries were often and keenly aware. It is obvious that there were infinite variations of these – every situation of daily life, every personal idiosyncrasy, caused such variations – but the dominant basic forms were as I have shown them. It is plain that all these forms are related to one another; they all represent tensions which arise from the central dichotomy of Man, that gap within him between rational intellect and irrational processes (faith, intuition, imagination, anger, love, etc.) which modern science suggests is represented by the two halves of our brain. The basic conflict, in fact, is between control of the self and lack of control. This we still experience today, and this fact enables us to understand much of the nature of our Elizabethan brothers and sisters; it also allows us to appreciate and enjoy the drama in which they found (as we can find) a way of coming face to face with the conflicts within them, and, perhaps, in the process of sharing and feeling the human strife upon the stage, of finding some kind of personal resolution of the anomalies of their nature.

PART TWO

The main forms of human conflict of which Elizabethans were aware have been described. Now, as a necessary preliminary to seeing their importance in the plays of Shakespeare, we have to mark the presence of such forms in the beginnings of English drama (section a), and then in the plays of Shakespeare's contemporaries (section b).

This background is vital if the significance and the nature of Shakespeare's plays are to be understood in their proper context. They formed a part of the dramatic tradition of their age, and that tradition had evolved from the methods and outlooks of all previous English drama. Shakespeare used the dramatic techniques and approaches of his age, no matter how far he developed and adapted them for his own purposes; to that extent he was a dramatist of his age. Nothing, perhaps, has so falsified our modern understanding of his plays as a tendency, at times, to see our greatest dramatist as a lonely phenomenon located uneasily in a distant and, to us, somewhat alien period of drama. The deepest understanding of genius consists in realising how it can rise into universality while yet remaining also of its time. In Shakespeare's case, we shall see that universality based on the truths of human nature was part of the tradition which he inherited; to appreciate this fact is to be able to realise fully the true quality of his genius in using that tradition.

(a) HUMAN CONFLICT
IN EARLY ENGLISH DRAMA

The earliest formal drama in England arose from an attempt to show the people, in a vivid and impressive way, their relationship to God, their part in God's work in the world, their propensity to sin and their hope of salvation, as portrayed in a succession of dramatised examples of God's dealings with Man, from the Creation and the

29

Fall through to Christ's sacrifice, the Resurrection, and the Last Judgement. What we may call the basic religious expressions of Man's warring state were always explicit, often plainly stressed, throughout this dramatic sequence, reinforcing the fundamental teachings of the Church.

For a spectator, behind the surface interest and excitement of the drama in the street before him lay the inescapable repetition of the facts of his human condition under God. The examples of the drama made him aware, once more, that he was by nature prone to sin, constantly from age to age rejecting good and seeking evil, and immeasurably inferior to God – yet he had to believe, it seemed, that the world was made for him alone, that the whole of his Maker's creative purpose was concerned only with him, that solely for his salvation perfect goodness could transfigure the evils of pain and death through Christ's redemption of him on the Cross. He had to accept, as the drama showed, that the everyday fact of death and dissolution was no final fact at all, that the constant battle within himself between good and evil was a necessary part of God's plan for humanity, was indeed the only way by which he could progress from half-beast to sanctified soul. In episode after episode as the Biblical pageant passed before him, he saw how so many creatures like himself had believed (as he himself so often believed) that they were masters of their fate, and had been shown by suffering, even by damnation, that Man's freedom lay within the purpose of God. The drama reminded him, too, of the ever-present incongruous nature of sin in his daily existence. It had entered the world through a fallen angel (how unsettling to be shown that even an angel could fall!) whose enmity to God, within God's foreknowledge, had been permitted to use the instability of Woman to lead Man into the Original Sin, and it was shown that this Original Sin was motivated by physical passion, that passion with which, and through which, he and all his fellows had been born, yet which, it appeared, both made him human and could make him less than human. So with the many other sins which the dramas of Biblical story portrayed; greed, lust, anger, and so on – they were all potentially in his human nature, lying uneasily with those powers for good which only the grace of God could develop into salvation. Thus, as he watched, he felt more keenly the evil and the good, the despair and the hope, the possible disaster and the inexpressible success, which constituted his human condition, and which, when the drama had passed by, were still present and working through his daily life, through his every contact and relationship with his companions, affecting all the business of living on this earth. They lay also within the nature of his mind, so that throughout his waking life, and often in his dreams, no doubt, there were present inner as well as outer conflicts.

Of course, the active consciousness of these conflicts was not always with him; his human nature had its own methods of distracting him. Indeed, the dramatic entertainments of the religious cycles themselves offered him the novelty, the excitement, the pleasant anguish and the laughter, of their vivid recreation in action and dialogue of the Biblical stories which he had so often heard in church. Moreover, he was the earliest Englishman, possibly, to taste the curious psychological experience which is the very essence of watching and hearing drama, and which lies at the root of the 'pleasure' that an audience should derive from effective theatre. Part of him became identified with the actors in their roles, with some only superficially, with others (the most moving, the most appealing) very deeply. In a strangely 'real' sense he might become Abraham torn within by his need to choose between obedience to God and his love for his son Isaac; he and his friends knew of such struggles between duty and love, even if far less dreadful, in their daily lives. Part of him would be, then, within the heart and mind of Abraham at that moment of choice, but part of him would feel outside and 'above' the action on the stage, for he could understand the complete setting in which Abraham's struggle was taking place, the 'before-and-after' which the play was showing as a whole. Thus (and this is true and important for members of an audience in any age) he was at one and the same time himself, also the special individual on the stage within whose being he had penetrated, and, in addition, a kind of temporary superior creature, even a sort of god, who stood above the stage action and realised causes and foresaw consequences. As we shall see, this 'spectator experience' will be extremely important in considering later, and especially Shakespearean, plays.

Following the plays of the religious cycles, there arose what was also a religious play, but one in which there was a more direct moral teaching. The 'morality plays', unlike the earlier drama, did not use ready-made, known Biblical stories; they personified the good and bad qualities which every member of the audience, as we have seen, felt to be inherent in his human nature, and the 'plot' was the direct dramatisation, the acting-out, of the conflicts inevitably arising from the mixed nature of Man. The climax was equally inevitably the happy or fatal outcome of those conflicts, usually with the salutary lesson of how, after evil or folly had brought Man to the brink of damnation, repentance restored the hope of salvation. From such a play, the ordinary spectator could derive a great deal of simple excitement and pleasant suspense as well as moral improvement. *The Castle of Perseverance*, which appeared in the first quarter of the fifteenth century,[1] was designed for production in the open air in a large circular playing-space, with the Castle of Perseverance (the refuge of Man) in the centre; around it on the perimeter were located God, the Devil, the World and the Flesh. The large amount of movement, the costumes of the characters (the Devil with burning fireworks attached to him), and the physical encounters between good and evil, must have been in themselves a fine large holiday spectacle. But the Banns, the explanatory prologue, make very clear the serious moral struggle which is to be portrayed in the action of the play:

> Þe case [theme] of oure comynge ȝou to declare,
>   Euery man in hymself forsothe he it may fynde:
> Whou [How] Mankynde into þis werld born is ful bare
>   And bare schal beryed be at his lasy ende.
> God hym ȝeueth to(two) aungelys ful ȝep [alert]
>   and ful ȝare [active],
>   Þe Goode Aungel and þe Badde to hym for to lende.
> Þe Good techyth goodnesse, þe Badde synne
>   and sare [misery];
> Whanne þe ton hath þe victory, þe toþyr goth behende,
>   Be skyll [logically].
> Þe Goode Aungel coueytyth euermore Mans saluacion
> And þe Badde bysytyth [assails] hym euere to hys
>   dampnacion,
> And God hathe govyn Man fre arbitracion [choice]
>   Whethyr he wyl hymself saue or hys soule spyll
>   [destroy][2]

Here is the essence of the human condition; the never-ceasing need to choose between the good and the bad will continue to be the basis, implicit or explicit, of English drama through the years from this play to Shakespeare and, in fact, to the present day. The Banns continue by giving a summary of the main action, the struggle of Humanum Genus and his Good Angel, helped by the Christian Virtues of Humility, Patience, and so on, against his Bad Angel and the seven deadly sins; victory for the Good follows, then the back-sliding of Man, and finally his salvation through the mercy of God.

In this play the theme of Man's struggle in this world is shown in relation to God's ruling presence, and his intervention in mercy at the end. Soon the emphasis appears to shift. The next extant morality plays, *Mankind* (about 1465–70) and *Wisdom (Mind, Will and Understanding)* (second half of the fifteenth century) are still of course centred on Man's moral strife, but now this battle is shown in terms simpler and, significantly, more directly addressed to the everyday business of living.

Mankind has the typical morality pattern of rise–fall–rise: Mankind listens to Mercy and is good; he listens to Mischief, Nought, New Guise, Nowadays (the evils of the ordinary world) led by Titivillus, a devil, and falls into sin; he repents, and is helped to goodness by Mercy. Much broad humour, fighting and vigorous stage action, especially around Titivillus, keep the moral lesson firmly attached to the human world of the audience. This moral lesson stresses one of the main forms of 'human incongruity' (Part 1, section (a) of this study, pp. 1–2), the conflict between the soul and the body as they exist in uneasy combination in Man. As Mankind says:

My name ys Mankynde. I haue my composycyon
   Of a body and of a soull, of condycyon contrarye.
Betwyx þem tweyn ys a grett dyvisyon;
   He þat xulde [should] be subjecte, now he hath þe victory.

Thys ys to me a lamentable story
   To se my flesch of my soull to haue gouernance.
Wher þe goodewyffe ys master, þe goodeman may be sory.[3]
   I may both syth [sigh] and sobbe, þis ys a pytuouse
         remembrance.

O thou my soull, so sotyll in thy substance,
Alasse, what was þi fortune and þi chaunce
To be assocyat wyth my flesch, þat stynkyng dungehyll?[4]

A little later, Mercy, warning Mankind, specifically links the body–
soul incongruity to the battle of the life of Man:

The temptacyon of þe flesch 3e must resyst lyke a man,
For þer ys euer a batell betwyx þe soull and þe body:
   'Vita hominis est milicia super terram'.[5]

Wisdom is even simpler than *Mankind* in its use of the morality formula; it shows how Mind, Will and Understanding (the 'Mights' of Anima, the soul), despite a warning by Wisdom, are led astray into worldly sins and pleasures by Lucifer, and then, after Anima's repentance, with her are saved from sin. Here the plot is diversified by an effective use of stage pageantry, dances and striking symbolic costumes and masks, techniques of popular and upper-class entertainment already assimilated to drama. Wisdom, identified as Christ who is both God and Man and partner of the Soul, is the exponent of the moral of the play, which concerns the 'reason-unreason' form of human struggle: Anima, the soul, has Mind, Will (irrational desire) and Understanding, and these are led into sin by failing to follow true Reason.[6]

In Henry Medwall's *Goodly Interlude of Nature* (c1495) this theme of the struggle in Man between reason and unreason is expressed at far greater length,[7] and in more detail, than in *Wisdom*. In each Part Man is drawn into sin by unreason (in Part 1 by Pride and Sensuality, in Part 2 by the seven deadly sins), and in each Part finally returns penitent to Reason, and is forgiven and reinstated. Man himself, near the beginning of Part 1, states clearly his dilemma in being part of the natural world of plants and animals, yet given understanding and free will that make him almost equal to the angels,[8] and shortly after, Nature (who appears only in this opening of the play) defines the importance of reason to this creature Man with his incongruous mixture of animal and near-divine qualities; as he says to Man:

> Let Reason thee govern in every condition;
> For, if thou do not to his rule incline,
> It will be to thy great mischief and ruin.
>   I wot well Sensuality is to thee natural,
> And granted to thee in thy first creation.
> But, notwithstanding, it ought to be over all
> Subdued to Reason, and under his tuition.[9]

Medwall goes further in this exposition of Man's nature; he lets Sensuality make the disturbing and inescapable point that Man cannot be human without his non-rational feelings. Sensuality tells Nature:

> Ye clepe [call] him [Man] lord of all beasts living;
> And nothing worthy, as far as I can see.
> For, if there be in him no manner of feeling,
> Nor no lively quickness, what lord is he?
> A lord made of clouts [rags], or carved out of tree;

And fareth as an image graved out of stone[10]
That nothing else can do but stand alone.[11]

To this Nature replies that Sensuality must have a part in Man, but
that Reason must have the control: thus Man is left in his free will to
keep the fine balance between his reason and his irrational human
desires and feelings.

Everyman, (*The summoning of Everyman* as the play is described
by the Messenger-Prologue) dates from about 1495. It stands apart
from all other English morality plays because of its special theme and
its exceptional dramatic force. In fact, the theme and its impact are
inter-related, for this portrayal of how every man encounters the
sudden realisation of the inevitability and imminence of death, and
desperately discovers that the things of this world are valueless at
such a moment, has a naturally terrible and universal power, and
must progress with gathering momentum from its start to its end. We
have seen that a basic strife arises from Man's constant knowledge
that he is mortal, and his equally constant tendency to think and live
as though he were immortal. Religion, as in *Everyman*, tells him that
his soul is indeed immortal, and, after proper penitence and forgiveness, can live in glory forever – but it is the ordinary man as he lives in
this world (and as he is shown in the earlier part of *Everyman*) who
has to suffer the shocking truth of his situation as he feels it. This
awareness of inevitable death is present in a great deal of Elizabethan
drama, often as a mere unexamined truism, sometimes as an anxiety
deep beneath the surface of the play, sometimes (but most rarely)
with the full agonising realization of *Everyman*. When this realisation is accompanied by a complete absence of any kind of religious
hope (as in Webster's tragedies), or by the psychological inability to
feel faith (as in Marlowe's *Doctor Faustus*),[12] it has only a dark and
terrible despair (far from Everyman's final understanding) as its
outcome.

The problem of reason–unreason, already seen as the theme of
Wisdom and of *Nature*, is one of the major incompatibilities of our
human condition, and was recognised as such by the Elizabethans
and their precursors. It is not surprising, therefore, that it should be
implicit in sixteenth-century and later dramas, which all deal with
human life in human terms. In some of the sixteenth-century 'moral
play's the theological approach is still clear, but a difference of
attitude can still be seen. In Part 1 I have emphasised the concern of
sixteenth-century man, in England, with his human incongruity as it
affected the everyday business of living. Although the need for

spiritual salvation was always part of his consciousness, for him as for all of us today in our different age, the need to live well in practical terms from day to day occupied the forefront of his attention. Thus one can begin to see in sixteenth-century England a greater and increasing stress on 'social morality', on the best ways of living a good life amid contemporary social conditions.

Yet one should remember that the miracle cycles, with what must have appeared their old-fashioned Biblical framework and religious tone, lingered on in public performance well into the second half of the sixteenth century, despite official opposition after the Reformation.[13]

A relatively large group of the 'new' sixteenth-century moral plays deals with the very practical and everyday problem of the control of the irrational in the young, in other words, the perennial difficulty of bringing up one's children properly.[14] It is assumed, of course, that the father, on whom the responsibility ultimately rests, is aware of the dangers of reason–unreason in himself, and therefore the more afraid of those dangers affecting his child. An early example of such plays, the anonymous *Youth* (*c*1520), is comparatively simple in its lesson; it shows how Youth can be brought to reason by Charity and Humility helping him against the disruptive and irrational forces of Pride and Riot. Although the reformative purpose is plain, nearly two-thirds of the play are comic or light in tone; the belief that drama, however lofty its moral aim, must also be entertaining goes back to the mystery cycles, and is strong (and growing stronger) in the plays we are now considering. Richard Wever's *An Enterlude called Lusty Juventus, Lyuely Describing the Frailtie of Youth: of Nature Prone to Vyce: by Grace and Good Counsayll Traynable to Vertue* (*c*1550) sufficiently indicates in its title the author's moral and social purpose, and suggests his emphasis in the play on the natural depravity of Man and the importance of God's grace rather than good works, a Calvinist doctrine. Juventus is led astray by the Devil, Hypocrisy, Fellowship and Abominable Living, but is finally brought to good life (and a lengthy account of his folly and repentance) by the efforts of Good Counsel and Knowledge (of God's Verity). All this is lightened by some thumping satire against Papists, and lively 'wicked' passages, but what one remembers most is the human, moving admission of youth's natural desire to enjoy life, expressed in the song sung by Lusty Juventus and his bad companions:

Why should not youth fulfil his own mind,
As the course of nature doth him bind?
Is not everything ordained to do his kind?
    Report me to you, report me to you.[15]
Do not the flowers spring fresh and gay,
Pleasant and sweet in the month of May?
And when their time cometh, they fade away,
    Report me to you, report me to you.
Be not the trees in winter bare?
Like unto their kind, such they are;
And when they spring, their fruits declare.
    Report me to you, report me to you.
What should youth do with the fruits of age,
But live in pleasure in his passage?
For when age cometh, his lusts will suage.
    Report me to you, report me to you.[16]

Here human conflict is admitted in frankness to an audience which knows the truth of it; reason may convince one of the ultimate need for wise living, but sometimes one's very nature fights against it.[17] Two other moral plays on this theme of the need to control children are alike in their simple moral pattern. The anonymous *Nice Wanton* (*c*1550) is the exemplary tale of how a good son, Barnabas, saves from suicide his mother whose heart has been broken by her bad son, Ishmael, who is hanged, and her bad daughter Dalilah, who dies of the pox. Thomas Ingeland's *The Disobedient Son* (or *Child*) (*c*1560) also deals with the problem of the recalcitrant son; here he marries without his father's permission, and ends in poverty and repentance. A late example of this type of moral play is *A mery and pleasaunt Comedie called Misogonus* (anonymous ms, *c*1560–77). This is a long play; the main theme shows how Philogonus, a worried and verbose father, learns from the bad behaviour of his son Misogonus (who, however, reforms at the end of the play) the folly of not bringing children up strictly. Although one can appreciate the human anxiety and self-reproach of Philogonus, who begins to live as a real person in the latter part of the play (like that later much-tried father Leonato), the chief attraction for the audience must surely have been the large amount of 'village' humour which is offered. The simple joking of John Heywood (e.g. his *Johan Johan* of the 1520s) has in this play become a series of low-life, vivid comic scenes scarcely connected with the main story, but full of the human characteristics of the common people: indeed, the major part of Act 3, Scene 3, where Cacurgus pretends to be a learned doctor-magician in order to dupe the simple peasants Isbell and Madge, can be considered a worthy precursor of the far more brilliant, but similar, stage-spectacle of Volpone acting the mountebank. Thus by the 1570s the moral lesson of *Youth*, still attached to abstract conceptions of 'religious' morality like charity and humility, has become firmly rooted in the 'social' morality of everyday life and its problems, where the underlying battle of reason–unreason is still and always present. As we have seen, the Elizabethans were well aware that failure to control unreason by reason could cause disorder and evil in society generally, as well as in the home. This belief shapes the themes of a number of moral plays of this period. Dishonesty and, especially, greed (a prime example of personal desire, uncontrolled by the higher reason, becoming a social evil) are used as effective dramatic material, for dramatists had long been aware that the portraal of roguery and cunning were always entertaining as well as salutary. *Hycke Scorner* (anon. *c*1513), another early example of the movement towards 'social' morality in drama, has a lesson drawn from the process by which Freewill and Imagination, bad but amusing and lively characters, are brought to repentance, which in this case means that personal freedom of impulse is curbed, but nearly two-thirds of the play are devoted to direct description of, and comment upon, the evils and trickery of the contemporary world. *A New Interlude of Impatient Poverty* (anon. *c*1547) shows again the emphasis on social morality: Impatient Poverty (surely a character-name for any age) is helped by Peace to reform, and is named Prosperity; he is then misled by Envy and Misrule, repents, and is renamed Prosperity by Peace. The moral is plainly that good self-controlled behaviour leads to wordly success. The description of Ulpian Fulwell's *Like Will to Like* (*c*1568) in the full title shows the same purpose: 'Wherein is declared not onely punishment followeth those that wil rather followe licentious liuing, then to esteem & followe good councel: and what great benefits and commodities they receive that apply them unto vertuous liuing and good exercises'. Similarly, Thomas Lupton's *Moral and Pitiefvl Comedie, Intituled, All for Money, Plainly representing the manners of men, and fashions of the world noweadayes . . .* (*c*1577) is based on the theme that in the contemporary world money seems able to do anything: the passion of greed, with the related self-indulgences like Pride and Gluttony, is shown controlling the lives of modern men; their sin, of course dooms them to damnation, and Godly Admonition, Vertue, Humilitie and Charitie have the last word but the lesson is certainly more social than religious.

Following from the concern with the effects of personal unreason on society, there was the wider 'political' interest in the well-being of the state as a whole, including, of course, the importance of the ruler in this respect.[18] A number of moral plays of the first seventy years or so of the century relate to this interest, even anxiety. The anonymous *Godly Queene Hester* (*c*1527), in one sense, looks back to the older fashion of the dramatisation of Biblical stories (which George Peele was later to revive briefly), but the story chosen is of how the good Queen, in all humility, had the moral strength to tell her husband, King Assuerus, that he had failed as a ruler in letting himself be led by the wicked Amon into wrongly persecuting the Jews of his kingdom; the main lesson of the play is that the responsibility of a king is to deal justly with his subjects, and not to be deceived by false advisers. Indeed, the King himself begins the final moralising of the play with this lesson:

> My Lords! by this figure [example] ye may well see
> The multitude hurt by the head's negligence.
> If to his pleasure so given is he,
> That he will no pain take nor diligence,
> Who careth not for his cure (responsibility) oft loseth credence;
> A proverb of old some time in usage;
> Few men that serve but for their own advantage.[19]

Of the . . . *merry play, both pithy and pleasant, of Albion, Knight* . . . (*c*.1537) there is known only an anonymous fragment (seven leaves) of the printed text of about 1565, but this remnant offers another approach, and an interesting one, to the subject of political-social discord. There is a long passage[20] in which Division describes to Injury (in surprisingly frank detail) how he will set at loggerheads the commons and Principality, and the lords spiritual and the lords temporal, by playing on the pride and suspicions of each group: in this way Peace and Justice will be weakened. The point that social and political confusion arise from the lack of reason is epitomised in Division's astonishment when Injury tells him that he must pretend to be wise (calling himself Policy):

> *Injury*
>   Then must thou dissemble thyself wise.

Division
    I make God a vow, that is impossible!
    That I, and wisdom, should knit in one quyneble
                                    (Ed. musical part)
    Or, in my brain to print such abusion
    That wisdom and I should be in one conclusion;[21]

In *Respublica* (1553) (possibly by Nicholas Udall), a long play of
some 2,350 lines, the treatment of older drama, first of Man's
personal salvation, and then of his moral behaviour in this world,
has shifted to a direct presentation of the dangers to the state of
power-seeking and greed: there is no emphasis on individual sin. The
play shows how Respublica (the state), a widow aware of her decay,
is persuaded by Avarice (calling himself Policy) that he and his
friends Honesty (i.e. Adulation), Authority (i.e. Insolence) and Reformation (i.e. Oppression) can reform and save her: the rogues
thrive, and People has to appeal to Respublica. Finally she is
supported by Compassion, Peace and Justice, and the villains are
punished by Nemesis (Adulation reforms and is allowed to survive as
Honesty). This very bare outline does little justice to the actual
dramatic strength of the play; although the moral purpose may
weigh a little heavily at times on a modern reader, there is much lively
roguery and strong irony in the drama. Avarice, particularly, is
almost a fully human personality of an amoral type that is always
with us,[22] and Respublica, well-meaning but weak, and the sturdy
and irrepressible People, are vividly and movingly real. *Wealth and
Health* (anon, *c*1554), in contrast, is very short (about 850 lines),
and has little of the richness of *Respublica*, although there is a great
deal of popular fun in the friendly hits at 'aliens' working in London,
expressed in the (to me, at least) almost incomprehensible English–
Dutch gibberish of Hance the Dutchman. Nevertheless, the chief
point is the welfare of England: Wealth and Health (of the state) are
deceived by Ill-Will and Shrewd (cunning) Wit, repent, and are saved
by Good Remedy. This is the simple formula of, say, *Youth* applied
not to personal, but to social, moral teaching. *Gorboduc* (1562) can
be regarded as another transitional example, but of a special kind: its
joint authors, Thomas Sackville and Thomas Norton, were writing
for an educated audience of the Inner Temple who were well
acquainted with the recently published *The Mirror for Magistrates*,
and with Senecan tragedy, the inspiration of the play's moral purpose, of which, no doubt, they fully approved. The play sets out to

show the historical and political results of the greed for power: the moral, brought out in rhetoric, violent action and moral dumb-show, is that rulers without political wisdom, unable to control themselves by reason, can cause disorder in the state, unrest and civil war, and personal disaster to themselves as well. But the play must also be seen as anticipating the approaching dramatic fashion of the fully-fledged history play, in which, as we shall see, history provides a framework which is fleshed out, with increasing depth and complexity, by the dramatic exposition of the personal incongruities of those who make history, or are made or unmade by history.

In this same period, of course, there were many plays which had virtually no specific moral purpose. I am thinking of the 'entertainment dramas' which appear between (say) John Heywood's *The Pardoner and the Friar (c*1519) and George Wapull's *The Tyde Taryeth No Man* (1576).[23] In such plays there is, naturally, some implied moral purpose in the display of the follies, sins and roguery of ordinary folk (*The Tyde Taryeth* has an explicit moral lesson at the beginning and at the end), but it is clear that the authors were aiming chiefly at the amusement of ordinary audiences. Even so, one must remember that these popular dramas deal with the perplexities of existence, those everyday forms of human incongruity which always bedevil Mankind, and which have their affinities with the deeper and more disturbing forms that we have been considering. For example, *Tom Tyler and his Wife* (anon. *c.*1560) shows the unsuccessful struggle of a peasant husband against his bullying wife, the subject of comedy throughout the ages, but the general point of the play, that one's life is ruled by destiny, and that one had better learn to make the best of it, shows a realisation of that opposition of fate and freewill which lies at the root of some of the greatest drama.

Finally, before we turn to the plays of Shakespeare's contemporaries, the highly idiosyncratic dramatic works[24] of John Bale must be briefly considered. He was Bishop of Ossory, and wrote his plays deliberately and openly as a means of presenting his theological beliefs, attitudes emphatically Protestant and virulently anti-papist. Thus his drama stands apart from other plays of the period which have a religious tone of a more general moral kind, and without Bale's marked polemical purpose.[25] Bale's plays have a special interest in that they show very clearly the close link between religious teaching and human nature at work in this world. *John Baptist's Preaching* has a passage, spoken by John Baptist, which describes the hoped-for effects of the Gospel upon Man's worldly behaviour:

All that, aforetime, untoward did remain,
The rule of God's word will now make straight and plain.
The covetous juror shall now be liberal;
The malicious man will now to charity fall;
The wrathful hater shall now love earnestly;
To temperate measure men will change gluttony;
Pride shall so abate that meekness will prevail;
Lechery shall lie down, and cleanness set up sail;
Slothfulness shall slide, and diligence arise
To follow the truth, in godly exercise.[26]

Here is brought to a point the conflict which sixteenth-century man knew existed between his spiritual aspirations, as formulated by religion, and his human weaknesses. Similarly, the lesson of *The temptacyon of our lorde and sauer Jesus Christ* is the importance of Christ's rejection of Satan's offer of the wordly lures of greed, arrogance and power. *Thre lawes* deals with what we have seen as a common theme in drama, the danger of disruption of good order in the realm; needless to say, Papistry is the cause, while Protestantism stands for the essential rule of God's law joined to human law in ensuring order. *The Chief Promises of God unto Man* is a dramatic sequence, throughout the Biblical history of Man, of the occasions when God grew tired of Man's constant disobedience and sin, but was persuaded to give him yet another chance of salvation. The play shows Christ's coming as the sign of God's decision to turn from strict justice to mercy in dealing with Man, the religious side, as we have seen, of a powerful form of human tension (see Part 1 section (j) pp. 26–8). It was still the subject of discussion, in religious poetry, in 1610.[27] Finally, *John, King of England*, a long play (2,783 lines) in two parts, is especially interesting in that it deals with human conflict in both its 'private' and its 'public' effects in a way anticipating the later Elizabethan history play of Shakespeare and his contemporaries. It amplifies the religious–social theme of *Thre lawes*, that papistry means disorder in the state and Protestantism order, by linking it to the figure of John and the troubles of his reign. The social evils resulting from papist control, and especially the cunning and arrogance of papistry in ruling the political scene, are very fully and effectively presented, but at the heart of the play is the problem of kingship. The God-given and unquestionable authority of a king is stressed throughout, but alongside this common view, prominent later in the Homilies, there is presented the actual nature of John. He is shown as a very human ruler trying to solve a dilemma which, to him, is insoluble, the choice between bringing the evils of war upon his country, and giving up his power to the Papists. England, a widow (as in *Respublica* later) representing the people scorned and oppressed by the papal powers, reveres and yet pities John; it is evident that a king is but a man, and may be inadequate for the burden of command which God has placed upon him. In fact, the Popish force of Sedition is finally conquered only by the intervention of an 'outside' figure, Imperial Majesty, the abstract quality which John all too humanly lacked.

(b) HUMAN CONFLICT IN PLAYS OF SHAKESPEARE'S CONTEMPORARIES

It is in the 1570s that one can see the beginnings of the truly professional drama in England, marked by the building of the first purpose-built theatre in 1576–77, in the London country 'suburb' of Shoreditch. The drama offered grew continuously in variety of stage-technique and play-material, catering for many levels of taste both in the same theatre and in separate theatres. In other words, drama became an organised response to a public interest, and that very fact meant that there was no radical break in continuity with earlier drama. Drama in England had always had a function as entertainment; it had always had, too, a more serious purpose, of a religious and spiritual, or of a more social-moral, nature, often both, and this purpose, as we have seen, was itself a reflection of the basic nature of Man, and of his spiritual and practical awareness of the struggles of his nature. By the closing decades of the sixteenth century, the spiritual-religious bases of human conflict had largely, but not entirely, ceased to provide the main material for drama: the emphasis in drama on the everyday social-moral conflicts as they appeared in, and affected, normal life in this world, had grown rapidly in the sixteenth century, and remained dominant with the appearance of the 'new' professional London theatre (and its country secondary activities). This theatre was 'new' in its wider appeal and greater complexity of method and organisation, a sophistication evoked by a large urban potential audience with the diversity of class and taste which one would expect in a capital city. Yet that audience, however large or various, was still an audience of human beings all with the personal and social interests and concerns to which their common humanity inescapably committed them, as it had committed their forebears. Moreover, this was an Elizabethan audience, that is, one composed of people who seem to have been especially aware of, and extremely interested in, the incongruities and complexities of their common human nature, eager for guidance in avoiding the personal and social dangers which that human nature presented, and even more eager (like all human beings) to enjoy, safely because vicariously, the spectacle of the evils into which one's humanity could lead one. This special curiosity about life is an Elizabethan characteristic which no student of the contemporary literature, sermons, poetry, letters or memoirs (that is, sources in addition to drama itself) can fail to accept as a fact. For a Londoner, in particular, the public drama became the most vivid and immediate means of satisfying this deep interest; it gave enjoyment, sometimes only superficial enjoyment, but there was always some presentation of the facts and conflicts of human existence. Often, as the drama made new explorations of that human material, the audience must have found once again, as its ancestors had in seeing earlier drama (although in a different context), that to realise one's own human quality, to suffer and to strive with Man's dilemmas in sympathy with an actor on a stage, was a liberating and desirable 'pleasure'. Human conflict was thus, more than ever before, the basic material and inspiration of the drama which we have now to consider, the drama around Shakespeare, and it was used to produce every effect from the lightest comedy to the deepest tragedy.

First let us take two plays, one early and one much later in this period, which show the dramatic use of that inner conflict between a sense of power and actual impotence which we have shown to be a common concern (see Part 1, section (c), pp. 3–5). For an Elizabethan it was pleasant, even pleasantly shocking, to see Pisaro[28] the would-be domineering father convinced of his parental power, reduced to having to accept the fact that his three daughters had all upset his plans, had chosen husbands for themselves, and had scorned the rights of a father: that Pisaro was a foreigner (a 'Portingale') and a usurer heightened the pleasure with an appeal to Elizabethan popular prejudice.[29] In the much later play,[30] the father was Sir Giles Overreach, a man Volpone-like in his greed for wealth, and almost a Tamburlaine in his lust for power over those around him. Here the self-deception of Pisaro has grown from the delight of mild human incongruity which an Elizabethan could laughingly identify within himself, into the shock of extreme human incongruity where the fantasy of power collides head-on with the reality of power-lessness. By that unbearable collision the personality of Overreach is destroyed. Massinger's play is technically a comedy, for Overreach's daughter and her lover are happily married by the end (and the play is full of comic moments), but it is still true that Overreach ends in futility and madness; he is not a tragic figure only because the discrepancy between his belief in his power and his actual weakness operates outside his character, and is never recognised within himself: as we shall see, true tragedy always shows, or at least suggests, a deeper awareness of the conflict within the tragic figure.

We have earlier seen that much human struggle was connected with the relationships between men and women, as one might expect (see Part 1, section (f), pp. 12–16). In the more 'popular' comedies of the period,[31] a love-theme is common; it is usually simple, pleasant and normal in its portrayal of a young man and woman in love, attaining their goal of marriage in spite of difficulties: love is accepted, indeed welcomed, with little serious internal conflict, as an incongruity which is part of everyday life, and which (it is fondly believed) achieves its resolution when the lovers are united. Of course the struggles of true love are used as a framework for comic intrigues and social comment, but the main point is that falling in love is seen as one (the most pleasant and acceptable) way in which men's desires and passions may sometimes be allowed to rule their reason. In these plays love remains an effective vehicle for comedy, for the portrayal of human happiness, because here it is usually accepted without any fully realistic analysis of the potentialities of human passion. Sometimes in such plays, although rarely, there is a suggestion of a more profound truth: for instance, in John Cooke's *Greene's Tu Quoque* (1611) there is the contrast between Gertrude, the woman in love and unable to hide it, and Joyce, her sister, who rebels against the traditional female submission to love and Man's dominance in love. The latter owes something, no doubt, to Shakespeare's Beatrice, and, like Beatrice, she finally succumbs happily to her fate of loving and being loved. The following passages show how these two characters touch (but only lightly) on that inner conflict between reason and passion which was so disruptive in other contemporary plays:

> GERTRUDE [*solil*]. But arts we [women] know not, nor have any
> skill
> To feign a sour look to a pleasing will;

> Nor couch a secret love in show of hate:
> But, if we like, must be compassionate.
> Yet will I strive to bridle and conceal
> The hid affection which my heart doth feel.[32] . . .
> JOYCE (*solil*.] To wrastle 'gainst the stream of our affection,
> Is to strike air, or buffet with the wind
> That plays upon us. I have striv'd to cast
> This fellow from my thoughts, but still he grows
> More comely in my sight: yet [is] a slave,
> Unto one worse-condition'd than a slave.[33]

Later she capitulates to Staines, the man she loves, in the very tone of Miranda to Ferdinand:

> Sir, I do know you love me; and the time
> Will not be dallied with: be what you seem,
> Or not the same; I am your wife, your mistress,
> Or your servant—indeed, what you will make me.[34]

Another approach to this love form of our human strife is that which characterises a number of the 'romance' plays of this period. John Fletcher's *The faithful shepherdess* (c1608) neatly but superficially portrays the spectrum of emotion from the pure chastity of Clorin and her lover Thenot, through the average passionate man Alexis, to the extreme lust of Cloe and the Sullen Shepherd. The play is a cleverly contrived pageant rather than a drama of the battles of human emotion, and the conflict of reason and passion goes no deeper than the surface contrast between pure and unchaste love, with somewhat formal admiration for the former and disgust for the latter. In such plays, considerations of plot-elaboration alone bring the pure into contact with the impure, and then only in the safety of innocence, as when, in Beaumont and Fletcher's *Philaster* (c1609), the virtuous Princess Arethusa is accused of unchastity with her page Bellario: there can be little surprise (certainly not for the contemporary audience) when Bellario is found to be a young maiden, and Arethusa and her noble husband Philaster end the play in happiness. *The Two Noble Kinsmen* (1613)[35] comes closer to a portrayal of the oppositions of life, for most of this long play is based on the struggle between the conventional code of friendship of companion knights, and the irrational irresistible pressure of love: in fact, the dilemma is so evenly poised that only the accidental death of Arcite cuts the knot, and gives a happy ending with Palamon marrying Emilia. The human conflict, in the highly contrived situation which evokes it, is made strangely real, so real that it jars with its setting – one is reminded of Shakespeare's difficulties.

At the opposite pole from this 'romance' world of high sophistication (unreal, yet at times beautiful in language and assured in tone), there are some plays which painstakingly, and with few pretensions to imagination or beauty, seek to show the encounters of emotion and reason as they can and do occur in the real world. Thomas Heywood's *A Woman Killed with Kindness* (1603) is usually remembered only as the curiously moving but ironic story of Frankford's treatment of his unfaithful wife. His reason resists the natural passionate impulse to revenge, and he puts her into a separate house, where she soon dies, repentant and finally forgiven. Such 'mercy' appears to us today more cruel than violence, and perhaps some Elizabethans may have felt the same, for we know that they were well aware of the dangers of cold reason, and feared it. This is the main plot, but the sub-plot which few remember is also significant, for it gives a comment on the reason-over-emotion theme of the main story: Sir Giles Mountford is a man whose violent anger leads him to kill two men in a quarrel, and who is thus reduced to poverty and imprisonment (although afterwards saved). Perhaps nearer to the realities of worldly evil, and certainly direct and simple in their approach, are the two anonymous plays *Arden of Feversham* (c1591) and *A Yorkshire Tragedy* (c1606); each is based on an actual crime, and each portrays the personal evil and suffering caused by the passions. The former, on the face of it, is crude and melodramatic, but it has a curious intensity: passion drives Alice Arden and her lover Mosbie, but particularly Alice, to commit murder with a kind of clumsy, blind stupidity that is almost animal-like, and the murdered husband, too, has the narrow, obtuse nature of a man obsessed by greed. There is little that is admirable, no larger hope, in this small world concerned only with its own mean desires; it is curiously akin, but in a bourgeois setting, to the 'Court' world of Webster's tragedies. *A Yorkshire Tragedy* goes more deeply into the nature of murder by showing the struggle between reason and unreason in the murderer; his soliloquy in Scene 4 is a tragically true expression of Man's recognition of his inner dichotomy, of the fact that he can see the good he should follow, and is given passions which prevent him from following it:

Oh thou confused man! thy pleasant sins haue

vndone thee, thy damnation has beggerd thee!
That heauen should say we must not sin, and
yet made women! giues our sences waie to finde
pleasure, which being found confounds vs. Why
shold we know those things [which] so much
misuse vs? – oh, would vertue had been
forbidden! wee should then haue prooued all
vertuous, for tis our bloude [instinct] to
loue what were forbidden.[36]

George Wilkins's *The Miseries of Inforst Marriage* (1606) is also
based on the same true story of the murderer Walter Calverley, but to
far different effect, for it has a happy ending. Yet the play's title, and
its motto 'Qui alios (seipsum) docet' ('Who teaches others teaches
himself'), suggest the serious underlying purpose of the work. It
shows very convincingly (despite the elaborately contrived reconcili-
ations of the ending) the potential evils of the social custom of
arranged marriages, by which a man had to accept a union manipulated by hardheaded relatives, without any consideration of love.
Here human incongruity is viewed from the other side, and it is the
calculating 'lower' reason which nearly proves disastrous when it
deprives true love, true passion, of its fulfilment. A more sophisticated dramatic treatment of this reason–unreason incongruity is
George Chapman's *The Widow's Tears* (c1605) in which the comedy arises from a persistent vein of cynical 'realism' about women
and their love. The dominant figure of the play, Tharsalio, is almost a
comic Iago, stripping away any pretensions to genuine feeling that
women claim, and reducing their love to mere selfish lust. Obviously,
Chapman is employing to the full the cynical implications of the
source-story by Petronius, but he is doing so with an underlying
suggestion of disgust which one would expect from a dramatist with
his strong moral views. Elizabethans at this time seem to have been
more than ever aware of the conflict between the coldly-rational and
the emotional views of love: Shakespeare was using it effectively in
his plays, and not only for comedy. But this awareness could be
expressed without undue seriousness; the anti-idealistic, anti-
Petrarchan reaction to the more feeling sense of women's love, as
seen for example in certain Shakespeare sonnets and in Donne, was
at least partly the use of a deliberately 'shocking' fashion, and the
contrast could be expressed as little more than a comment on the
nature of contemporary love. For example, the 'moral' of Fletcher

and Beaumont's *The Scornful Lady* (c1613) is that society women should renounce their tricks and affectations of love, and offer their lovers the honest, plain affection that men need from their chosen wives. Yet Chapman's comedy had suggested something of the disruptive, pessimistic mood that a fuller realisation of the warfare of reason–unreason in men and women could produce, and in Webster we shall see the full complex effects in tragedy of such a realisation.

Meanwhile, we must return to earlier plays, of the 1580s, where the tension in Man between reason and unreason had been shown in its most direct, violent and exciting form. Popular melodrama obtained a brief furore by pouring out, with vigorous action and emphatic stage-craft, almost every obvious example of the savagery and wickedness which passion could produce when beyond the control of reason. Thomas Kyd's *The Spanish Tragedy* (c1587) (in the 1597 revision by Jonson) is the archetype of such drama, wherein violence begets violence, cruelty leads inevitably to the further cruelty of revenge, and the passions are shown in unrestrained command of Man's (and Woman's) actions. This play was certainly an obvious, over-simplified display of emotion triumphing over reason, but it was nevertheless a valid one for Elizabethans; they knew (as perhaps we are beginning to realise anew today) the blind violence and stupid cruelty of which men who feel without thinking are capable – countless so-called 'witches' had been and were being consumed alive in fires lit by fear and spite and superstition in England and throughout Europe. Christopher Marlowe's *The Jew of Malta* (1589) resembles Kyd's play in its sequence of the melodramatic results of unrestrained passion. Here the destructive greed and spite of the Jew Barabas meet head-on the equally irrational blind malice, prejudice and pride of the 'Christians'; the result is the most obvious popular entertainment, plain melodrama perhaps, but a melodrama uncomfortably akin to the actual truth of contemporary attitudes and ever-present human nature. Such plays, amid the growing sophistication of playwrights and audiences, could not long continue popular in their original naïvety, but they may have reminded later Elizabethan dramatists of the vast wealth of materials for more deeply exciting plays that lay within the warring hearts and minds of both themselves and their audiences. In the past, the drama of human conflict had had its tragedy of lost salvation and its melodrama of the devils of Hell; now it was intent on the torments within a man and between a man and his society. Those plays of this period which were centred on reason–unreason appear to vary between these two contexts. But man can never be effectively portrayed on the stage in complete isolation – even a soliloquy concerns more than the speaker – and these tragedies show that, however imperfect the balance may be, their writers were aware that tragedy on the stage, as in life, involves the stresses outside as well as within the man at the centre of the struggle. Moreover, the difference of emphasis, as well as of balance, produced a variety of tragic, near-tragic and even melodramatic effects.[37] John Marston's *Antonio and Mellida* (*c*1599) and its sequel *Antonio's Revenge* (*c*1600) provide a point of departure. Both plays show the battle in man of his passions and reason. In the first play (Act 3 Scene 2) Feliche, seeing Man as a mixture of conflicting goodness and badness, is glad of his own freedom from extremes, but immediately afterwards he falls into jealous anger at Castillio's success with women. In the next scene (4.1) Andrugio first speaks philosophically of the virtues of a 'true right king', and then, a moment later, loses his temper when Lucio mentions the Genoese: the point is stressed when he adds:

> Spit on me, Lucio, for I am turn'd slave,
> Observe how passion domineers o'er me.[38]

Similarly, in *Antonio's Revenge*, Pandulpho on two occasions early in the play (1.5 and 2.2) speaks of how the man of true valour is above anger and violence, his reason unaffected by the effects of mere chance. Yet in fact he takes part with Antonio in his bloody revenge on Piero, and himself admits to Antonio (4.5) that his manly passion has overcome his reason: as he says, 'Man will break out, despight Philosophie'.[39] This might almost be the motto of the two plays. They are essentially popular melodrama (somewhat less crude, it is true, than Kyd's play), but now characters have been shown to be aware of their human nature at odds within themselves; this modifies the melodramatic tone with something approaching a tragic quality. Tourneur's *The Revenger's Tragedy* (*c*1606) is a hurrying, breathless pageant of wild sexual desire, centred around the Duke, and spreading outward to his Duchess, his son, and his bastard son; on the surface it is a melodrama of lust, and doubtless it excited and satisfied its audience at that level. But in the character of Vendice, the revenger, and his constant comments on the evil in man and in society, there is at least a suggestion, running through the play, of the wider relevance of that evil; lust is seen to destroy both individuals and the world in which they live, and die. By the end of the play, only the good Antonio lives to succeed the Duke; some kind of resolution has been achieved; Man has been shown as more (if only a little more) than a mere greedy, unthinking animal. Yet, when that has been said, this play of Tourneur's (and the same is true of his *The Atheists's Tragedy* (*c*1609), still remains barely on the edge of true tragedy; it is good 'theatre' of an obvious kind, but there is little expression of the deeper, universal truths of human nature, and thus little to draw each member of the audience into the action – and it is when this happens that true tragedy begins.

Webster's *The White Devil* (*c*1612) and *The Duchess of Malfi* (*c*1614) have a quality distinct from that of all the 'tragedies' we have so far considered, although the events in them are just as extraordinary, just as violent and destructive, and the theatricalism of special stage effects is equally obviously aimed at popular taste. But the essential impression of these plays is much more deeply disturbing, because it is far closer to part, at least, of universal human truth; Webster is showing something of a sense of human disruption which the audience feel within themselves. At the crucial moments in these two plays, a true tragic bond between play and audience is created, in which the individual spectator feels himself inside the play, sharing the feelings and interaction of feelings of the characters, and yet also outside the play, able to see the inevitable human pattern of that interaction, and its consequences for the humanity on the stage and in himself. The protagonist of each play is a woman, and a woman of a vital quality, that stubborn, instinctive assertion of personal rights which, in a woman in the arrogant male world of these two dramas, becomes a rare form of obstinate courage. Each is driven from within by human pressures, in Vittoria's case sexual desire and the passion for social greatness, in the Duchess's a much more moving, simple woman's need to live in peace with the man she loves and their children. However appealing they are, we must remember that the Duchess, in the view of many Elizabethans, is at fault in pursuing her personal desires at the expense of the duties of her station (her brothers have that much worldly justification),[40] and Vittoria is an acquiescent, even eager, part of the amoral society without which she cannot exist – and because of which she ceases to exist. Neither was wholly admirable, then, in Elizabethan moral terms, yet their weaknesses were human ones which the audience could experience and acknowledge within themselves. Each is caught up in a closing mechanism of plotting, and finally dies, but neither has been destroyed within; each retains to the end a self-awareness, an ability to face both good and ill, that stands above the painful destruction of all hope. Thus the cruder conflict of passion and reason of Tourneur has now a greater subtlety and scope, a new universality in terms of human experience; passion is still shown as a dangerous irrational force, but it is our passion as much as Vittoria's or the Duchess's, and now the rational side of Man, when it becomes divorced from all human feeling, the coldly employed tool of arrogance and selfishness, is felt to be a 'lower reason' far more truly evil than passion, however regrettable that passion may be. For Man in his ever-continuing contest between reason and unreason, here is some dramatic suggestion of the complexity of the struggle, and the pity of it – and the challenge. Perhaps the Elizabethan audience may have seen Webster as confusing moral values when he seemed to wish to show that Vittoria's lust and self-seeking, for example, were at least more acceptable, as human qualities, than the evil of those around her – but they would be convinced in their hearts. The fact was that Webster had shown (as Shakespeare so often showed) that, for tragedy, moral values must be felt in personal, not legalistic, terms; personal sympathy moves us more deeply with its conviction of truth than any mere formula of right and wrong. Which is perhaps to say (as an Elizabethan would have expressed it) that tragedy must have something of the all-comprehending love of Christ, the New Dispensation of Mercy rather than the Old Dispensation of Justice: perhaps it is only in understanding and mercy that an audience can feel, at last, some resolution of its own discords.

The theme of emotion–reason was being used, of course, for light popular drama of a far less searching kind than Webster's, or even Marston's. An interesting example is provided by two plays of similar title and pattern, Fletcher and Beaumont's *Cupid's Revenge* (c1608) and John Stephens's *Cynthia's Revenge* (1613): they are both entertaining medleys of passion and violence (the latter far longer and more unrestrained than the former), but it is noteworthy that each is based on showing what happens when there is a breakdown of reason in society. In *Cupid's Revenge* the worship of the god of love is banned by Hidaspes, the daughter of an old Duke; in revenge, Cupid causes virtually everyone (at the Court, that is) to fall into wild and foolish loves, which are followed by intrigues, murders, suicide and so on: the play becomes almost a morality-drama of the dangers to the moral and physical good order of society when Man seeks arrogantly to deny his natural desires.[41] Stephens's play similarly tells of the madness, revenge, killing, intended rape and other entertaining disasters which occur when Cynthia (the moon, patron of the fantasies of love) shows her displeasure with mortals. The lesson is obviously that love is not to be ignored or despised by rational arrogance. It is characteristic of the age that, although the play is full of inflated rhetoric and improbabilities, it also has a thread of quite sober comment on the follies and evils of society, and two lines which epitomise human dichotomy of a kind already noted:

> Yet on our state's imposed a slavish curse,
> To see things good, though we connive at worse.[42]

The use of this theme of reason—unreason continued, of course, in drama beyond Webster, but only rarely with anything of the Websterian tone of pity for the sufferings of human beings in the grip of their inner struggles. One or two of the later 'tragic melodramas' have this authentic tragic note, and most unmistakably Middleton and Rowley's *The Changeling* (1622), in its main plot. This centres around Beatrice, a lady about to be forced by her parents to marry Alonzo, yet deeply in love with Alsemero; passion drives her to find a tool, Deflores, to kill Alonzo; then, after the murder, Deflores reveals that he, too, is driven by passion, and Beatrice has to give herself to him. Violence and intrigue follow, and culminate in Deflores's killing of Beatrice and of himself. Only in *Macbeth* has the awful logic of passionate blind desire, working through violence, been shown more truly and more terribly; moreover, Beatrice has something of the dreadful amoral 'innocence' of Lady Macbeth.[43] In *The Changeling*, as in the Webster plays, we are taken into the inner heart of the protagonist, and made to feel how that heart is impelled by its own needs: the results of the passionate necessity are cruel and dreadful, but our understanding of the pressure of her warring impulses on Beatrice creates a deep pity which, as I have suggested, is merciful rather than just. That the 'comic' sub-plot counterpoints ironically Beatrice's passionate unreason by showing a man using simulated and calculated 'madness' to obtain a desired woman, may not even have been intended by the dramatists, but the irony is there if the play is given in its entirety.

A series of plays by George Chapman written in this period[44] shows another approach to the portrayal of human incongruity in drama. If the plays which we have just been considering suggest how much some playgoers enjoyed the violence and horrors produced when passion had its way unchecked by reason, the existence of these Chapman plays reveals that some audiences, at least, were prepared to see Man's human struggles treated more analytically, more 'philo-sophically', in dramas where these struggles may still produce pain and violence, but where the sufferers can sometimes glimpse the reasons for, and a possible answer to, their sufferings. Even so, the dramatic world of Chapman, too, has its moments when characters express merely an uncomprehending and intuitive awareness of the painful mystery of life. When Tamyra, a relatively secondary figure (like all the women in Chapman's plays) says:

> Man is a tree that hath no top in cares,
> No root in comforts; all his power to live
> Is given to no end, but t'have power to grieve.[45]

it could be the later Duchess of Malfi speaking: when Byron meets his execution with

> Never more
> Shall any hope of my revival see me;
> Such is the endless exile of dead men.
> Summer succeeds the Spring; Autumn the Summer;
> The frosts of Winter the fall'n leaves of Autumn:
> All these and all fruits in them yearly fade,
> And every year return: but cursed man
> Shall never more renew his vanish'd face.[46]

for a moment Chapman and Webster are one in their poignant acceptance of the ultimate incompatibility of Man and death, one which only religious belief or philosophical conviction can even attempt to resolve.

The world of Webster has neither, but throughout Chapman's there is usually the steady assertion that Man can rise above his sense of littleness and impotence in face of the narrow cunning and passionate violence of men. He can meet the incongruity which makes Man a battlefield of reason and unreason with the Stoic expedient of making reason quell unreason; he can then be a king among men, the superior of earthly kings when these unworthily allow themselves the passionate weaknesses of their ordinary sub-jects.

In the figure of Strozza (*The Gentleman Usher*) Chapman shows how the Stoic man's mind can control the 'frailties' of his physical body when in pain; thereafter his dramas widen the possible range of the mind's dominance, yet show how rare such dominance is. In *Bussy d'Ambois* (II.i) Nuntius (the Messenger) compares Bussy to

Pyrrho in his mastery over the fear of death and love of life, and later in the same scene Bussy himself claims superiority to law, but he is treacherously killed at the end of the play because he has in fact allowed passion and pride to master him. In the sequel, *The Revenge of Bussy d'Ambois*, Clermont, the brother of Bussy, is presented as the truly dispassionate Senecan man, superior to Bussy (as Guise says)[47] because he has the learning that can control passion as Bussy could not. He is the rational, prudent man who can disdain fear, but without rashness (as, again, his brother could not), and love to him is far above mere passion. He sees the world as controlled by God's good purpose, which the wise man willingly accepts and will not seek to oppose to satisfy his own desires. As he says before killing himself, he considers the body merely the outermost barrier hiding the spirit, the soul, and finally, at the core of Man, the mind, and his suicide is therefore reasoned and deliberate. The inner conflict seems to have found its resolution in Clermont, yet he has been forced by the circumstances around him, his situation, to avenge his brother's death, to act against true reason – the justification is that he has done so with reason, with full awareness of what he is doing. In *The Conspiracy and Tragedy of Charles, Duke of Byron* the disruptive power of passion and unreason is again shown; in these two plays Byron is a man possessed by his own pride and ambition,[48] and fatally unable to control these passions; the irony of his downfall is that he believes himself to be the truly right and rational man who needs no control. He is thus the second of Chapman's examples of the man who, however striking he may be in the fine rhetorical expression of his rational superiority, is in fact the victim of his own passions; we have already seen the irony of the would-be but imperfect Stoic in Feliche and Andrugio (Marston's *Antonio and Mellida*) and in Pandulpho (*Antonio's Revenge*). Both Marston and Chapman have an Elizabethan sense of the continual pressure and power of human incongruity; in *The Tragedy* (5.3.189–98. T.M. Parrott (ed.) (1910) *Tragedies of G. Chapman*, London. Routledge) Epernon, commenting on Byron, sums up this condition of Man in terms akin to those of Fulke Greville (see note 36):

> Oh, of what contraries consists a man!
> Of what impossible mixtures! Vice and virtue,
> Corruption, and eternnesse, at one time,
> And in one subject, let together loose!
> We have not any strength but weakens us,

> No greatness but doth crush us into air.
> Our knowledges do light us but to err,
> Our ornaments are burthens, our delights
> Are our tormenters, fiends that, rais'd in fears,
> At parting shake our roofs about our ears.

Here is expressed the more common, more tragic conception of the futility of human striving in a confused and evil world, yet Chapman had already shown, in *Caesar and Pompey*, the truly philosophical man as able to live in the world unconquered by it: Cato is set against the figure of Pompey, again the would-be master of himself whose self-sufficiency is inadequate; following the advice of others, and against his better judgement, he attacks Caesar's army and is conquered. Cato alone is impregnable in his conviction of his own rightness. Similarly, Chabot, in Chapman and Shirley's play about him, moves amid the plotting and injustice of the French court with calm confidence in himself. When attacked by the cunning of the Chancellor and the Lord High Constable, he refuses to retreat; his inner certainty of rational innocence is a kind of moral virginity, akin to that of the Lady in Milton's *Comus*; as he says to Allegre:

> I walk no desert, yet go arm'd with that
> That would give wildest beasts instincts to rescue
> Rather than offer any force to hurt me –
> My innocence, which is a conquering justice
> And wears a shield that both defends and fights.[49]

This is Chapman's assertion against despair, but Chabot is so exceptional that one wonders whether the ordinary member of Chapman's audience was wholly convinced. As I have already suggested, when Chapman's heroes are truly philosophical, and suceed in mastering their weaker, irrational selves, they are admirable, but inevitably somewhat inhuman in their exceptional integrity: Cato and Chabot are at times oddly like the impossibly noble heroes of such 'romance' plays as *Philaster*, but with the essential difference that their 'greatness' is explained by the dramatist as being the result of reason's power over unreason, not merely stated as an axiom of romance.

Chapman, in short, had used many of his plays for the repeated assertion that the determined use of reason alone could resolve the reason–unreason struggle which caused so much of Man's pain in this world. But he had not expressed the deeper reality which

Shakespeare, as we shall see, was suggesting, the fact that, if Man is to remain truly and uniquely human, he must accept his discords as the essence of being human, and, even while struggling with their consequences, realise that other parts of his complexity – love, courage and truth especially – may transform those consequences, however terrible.

The comic world of Ben Jonson may at first seem a long way from the world of Chapman's dramas, yet beneath the obvious differences, the dramatists' intentions are remarkably akin.[50] Like Chapman in his tragedies, Jonson in his comedies has a plain moral purpose, in his case to show his audience their follies, doing so, of course, by following Sidney's precept to join entertainment with instruction. So Jonson's comedy is usually the wittily true portrayal of the London bourgeois and lower-class world as a pageant of human follies and frailties; the 'humours' on which his comic technique is based are, in fact, types of obsession, where a dominant desire or irrational belief overcomes the rational actions and outlook of a character. Jonson's comedies show the comic use of the human truth that unreason may control a man's reason, but unreason here leads a man, not to tragedy, but to his defeat in everyday worldly matters, to his becoming a fool whom men who employ 'lower' reason to get their desires can manipulate at will. Thus in Jonson's comedies we find a gallery of type-figures (largely two-dimensional because their characteristics are selected and exaggerated), each marked by an urge beyond reason. In *The Alchemist* (1610) Mammon is ruled by lust, Ananias and Tribulation Wholesome by a sectarian greed for power, Dapper and Drugger by avarice (of a very mild sort, admittedly), and Kastril by vanity. The rogues who do the 'gulling' are themselves greedy, but cunning, and Face, in the end, has the rational wit to escape the consequences of his knavery. So also in other typical Jonsonian comedies, but sometimes a character can have a certain awarness of his weakness: Kitely, in the English version of *Every Man in His Humour* (c1612), is ruled by jealousy, yet he understands how his reason is overcome by this irrational passion, an 'infection', he says,

> Which as a subtle vapour spreads itself
> Confusedly through every sensitive part,
> Till not a thought or motion in the mind,
> Be free from the black poison of suspect.
> Ah! but what misery is it to know this?

> Or, knowing it, to want the mind's erection [power]
> In such extremes?[51]

In comedy, Jonson can merely touch on, here, the agonies of jealousy which *Othello* had so carefully analysed and portrayed, but even the shadow of a darker truth gives a different edge to the laughter. In the much earlier *Every Man out of His Humour* (1599), although Sordido is ruled by meanness and greed, Deliro by uxoriousness, and Fastidious Brisk by ambitious vanity, Macilente, the man originally given to envy, at the end of the play has learnt to overcome his obsession. So the dramatist allows that sometimes the rational part of man can see his unreason, and yet, like Kitely, be unable to control it, or succeed like Macilente: all depends on the strength of a man's reason; as Horace says in *The Poetaster* (1601):

> But knowledge is the nectar that keeps sweet
> A perfect soul, even in this grave of sin[52].

Given Jonson's underlying knowledge of human nature, and of the power of the irrational when it rules a man, it is clear that his comedy could never be entirely safe from the intrusion of a serious truth that might change its effect. To maintain a laughter that was relatively care-free, he had to portray the truth of human folly, contemporary London life, as a surface reality with no deeply disturbing implications, and, of course, it was mainly his magnificent command of colloquial language, of the rhetorical force of heightened everyday speech, that usually succeeded in overwhelming any intrusion of serious human concern. But such intrusions do suggest themselves at times: Surly in *The Alchemist* is dangerously near to being a decent, ordinary man in a setting of fools and rogues; although he wants to get Dame Pliant and her money, he lets his moral scruples overcome his greed, and wins merely the lady's contempt. This is only just laughable, in the cynical atmosphere of that play. But in *Volpone* (*c*1606) the moral implications are far more serious and disturbing. In fact, Jonson suggests this in his Dedication of the play, and defends the gravity of the ending by asserting that it is 'the principal end of poesie [drama], to inform men in the best reason of living', and that 'the office of a comic poet [is] to instruct to life'. What is really shocking, far more shocking than a mere revelation of the easily acceptable comic truths of life of every day, is Volpone's obsession, not so much by greed as by his lust for power over others (Tamburlaine's seems healthy and natural beside it), and by the world of uncontrolled, vicious, selfish desire which this obsession delights to dominate and control. It is only at the very last moment that the rational power of the state reasserts order over anarchy, and then only because Volpone's supreme arrogance prefers exposure to accepting the dominance of Mosca. Here is portrayed a world brought to the edge of disaster by the force of selfish unreason, and the effect is akin to that of the world of Webster. Here in Jonson, the comic writer, we have seen for a moment the contemporary deep social anxiety recognised by many other dramatists and other writers of the time, that human unreason might perhaps be beyond the control of human reason, that first individuals and then society itself might crumble into anarchy as a result of a collapse of Man's power to deal rationally with his divided nature. It is an anxiety that a later age knew,[53] and which we can well understand today.

I have just referred to the underlying awareness of the Elizabethan age, including both dramatists and audiences, of the dangers inherent in the conflict of reason and unreason as it affected individuals and, through individuals, society as a whole. Indeed, Man and his society had long been seen as intimately connected; Donne's 'No man is an island' has impressed our modern age as the special insight of a great poet – it is no less impressive if we realise that the idea had been widely current for generations before Donne expressed it thus. It is therefore almost predictable that the age would be keenly attracted by plays which dealt directly with the history of rulers and ruled, and that so many examples of the popular genre of 'history plays' should have been concerned, explicitly or implicitly, with the social expression of the struggle just mentioned.

In fact, for the dramatists and play-goers of Shakespeare's time, secular history had largely taken the place of the Bible as the source of stories for drama. The method of using such stories had of course changed. Medieval Biblical drama had used the Bible's tales explicitly to resolve Man's conflicting drives in religious, spiritual terms; Shakespeare and contemporary dramatists, when they used historical stories taken from the nation's past, did so first to provide the more obvious entertaintment of exciting situations and vigorous incidents (never to be underestimated in any valid consideration of Elizabethan drama), and then, on a deeper level, to show, or even explore, the tensions between Man as individual and Man as ruler. As we have seen, Aristotle had written his *Nicomachean Ethics* as a prelude to his *Politics*, thus dealing first with the necessary qualities of the 'private' man before showing the qualities required by the 'public' man, and he had quoted approvingly '. . . the saying of Bias "Office will prove the man" '.[54] Thus the use of historical material for a play reinforced an Elizabethan interest, and, when developed (especially by Shakespeare), was to add a special human depth and subtlety to many contemporary dramas. By the very fact of using historical material, a dramatist was almost required, certainly encouraged, to see and present his characters both from within and from without; it was especially in a drama of historical 'fact' that the audience came to expect, first an account of how people of the past acted and interacted to produce the known historical events, and second, some exposition of the inner personal nature of historic individuals and its effects on their public historical actions. Remembering the plays of Webster and Chapman, and others, it is plain that, in this context, any drama which tells of individuals caught up in the wider life of courts and kings must be considered akin to more obviously 'historical' plays: as we shall see, all the main Shakespearean tragedies, and many of his more serious plays which are not, technically, tragedies, are effectively 'history plays' in this sense, and derive much of their special human complexity from this fact.

Returning to a consideration of contemporary Elizabethan history plays of the usual definition, what strikes one most about them is the way in which historical themes lent themselves to the expression, conscious or subconscious, of so many forms of human conflict. Of these, the order–disorder problem in personal and public life[55] was, I believe, the major *angst* of the time, which lay beneath much of the savagery of reaction to such nonconformities as heresy, papistry, treason and witchcraft. Of course, always connected with disorder and rebellion in the context of 'history' plays, was the conflict of reason and unreason which makes men (now as then) believe that peace, order and justice can be achieved by the injustices and disorders of violence and war – from which proceeds inevitably the ironical and fatal fact that the use of violence to obtain non-violence, 'peace', establishes the precedent for its own overthrow by violence. This irony is implicit in the genre of Elizabethan 'history' plays, and is not often openly expressed; the best example of an explicit reference is a passage in *Sir Thomas More*, from a lengthy speech by More which finally persuades the rebels to give in. Suppose they had obtained their demands, he says to them:

What had you gott? I'le tell you: you had taught
How insolence and strong hand shoold preuayle,

How order shoold be quelld; and by this patterne
Not on [one] of you shoold lyue an aged man,
For other ruffians, as their fancies wrought,
With sealf same hand, sealf reasons, and sealf right,
Woold shark on you, and men lyke rauenous fishes
Woold feed on on [one] another.[56]

An early borderline example of a 'history' play is, in a way, an exception, in that it was written and acted by amateurs, and not for a public or popular audience. *The Misfortunes of Arthur* (1588)[57] was a special dramatic show written to entertain the Queen; perhaps because of the occasion, and the interest in law of the devisers, there is a strong emphasis on the necessary qualities and responsibilities of a ruler, a tone which reminds one of Baldwin's dedication of *A Myrrour for Magistrates*. A brief quotation from Act 2, Scene 1 will serve to show the attitude:

MORDRED	He is a fool that feareth what he may.
CONAN	Not what you may, but what you ought, is just.
MORDRED	He that amongst so many so unjust Seeks to be just, seeks peril to himself.
CONAN	A greater peril comes by breach of laws.
MORDRED	The laws do licence as the sovereign lists.
CONAN	Least ought he list, whom laws do licence most.
MORDRED	Imperial power abhors to be restrain'd.
CONAN	As much do meaner grooms to be compell'd.
MORDRED	The fates haue heau'd and rais'd my force on high.
CONAN	The gentler should you press those that are low.
MORDRED	I would be fear'd.
CONAN	The cause why subjects hate.
MORDRED	A kingdom's kept by fear.
CONAN	And lost by hate. He fears man[y] himself whom many fear.[58]

This dialogue between the wicked and traitorous enemy of King Arthur and the good Conan may seem old-fashioned and even naïve, but it contains much of the essence of the conflicts used by later and more complex 'history' plays.

The other more popularly designed 'history' dramas of the 1580s and 1590s are also very much concerned with the nature and duties of kingship, and with the conflict between personal weaknesses and public responsibility. Regarding the anonymous *Edward the Third* (c1590), I would stress the fact that the two lessons of the play for rulers are that a king must not give way to desire, and that power does not excuse the breaking of an oath – all this contained within a patriotic, exciting story of the valour and martial success of King Edward and the renowned Black Prince against the French. Robert Greene's *The Scottish History of James IV* (c1590) tells how James lusts after the virtuous Ida, and, through the prompting of this desire and of the Machiavellian villain Ateukin, almost seeks to murder his Queen, Dorothea: only the invasion of Scotland by English forces brings James to repentance, and the play to a happy ending. Marlowe's *Edward the Second* (c1592) is in a class of its own among such plays, and of a quality to compare with that of Shakespeare's *Richard II*: it foreshadows the way in which the 'history' play would develop in human depth and feeling in the hands of a great dramatist. The usual framework of historical legend is employed in *Edward the Second*, used, of course, for the more obvious and popular dramatic appeal of the play. But there is also the special treatment of the tension between the human frailty of the private man and the duties of the public man which raises it to a new importance, and in this work the 'history' play grows in human truth and complexity to a stature little short of great and genuine tragedy. Tragedy, as we shall see in Part 3, is in its essence the display of human nature (seen living and striving in and around a special personality) in a situation which presents that human nature with pressures which, for that particular personality, are of special danger. Marlowe must have realised from his material that the private man–public man antagonism inherent in it could be developed into a deep and satisfying dramatic interest. Marlowe had understood, too, I believe, the reason why tragedy had always been associated with the lives of 'great ones': in examining Shakespearean tragedy we shall see that the greatest tragedy requires both the outer dramatic potentialities of the public man and the inner dramatic universality of the private man. *Edward the Second* shows how the homosexual desires of Edward as a private person are inevitably disruptive of his wife's love, and fatal to his public status as a king. His decline is fully displayed, but a similar 'secondary tragedy' is only suggested in the case of Queen Isabella. Her private love for her husband, admirable if pitiable in itself, in her situation leads her to encourage him in his devotion to homosexual favourites, to her subsequent capture by the calculated attractions of Mortimer, and to the final disastrous loss of her two loves, and her imprisonment by her son. In short, Marlowe has learnt the secret (which later dramatists exploited) of finding within the historical action of his plot the essentially tragic potential which can transform the play. Another play of this time, the anonymous *Woodstock* (which survives as an almost complete manuscript written between 1591 and 1595) presents an interesting contrast to Marlowe's play. It deals with the story of Richard II and his favourites, the evils caused to the common wealth by these favourites' power over the King, his repentance after the death of his Queen, and the defeat of the favourites by the nobles. Thomas of Woodstock, Duke of Gloucester, one of the King's outraged uncles, is foremost in his open disapproval of Richard's weakness, and is murdered shortly before the end of the play (as it now exists). This outline of the play is too cursory to do justice to the human characterisation of Woodstock especially, or to the quite exciting dramatic movement of the play, but it is true, nevertheless, that a political and private situation very much like that of *Edward the Second* is treated virtually without any emphasis on tragic implications present in both plays. *Woodstock* thus remains a good entertainment as a 'history' play, containing many implicit references to the stresses on private men in public positions (especially in the domestic and political situations of Woodstock himself), but little more than this.

There are two plays (both of about 1591) which as 'history' plays show a special stress on the matter of rebellion and consequent disorder in the state. Of course, the plays that we have just considered all suggest or display the disorder which arises from the inadequacy of kings, but the anonymous *The Life and Death of Jack Strawe a notable Rebell* shows such disorder from another angle – it is a very direct account of the Straw rising, its beginning, progress and collapse. It has the Homily tone, with a strong lesson of the dangers of mob violence and of the King's vital role as the final defender of the state against disruption. As before in the sixteenth century, the common people are shown as moved only by unreason, and although there is a certain sympathy and understanding shown for them as a whole, it is made quite plain that, for the good of the state, they must be strictly controlled. *The Lamentable Tragedie of Locrine* (*c*1591, perhaps by Peele or Greene) is a much more pretentious play, with rhetorical passages in the popular grandiloquent tone of the recent *Tamburlaine* plays, 'rich' descriptive language, and even a thread of coarse comedy. It is obviously aimed at contemporary popular taste. So it is a significant indication of that taste that the theme of the play is civil war in England, and that Ate, the classical goddess of discord, appears in the Prologue to each act, and has the final moral comment (C.F. Tucker Brooke (ed.) (1908) *The Shakespeare Apocrypha* Oxford: Clarendon Press, p. 65):

> Lo here the end of lawless trecherie,
> Of vsurpation and ambitious pride;
> And they that for their priuate amours dare
> Turmoile our land, and set their broiles abroach,
> Let them be warned by these premisses [the foregoing play].
>
> And as a woman was the onely cause
> That ciuill discord was then stirred vp,
> So let vs pray for that renowned mayd,
> That eight and thirtie years the sceptre swayd,
> In quiet peace and sweet felicitie;
> And euery wight that seekes her graces smart,
> Wold that this sword wer pierced in his hart!
>
> *Exit*

Ate's warning is against the national disorder caused by personal passions, in 'great ones' of course, and Queen Elizabeth is praised as the exceptional woman, the 'mayd', who has brought a long period of peace to England. Whatever the complicated personal and political reasons for her celibacy, I think that many Elizabethans saw her as a special type of female, womanly in her almost maternal concern for her subjects (which was a fact and no mere piece of government propaganda), but, in her unwomanly refusal to marry, apparently free of the female weaknesses of passion which might have caused trouble in the country (witness Mary Queen of Scots). That so many of the time increasingly feared the absence of a direct heir to the throne, was another, purely political matter.

These are what are obviously to be classed as 'history' plays (outside Shakespeare), and such plays had ceased to appear by about 1600, but, as has been suggested, there were many other contemporary plays which, while not 'history' plays in the usual sense, are nevertheless set in the framework of rulers and ruled, and, like 'history' plays but without the emphasis on history as such, explore the incongruity of the private man and the public man. Chapman's two Bussy plays, his two Byron plays and his *Chabot*, which we have already considered from a different but connected point of view, are examples, as are so many of Shakespeare's plays.

Finally, we should remember that a fashion for plays based on classical history succeeded in the 1600s to the popularity of the English 'history' plays. Leaving Shakespeare aside, we can see in other plays of this genre a renewed emphasis on the personal causes of public danger or disorder; indeed, it seems that the classical material was chosen with this in mind, for it had already been used by well-known classical writers like Cicero for this purpose. An example, Jonson's *Sejanus, his fall* (1603), follows closely a notorious episode in Roman history which reminds one of the tales used in *A Myrroure for Magistrates* for a similar end: it is the account of the growing arrogance of Sejanus (the favourite of the Emperor Tiberius), its destructive effect on justice, peace and goodness in Rome, and his sudden final downfall, and his death at the savage, undisciplined hands of the mob. In fact, the lesson of reason and unreason goes deeper than this; the Emperor emerges towards the close of the play as the epitome of the 'lower' reason, a political cunning that alone, in such a world of political struggle, can cut short the personal lust for power of Sejanus. Even then, the end of the drama ironically shows the first savage excesses of Macro, the would-be successor to the aims and methods of Sejanus. Jonson's *Cataline, his Conspiracy* (1611) is another example of the same theme, but with the difference that in this play (following the historical facts, of course) there is an affirmation of the power of reason and justice to prevent the dangers of an unbridled egoism.

The whole of the preceding section has been intended to furnish background material which may aid the reader to see (in Part 3) Shakespeare's plays, the main subject of this work, in their proper setting. Many more examples and details could have been given, but I hope that enough has been offered to show later, by comparison, that Shakespeare's dramas are indeed part of their age, and yet shaped uniquely and unmistakably by the special insight and powers of this dramatist. He certainly shared those Elizabethan awarenesses of Man's inner conflicts which I have described and illustrated, but his importance as a playwright consists in the plays which he created from his personal sense of those awarenesses. To help the reader to understand and feel more deeply the manner of that creation, is the purpose of Part 3.

PART THREE

Human Conflict in Shakespeare

Introduction

Before examining in some detail the many ways in which human conflict appears in the plays of Shakespeare, it is necessary to explain certain factors which apply especially to this dramatist.

The first point to make is that Shakespeare remains today pre-eminently the dramatist of human life in this world, and the one who displays most fully and truly in dramatic terms the many complexities of that human life. Thus, whereas earlier dramatists, and his contemporaries (as we have seen), at most use only a few of the many effects of Man's contradictions as material for their plays, and even then, often in an over-simplified or tendentious manner, Shakespeare is unique in showing on his stage a wide and full interaction of these human stresses even in a single play, and certainly in his work as a whole. This difference of range and variety becomes a qualitative difference as well as a quantitative difference. His is the only large body of dramatic work in which it is possible to see a particular form of personal struggle in action, not only in one set of circumstances, one play, but in others as well, and then to compare the nature and results of this particular form in one play with those in another play or plays. A Shakespeare play, moreover, often contains a variety of kinds of human incongruity, in minor as well as major characters, and each kind may link to, or contrast with, similar or variant kinds in other plays. In addition, each example is given a dynamic, not a static, exposition: it is modified, developed, often changed in the course of a play always in conjunction with other examples which are themselves affected. So any attempt to understand the entire nature of a single Shakespeare play would require, strictly speaking, an understanding of every Shakespeare play, even if one confined one's attempt to realising his use of his basic material, the battle within Man, and largely neglected the essential consideration of the effects of his language and stage-craft. Thus, in this present section, the main part of this work, I shall examine virtually all the plays, and so try to achieve an overall view of the ways in which Shakespeare's drama as a whole is permeated by that basic material, which of course is much more than mere material, for it includes the entire 'ethos', tone and manner of Shakespeare's dramatic creativity. I shall examine a number of the plays in detail, for only in that way can one begin to understand how, within one play, expressions of human conflict change and interact and, in the process, constitute the play itself.

In thus examining Shakespeare's plays, we shall see that, in fact, Man's dichotomy links comedy and tragedy. It is in their dependence on this dichotomy that comedy and tragedy can be recognised as akin, despite their obvious differences. The forms of natural inner conflict outlined in Part 1 all present deep and disturbing problems to human beings, and are perhaps more likely, therefore, to be portrayed and explored in tragedy, but such problems also demand the relief of laughter and tenderness of the comedy which will remind the audience that their conflicts can also produce the true happiness of which Mankind is capable. The essence of the matter is that the shock of realising once again the incongruities of human nature, and their effects on our life, is the source of both the deepest tragic awareness and the most satisfying comic delight.[1]

There is a further consideration which, I hope, will be ever-present in the reader's mind in reading this section. I have already referred to it briefly in relation to the earliest drama, but it is of chief importance in understanding the effects of Shakespeare's plays, especially in performance. It is related to the very nature of the theatre and of plays written for performance in a theatre: it concerns audiences in any period, including our own. It is best explained by taking an Elizabethan play-goer enjoying a Shakespeare play. The play deals with some aspects of fundamental human nature in action. Our Elizabethan play-goer has been prepared, by previous and contemporary dramatic practice, to expect recognisably human characters, characters which he feels could exist, even if he has not met any such, and which he accepts could have lived in the Forest of Arden, or in the Rome of Julius Caesar, without being radically different from the people of his own London. He also expects a dramatic story to be acted out by these characters; this story will attract and hold his attention, but on the more superficial level; he will no doubt enjoy a murder, for example, but the main interest will be why and how a character murders or is murdered. Characters, for him, must be characters in action, or approaching action. He will identify with some, perhaps all, of the characters, but this strong empathy will be only part of a complex experience. He will 'feel' himself to be Othello (and/or Desdemona, Iago, etc), but at the same time he will also be himself, enjoying a play at the Globe as part of a busy and stressful London life. He will be in Othello, in Iago, in himself, in Cyprus, in London – that is, both inside and outside the play. From this curious psychological experience in the theatre will follow another, if the 'life' on the stage is sufficiently true to the inner realities of actual life in the world: there will be moments, often caused by the play's comments on life, when he will also feel himself as sitting 'above' the play, moments when he will see an intricate pattern of human behaviour taking shape before him. Of that fabric, in some strange way, he will feel himself one of the threads, and yet able to realise and appreciate the design as a whole. This experience, I believe, is evoked especially by the immediacy and human contact of drama, but something akin surely takes place when a novel is read with sufficient concentration of thought and feeling. In the theatre, the experience must be quasi-religious; our Elizabethan spectator will extend his consciousness to be, firstly more aware of others, then more aware of himself in others, and finally, aware of himself and others as part of a supra-human realisation. All of this depends on the fact that Shakespeare is using human nature, human experience, as the stuff of his drama; thereby the play-goer's recognition (itself partly thought, partly feeling) of his own human incongruity as part of that shown on the stage, and part of the nature of Mankind generally, brings about the 'three-fold vision', of personal life, 'play life', and universal life. Perhaps this curious expansion, almost disruption, of the spectator's personality, a kind of mild nervous breakdown, is what produces that strange and special exaltation which is the effect of all great, even merely effective, drama.

Comedies

Love's Labour's Lost (c1595) is a convenient early point at which to begin an examination of Shakespeare's use of inner tensions in comedy, for it starts with a situation, contrived of course, in which a group of privileged persons (a king and three courtier-friends), out of their ample leisure and freedom to indulge their fancies, believe that they have decided to confront and resolve what is in fact a basic human conflict. They make their first mistake in over-simplifying the problem; they see themselves as forced to choose between their natural desire for love and the satisfaction of their intellect. From the moment when the group apparently commit themselves to the latter, the audience, knowing from its own experience that human nature cannot be treated so naïvely, prepares itself to enjoy the inevitable failure of the attempt.[2] The audience's spokesman is Berowne; unlike his companions he sees the dangers of this attempt at un-natural rationality, yet he supports for the moment their airy com-mitment to a monastic regime of intellectual endeavour. It is all very plainly a game, based most precariously on a mixture of youthful idealism (of no very serious sort) and an almost complete lack of self-knowledge in all the men except Berowne. The group, by the end of the play, will have come to know themselves and the nature and strength of their human discords a good deal better, and as the love that they have so lightheartedly rejected at first, proves to be a very civilised and moderate passion, the process of self-recognition will not be tragic or devastating in its effects. Around the men's group, and the corresponding group of women (the Princess and her ladies), but above all around Berowne, Shakespeare quickly builds up an atmosphere of intellectual word-play which nicely expresses the quality of the incongruity with which the play deals; there is a growing ironical suggestion that it is not intellect in monastic seclusion which is the real enemy to true feeling, but cold intellect itself, shown in intellectual wit. Although all the men and the ladies are skilled in repartee (after all, it is a large part of the 'surface' delight of the play), in Berowne wit is an intellectual commitment and of the essence of his masculine pride; it is Berowne who, with the beginnings of self-knowledge, expresses the basic, traditional male dilemma of reason and love in his soliloquy in Act 3, Scene 1, beginning 'And I forsooth in love . . .' where his conception of himself as the cool, rational master and critic of emotional 'weak-ness' starts to crumble under the pressure of the emotion within himself. Later, at the beginning of Act 4, Scene 3, Berowne's conflict is again expressed in soliloquy, this time in prose, and we are reminded how full of humour such personal internal arguments can be, remembering also the struggle of Launcelot Gobbo's reason with his conscience (*The Merchant of Venice*, 2.2), and, best of all, Falstaff's rational dismissal of the fantasy of 'honour' (*Henry IV, Part I*, 5.1). Berowne is the comic centre of the play, and the laughter he arouses derives from both wit and humour: 'wit' may be briefly defined as 'human incongruity recognised by the intellect', 'humour' as 'human incongruity felt emotionally'. Thus it is significant that

Berowne, as the play unfolds, moves more and more from being witty to being humorous; by the end, he is almost ashamed of his former taste for wit, and shows a new sensitivity in his response to the task given him by Rosaline:

> To move wild laughter in the throat of death?
> It cannot be; it is impossible;
> Mirth cannot move a soul in agony.[3]

Here he has been made to recognise, at last, that 'a gibing spirit' (as Rosaline calls it) is merely a matter of intellectual cleverness, with no human emotional adequacy, and is indeed a symbol of the barren victory that would have resulted if he and his friends had persisted in cultivating intellect at the expense of feeling. Here is the Elizabethan realisation (see Part 1, Sections (e) and (f), pp. 5–16) that reason without unreason is as dangerous and, worse, inhuman as unreason without reason.

Opposed to the men is the group of ladies headed by the Princess. To the Elizabethan (perhaps even to some people today) the conflict is an obvious and accepted one: on one side Man in his intellectual arrogance and sexual desire, and on the other Woman with her traditionally dangerous gift of emotional unreason controlled yet sharpened by that human logic which is so often far more than mere common sense (Shaw's comedies make continual use of the contrast). When the ladies, especially the Princess, jest with or comment on the men, therefore, their remarks are rarely merely witty. Critics have often pointed out that the play is brought down to earth suddenly by the news of the death of the Princess's father, but in fact the movement from intellectual make-believe to a feeling recognition of real life had been in progress, through the ladies, long before that; the reminder of death links up with hospitals and the dying, at the end of the play, to drive the lesson home to the men.

It is an obvious, but effective, part of the pattern of the play that the dramatist has made 'low-life' characters, especially Costard and his Jaquenetta, a variation and a comment upon what we see happen to the upper-class groups. I think our modern embarrassed dislike of the idea of different social classes (different in having or not having wealth and education) may hinder our obtaining from this play a delight which an Elizabethan, rich or poor, would have felt at once in such a play as this. The 'low-life' people in this comedy, for Shakespeare's audience, are there to be laughed at, for Elizabethans took it for granted that uneducated poor folk often seemed merely stupid; they also took it for granted that educated, rich, and important 'great ones' were often stupid, and they laughed as heartily at Polonius as at Dogberry. What is essential, for this play, is the fact that Elizabethans could see, in the juxtaposition of these upper-class and lower-class characters, almost a morality-type emphasis upon the universality of reason versus unreason. Underlying all this is the suggestion that one need not admire only reason or unreason, learning or simple ignorance: at the end of the play, characters have learnt a new balance, a resolution (partly at least) of their contradictions – the King and his men have been brought to feel more truly and humanly, Costard and his group to think more wisely – life is made up of opposites, the Owl and the Cuckoo, Winter and Spring, as the final moments of the play remind us.

Another strand in the play remains to be noticed, related in a way to the class-distinction already mentioned. The formal balance of the drama is between a King and a Princess, and the nominal cause of their meeting is an official, indeed mercenary, matter of state affairs.[4] It would be misleading to over-emphasise what is largely an expedient of the plot, but it is interesting to note that the King and the Princess are something more than mere comedy-types: one is a ruler, and the other the daughter and ambassadress of a ruler. That being so, it is of some significance that the King, although a pleasant and courteous gentleman, is shown as little more than a high-spirited gallant among gallants; in Act 2, Scene 1, he sounds, for a moment, like a serious ruler, intent upon retaining his territories, but the overall emphasis is upon the human quality of a man, yet a man who is a king. There is a foretaste here of Prince Hal – Henry V, a touch (delicate as befits this comedy) of the wider, more serious theme of human divergencies in the rulers of men. On the other hand, the Princess is revealed as a woman of quiet gravity and wisdom, quite distinct from her ladies, and it is around her that the play centres, and conflicts are finally resolved. It is fitting that she should speak the key lines of the drama:

> And out of question so it is sometimes:
> Glory grows guilty of detested crimes,
> When for fame's sake, for praise, an outward part,
> We bend to that the working of the heart.[5]

'Glory' here means pride, vanity, even arrogance, and this is a complete comment upon the main theme of the play, an epitome of the original mistake of the King and his companions. More than this, we have here an anticipation of an attitude to life and its problems that is to shape and colour a great deal of Shakespearean drama yet to come.

Love's Labour's Lost, then, represents the moment at which Shakespeare's characters are just beginning to deepen from superficial types to something approaching real people – human nature can be recognised at work in them. In his earlier comedy, the dramatist had been content to create laughter largely from the manipulation of simple type-figures in continuous variations of plot; it was a comic method going back to *Gammer Gurton's Needle* and to Plautine comedy, and its appeal was chiefly to the mind. Audiences in many ages have been perfectly content with the intellectual satisfaction of following the intricacies of the interaction of characters, and of being surprised at unexpected (but scarcely motivated) twists in the plot. This type of drama, which may of course be made to provoke horror as well as laughter, is akin to the simplest of all acted narrative: children creating their own imagined world of action in 'play' are less concerned with character than with action; people are simply good or bad, and what they do, the more exciting and surprising the better, is what chiefly matters. Much of Elizabethan and Jacobean drama (with magnificent exceptions) is basically of this sort, and the mode persists, always popular, to Restoration period examples, to Victorian farce and melodrama, and on to the modern 'thriller' on stage and television, and the 'west-end farce'. It has always been slighted (and perhaps secretly envied) by the serious dramatist, and critics have usually approached it with a certain condescension. It is quite mistaken to consider *The Comedy of Errors* (*c*1592) and *The Two Gentleman of Verona* (*c*1595) in this spirit; both of them show a grasp of stage technique, of plot-manipulation, surprising in a young dramatist, and the characters, although for the most part frankly simple counters in a game of movements, are better so.

'Better so' – this is the point. Imagine, if you will, the child's story of 'Goldilocks and the Three Bears' as dramatised today by a 'serious' dramatist. You recoil in horror, I hope, as you realise the consequences: Goldilocks becomes a complex young soul torn and tortured by Freudian, post-Freudian and, no doubt, other psychological stresses, and the Three Bears (their extraordinary concern with personal possessions duly noted) are equally loaded with all the conflicts of human nature as currently 'explained' and systematised – and the original story, its special simple appeal that has lasted through the centuries, has disappeared. This example is surely merely ludicrous in itself (although I should not be surprised to see the modern stage version appear shortly), but it is crucial to an understanding of Shakespeare the dramatist.

The fact is that Shakespeare's earliest comedy, little more than 'plot-comedy', could work successfully with only the barest treatment of human character; to have incorporated the complexities of inner conflict into plots of a fairytale nature would have raised serious problems for the dramatist, and, worse still, dangerous uneasiness in the audience. Such results did in fact happen in later plays.[6] Through his increasing use of the reality of human life as material for drama, Shakespeare moved from a drama in which limited type-characters were appropriate to an emphasis on plot, to a drama in which the action grew from complex human beings; why they acted as they did, and the human consequences (to themselves and others) of what they did, were more important than the 'plot' in its older sense. But of course that plot was still carefully devised, and theatre-goers of simpler tastes could enjoy 'the story' without being fully aware of the inner, deeper human truths which worked throughout it; certainly there are still many today (despite the well-meant efforts of critics and expositors) who can enjoy the exitements of, say, *Macbeth* without the need to think and feel very deeply.

The Comedy of Errors is of a piece and consistent in tone; the characters exist as necessary parts of a complicated mechanism which has a certain delight for the mind observing from outside the play, for there is little more searching human truth to draw our thought and our feeling into the drama. Such human stress as exists in this play is true to life, but only in simple, one might say stock, terms: the near-execution of Aegeon, and the perplexities of the twins and their mother before the recognition scene, seem superficial beside later Shakespearean events and characters. But *The Comedy of Errors* works well within its obvious, and popular, limitations, and its author, after all, was fortunate to be writing in happy ignorance of the later demands that critics tend to make of geniuses.

The Two Gentlemen of Verona (c1595) is simple enough to create very little of the uneasiness referred to above. But Shakespeare, already beginning to show his insight into human nature, is approaching the edge of difficulty. The four lovers, at times, are very near to being real young people wrestling with recognisable passions, something too large and disturbing for the plot which they should merely serve: Launce, certainly, the first of the dramatist's memorable comic characters, has at least one moment when he foreshadows the greater human quality of Dogberry or even Falstaff. In Act 3, Scene 1, he has an address to the audience which is a comic accompaniment to the speech of his master Proteus in Act 2, Scene 6;[7] it shows him in the clutch of a true form of human dilemma, the perennial conflict between common sense, reason, and irrational love, and the struggle is followed up in the rest of the scene. But Launce is not an essential part of the plot, and his touch of deeper human truth does not upset the general tone of the play.

At about the same time, *The Taming of the Shrew* (c1594) is an amusing 'plot-drama' where Shakespeare is still prepared to keep his characters safely in tune with the nature of the story. It is what one might call a 'social love morality', and has the basic human theme of the 'love–hate' relationship between men and women in any age, and marriage as a part of it. But it is a play of one situation, not of development, of a broad truth not a personal one, and it is enough that Petruchio and Katharina should be vivid, witty, and tempestuous types. Once let those types move into the inner struggles of real men and women, and we shall be in the world of Benedick and Beatrice – further along the road of deeper exploration, we shall be with Othello and Desdemona.

A Midsummer Night's Dream (c1595) illustrates markedly the stirring within Shakespeare's comedy of this 'danger' from overmuch truth to life which we are considering. To a world of 'romance' figures, a Duke Theseus and his bride-to-be Hippolyta and two pairs of perplexed lovers, the dramatist adds a parallel world of fairies, whose King and Queen, quarrelling as only husband and wife can, offer a neat comment upon the lovers' quest for married bliss; as the play was perhaps originally written for an actual wedding celebration, there may be further local ironies at work. But only ironies, and benign at that; the full human reality of passion and love and marriage would have been unsuitable in such a context. Yet the suggestion of this reality does intrude upon the masque make-believe; it is kept in balance, however, with the rest of the play, and indeed it adds a special mixed quality of the mingling of real and unreal. The confusions of the lovers are little more moving than the speculative debates of academic philosophy on the differences between 'loved, not loving', 'loving not loved', and so on, but when Bottom speaks, the Elizabethan feels at once (as we do) that his own human reality is to have its say. Bottom shows the convincing truth of a man who cannot really believe that this fairy creature, Titania, loves him, yet is wonderfully delighted at being thus courted – there is something of the later Malvolio's surprise and smugness at being admired by Olivia, but without the touch of pain to come. Bottom's response to Titania's 'I love thee' is the pinpoint of prosaic truth that might almost prick the bubble of fantasy on which the play is poised:

> Methinks mistress, you should have little reason
> for that. And yet, to say the truth, reason and
> love keep little company together now-a-days. The
> more the pity, that some honest neighbours will
> not make them friends.[8]

This is reason encountering fantasy, a powerful form of human incongruity ideal for satire,[9] and from this point fantasy begins to modulate into the ending of the play. There, romantic love-play is brought down to a world where the dramatic cleverness that has maintained the fantasy is deliberately contrasted with the everyday naïvety of the sad tale of Pyramus and Thisbe, and the audience is withdrawn from the fantasy. A few moments later, Puck performs the delicate function of all Shakespeare's Epilogues, of making the transition from the stage world of make-believe to the real world of an audience preparing to leave the theatre, and reality has finally, for the moment, ousted imagination.

Once again Shakespeare had brought reality into contact with fantasy, and had added an extra dimension to his drama by reminding the audience of their own conflicts between reason and love, fact and imagination. Through the further experiment with this in *As You Like It*, Shakespeare will come to the ultimate perfection of balance, in *Twelfth Night*, between what man dreams, and what man knows, he is, a fundamental form of that complexity of which his life is fashioned.

In *As You Like It* (*c*1599), as the title suggests, there are the main ingredients which the Elizabethans most enjoyed in love-romances, as Lodge had known and Shakespeare also realised: his play has lovers, wicked opposition to their love (which itself changes to love at the end), difficulties in the way of the properly heroic yet not too clever hero and the witty yet not too intellectual heroine, disguises, and the final perfect happiness of all (although there may be doubts about a Touchstone married to an Audrey). The Elizabethan audience liked these things, but they also liked real-life comment on romance, existing side by side with it without destroying it. As we have just seen, Shakespeare had already learnt how to satisfy this desire for incongruity, and *As You Like It* shows a further advance of his skill. Orlando is almost the ideal romantic lover, but not quite; when, in his courtship game with the disguised Rosalind, he reaches the point of self-awareness where he can say to her 'I can live no longer by thinking',[10] the convention of stage-pretence is almost broken (one remembers the Marx Brothers' 'shocking' asides to the cinema audience); the intricate artificiality of a boy acting a woman, Rosalind, who is pretending to be a young man, 'Ganymede', who is playing the part of Rosalind, delightful as all this is, has almost reached its breakdown; the play is moving into its last phase, and shortly all pretence and misunderstanding will yield to true aware-ness of love. In such a popular play of the fantasy of love set against the truth of love, and of 'romance' villainy set against genuine stresses of feeling, the battle of reason and fantasy which is also part of the human nature of the audience produces an empathy which makes the play much more than a mere amusement: at its final settlement of confusions and conflicts, the play brings to the specta-tors some vicarious sense of the resolution of their own inner conflicts.

In his career in stage comedy, then, Shakespeare has so far been using, increasingly, real characters set in conventional 'romance' patterns of action. Moreover, he has learnt to use prose and poetry as the symbols of, and media for, these two tones of his comedy; it is significant that the ironic passages between Orlando and 'Ganymede' are in prose, and that the moving overtones of genuine feeling are suitably expressed in poetry. Against this, of course, is set the revealing parallel of Touchstone and Audrey, where, in another way, the audience recognises the dilemma of all men's love – prone to idealisation while still aware of the folly of allowing reason to be a slave to desire. At this point, in *As You Like It*, the reality of the characters has increased, but the balance of truth and fantasy is still working well and acceptably, with the beginnings of a special comic quality.

In *Twelfth Night* (*c*1600) that special quality is fully achieved; the balance reaches its most delicate and effective form, and gives the play an appeal which the dramatist never exceeded in this kind. The plot-mechanism is still one of 'romance'; the 'fantasy' of Olivia's vow, of the identical twins Viola and Sebastian, of shipwrecks and mistaken identities leading to final recognitions and inevitable pair-ing of lovers – all this is plainly within the formula, say, of *Friar*

Bacon and Friar Bungay earlier and *The Faithful Shepherdess* later. But in *Twelfth Night* Shakespeare has taken the puppets who would have been at least adequate in such a plot, and has transformed the chief ones into characters of human reality, moved from within by personal pressures known in themselves by the audience. Orsino, it is true, remains almost entirely a 'romance' type figure, and so at the end of the play one feels a jar of discrepancy and disappointment when he is paired off with the living, loving Viola; a similar uneasiness arises when the colourless stock figure Sebastian almost casually consents to a rich marriage with the movingly human Olivia.[11]

Love is the chief motive-force of the play. Love in real life is made up of many of the most disturbing, yet wonderful, effects of our mixed nature, as the Elizabethans recognised, and here Shakespeare shows such effects at work. In Viola, the most lovingly patient of all Shakespeare's heroines, her devotion to Orsino forces her to woo Olivia on his behalf – love wars with itself; although this conflict is caused by a contrived situation, it is made into an insight into human truth, here mildly and tenderly presented, as befits this comedy. More striking is the human conflict of Olivia; within her is shown very vividly and exactly, stage by stage, the struggle between the personal pride and intelligence of a very dignified and self-possessed lady, and her sudden, almost girlish, passion for 'Cesario'. As she says to 'him' at the moment when her self-control is thrown to the winds:

> I love thee so that, maugre all thy pride,
> Nor wit, nor reason, can my passion hide.[12]

She admits that pride, intelligence and reason are powerless against her love, and most members of the Elizabethan audience would have recognised, in their own lives, the fact, or the possibility, of such a struggle and its outcome. In the present context of happy-ending romance-comedy, the audience's recognition would have been part of its involvement in the play, of its happiness in that involvement; in other contexts, as we shall see, the recognition is more disturbing and painful, even if ultimately essential.

In Malvolio, Shakespeare comes nearer to disturbing the perfect balance of the play. He first appears as a pompous, self-satisfied Puritan, highly satisfactory as such to the audience; his clash with Aguecheek and Belch is a nice obvious use of their knowledge of the strain always present between control and indulgence, and it is linked neatly to the trials of Olivia. Left at that level, Malvolio would still have been part of a true comment on life, but Shakespeare, very tentatively, goes deeper into the man, creating a comic situation enriched with human truth. In Act 2, Scene 5, Malvolio enters in the grip of a daydream, a fantasy about Olivia's secret regard for him; his vanity, the anomaly of such vanity in one so outwardly reserved and prudish, is absurd and already pathetic; for a moment, both he and his mistress are alike in their impossible hopes. Shortly after, he reads the letter forged by Maria, and in a kind of revelation he sees all his fantasy changed suddenly. When he says to himself,

> I do not now fool myself to let imagination
> jade [trick] me; for every reason excites to this,
> that my lady loves me,[13]

it seems almost shocking that such an instant of self-revelation should be overheard by Sir Toby and the others. The past secret history of the steward's vanity is opened up in that emphasised 'now'; for so long fantasy had persisted in spite of reason, and now 'reason' (really a new fantasy) has shown fantasy to be 'fact'. This display of human conflict has moved Malvolio into real humanity, and it makes us, at the end of the play, feelingly echo Olivia's 'He hath been most notoriously abused'.[14] There is an anticipation here of the way in which, later in Shakespearean tragedy, our identification with a character through our shared incongruity makes us suffer with him. In the clash between reason and unreason, Malvolio is approaching tragedy, is a distant relative of Antony.

So in *Twelfth Night* the balance of fantasy and fact, laughter and tears, is only just kept, and indeed the sense one has of treading a borderline gives a great and special appeal to the play. We should remember that this borderline feeling was characteristic of the Elizabethan view of life, a life where all, at different levels of society, lived between folktales and bad harvests, poetry and the daily chance of death, the Christian vision and sectarian political warfare. But borderline living of this sort is, of course, an accompaniment of our awareness of human discords in any age; it is not mere chance that the 'love–death' theme so common in Elizabethan poetry and song is echoed in our modern equivalents, popular songs and the novel of cynical realism.

But we must now turn to another sign of Shakespeare's growth as a dramatist, one which is closely related to what we have already seen, and which had already shown itself before *Twelfth Night*. *The Merchant of Venice* (c1596) is, obviously, quite different in its effect from the two comedies which we have just examined, different for Elizabethans as well as for us, although the central theme is love in all three. The manner of treating love (reason against emotion) in *The Merchant of Venice* would have seemed to the contemporary audience part of a 'modern' tendency to enjoy stressing the reason half of the tension, while *Twelfth Night* would have seemed somewhat old-fashioned in its care for the emotion half. But both approaches to love were not new in drama,[15] and both have continued to the present day.

The Merchant of Venice has in its very title a hint of what is to be one of the forms of contradiction shaping the play; it suggests a matter-of-fact theme, yet from the opening the tone is far different. Antonio is a curiously sensitive, withdrawn gentleman (akin to the Orsino of *Twelfth Night*), and the trading by sea of this 'merchant' is quickly rarified and adorned in a profusion of fancy by Salerio and Solanio. The world of realist commercial risks is placed in contrast to the elegant moodiness of the gentleman; the prose and poetry of life are in conflict around Antonio. The contemporary audience would have felt the discrepancy; although by the 1590s it was accepted that a gentleman could take part in commerce, there remained a lingering tradition against it. For example, some ten years before the appearance of this play, a gentleman writing on the special status and responsibilities of gentility, could refer scathingly to this very point, in connection, in fact, with the commercial customs of Venice:

> For the Gentleman of Venice (which, as
> a faction, seeme altogether seuered from
> all traffique or dealings, with the
> common and plebian sort of people)
> tradeth merchandize: yea, the degree of
> *Some people* knighthood (saith *Pogius*) deemeth it
> *take it for* best fitting their honors, to be
> *an honourable* Merchants, a most vile and base
> *trade.* iudgement.[16]

From this initial incongruity concerning Antonio, in a sense, the whole nature of the play develops, as related incongruities spread throughout the action. Antonio is too much the fine gentleman in whom the emotion of friendship (for Bassanio) is paramount, to allow himself to bother about Shylock's possible enmity in the terms of the loan. The Antonio whose genteel scorn for the Jewish use of usury has led him to harm the trade by lending without interest, is incongruously the Antonio who for the sake of a friend consents to employ a usurer.[17] The opposite incongruity affects Shylock: the Jew who believes that money should beget money, contrives a loan for Antonio from which, as he himself points out, he expects no material gain.[18] So Antonio and Shylock are akin in their tension between reason and unreason: the emotion of friendship, for Antonio, is stronger than reason, as hatred is for Shylock. Already in the play the fine unreason of love and friendship, the exciting melodramatic unreason of hatred and revenge, have been placed in contrast with the reason of everyday life; taken too far, such a contrast could become seriously disturbing. Similarly Bassanio, who is surely the romantic hero, is shown as a levelheaded young man in search of a wealthy wife (just like, no doubt, some young men in the audience). Shakespeare gives him the offhand excuse that he 'nobly' needs money for the honourable repayment of his family's debts. The curious hardheaded tone is echoed in Portia's attitude to her father's 'storybook' conditions for her choice of a husband. Shakespeare makes it quite plain (no deep analysis of her psyche is required) that she is largely a very sensible woman, quite determined to protect herself against being saddled with an impossible husband. The 'fairytale' quality of the casket test is firmly brushed aside once Portia knows that Bassanio is her man, and any straightforward stage interpretation of Shakespeare's text makes it clear that he is helped by the song not to choose a casket by its appearance, as his rivals have done. After he has chosen correctly, Portia accepts his love, and for a moment we are back in the world of Rosalind and Viola; her aside, and especially her speech later to Bassanio ('You see me, Lord Bassanio, where I stand . . .[19]) form the one place in the play where she becomes a woman of love and simple faith; Bassanio's reply is far more rhetorical and far nearer to the general tone of the drama. This is the only appearance in the play of the fine, unreasoning conviction of true love in Portia; the tone of this 'romance' plot requires a heroine who can use rhetoric rather than deep feeling to save Antonio from the villainous Jew. But even when Antonio has been saved, there is no return to any simple emotion: the end of the play echoes the tone of its opening. Lorenzo and Jessica, in the passage that opens Act 5, Scene 1, laughingly (almost callously after the treatment of Shylock) take romantic love down step by step through the tragic fervour of Troilus and Cressida, the naïve figure of Thisbe, to the love-grief of Dido (betrayed by the levelheaded Aeneas) – and then immediately to the deliberate anticlimax of the merely flirtatious Jessica–Lorenzo 'love' passage. This is of course a neat and highly popular debunking of all that romantic love-comedy asserts;[20] love is seen as a game which the clever win, and the defeat of Jessica's father is just such another game. The play ends in equally popular sexual cynicism, playful jesting on rings and marital infidelity. Here romantic love is put aside in favour of the other part of the audience's experience – everyday reason triumphs over the unreason of emotion. There is nothing deeply disturbing in this, but it means that Shakespeare has had to avoid the emotion which might have disrupted the tone he was seeking. So Antonio, Bassanio and even Portia come dangerously near to being mere 'plot-comedy' types, and, not surprisingly, the most vivid and living character is the minor figure of Launcelot Gobbo.

Except for Shylock – and it is an exception which, at odds with the 'love' theme, changes the nature of the play as a whole. Against the near-types stands the reality of the Jew. Of course, the Shylock we see, and feel, today is not entirely the man that the Elizabethans would have experienced. For many of that audience, as we know, Jews were still the murderers of Jesus; perhaps more important for the average Elizabethan, a Portuguese Jew, Roderigo Lopez, had recently tried to poison the Queen. But even Marlowe's Barabas, in the popular *The Jew of Malta* obviously designed to exploit the common prejudice against Jews, has his villainy explained, if not excused, by being shown as a human being reacting to the callous pressures upon him of Gentile society, and Shakespeare's development of this 'humanising' of the Jew-type must have found many of his audience ready to understand and accept its truth. So Shakespeare is on dangerous ground. The bond-theme is the main framework of the events of the play, and being far-fetched and remote from human reality in its action, it needed only a type-Jew, to scheme against the good Gentile and to be cleverly, and rightly, caught in the very law-machinery which he himself had sought to use. This would have been, as it stands, entirely acceptable to many of the audience: as one worthy Puritan preacher wrote some ten years after *The Merchant of Venice*:

> Lastly, Christian Monarches & Magistrates
> must not only by enacting and execution of
> seuere lawes, represse their [Jews'] vile
> and intolerable vsuries, whereby they plague
> & oppresse many poore Christians, and punish
> with al sharpnesse their horrible blasphemies

against Christ and his gospell, but cause
them being vnder their authority & subiection
to be by degrees instructed in Christian
religion, and for the sooner effecting of it,
to compell them to heare the gospell.[21]

This outlines the dominant attitude of the Gentiles to Shylock in this play, and, indeed, almost prescribes his final sentence.

But Shakespeare plainly goes more deeply than this into the human truth of the Jew's nature and situation. The struggle in Shylock between his love of money and his hatred of Antonio, reason against unreason, already mentioned, is shown as part of a wider incongruity between Shylock the thinking man and Shylock the man of feeling. When the Gentiles are amused at 'my ducats and my daughter', the dramatist has given us enough insight not to laugh without uneasiness at this epitomising of his inner conflict. Jessica's willing robbery of her father and elopement with Lorenzo, which could so easily have been seen as the delightful, condign punishment of a bloodthirsty 'Jew-villain', become, once Shakespeare has suggested the unbearable pressures of his human situation, almost the makings of tragedy. It is true to say that Shylock is akin to Lear in terms of destructive human conflict; of course he is not intended to be a Lear, is not allowed to approach Lear's truly tragic status, but, as I have said, tragedy and comedy are often related through human incongruity, and all the greatest comedy has within it the potentialities of tragedy.

The Shylock theme reaches its full development in the Trial Scene; it is here that the uneasiness of the discrepancy of plot and character reaches its height and, perhaps even for an Elizabethan, overshadows the 'comedy' of the play. At this point, incongruities already present in the play, suggested rather than explored, focus into a form of human dilemma of deep significance. If we look beneath the conventional surface, beneath the twist of plot by which a villainous Jew gets his due punishment, we realise that we are being presented with the problem of justice and mercy. There is direct reference, indeed, to justice and mercy in this scene, but the deeper truth of the situation makes this reference strongly ironic, and this very irony emphasises the actual problem that is present. As we have seen in Part 1, Section (j) (pp. 26–8), justice is a matter of formal thought applied within a framework of logical cause and effect: mercy is an emotional force moving far beyond the scope of rational thinking. As Portia truly says: 'It is an attribute to God himself', and the whole point of God's mercy is that it is free and unmerited, the gift of love, not of cold judgement. So Portia's famous 'mercy speech' has the most disturbing irony at its core. Shylock has appealed to the logical process of the law, and is about to be trapped in even more finely-spun legal logicality: neither the Gentile court nor even Shylock himself really wants to give or accept true mercy. To be genuinely loved and forgiven by the Gentiles who had filched his money and his daughter, to be offered the incredible loving mercy of the New Dispensation rather than the strict justice of the Old – both are impossible for the Shylock created by Shakespeare. In the end, of course, the Jew gets a slightly mitigated sentence in terms of strict justice, and then any remnant of Christian mercy or charity is destroyed when Antonio, with a fine show of generosity, leaves Shylock with half his former possessions – but on condition that all his goods shall eventually go to his renegade daugher and her Gentile seducer, and that the Jew shall become a Christian. Shylock has been broken from within and from without, and, like Coriolanus later, he can exist only by not being himself: the Reverend Thomas Draxe, and other Elizabethans, would have fully approved.

Obviously I have just been considering a Shakespearean character as if he were a living, real person, and I intend to do so constantly, in spite of the fact that some have regarded this as (with Milton's 'Fame' of course) the last infirmity of the critical mind. The plain fact is that Shakespeare, in Shylock (as in many other characters), has fashioned from words and acts and self-revelations a being who lives within the world of the play as we would live if we were in it, showing all the effects of the human difficulties which we know in ourselves. The character, and his part in the play, demand consideration in human terms. No sensitive play-goer, Elizabethan or modern, has ever regarded Shylock (or any other such Shakespearean character) as anything but at least an attempt to show a real person, one alive in the truest sense, whatever the contrived situation or make-believe society in which he may have been placed by the dramatist.

To an Elizabethan, then, *The Merchant of Venice* would have been a play largely based firmly in the popular tradition of comedy, with an exciting, unusual (even far-fetched) story in a patrician setting where servants and other commoners were vivid reminders of the lively commonsense humour of their class, and where the good were vindicated and the lovers united by the end of the play. But for the Elizabethans there would also have been something more than this traditional appeal: Shakespeare has plainly and deliberately shown a special interest in how such human beings really feel, and thus in what motivates their actions. This interest appears most fully in Shylock, to a smaller extent in Antonio and Launcelot Gobbo, but it is enough to shift the conventional comedy tone a little towards the human seriousness of tragedy; as far as Shakespeare is concerned, it is a movement towards what we must call 'tragedy-in-comedy' rather than 'tragi-comedy'. The latter term usually implies a mixture of serious and comic themes, whereas Shakespeare's 'tragedy-in-comedy' is much more than this; it is rooted in the dramatist's awareness of the real nature of human living, his sense of Man, and Woman, as that battleground of warring needs and drives, impulses and fears, described in Part 1. In *The Merchant of Venice*, therefore, the emphasis is moving from 'plot' to 'character-in-plot'. Shakespeare is not the only contemporary dramatist to show this, as we saw in Part 2, but his unique insight into human nature will carry him further along this road than any of his fellows. Shakespeare's comedies are a preparation (conscious or not) for the special perception of human incongruity of later, more serious plays, and *The Merchant of Venice* marks the point where both the advantages and the difficulties of his approach are beginning to be felt.

   Much Ado About Nothing (c1598) is akin to *The Merchant of Venice* in that, instead of the balance of incongruities one feels the stress of them, but in this later play the stress is more pervasive, more unsettling. To express the effect in general terms, one can refer first to the significant title (which can suggest only the main plot of Claudio and Hero). Then there is the actual story of these two lovers, and its curious ending. If the unrealistic 'romance' tale of Claudio's wooing of Hero, the villainous plot to spoil the marriage, and Hero's apparent death, had been presented on stage with suitable storybook emphasis on the excitements of the plot and its forseeable happy ending, and had employed merely ordinary types adequate for such a treatment, much of the play, and even Claudio's final remark to Hero, might have been good enough. But Shakespeare has clearly shown Claudio to be a realistic, 'modern' young wooer with, like Bassanio, an eye for a wealthy wife,[22] and a nice gift for cynical wit about lovers; unlike Benedick (or Berowne) he never realises, it seems, that love is emotional, not cerebral. His public repudiation of Hero, therefore, sounds to me more like spiteful annoyance than heartbreak. He is realistic, but not real. But then one experiences the disconcerting way in which Leonato, earlier a quite recognisable 'father-type', becomes suddenly, first at his daughter's disgrace, but especially afterwards, in Act 5, Scene 1, a human, suffering figure, more moving even than Shylock robbed of his daughter. Here a conventional story has been broken into by the genuine incongruity of his personal emotion at odds with his reason, and with the reasonable attitude of those unaffected by his grief. Later, in *Othello*, Brabantio will feel, and express more pointedly, a similar agony, but in a play where the realities of the human struggle are paramount, and where his sorrow is merely a hint of greater sorrows to come to all. So we find ourselves sharing the pain of Leonato, of Hero, of Beatrice; this is no longer just a story, as the play so far had suggested – after this the ending around Claudio and Hero rings strangely hollow.

Many play-goers and critics (including apparently Charles I) have felt that, while the main events of the play are centred, in terms of plot, on Claudio and Hero, the true life and appeal arise from Benedick and Beatrice. In considering this wonderful pair, one is reminded of *Love's Labour's Lost*. In this play, as we have seen, the humour arose from a simply expressed truth of human nature; human beings were torn between the ideal of reason and the fact of emotion, and to see the way in which they had to come to terms with the dilemma was heartwarming and amusing, for the struggle was not too serious or painful. In *Much Ado* a similar contest is far more complex, more finely balanced, and shown in neat and convincing diversity. Benedick begins as a worthy, gallant young man who shares the traditional attitude of his peers of desiring love and distrusting women in love: his precious individuality feels safe only in his rather narrow world of intellectual cleverness and cynicism. One might have expected his 'defeat', his acceptance of his own human nature, to have come from a woman who represented the Elizabethan conventional half of the situation, one whose character-istically feminine emotional demands on life would subdue his cynicism. But Shakespeare makes it more deeply human, far better than this: Beatrice is, by her nature, more than half a Benedick; as Hero suggests at one point,[23] she is unconventional and even un-womanly in her masculine wittiness and independence. So Beatrice and Benedick are both fighting against themselves, and the outcome cannot be the usual one (as in *Love's Labour's Lost*) where the man confesses himself overcome by the woman. The two lovers can finally come together only by accepting and sharing their common 'defeat', and this is what makes the last moments of the play not only amusing, but moving. I would add that this ending is the earliest example of Shakespeare's ability to show the happy resolution of human incongruity.

Before I leave *Much Ado*, mention must be made of Dogberry and his friends. Such lower-class characters, in the tradition going back through *Gammer Gurton's Needle* to the guild-cycles, represent the untutored, instinctive reaction to living, and often become, of course, an implicit comment on the natures of their 'betters'. This can be seen, not only within a play, but from one play to another: it is interesting to note that Launcelot Gobbo's 'soliloquy', already mentioned, is related to, say, Claudius's soliloquy in Hamlet. Both are based on the common conflict between right action and wrong, good reason and personal desire; Claudius's struggle is in essence the same as Gobbo's, however different they seem, and are meant to seem: one is terrible in its antecedents and its consequences, and is expressed in blank verse of an appropriate density and force; the other has the everyday, prose tone of lighthearted acceptance of Mankind's oddness. Yet both are equally valid and effective perceptions of human conflict. So Dogberry's stupidity and complacent acceptance of his own little social importance, expressed in the precisely correct prose tone, has the truth which makes us laugh because we, too, are his brothers, and it also reminds us that the more 'important' figures of the play have their own stupidity and complacency, show an equally human confusion and inadequacy. From such realisations grows the sense of universal truth that Shakespeare's work, as a whole, gives us.

We should now consider two plays of the period 1602 to 1605, *All's Well That Ends Well* (*c*1602) and *Measure for Measure* (*c*1604); the second of these is important for an understanding of the development of Shakespeare's use of his material, while the first acts as a prelude, in this context, to the second. Both these plays show the dramatist still employing plots of the traditional, popular sort, what I have called 'romance' story, and no doubt many Elizabethan play-goers would have been happily content with their excitement and obvious appeal. But Shakespeare is offering much more than mere variety of incident and situation; he has borrowed busy dramatic stories, but he is plainly seeking to display, within the limits of his stage, the confusions of motive and the psychological tensions which can be found at work in these stories, and which are now increasingly shown to be the manifestations of inner strife. In these two plays, and especially in the second, reason is shown at war with unreason, desire, and this conflict is joined to the social conflict between order and disorder; inevitably linked to these struggles of incongruity is the problem of the ruler, in which 'private man' and 'public man' are at odds – and all these forms of human incongruity are set against the primal form, the awareness of death.

To consider *All's Well* first, one central theme of the play is the working of sexual need in both Bertram and Helena. The nature of that need, and therefore the attempt to satisfy it, are different in each, but part of the deeper interest of the drama is our growing realisation that the apparent opposition of these two (in the simple terms of the sources, a sensually selfish young man faced with a loving, devoted young woman) is shown in Shakespeare's treatment to be the encounter of two human beings striving, each in his or her way, to resolve the battle between the rational and the irrational demands of their natures. Bertram is at first even callously 'rational' in his reaction to the wife imposed upon him; he is shown as balanced between the conventional class standards which for him make marriage to Helena impossible, and the material arguments for gaining the King's favour which goes with the impossible marriage. Like so many of us, he thinks he finds a way to take what he wants and reject the price. So far Bertram has not been subject to the irrational force of sexual desire, but the main part of the play is now concerned with the total collapse of his earlier strength of 'lower' (selfish) reason under the pressure of an irrational lust for the innocent Diana: by this he is finally brought to the surrender of his ring, the very symbol of that family pride which had made him reject Helena.[24] She, on the other hand, in order to satisfy her irrational love for a man who scorns her, employs all her rational cunning to make Bertram accept his marriage to her. Thus reason and unreason work together as well as conflicting; there is suggested a kind of resolution in which, as Helena says,[25] the end justifies the means. The end is not perhaps as satisfyingly conclusive as she believes; now that Shakespeare is raising questions of inner conflict in a simplistic story-setting, the end will never be as naïvely acceptable as in the original story. We are left merely to accept the suggestion that Bertram, at the end of the play, has suddenly learnt something of his own true nature, and loves Helena; what kind of love it is, whether it is as amenable to reason as Helena's, these are (we are told) dramatically unjustifiable questions which exist outside the play. But the Elizabethans would have asked them, as we do; it is Shakespeare who has made us ask them, and he will continue to do so, in varying degrees, in all the plays we have yet to examine.

The 'problem' of Parolles, to many modern critics and play-goers the most interesting part of the play, is strangely linked in human contradiction to the struggles of Bertram and Helena. At one level, Parolles is obviously an amusing character intended by Shakespeare to increase the appeal of the play, which has few light moments apart from him and the Clown. But, significantly, he has been made too real a human being, too truly a victim of his own discord, to be wholly funny, even to Elizabethans. In late-Elizabethan society, where earlier feudal assumptions regarding social and personal conceptions of 'duty' and 'honour' were being re-examined,[26] the question of cowardice in a soldier was a serious matter, however much the stock braggart-coward continued to raise laughs. Shakespeare of course had already touched on the point in Falstaff's soliloquy on honour in *Henry IV, Part 1* (3.1.), where the old assumptions regarding courage and honour of a Hotspur (matters of emotion and tradition) were amusingly analysed and dismissed by the worldly reason of a fat old man. The portrayal of Parolles goes deeper than this. The background to his cowardice is set in the discussion of 'honour' which in Act 2, Scene 3, arises from Bertram's rejection of Helena. The King warns Bertram to esteem honour and virtue by what they perform, not as mere tokens of an inherited status; as he says:

> Honours thrive
> When rather from our acts we them derive
> Than our fore-goers.[27]

On this definition, Bertram is later to dishonour the rank to which he gives so much importance; his lechery is as dishonourable as Parolles's cowardice. Indeed, it is far more so, for Lafeu makes it plain that his chief objection to Parolles is that he is a nonentity trying to mix as an equal with gentlemen.[28] So he is only pretending to have a gentleman's inborn respect for honour and courage, and has no true class obligation. Parolles's admission in Act 2, Scene 3, 'What I dare to[o] well do, I dare not do', gives a hint of his dilemma, which is made clearer in Act 4, Scene 1, when he admits:

> I find my tongue is too foolhardy; but my
> heart hath the fear of Mars before it, and of
> his creatures, not daring the reports of my
> tongue.[29]

This, and what follows, show the conflict from which he suffers; he has the imagination to see what deeds would be brave, with a tongue all too ready to say he will do them, but his 'lower' practical reason prevents him from facing the danger necessary to do the deeds. He shows, in fact, the workings of that conflicting quality which makes mankind emotionally see the better and rationally follow the worse. But the truly and surprisingly human moment of Parolles is his reaction to his public unmasking as a coward and a potential traitor. Just before he realises how he has been tricked, he gives an interesting comment on himself:

> Only to seem to deserve well, and to beguile
> the supposition of that lascivious young boy
> the Count, have I run into this danger.[30]

Here Shakespeare associates the absence of honour of Parolles with the dishonour of the gentleman who is so scornful of him, and an Elizabethan might begin to wonder which of the two is the more contemptible. Then Parolles's tormentors reveal themselves, and finally he is left alone with the realisation that all his pretensions are finished. This is his reaction:

> Yet am I thankful. If my heart were great,
> 'Twould burst at this. Captain I'll be no more;
> But I will eat, and drink, and sleep as soft
> As captain shall. Simply the thing I am
> Shall make me live.[31]

This is the chief of those places in the play where one has no doubt that the dramatist has moved decisively from the type to the full human person. Here we are shown a moment of self-realisation akin even to that which marks the final stage of all Shakespeare's great tragic figures, and its human truth for Parolles is no less valid than for them. We now fully understand all that we have been shown of the man up to this point; we see that he had been living as we all live sometimes, torn between what he thought he might be (or pretend to be) and what he really was. This collision of fantasy and fact could be resolved only by the acceptance of one of these two incongruities, and the rejection of the other. Parolles is 'thankful' because at least he has had to accept the fact that he is no hero; now that that is faced and accepted, he can live without stress as himself, the person he really is. Earlier the *Second Lord* had commented on him: 'Is it possible he should know what he is, and be that he is?.[32] Now

Parolles has found the answer, has had it thrust upon him. That he is accepting his own 'ignoble' nature, can be held contemptible only by those who see human beings as neatly divided into the 'good' and the 'bad'. An Elizabethan ex-soldier, writing years before Parolles was created, had described (yet with an understandable scorn) the crux of Parolle's final solution:

> Now to the contrary come to the nature
> and condition of a Coward, whose mind is never
> to do any noble act, for he that can bear the
> infamy and blot of that name, to be called a Coward,
> lives careless of all other villanies.[33]

A further point should be made about this play; it concerns the role of the King. Shakespeare's source[34] gave him the King who is cured by the heroine and, in reward, forces her chosen husband to marry her, but the King's last-minute offer to subsidise (in our crude modern idiom) Diana's marriage to anyone she chooses is an addition by Shakespeare. No doubt it can be seen as merely a minor consequence of the dramatist's modification of his source, a change which elaborated the tensions of the last scene by bringing Diana in person before the King, and therefore made it desirable to assure the audience that she was given a 'happy ending'. But Shakespeare had already, in the course of the play, made the reality of the main characters stronger than the old story could bear, and now this final touch has a curiously ironic effect. We are reminded, here in the closing moment of the play, of the earlier arbitrary power of the King to dispose, as he believed, of his subjects' private emotions; the result had been, not a mere exciting tale of a finally-justified heroine, but an uneasy portrayal of the tensions and indignities of human nature; inevitably we feel a doubt about the effects of such simple, and similar, 'generosity' towards Diana. This touch of ironic doubt, slight in itself, is an interesting anticipation of the far deeper, far more disturbing ironies of the somewhat similar ending of *Measure for Measure*, indeed, of that play as a whole. It helps us to realise that both these plays, because of the dramatist's emphasis on the complexity and strength of Man's contradictions, are alike in changing the almost nominal role of the ruler in the source into a much more ambiguous and doubtful function. In short, human incongruity is the problem of such plays.

Measure for Measure, like *All's Well*, is based on 'romance' material stories which usually sought to delight readers by unusual situations, unexpected developments of the narrative, and a 'happy ending', all dealing essentially with emotional episodes in the lives of upper-class characters. Such was the material used for *All's Well*, but it is significant that Shakespeare's main sources[35] for *Measure for Measure* are much more concerned than this with social and moral questions implicit in the story. Shakespeare, in using these implications, does so in a different way. Both Whetstone and Cinthio are explicitly writing for moral instruction: Whetstone, in 'The Epistle Dedicatorie' to his play, says:

> The effects of both [parts], are good and
> bad: vertue intermyxt with vice, unlawfull
> desyres (yf it were posible) queancht with
> chaste denyals: al needeful actions (I thinke)
> for publike vewe. For by the rewarde of the
> good, the good are encowraged in wel doinge:
> and with the scowrge of the lewde, the lewde are
> feared from evill attempts.[36]

Similarly, Cinthio claims in his Prologue to *Epitia* that:

> you will learn from it [his play] that lust
> leads its possessors to a wretched end, that to
> trust the faith of a person aflame with burning
> desire is vain, and finally that a gentle heart
> never does any injury which will abase it.[37]

Shakespeare's *Measure for Measure*, however, shows no such emphasis on moral teaching; his play has human situations leading to moral tensions and the problems these present to the characters, but no generalised moral dicta in action. He sees his material as a framework for a dramatic sequence of events interesting and exciting in themselves, but more important as the setting in which human beings can be shown wrestling with the incongruities which the dramatist, his actors and his audience share as the price of being human. I propose therefore to examine this play in some detail in the order in which it unfolds both as a dramatic story and as a developing exploration (in its first half at least) of inner discordancies.

Act 1, Scene 1, is one of Shakespeare's more direct and effective opening scenes. Within a few minutes of the beginning, an Elizabethan audience would be wondering what kind of Duke this is who admits that Escalus, a trusted old Lord, knows more about ruling than he does, and who is preparing (with no valid reason given) to hand over all his power, not to Escalus, but to Angelo, apparently solely because he is known to be a good man, 'good', that is, in that reason controls him. The Duke brushes aside Angelo's doubts, and leaves him and Escalus equally confused as to the exact nature and extent of their authority. Thus, in this storybook opening, there is already a suggestion of that discrepancy between private man and public man that will be so plain and crucial later in the opening of *King Lear*; already there is suggested the question whether a ruler, by a personal whim, can repudiate his responsibilities and still transfer them to an untried private person. The next scene displays vividly a major human and social problem which the Duke has neglected, and suggests its wider implications; the state's rational control over the irrational excesses of its subjects is linked to the individual's need for self-control; self-indulgence in the individual represents anarchy in the state, and the ruler's failure to control popular vice is equivalent to the individual's failure to control himself (see Part 1, Sections (h) and (i), pp. 18–26. Lucio, Mistress Overdone and Pompey directly, and entertainingly, create a tone of open acceptance of sexual indulgence as a human need and a human right, but this is quickly set against Claudio and his predicament. The situation is nicely balanced. Claudio admits frankly that personal licence inevitably swings finally to public repression, and even to self-destruction:

> As surfeit is the father of much fast,
> So every scope by the immoderate use
> Turns to restraint. Our natures do pursue,
> Like rats that ravine down their proper bane,
> A thirsty evil; and when we drink we die.[38]

Claudio accepts this consequence; what he plainly shows in talking to Lucio a little later, is that he resents the way in which the law, as exercised by Angelo, has caught him in its swing to severity, especially (a nice Elizabethan touch) as he and Juliet had delayed their marriage only for the most prudent financial reasons. Already there is a suggestion that reason in excess can be as dangerous as feeling in excess, that if passion needs the control of reason, reason needs the mitigation of feeling. In the next scene (1.3) this is pursued further: the Duke admits that for fourteen years he had neglected his duty to apply the law, and that this apparent mercy had brought the state to such anarchy that he himself is unable to control it. Furthermore, he suggests that he is using Angelo to take the brunt of the people's resentment (Claudio's resentment) when the law bites again. Finally he adds that Angelo's authority will test his apparent superiority to all human weakness. Thus rigid justice and merciful justice are being linked to rigid self-control and the admission of Man's frailty; strict justice and strict purity are no doubt admirable, but may need human modification at times. Man's justice–mercy and his reason–unreason conflicts are here beginning to be brought together as related examples of Man's inner struggles.

Act 1, Scene 4, completes the opening 'point-of-departure' design by bringing Isabella into the pattern. It is clear that she is presented as the female equivalent of Angelo; like him she has rejected the common human weakness of self-indulgence. As Lucio begs her to make an effort to persuade Angelo to pardon her brother, it is clear that even he respects the chaste quality of Isabella, but it is equally clear that Lucio sees her womanly beauty as a means to be used in winning her case:

> Go to Lord Angelo,
> And let him learn to know, when maidens sue,
> Men give like gods; but when they weep and kneel,
> All their petitions are as freely theirs
> As they themselves would owe [own] them.[39]

It is a hint of Isabella's pragmatic nature that she accepts without demur the suggestion that being a woman can help her to save her brother when appealing to Angelo the man.

Act 2 contains the crucial movement of the action, in which Isabella pleads with Angelo for her brother's life, and he offers it finally at the price of her virginity. This takes place in Scenes 2 and 4, but Scenes 1 and 3 of course have their bearing on the main action. Scene 1 starts by stressing again, through Angelo, the need to restore the full power of the law, but this is followed by Escalus's plea for a human and merciful interpretation of it. To this Angelo replies with a strictly legalistic distinction between wanting to sin and sinning; the law sees only the act. Again the emphasis is on the law as a logical and immovable process, contrasted with the law as subject to mercy; the irony of Angelo's imminent illegality is being prepared. The rest of this scene shows Escalus dealing with the Dogberry-like figure of Elbow, the elected constable, and Froth and Pompey (the comedy of their rambling ideas is that of the Nurse in *Romeo and Juliet*). Angelo asks a few brusque questions and then impatiently leaves, but

Escalus continues his patient, even friendly, inquiries, and finally promises to help the long-suffering Elbow to get rid of the duties which his neighbours have foisted upon him for seven-and-a-half years; the unwilling constable is a neat further comment on the question of authority. The lower world of Vienna is now seen through the understanding of Escalus, more intent on helping against sin than punishing it. Yet the scene ends with the warning that 'Pardon is still [always] the nurse of second woe'[40] – the problem of justice–mercy is finely balanced.

Act 2, Scenes 2 and 4 give the 'first pleading' and the 'second pleading' of Isabella's case for her brother. Between them is the brief scene in which the Duke makes his first reappearance in the play, disguised as 'Friar (Lodowick)' – even while Isabella argues, the process by which argument will be superseded by stage-intrigue has begun. The two scenes with Angelo and Isabella are the moral climax of the play, and the turning-point of the action. Act 2, Scene 2, starts with the completely self-assured Angelo already suggested earlier; Act 2, Scene 4, ends with an Angelo committed, with equal self-assurance, to a completely opposite attitude. Yet the two Angelos exist within the same man; that is the essence of human incongruity. Act 2, Scene 2, begins with the Isabella already briefly seen, strong in her beauty and purity; Act 2, Scene 4, ends with an Isabella who, after two scenes of her finely-spun and strangely innocent verbal battle with Angelo, finds that arguments can be swept aside by lust. In other words, Angelo and Isabella are curiously alike before their contest starts, when both are naïvely unaware of the power of Man's inconsistency; by the end of the battle, both have felt that power, Angelo through the innocence of Isabella, Isabella through the evil of Angelo.

Both these scenes deserve careful reading and skilful informed acting; they are much more than a mere dramatic encounter of innocence and lust. For an Elizabethan, beyond this obvious appeal they would have been a deeply interesting, even disconcerting, reminder of the conflicts at work within the individual and within society, and those conflicts are still potent today. So they need to be examined in some detail. Isabella's first 'argument' is a plain piece of casuistry, that Claudio's fault should be condemned, not Claudio; Angelo shows the weakenss of this; Isabella seems about to give up, but Lucio spurs her on. When she takes up the plea for mercy, Angelo replies that his will[41] is not for mercy, and so he cannot grant it; she begs him to copy God's mercy to forfeited souls, and he falls back on the claim that he is merely carrying out the law. Isabella now talks of pity, but he is ready with the well-known argument that the best pity is to stop people from committing sin. She is then given a most (poetically) effective passage on mere mortals in authority trying to show a power that God would never use, but she soon switches to a very different argument – great authority can afford to risk mistakes, for its power overrides its faults, a dangerous suggestion to a man like Angelo. She goes on to say that if he can feel any similar sin in himself, he cannot punish Claudio; this has been answered by Angelo in the previous scene, and there is irony in the fact that his point that the law does not consider mere intention is used at the end of the play, by Isabella, to ask mercy for him. At this stage in the argument, Angelo shows that his desire for Isabella has been aroused. Thereafter he is eager to end the debate, and, when the rest have gone, his soliloquy expresses, first his amazement that a pure woman, not a strumpet, arouses his lust (innocence itself becomes ironic), and second, his new understanding of how men can be overcome by passion opposed to reason.

Two other soliloquies by Angelo preface the 'second pleading'. In the first, which opens the scene, Angelo's struggle has reached the point where his 'will', his passionate intention, has reduced rational control to a mere conventional hypocrisy required by his social position; he even attacks this appearance required of those in authority; the 'private man' and his will are rebelling against the 'public man' and his essential reason. This links to the incongruities present around the Duke and his part in the rest of the play – the 'public man' who had deliberately avoided the demands of that role (so putting Angelo under the pressure that destroys him as a 'public man'), acts with the power of a 'public man' hidden in the guise of a 'private man'. In the contrived confusion of role-playing (itself symbolic) in the last scene of the play, the Duke alternates between the two personae until he can finally emerge as the 'public man' in decisive control of all around him – even then, he uses his authority as 'public man' to assume possession of Isabella, and satisfy the 'private man'.

The 'second pleading' hinges on the moment when Isabella will recognise what Angelo is demanding of her; the delicate suspense is highly effective dramatically. At first she seems to be ready to commit sin to save her brother, and even talks of giving her body. But the ambiguity is at once explained; she would give her body to punishment, not to sin; the only sin she will commit is that of pleading for a sinful brother; if Angelo is to sin in pardoning him, she will take that possible sin on herself. For a moment, Shakespeare makes us wonder whether such finely-spun 'theological' arguments are really as naïve as they appear, for we have already been shown that she is not wholly unaware of the real world of men and women. When Angelo, in understandable if not admirable impatience, suggests that she is being wilfully obtuse, Isabella is apologetic; he is forced to be blunt. The serious moral struggle is taking on overtones of the age-old battle of the sexes and its ironic comedy. Of course Isabella firmly rejects Angelo's offer, and, in contrasting 'lawful mercy' and 'foul redemption', actually admits that her earlier sympathetic attitude to Claudio's sin had not been her real view of it, but one assumed as part of her pleading. This, her first admission that she is less than perfect, at once leads Angelo to join her with himself in human frailty, and then to the significant comment:

> Since I suppose we are made to be no stronger
> Than faults may shake our frames.[42]

Here Angelo, not unlike Parolles, comes to terms with his own human frailty, recognises his human imperfection, and accepts the consequences – and Isabella herself is brushed by his awareness.

The long argument is virtually at an end. Angelo urges her to accept her own weakness as a woman, and grant his demands; she breaks out into indignant protest, and then tries to blackmail him. He, of course, is unmoved by her threats, and leaves her to consider Claudio's execution (now with the addition of torture) if she remains stubborn. She stands alone on the stage exclaiming against the way in which passion can override the law (but she herself had been trying to make pity greater than the law), and then she moves to the final lines of the scene:

> Then, Isabel, live chaste, and, brother, die;
> More than our brother is our chastity.
> I'll tell him yet of Angelo's request,
> And fit his mind to death, for his soul's rest.

The ideal 'good' of chastity is to be preserved by a brother's death – 'higher' reason is more important than human love. This is her decision, but enough inner contradictions have been revealed in the play already to make such an attitude highly suspect; in fact, Isabella spends the rest of the play showing (with the Duke's help) that clever plotting can save her brother, and that, ultimately, she has no rigid commitment to chastity if a good and proper marriage is available. This is not just a discrepancy of character necessary merely to contrive a 'happy ending', and easily accepted if she had been a storybook type. Given Shakespeare's portrayal of the human truth of Isabella in the first half of the play, it must be seen as an indication, however slight at the end, of the true discords of human beings.

So we come to where the third major character in the conflict is brought to a realisation of another form of human conflict, one which everyone has to face, the desire to live and the inevitability of death.[43] In the next scene, Isabella has to tell Claudio of Angelo's evil, and 'fit his mind to death', but the pressure on Claudio is prepared for in the opening part of the scene, where the disguised Duke gives the young man the traditional arguments in favour of being ready, even eager, to die. The *De Contemptu Mundi* approach to death was still a part of Elizabethan thinking: many of the contemporary audience would have recognised the Duke's reasons for why life is apparently not worth living, although they might have doubted, and rightly, Claudio's immediate acceptance of the Duke's argument. Where death is concerned, everyone (a Christian more than most) may acknowledge the logical reasons for not fearing it; yet here again, as in so much of our nature, reason is at war with deep emotional and instinctive pressure, and we know that life is sweet. An instructive comparison with Shakespeare's treatment here of this matter can be found in the anonymous *The Raigne of King Edward the Third*, written some ten years before *Measure for Measure*. In this play, another sober man speaks to a younger man about death, and convinces him:

AUDLEY   To die is all as common as to live;
The one in choice, the other holds in chase:
For from the instant we begin to live
We do pursue and hunt the time to die:
First bud we, then we blow, and after seed;
Then, presently, we fall; and, as a shade
Follows the body, so we follow death.
If then we hunt for death, why do we fear it?
If we fear it, why do we follow it?
If we do fear, how can we shun it?
If we do fear, with fear we do but aid
The thing we fear to seize on us the sooner:
If we fear not, then no resolved proffer

Can overthrow the limit of our fate:
For, whether ripe or rotten, drop we shall,
As we do draw the lottery of our doom.

PR. EDWARD   Ah, good old man, a thousand thousand armours
These words of thine have buckled on my back . . .
I will not give a penny for a life,
Nor half a halfpenny to shun grim death,
Since for to live is but to seek to die,
And Dying but beginning of new life.
Let come the hour when he that rules it will!
To live, or die, I hold indifferent.[44]

'Prave words', as Fluellen once said, and nicely in the tradition of heroic martial plays, but contrast with this the way in which Claudio finally faces the prospect of imminent death, and one realises the significant move from accepted conventional responses to the naked truth of how human beings react to the fear of death. Isabella, now that her standards and her trust in man's goodness are perhaps a little shaken, is right to fear, as she says, that Claudio will seek life even at the price of her dishonour: although for a moment he speaks almost as nobly as Prince Edward, his instincts soon sweep away all the reasonable restraint of accepted behavior, and pour out into the vivid physical–emotional imagery of his speech beginning 'Ay, but to die, and go we know not where'.[45] It is a passage which, in its feeling for the truth of human nature, deserves comparison with any of the great Shakespearean tragic speeches; it is so disturbingly real that even by itself it almost breaks the 'romantic-story' mould in which the play is nominally set.

But now that 'romantic story' takes over. The remaining half of the play is mainly concerned with the elaborate scheme of the Duke (using Isabella, Mariana and the Provost) to expose Angelo, the 'killing' of Claudio by Angelo's command (causing another complication in the Duke's plotting), and the outcome of it all in a long final scene where, ironically enough, Lucio is the only character to be suitably punished.[46] All this plot-contrivance is well handled as dramatic suspense and entertainment, and enriched as such by the low-life figures, especially Pompey and Barnadine,[47] but after the Claudio-Isabella confrontation in Act 3, Scene 1, the treatment and tone have changed. This is the reason, I think, why so many critics and audiences have felt somewhat puzzled by the play. The material was a story of far-fetched plotting, starting with an unlikely situation

and contrived to a happy ending; but in the first half of the play
Shakespeare had established the main characters as real persons
assailed by their disturbing inner struggles, and the starting situation
had thus become an epitome of real life, however unlikely the
setting. In the second half of the drama these characters had faded
into mere players in a plot, sufficiently alive of course, yet out of key
with their beginnings. But in tragedy, in *Hamlet*, Shakespeare had
already shown that he could use a plot to carry the reality of human
conflict through from beginning to end of a play; indeed, in *Hamlet*
that human conflict is the play.

English History Plays

During the 1590s when Shakespeare had been writing the series of
comedies from *The Comedy of Errors* to *Measure for Measure*, he
had also been making a number of plays dramatising episodes of
English history. In its presentation of the forms and effects of 'inner
incongruity', this group makes an interesting accompaniment to his
use of that incongruity in the comedies, and these two groups of
examples of his growing attention to human nature in his plays
establish a foundation upon which all his later drama is based in this
respect.

We have already seen in Part 2 how often the drama of
Shakespeare's precursors was concerned with questions of kings and
kingship, and how *A Mirror for Magistrates*, a popular work in
various editions from 1559 to 1587 (and after), gave examples of the
many ways in which rulers ('magistrates') could prove unworthy of,
or unsuited to, their supremely important office, and thereby fail.
Suggestions of the same theme, as we have seen, occur as part of the
human interest of some of the comedies; wherever a figure has a high
status in society, and proves unworthy of it, the wider problem of
authority is relevant.

However, comparing the comedies and the English history plays in
general, it is clear that different treatments of human conflict are
being used. In the comedies, the emphasis is on individuals striving
with this conflict within their personal lives; the partial exception to
this, *Measure for Measure*, where the theme of public authority is of
basic importance, comes last of these comedies, when Shakespeare
had moved from both normal comedies and history plays to the field
of tragedy. In the English history plays, Shakespeare is using material
known, in outline at least, to many of his audience; that audience had
learnt to see past English history as a sequence of dynastic struggles

out of which, finally and even miraculously, had emerged the relative peace and security of Elizabeth's reign. They knew that ambitious men or powerful interests, the rebellion of an Essex or the constant efforts of the Jesuits, could shake the country's hard-won stability, that before long their Queen would die, and that then the throne might be the focus of further power-struggles like those of the past.

Shakespeare's English history plays are dramatically concerned with their continuous theme of political struggle, of personal power-seeking and power-keeping, always related to the fate of England. So they deal essentially with the tensions revealed when an individual with personal strengths and weaknesses is forced by ambition or circumstances to use them, as best he can, in the dangerous arena of public life. The main question behind all these plays is, how will a certain political person, being what he is as a human being, act in his political situation?[48] The chief facts of the political plot are already known; Shakespeare's special skill lies in showing how personal factors largely determined the recorded course of history.

The main English history plays, then, display the inconsistency of Man in its common major forms affecting not only individuals, but thereby the course of public events, and especially the lives of the people who are England. Thus public figures are shown as striving for power while at the same time conscious of its burdens and dangers, and its transitory nature. So, too, they seek a power based on peace and order, yet ironically do so by creating a social disorder that holds the seeds of their own downfall. Sometimes they attempt to be 'private' persons still, although committed to 'public' positions; then their weaknesses as individuals may destroy their authority and strength as 'public' figures. The warring motives present in all Mankind, if not controlled or resolved can affect a person's life and the lives of all around that person – this is the substance of so many of Shakespeare's other plays; in the English history plays Shakespeare always makes us aware of this 'local' effect, but to it is added the far greater stress on the national and dynastic consequences. Moreover, in the world of these history plays, the human challenge of death, while being, as always, a basic conflict within the individual, becomes also an irony of political strife; in that strife it can be used as the ultimate means of acquiring power, yet the user is mortal, and will die; the ruler's unique power confers neither god-like wisdom nor immortality. With the king's death, often, the struggle for power follows once more the beaten path through death to death – and the world of ordinary men, the commonwealth of England, must tread the same path.

Shakespeare's English history plays of the 1590s should be considered in two groups.[49] *Richard III* (c1593) and *King John* (c1596) are akin in being largely chronicle plays dramatising a series of historical events, with the major emphasis on the 'story'. The 1597 title page of the first quarto of *Richard III* shows the contemporary view and appeal of the play:

> The Tragedy of King Richard the third. Containing, His treacherous Plots against his brother Clarence: the pittiefull murther of his innocent nephewes: his tyrannicall vsurpation: with the whole course of his detested life, and most deserued death.

The 'rise-and-fall' pattern suggested in this outline story is a traditional one, allied to the tales of *A Mirror for Magistrates* and to so many earlier 'moral' plays of the sixteenth century, as we have seen. Explicit in this story is just such a moral, that usurpation and murder inevitably and rightly bring disaster to the usurper. But the moral is political rather than personal, and the dramatising of the events of Richard's wicked career can be effective without any complex treatment of character. Shakespeare is obviously not attempting any such treatment. The play works very effectively with the 'villain' Richard as its centre, and an assortment of mainly type characters ranged around him as the predetermined victims of his villainy. He refers to himself (in Act 3, Scene 1) as being 'like the formal (traditional) vice, Iniquity'; the Vice of the earlier 'moral' plays, although plainly reprehensible, and inevitably unsuccessful in the end, was often, and deliberately, the most amusing and lively figure in a rather didactic and predictable moralising tale, and this is certainly true of Richard as he works steadily towards kingship. Of course he has to collapse into defeat at the end, and in so doing become suddenly and briefly a human example of frustrated ambition. In short, human conflict is shown in simplified form, the unfeeling reason ('lower reason') of Richard against the emotional fear and disgust of his victims; the reason is mechanical and inhuman, the emotion is luxuriant and verbose. The play, although brilliantly contrived, deals in simplified passions, sudden and brutal action, and conventional (if true) reactions, and in such melodramatic qualities it is akin to *Titus Andronicus*, a play of about the same date.

King John was Shakespeare's reworking of an earlier anonymous

play *The Troublesome Raigne of Iohn King of England*, published in
two parts in 1591. The reworking was designed chiefly to clarify and
strengthen the narrative interest and the historical emphases of the
earlier play; in tightening the action, indeed, Shakespeare went so far
as to omit what must have been, in his source, the highly popular
portrayal of the poisoning of King John; the overall effect of the
historical tale seems to have been more important to him than a
theatrical effect. The two title pages of the earlier play, like that of
Richard III, show its chief purpose and appeal:

> The Troublesome Raigne of Iohn King of England, with the
> discouerie of King Richard Cordelions Base sonne (vulgarly
> named, The Bastard Fawconbridge): also the death of King
> John at Swinstead Abbey. . . .

> The Second part of the troublesome Raigne of King John,
> conteining the death of Arthur Plantaginet, the landing of
> Lewes, and the poysoning of King John at Swinstead Abbey.

The plays are here presented as a dramatic story of political events
centred on King John, with full exploitation of the excitement of the
Bastard, the pathos of Arthur, the patriotic reactions to the French
invasion, and the theatrical appeal of John's death. Like *Richard III*,
Shakespeare's *King John*, following the general manner of its source,
is a play of traditional political moral force, but the emphasis is much
more on the wider question of the danger to England than on the
evils of John. John's usurpation, evil in itself, is seen as the beginning
of England's troubles; the death of Arthur is pathetic, but more
important is the fact that John's believed guilt leads the English nobles
to join the French against their own land; the final point of the play is
that the nobles recognise their mistake, force the French to with-
draw, and England is once more united under the new king, Henry
III. As part of King John's perplexities for England, the political-
cum-ecclesiastic power of the Pope is shown as almost successful
against the realm; the political attitude of Bale's *John, King of
England* is still obviously popular, although there is little of his
extreme Puritan purpose.

Although these two plays, *Richard III* and *King John*, are basically 'narrative-plays', and the characters in them scarcely more
complex than the roles require, by the very nature of those narratives
there is an implied presence of personal strife underlying the 'social'
forms. These 'social' forms are not yet yet joined to close portrayal of

the personal forms – indeed, the following English history plays will not link the two deeply, except in the case of *Richard II*, but they will show an increasing use of the personal forms.

With *Richard II* a shift of emphasis occurs which significantly changes the presentation and the effect of what is still, of course, history displayed in dramatic form. By the end of the first scene, we are aware that Richard is not just the King, but a man of a strangely imprecise nature in a crucial position of power. He proclaims, in effect, the confusion within him:

> We were not born to sue, but to command;
> Which since we cannot do to make you friends,
> Be ready.[50]

We suddenly realise the essence of Richard's inner discord, the fatal discrepancy between his assumption, as King, that kingship itself confers absolute power, and the conflicting recognition, as a man, that he has no power over the private feelings of his subjects. In Scene 3, authority is already beginning to be weakened by personal whim; the king has claimed power, then immediately admitted that individuals must settle what authority claimed to control, and has now resumed decision-making in a quite arbitrary manner. Bolingbroke's 'such is the breath of Kings' notes at once the power of kingship and its personal human unpredictability – and perhaps suggests his dawning desire for such power.

For the rest of the play, the struggle lies not between 'The King' and 'The Usurper', but between the man Richard who is the King and the man Bolingbroke who becomes the usurper. We are moving from the historical-political world of *Richard III* and *King John* partly towards and into the 'private' world of, say, *Othello*.[51] The treatment is still a mingling of the historical and the personal, usually with the emphasis on the former, but from that mingling are coming important results; historical drama is moving from the historical 'story' to the historical 'novel'; the movements of history are beginning to be realised by the audience as the interplay between events and character.

Thus *Richard II* steadily becomes a play shot through with comments on, and displays of, personal human incongruity and also (because these persons are 'great ones', men whose aims and actions affect the whole state) that wider 'social' form of human incongruity which determines the stresses under which both rulers and people live. The central emphasis of the play is on showing Richard's conflict between his personal self and his political self living within one man, already hinted at in the opening of the play. In Act 2, Scene 1, the dominant thread is pursued. York, who throughout the play is the epitome of belief in legal right and the unquestioned authority of kingship (a belief later made part of his conflict), says to the dying Gaunt:

> Then all too late comes counsel to be heard
> Where will doth mutiny with wit's regard.[52]

This applies the common Elizabethan sense of 'will' (desire, irrational intention) as the dangerous enemy of 'wit' (intelligence, reason), a basic dichotomy, to the self-indulgent behaviour of the King, and it is reinforced shortly afterwards by Gaunt's words to Richard:

> Landlord of England art thou now, not King.
> Thy state of law is bondslave to the law'.[53]

Gaunt's point is a fundamental one; the King who should be the law, and above the law, through his personal greed has reduced himself to a mere landowner, a businessman subject to the law. This view of Richard's weakness as a King is supported by what we are shown in this scene of his almost childish, selfish obstinacy in pursuing his own ends. When he arrogantly seizes Bolingbroke's inheritance from Gaunt, York has to tell him the danger of what he is doing so impulsively; by breaking the natural law of inheritance from father to son, the King is in fact undermining the accepted law of succession on which rests his own tenure of the throne – and in fact his action drives his nobles to support Bolingbroke. Thus Richard has been presented plainly as both the selfish individual and as the anointed King who believes that his power comes by divine right. Such a man is not unusual among English kings; the question now is whether the individual is capable of remaining the King.

Before Richard undergoes his final test as the man who is also a king, the almost symbolic events of Act 2, Scene 3, point forward to that test and, indeed, prepare the outcome of it. York is confronted by Bolingbroke and his growing popular support: he admits that Bolingbroke's claim to his own inheritance is just, and can only argue that force must never be used against a king. But he has no power with which to buttress Richard's traditional rights, and quickly he slides from a pathetic attempt to be neutral to an acceptance of the fact that he must follow Bolingbroke. This is a pointer to Richard's dilemma; he can afford to believe in his God-given right to rule only if he is prepared to fight for that right as stubbornly as if it were not God-given. Bolingbroke has no such dilemma, no struggle between belief and reason; he has the power to seize the throne, the opportunity, and the will to use both power and opportunity.

The conflict in Richard is again shown, very clearly, near the beginning of Act 3, Scene 2, the scene in which he cracks under the strain of his own 'human incongruity'. Richard has marked his return to England with a somewhat over-emotional, 'poetic' assertion (very effective on stage) that the very soil and its creatures will fight for their true lord, ending:

> Mock not my senseless conjuration, lords.
> This earth shall have a feeling, and these stones
> Prove armed soldiers, ere her native King
> Shall falter under foul rebellion's arms.[54]

Richard, among his fighting lords, has indulged in a fantasy which, no matter how beautiful, is certainly irrelevant in practical terms for a King facing armed opposition: his supporters present must feel amusement or dismay. The Bishop at once suggests that God helps those who help themselves, and Aumerle more bluntly stresses the need to meet Bolingbroke's power with power, and quickly. What is Richard's response? An even more wonderfully emotive and rhetorical speech, ending:

> Not all the water in the rough rude sea
> Can wash the balm off from an anointed king;
> The breath of worldly men cannot depose
> The deputy elected by the Lord.
> For every man that Bolingbroke hath press'd
> To lift shrewd (perverse, wicked) steel against our golden
>   crown,
> God for his Richard hath in heavenly pay
> A glorious angel. Then, if angels fight,
> Weak men must fall; for heaven still [ever] guards the right.[55]

Richard's confusion between his kingship and his situation has become all too apparent, and it is the crux of the play: as an individual he has qualities of emotion and imagination (thanks to Shakespeare's poetry) which, if he were in another position, might be suitable and admirable;[56] in fact, from now on to the end of the play, the audience may admire and pity him, but they are shown that he is ineffectual in his political role.

The rest of Act 3, Scene 2, and its sequel, Scene 3, show the practical consequences of this. Richard, firm in his assurance as an anointed King, is now subjected to one of Shakespeare's effective 'hammer-blows' sequences:[57] Richard hears that Salisbury's 12,000 men have gone over to Bolingbroke, then that Bolingbroke is gaining general support, and that Bushey and Green are dead. Here his precarious balance between Man and King is directly affected, and the result is significant; his feeling swings to a sudden sense of his littleness as mere Man, turns to thoughts 'of graves, of worms, of epitaphs', and he dismisses his kingly convictions with:

> For you have but mistook me all this while.
> I live with bread like you, feel want,
> Taste grief, need friends; subjected thus,
> How can you say to me I am king?[58]

Within a moment or two, with the encouragement of the Bishop and of Aumerle, he has swung back to renewed belief in his kingship, but only briefly – Scroop delivers the last blow, the news of York's defection to Bolingbroke, and Richard not only reverts to his sense of personal inadequacy, but renders it final by an irrevocable step, the order to disband his army. His anointed kingship has proved to be dependent upon worldly power, and crumbles with the loss of that power when Richard shows himself unable to admit the fact and use the power.

Bolingbroke has not beaten Richard; the King's personal inner contradiction has resulted in a surrender of his kingly duties and responsibilities, and he has himself forsaken his kingship. Act 3, Scene 3, and Act 4, Scene 1, are only the practical, political working-out of this internal disruption, with Richard hastening to give up his crown, but the two personae are still at futile war within him, and this is the beginning of his last phase, the final and open display of that underlying doubt as to his own identity, his own role, which has been implicit almost from the first. Thus, in Act 3, Scene 3, he says:

> O that I were as great
> As is my grief, or lesser than my name!
> Or that I could forget what I have been!
> Or not remember what I must be now![59]

and in the next scene but one (4.1), after he has given Bolingbroke the crown, but with a wild and bitter reminder of the sanctity of kings, he can comment:

> Nay, if I turn mine eyes upon myself,
> I find myself a traitor with the rest;
> For I have given here my soul's consent
> T'undeck the pompous body of a king;
> Made glory base, and sovereignty a slave,
> Proved majesty a subject, state a peasant.[60]

Even near the end of the play, in Act 5, Scene 5, just before his murder, he is still wrestling with his divided self:

> Sometimes am I king;
> Then treasons make me wish myself a beggar,
> And so I am. Then crushing penury
> Persuades me I was better when a king;
> Then am I king'd again; and by and by
> Think that I am unking'd by Bolingbroke,
> And straight am nothing.[61]

Thus Richard ends as the victim, destroyed from within, of a far more dangerous form of incongruity than merely that between 'private' man and 'public' man, although this is its origin. It is a form whereby a man is caught between fantasy and reality;[62] being the man he is, he cannot break out of the trap, resolve the dilemma by committing himself to either fantasy or reality. So Richard dies as a man given by God the divine right of kingship and therefore protected by Him from usurpation, but also as a man who knows, but will not admit, that to half-believe in such supernatural support is not to have it, and to need instead the brutal reality of political and military power. *Macbeth* shows us a man who, at first, is caught in a similar conflict; he has a similar (but of course evil) assurance of supernatural support for kingship, but he cannot, not being a Banquo, trust to this, and must resort to aiding the supernatural by violence. Here the similarity ends: Richard dies as a weak, divided personality destroyed by that inner division; Macbeth ends as one who has deliberately reduced himself to the stark simplicity of a man of violence, and dies by violence. Shakespeare and his audience know how rarely human conflict can be resolved fully, and what varied disasters can come upon a man, and upon his society, if resolution does not take place. But death, of course, the final resolution, can always be relied upon to end a man's struggles, and a play.

The immediate dramatic effect of *Richard II* has been as a portrayal of historical events, political warfare, with stirring scenes of physical action prominent. But the inner theme of 'man-in-history' has been stressed around the figure of a king. From *1 Henry IV* to *Henry V* the examination (always in dramatic, entertaining terms) of inner strife in history is wider, more diffuse, less concentrated on a particular person.

Thus the move from *Richard II* to *1 Henry IV* is significant, chiefly because the emphasis of this dramatised history is increasingly on the ways in which, politically and in human terms, a great and successful English king is created, and the effects of this on England. Of course, for a large part of the audience the main interest of the process lies in the physical events, the successes and failures of war, yet battles are admitted to be impossible to portray realistically on the Elizabethan popular stage,[63] and the struggles of personal discords can be shown much more effectively in speech rather than action. Moreover, the human incongruity of less important, less 'historical', figures begins to appear more markedly from *1 Henry IV* on; that they often represent comedy for entertainment does not make them any less true to human nature. The move from the Gardener of *Richard II* (3.4) to Falstaff and his companions in *1 Henry IV* is typical of the change of tone and emphases between the two plays. The Gardener represents 'the Wisdom of the People' commenting on the actions of their superiors; he is very near to the old 'moral play' characters, and he is scarcely a living individual. Every member of the tavern world in *1 Henry IV*, and increasingly in *2 Henry IV*, is a human being subject to the repercussions of political events invading their private lives.

These political events, beginning in *1 Henry IV* (although springing from *Richard II*) are now shown as the outcome of the tensions within a number of personalities. There is still the main stress, of course, on the 'man-become-king', Henry IV, and the 'man-becoming-king', Hal. In both cases we are shown the private man in the public situation; in the presentation of Hal–Henry V especially, the two worlds in which he at first moves are dramatically illustrated and contrasted, and his final rejection of the private world is prepared for from almost his first appearance. Henry IV is shown as confronted, like any ordinary private man, with the incongruity between will and wit, between desire and the logic of the events put into motion by that desire. In getting the crown, Henry had used both his own determination and the divided weakness of Richard, using physical force (and the threat of it) to defeat Richard. In *1 Henry IV*, the audience is reminded of what they have so often been told, that the usurper who uses force to gain the throne offers an example and a justification to any future seeker after power. More than this, Shakespeare has carried on and developed from *Richard II* the old 'fitness-for-authority' question; how can a man desiring or possessing public power so control or modify the pressures of his natural 'human incongruity' that he becomes worthy of that power? The answer is made plain, not argued didactically, in the three English history plays following *Richard II*; the man in authority, torn as we all are between reason and unreason, must choose reason, and even use unreason rationally – the successful King Henry V needs a bond of patriotic emotion with his soldiers; where the friendly emotion of friendship may become dangerous, as at the end of *2 Henry IV*, to the status of a king, it is rejected. Much is made in these three plays of Henry IV's fear that Hal will follow the emotional weakness of Richard rather than the rational path that he had found so successful in gaining the crown, but we already know that Hal is more single-minded than even his father; his soliloquy at the end of Act 1, Scene 2, of *1 Henry IV* has made that plain. So there is no doubt that Hal will prove to be fully equipped psychologically for the status of triumphant conquerer and beloved King of England that the audience know he achieved, and which is fully and vividly shown in *Henry V*. Thus there is no inner conflict in Hal–Henry V; the tavern world becomes a source of comedy, not a testing-ground for Hal, but it gives more than comedy – it becomes the human counter-balance to the calculating reason required in the world of successful power-seeking and power-using.

The Elizabethan audience, enjoying to the full the rich comedy of Falstaff and his cronies, would have seen, partly at the dramatist's prompting, that these figures are representatives of the anonymous world of 'the common people' around whom, through whom, all the struggles of 'great ones' take place. This is no matter of imposing Marxist or other doctrinaire interpretations unknown to the audience, upon the life created by Shakespeare; he is expressing a truth of social existence that men had learnt by experience over the centuries, and had accepted as part of their own humanity. The Elizabethans knew that ordinary people had to accept their own inner discords in order to go on living in this world; they also knew that such discords were at work in the great, and that on their ability to handle these discords depended the order or disorder of every man's life. Falstaff and his friends are deeply comic, not merely funny, because they show human complexes working at an ordinary, everyday level with apparently almost a complete disregard of what similar complexes are doing at a higher, political level. If the comic world of the tavern could have stayed unaffected within its own limits, we might have had the almost care-free laughter of, say, *The Merry Wives of Windsor*, but Shakespeare now seems committed to a deeper reality of life, in which laughter is never wholly care-free. Thus it is inevitable that the laughter is not 'free', is more and more affected by the political world 'above'. Indeed, Prince Hal, after his early soliloquy, shows the influence of that political world; the tavern laughter is never wholly free of it, for the king-to-be is always felt as a presence. The gradual change in the tone of Falstaff and his laughter symbolises what is happening. In the earlier part of *1 Henry IV*, Falstaff is a special individual with a special form of universal comedy built around him; his human incongruity is the lovable, common (but heightened) one of the average man who knows he is old, but feels he is young, who is proud of his cleverness, his 'lower reason', but who cannot resist the desire for too much food and drink. Even when war intrudes upon him, he can manage to assimilate it, with laughter, to his own view of life. Then the 'greater' world above the tavern begins to sharpen and modify that earlier comedy; Falstaff shows more and more awareness that his young Hal will be king; however much ironic laughter has already arisen from the proximity of tavern and Court, this is a serious business. By the final stage in *2 Henry IV* of Hal's progress towards kingship, Falstaff's earlier easy acceptance of his comic role of lord of the tavern has clouded over with a striving towards the greater things that the new King's old friendship must surely give him: Shallow's naïve comedy of the old man remembering youth is an echo of a Falstaff who no longer exists. The earlier Falstaff would have laughed, with a certain respect of course, at the Hal now emerged into the purposeful, responsible King Henry V, and would have called for sack as he laughed; the final Falstaff, having contemplated the 'greater' world of power and ambition, has lost that 'innocence' which was the core of his laughter. That his heart was at last 'fracted and corroborate', as Pistol said, marks the human tragedy of a man who, in his human confusion, had tried to move from his private world of emotion and unreason into a harsher world where reason carefully balanced emotion against expediency – and found him no longer necessary.

The tavern group, we must remember, however funny, represented to many of the Elizabethan audience that disorder which was a constant offence to some, and a real danger to the social order of all. The new King is rationally a good king in controlling them, even abruptly and harshly. It is acceptable and right, where successful and glorious kingship is concerned, that the common people should now be represented by independent yet dependable and disciplined soldiers like Bates, Williams and Fluellen – military glory, the quasi-apotheosis of Henry V, is not built upon Pistol and his like.

Something has happened to kingship, too, in the movement from Henry IV to Henry V. Henry IV had soliloquised, in well-known traditional terms, on the anxieties of kingship and the happy freedom from responsibility of the common man,[64] but it was plain that he had schemed and fought to obtain kingship, and was desperate to hand it on to his son. When Henry V soliloquises on the same theme,[65] one feels a shift of attitude; the King is bitter at the way in which the common people lay their private responsibilities upon him, and regrets that 'Ceremony' cuts him off from the peace of common folk. For a moment there is a suggestion that even the great Henry V is affected by some inner strife between the ideal glory of kingship and the reality of being a king; the fact is that the goal is now something beyond mere kingship, it is kingship used for the glory of England. That end justifies, for the King and his people, the use of patriotic persuasion in the 'Crispian' speech, for it leads to the triumphant defeat of the French.

And yet. . . . After this triumph, what follows? The curiously casual courtship by Henry of the French Princess Katherine, the glory of conquest in war subsiding into the old tradition of the woman's power in love over the man, here in the uneasy context of a political match. The scene is of course neatly and effectively amusing, but it cannot avoid being an ironic comment on all that has preceded it. The irony is strengthened almost to cynicism in the epilogue by the Chorus:

> Small time, but, in that small, most greatly lived
> This star of England. Fortune made his sword;
> By which the world's best garden [guerdon, reward] he
>   achieved,
> And of it left his son imperial lord.
> Henry the Sixth, in infant bands crown'd king
> Of France and England, did this king succeed;
> Whose state so many had the managing
> That they lost France and made his England bleed.

All that four plays have shown of the struggles of men's human nature in power, or in getting and keeping power; all the dramatic display of the attempts of men to suppress their inner human weaknesses and use their political strengths – all this has produced a wonderfully successful and dramatic succession of human and political action and reaction, but this pageant of Man's seeking for power, and his use of it when obtained, has ended in this wry prospect: the passing of a triumphant 'king, the inadequacy of the next (or his statesmen), and in a few years the spoils of glory lost, and England once more as distressed as she was at the beginning of *Richard II.* One cannot be sure that such cynical awareness of the littleness of Man's worldly efforts is part of the dramatist's view of life; even if it were, he would have shared it with his audience and his age, all heirs of a tradition of the religious emphasis on the unimportant transitory nature of all the Man seeks for in this world. But it is interesting, at least, to realise that much of Shakespeare's later work emphasises the human struggle to achieve worldly success or avert worldly disaster, and makes us feel that it is not the success or disaster that finally matters, but the struggle itself.

Classical plays

Timon of Athens (*c*1607) can best be considered as an exceptional play, a marked contrast to the other three plays[66] dealt with in this section. I would agree with most critics in regarding it as an unfinished play, an outline sketch to which the busy dramatist never returned. Because of its consequently simple plot and emphatic contrasts, it reminds one of the earlier 'moral' plays of the sixteenth century. In fact, all the characters could be regarded as typifying moral concepts by their actions in the play. Looked at in this way, Timon becomes a brutally direct representation of Foolish Trust changing to Misanthropos, the earlier 'friends' of Timon are Flattery, Greed and False Friendship, Flavius is Trusty Service, Apemantus is Spite, and Alcibiades might well be Custom or Worldly Wisdom. But this 'morality' has no moral; human nature seems to be shown in the broad, bold lines and simplified tones of a caricature, with the limited truth of a caricature, but with no firm suggestion of any deeper truth.

 Timon of Athens is more important than this, not in itself but in relation to other Shakespeare plays of this period, the early years of the new century when he was writing, not only the 'classical' plays, but his mature comedies, the 'darker' comedies, and the great tragedies. Certainly at this time in Elizabethan London there was a tendency to welcome a cynical 'realistic' view of human nature; the appearance on the London stages of such plays as Marston's (and Webster's) *The Malcontent*, Chapman's *The Widow's Tears*, Jonson's *Volpone* and Tourneur's *The Revenger's Tragedy* shows something of a taste and outlook that was to deepen later into the tragic despair of Webster's *The Duchess of Malfi*. In such plays, in such a mood, human conflict was being accepted as the inescapable fate of Man and Woman, something to be recognised without hope, which destroyed any human pretensions to fineness or wisdom, which could be faced only with savage laughter or the empty dignity of admitted defeat.[67]

Timon of Athens, then, represents a moment when Shakespeare, casually almost, moved into that mood, recognised its partial validity and truth, but had already passed beyond it into a deeper realisation that this was by no means the whole truth. All Shakespeare's plays of this period contain something of *Timon of Athens*, just as the finished portrait embodies the rough sketch; Shakespeare is now finding the ability to show in dramatic form the complex joys, and terrors, of Man's constant strife with the incongruities which make him truly human. *Timon of Athens* merely demonstrated, almost in the didactic manner of contemporary preachers, that Man's nature could swing him between an irrational faith in the goodness of his fellow men, and an equally irrational conviction that all Mankind is contemptible and worthless. As Apemantus says to Timon, 'The middle of humanity thou never knewest, but the extremity of both ends'.[68] Timon is truly limited to an emotional realisation of those extremes of human nature between which we struggle. Shakespeare left him at that point, for there was nothing in the naïve story to evoke deeper awareness, wisdom, in the protagonist. But Hamlet, too, experienced irrational trust in human goodness and irrational disgust at human evil – and fought beyond these passions to the verge, at least, of seeing that they were only part of the truth about Man.

Keeping *Timon of Athens* in mind, let us turn now to the three 'classical' plays with which this section is chiefly concerned, considering them in the order in which they were written. These plays are all in a 'story' sense, history plays, and it is worth comparing them with the group of English history plays which we have just considered. As we have seen, Shakespeare moved from emphasising, in *Richard III* and *King John*, the chronicle material of the plays, with very little detailed concern for the characters, to the *Richard II–Henry V* group where the course of history is shown, at least partly, through the inner discords of the great and their effect upon both rulers and ruled. Yet even here, after *Richard II* the workings of these discords seem incidental to the process of showing the course of history; we are taken more deeply, and movingly, into the nature of Falstaff than into that of Prince Hal – Henry V; the dominant theme of kingship, of fitness for power, tends to become more a matter of politics than of individual human behaviour.

In the 'classical' plays, however, although the events of history are of course their framework, the truths of personal character, of the inner struggles of persons in a public setting, are the essence of their dramatic force, as they are of the material on which the plays are based. Thus the three 'classical' plays of this section show a different quality, a different tone, from that of the English history plays. To the Elizabethan, classical history had never been striking and important merely as the record of events; as such, it was far more remote and alien than the accounts of the Tudor rise to supremacy of which the Queen was the pinnacle. But from the Renaissance in England (and before, in medieval thought) the history of Greece and Rome had been a wonderful storehouse of episodes and tales of general appeal, and thence of salutary examples used by classical philosophers and moralists, and following them, by English commentators, to illustrate the wisdom and folly of human nature, and especially the best way of dealing with the business of living.

As examples of contemporary English comments on classical history, it is interesting to note a few concerning Shakespeare's actual protagonists in these plays. In 1573 a moral writer refers to Caesar's failure to heed the assassination warning as a sign of pride,[69] while another writer in 1590 sees the same incident as revealing the inevitability of one's destiny, and Caesar's unique power as the cause of the Brutus-Cassius conspiracy.[70] A writer in 1576 stresses the fact that the conspirators against Caesar never prospered afterwards,[71] and a popular author in 1587 goes further and points to the violent deaths of Brutus and his fellow-plotters as examples of God's vengeance on murderers.[72] The psychological subtlety of Chaucer's account of the love of Troilus and Cressida had come down to the Elizabethans as little more than the over-simple tradition of Cressida as the faithless woman; at most, Troilus and Cressida were seen merely as victims of love.[73] As for Coriolanus, his story was used early in the Elizabethan age by William Painter in his popular collection of stories, *The Palace of Pleasure* (1566), and the emphasis is on the fact that only the persuasion of his mother, with that of his wife and children, stopped him from destroying Rome.[74] Some thirty years later a serious moral writer, making the point that

> vertuous men should be such, as no disgrace, or
> disdaine done by the wicked, should driue them to
> forsake the performance of those duties, which to
> God, and to the common wealth they owe,

takes as his example Coriolanus, who, because of the disgrace of being banished from Rome, 'became an open enemy, and chiefe leader against his countrey': but his mother showed him his error, he laid down his arms, and 'dyed with griefe of mind'.[75] Similarly, the author of *The Picture of a perfit Common Wealth*, a few years later, observed that, if Coriolanus had died in infancy, he 'had not so treacherously, & unnaturally borne armes to the ruine of his own naturall countrey'.[76]

These examples are only a few indications of the contemporary 'moral background' to the material which Shakespeare used in these 'classical' dramas; this material was an important influence on him, especially the 'Parallel Lives'[77] of Plutarch, whose interest was above all in the various ways in which great men made history, and their personal reasons for their actions. Apart from the possible influence upon Shakespeare of contemporary attitudes to his stories, he had already shown, before *Julius Caesar*, an increased interest in the clash of human motives within history, and already-debated and readymade Plutarchan material which he uses for the 'classical' plays certainly encouraged this interest (in his audience as well as in himself). We should remember at this point (as one should always in any consideration of Shakespeare the dramatist) the dramatic potentialities of the source-stories; all three of these classical tales are admirably suited to providing the basic ingredients of popular, as well as more complex, dramatic entertainment. Each of them has strong theatrical situations, suspense and action, debate and emotion, and an effective ending, together with impressive 'great ones' (although virtually no comic plebians) embroiled in the confusions from which world history emerged. That all the audience probably knew the final outcome of, at least, *Julius Caesar* and *Troilus and Cressida*, did not matter, any more than it had in the case of, say, *Henry V*; most audiences, in any age when drama is more than light entertainment, prefer the 'how' and 'why' of plot-events to the mere events themselves, however immediately exciting these may be.

Considering the three 'classical' plays, for a moment longer, as a group, the first thing that strikes us is that all of them display, with various emphases, that form of human tension which we have noted as the conflict between 'the private man' and 'the public man'. That tension had been shown in some depth in the figure of Richard II, but only in general and predetermined ways in Hal–Henry V. The second marked quality common to these three plays is a pervasive tone of irony which is certainly to the taste of many in his audience, but which is in itself the natural outcome of Shakespeare's material and his approach to it; as these plays show the personal and political results of a man's failure to adapt his nature effectively to public demands upon him – and yet these political results are, by their very nature, often remote, inconclusive, even pointless in their own terms – deep irony is bound to arise.

Julius Caesar presents in some detail the human factors involved in the making of a political conspiracy, then assassination as the immediate aim and result of that conspiracy, and finally the inevitable consequences, not so much of the killing of Caesar, as of the ways in which that killing is used for political ends. Thus the play divides into two parts at the end of Act 3, Scene 2, at which point Antony has out-manoeuvred the conspirators, and the war of words and ideas develops into the war of military action: there is an accompanying change of tone from the close intensity of the struggle of motives within Rome to the simpler, more open strategies and actions of the campaign leading up to Philippi and the defeat and deaths of Brutus and his companions.

In the first 'half' of the play there is no question as to whether Caesar will be assassinated – even the groundlings knew that the great Julius died thus; what matters dramatically is Brutus and his part in the killing, his effect on that killing. Shakespeare, after establishing in 1.1 the fact of Caesar's predominance in Rome, and the ordinary political man's fear of his power, places side by side Cassius and Brutus. Cassius is clearly the naturally 'political' man whose hatred of Caesar is nevertheless intensely personal and emotional; he can move from his private feelings to political considerations instinctively and easily: the 'public' man and the 'private' man work together in him without conflict, interacting to the advantage of both. Brutus is a different matter: he is the patrician whose personal family pride is rooted in the traditional ideal of liberty, and all his decisions must be justified in that sense. But his idealism, however noble, is shown to be somewhat abstract (he finally decides that Caesar must be killed, not for what he is, but for what he might become), and it is certainly remote from practical political realism. It is one of many ironies that Cassius uses great skill to draw him into the conspiracy as a man whose 'nobility' of motive is essential for the popular acceptance of the assassination, yet that it is this 'nobility' which rejects Cassius's wish to kill Antony as well as Caesar, and so causes the ultimate collapse of the conspirators. Later too, of course, the worthy and grave Brutus shows himself an inept tactician before Philippi. He is a man fatally committed to the conviction of his own complete rightness, so is led to assume that he can step from his private world to the public political world without changing in any way; his certainty that the death of Caesar will of course be seen as the rational means of protecting 'liberty' does not even suspect the fact that politics deals in emotion as well as reason, and Antony's manipulation of the mob is merely the final proof of Brutus's unfitness for the Roman political scene which he seeks to control. Brutus, who might have been made a figure as tragically self-divided as any Hamlet, remains throughout the play (once he has decided that it is right to kill Caesar) completely convinced of his own justification. Yet he speaks of himself in Act 1, Scene 2, as 'poor Brutus, with himself at war', and the dramatist gives him, in Act 2, Scene 1, one of his most terrible insights into human nature:

> Between the acting of a dreadful thing
> And the first motion, all the interim is
> Like a phantasma or a hideous dream.
> The Genius and the mortal instruments
> Are then in council; and the state of man,
> Like to a little kingdom, suffers then
> The nature of an insurrection.[78]

It is as if Shakespeare is on the brink of creating a complex human Brutus who will dominate the play, but that would be to reshape his source and common tradition; in fact the play gives no further indication that Brutus fought any great interior struggle before deciding to join the conspiracy, and he leaves the play (and this world) entirely satisfied with what he has done: the 'tragedy' of Brutus is not true tragedy. He has been seen, of course, as too fine a man for the company he keeps, too good a man for political action, but many of Shakespeare's audience would have been cynically yet painfully aware that in the ruthless jungle of politics a self-satisfied 'idealist' can often cause more unrest in society than even a cunning political opportunist like Antony, as the current Elizabethan strife between religious faith and government pragmatism showed. If one sees clearly the Brutus that Shakespeare presents, it is very hard not to believe that Shakespeare's audience saw a certain ironic quality in Antony's final words on the 'noble' Brutus:

> This was the noblest Roman of them all.
> All the conspirators save only he
> Did what they did in envy of great Caesar;
> He only in a general honest thought
> And common good to all made one of them.[79]

This is the traditionally accepted view suitable for an epitaph, but the audience had been shown that Brutus had given the Romans civil war and the dominance of the power-seeking Antony instead of the liberty he had promised,[80] and that the man who praised him here had been quick to profit by the political ineptness that accompanied his idealism. Indeed, the irony grows deeper when one considers the contest of reason–unreason shown at work in this play. Brutus, the man admired for his high, logical principles, is in fact motivated by 'ideals' which are shown to be really a kind of emotion that will accept even the major unreason of assassination; the only moment in the play when he attempts to employ rational argument is in addressing the mob after Caesar's death, precisely the moment when, as Antony shows, practical policy demands emotion not reason. Cassius, who at the beginning of the play reveals plainly the emotional nature of his hatred of Caesar, is nevertheless rational enough in his grasp of the political dangers and demands of the conspirators' situation; yet by the time of the quarrel scene with Brutus, his emotional respect for the latter has entirely overcome his practical knowledge of their tactical position, and the 'idealist' is allowed to lead his ideals to defeat at Phillipi. Many of the Elizabethan audience must have been left wondering at the irrational springs of violence and war, and at the tragic and ironic inability of even 'great ones' (perhaps especially 'great ones') to choose reason rather than unreason in deciding the course of history.

In *Troilus and Cressida* there are both the irony and the pressures of the mixed nature of Man that are present in *Julius Caesar*, but the tone and emphases are different. The play of course gives an account of the traditional story of unhappy love, but the Prologue stresses its setting in the siege of Troy, where the Trojan and Greek leaders are not fighting, but busy debating attitudes and motives. The siege of Troy lasted ten years, a memorable stalemate ended at last only by treachery and cunning. Thus the historical material of the play was in itself inconclusive, remote enough to be seen realistically, and with its own cynical implications. The story of *Julius Caesar* had been clear cut and much more impressive as historical action than *Troilus and Cressida* could ever be; Shakespeare in fact exploited the apparent weaknesses of the latter to create an entirely different play.

The first two scenes of the play enter straight into the situation of Troilus, a gallant and high-born young Trojan whose fighting spirit has been sapped by falling in love with Cressida, a Grecian hostage in Troy. With Troilus is Cressida's uncle Pandarus, his name and function already well-known to Elizabethans. These two scenes are largely a display of 'wit' on the subject of women and love, and particularly Troilus's love. 'Wit', for Elizabethans, was an ambiguous term; basically it signified intelligence, but it had long had also our modern sense of the word, the amusing verbal expression of a clever mind. This overlapping double meaning of 'wit' is an indication of the Elizabethan double attitude to love, the favourite subject for 'wit'. For an Elizabethan, desire can ruin a man's life, so love-stories can obviously be considered rationally as serious examples of this danger, and are often moralised upon as such.[81] But a less serious Elizabethan attitude is that a man's cold practical reason is often, and rightly in human terms, powerless against love – everyone knows that, and it is a natural cause of laughter. This laughter can be benign and heartwarming (as so often in Shakespeare's comedies); it can also be a laughter soured by the cynicism which so frequently proceeds from wryly accepted disgust, even fear. It is this latter kind of laughter which is present in these first two scenes of this play; it is not very far from the open and bitter realisation of man as a stupid animal[82] which colours the continuing comments of Thersites throughout the play.

So the human struggle of reason–unreason, in love, permeates, from its beginnings to its end, that part of the drama which deals with Troilus and Cressida and their love, but the possible cynical laughter is modified by the dramatist's characteristic display of both sides of this human equation, as Chaucer had shown them. Troilus is more than a mere fool led astray by passion; Cressida, especially, is more than mere sexual attraction and weakness; in her soliloquy which ends Act 1, Scene 2, there is the moving suggestion of a real

woman (an Elizabethan woman, indeed) in a male-dominated society where the woman has power against the man only as long as she
represents his unsatisfied desire – an Elizabethan (even a modern)
truth that is present, in different ways, in every Shakespearean
woman-in-love.

Thus the play opens, and then the love story is thrust into the
background until Act 3, Scene 2, where Troilus at last wins sexually a
Cressida already won in her heart. In its place are given two long
'philosophical' debates, the first among the Greeks (1.3), the second
among the Trojans (2.2), with a 'comic interlude' (2.1) which has its
relevance to both debates.

The Grecian debate is centred on the Ulysses speech on Disorder,
wonderfully impressive in its grave rhetoric, but, as we shall see, all
the more ironic because of that. In itself, it is a revealing expression of
that Elizabethan concern for the rule of reason and good order in
society which I have already discussed as an example of deep-seated
human conflict (see Part 1, Section (i), pp. 24–6. But in its relevance
to the play as a whole it is no less important. Ulysses's speech
reaches its climax in the lines describing the effects of 'discord':

> Force should be right; or, rather, right and wrong –
> Between whose endless jar justice resides –
> Should lose their names, and so should justice too.
> Then everything includes itself in power,
> Power into will, will into appetite;
> And appetite, an universal wolf,
> So doubly seconded with will and power,
> Must make perforce an universal prey,
> And last eat up himself.[83]

Ulysses has earlier seen the final disaster as the result of the loss of
'degree', that hierarchical order which the heavens and men must
alike observe. The Greeks, he warns, and particularly Achilles and
Patroclus in their lack of respect for their leaders, are breaking up
good order and discipline, and leaving men to fight as and when they
wish. But what he describes above has deeper implications; it
suggests that when force is divorced from justice, and is joined to
'will' (personal desire), together they serve only to enable Man's
blind greed ('appetite') to rule the world, until it finally destroys
itself.[84] Thus war must be seen as the merely irrational and destructive servant of passion, unless it is motivated and controlled by the
rational sense of right and justice.

Remembering this view of war, let us turn to the Trojan debate about whether or not to keep Helen, that is, whether the Trojans should fight on. It is, in effect, an illustration of the reason–unreason incongruity, with admitted reason set against the frank unreason of the thirst for honour, which finally wins. Troilus throughout the debate is the determined champion of 'honour', seeing only the shame of giving up the struggle to keep Helen; he ignores all argument, even the warning of Cassandra's prophecy that Troy will burn if Helen is not returned; to him, reason merely spoils 'manhood and honour'. Paris speaks of the shame of giving up Helen, but he has just made it clear that the Trojans' help is his only hope of keeping her. Hector's key speech [85] is almost shocking, remembering that of Ulysses. Quietly and logically he shows conclusively that the Trojans, in supporting Paris's theft of Helen, have helped 'will' (passion) to break the established social law; Helen is the wife of Menelaus, and 'these moral laws/Of/nature and nations' demand that she should be returned to him. Then comes the dramatic, and quite un-ashamedly irrational *volte-face*; he concludes by supporting the move to keep Helen,

> For 'tis a cause that hath no mean dependence
> Upon our joint and several dignities.

Troilus's response is:

> Were it not glory that we more affected
> Than the performance of our heaving spleens [angry
>   passions],
> I would not wish a drop of Troyan blood,
> Spent more in her defence.[86]

Reason is out of court; 'glory' is as much emotional self-indulgence, in this context, as any passion.

Thus by the end of Act 2, Scene 2, the central point of the play has been established. Both Ulysses and Hector have stated the need for the rule of reason, the former in general terms, the latter specifically concerning the fight to keep Helen; but both have regarded this view merely, it seems, as a platitude, and Hector has immediately shown that, to him, preserving 'dignities' is more important than following reason. Troilus says openly that 'honour' alone matters – reason has nothing to do with it. Hotspur had shown a similar zest for 'honour', but in a context far more truly noble. So the war is to continue, against the obvious claims of reason and justice, and solely to preserve the warriors' pride and honour. The irony of the commitment to this 'honour' is deepened in Act 3, Scene 3, when Ulysses comments on honour and reputation to Achilles. He is the traditional crafty Ulysses working upon Achilles's pride, of course, but what he says is disturbingly true in this context – 'honour' is merely a matter of the interest and estimation of the public, which prizes only the latest and most active of the claimants, and quickly forgets what it has prized. If this is the 'honour' which both Trojan and Greeks put above reason, the war-leaders are stupid even in their gallant courage, and the war is merely an exercise of childish emulation. In fact, all the rest of the play is coloured by the bitter irony that these so-called 'great ones', pursuing a 'famous' struggle, are but very ordinary, foolish men, as confused by personal pride as the later 'hero' Coriolanus, and without his justification.

Against this beginning, how in fact does the play develop? Plainly in spite of its title, the major place is given to the warring world in which the love-story lies embedded, indeed, almost buried. That world is shown as mainly concerned with Ulysses's elaborate manoeuvres to spur Achilles into fighting once more for the Greeks; his methods are far from noble (in fact, akin to those of a cunning schemer in classical or Jonsonian comedy) – and their result? The great Achilles finally fights, and in the end orders his followers to kill the defenceless Hector in what was supposed to be honourable single combat; all Hector's honour is shown to be irrelevant in face of brutal cunning and ambition.

And what of the love story lying at the heart of all this futile eloquence, courage and chicanery? From its beginning, it bears the slur of the very name of Pandarus. Let us contrast with it another love story, that of Romeo and Juliet. This tale of unhappy love, too, is set in a world of stupidity and strife, and has a go-between eager to help the lovers. But compare the reality of the world of Verona and the wordy posturing of the world of the Greeks and Trojans; compare the naïve yet feeling amorality of the Nurse and the smug, ostentatious cynicism of Pandarus. Obviously, in spite of moments of human truth, the story of Troilus and Cressida had no chance of being either a moving account of true love at its beginning, or a truly tragic tale of love betrayed at its end. Shakespeare has been led by tradition, perhaps by a new public taste for 'realism' some seven years after *Romeo and Juliet*, to give the 'political' theme the greater emphasis, but the love-story still has an importance in its wider truth to human nature.

His treatment seems designed to suggest that, in a warring setting which so much of the play portrays, only the most complete and unshakeable love can survive, and only then by a miracle of faith.[87] We can expect no such miracle here; this love is a very ordinary love, pathetic rather than grandly tragic. Shakespeare's sources gave him a Cressida who was still a byword for faithlessness in love, but of course as always he interpreted the fact, and showed the human nature behind it. His interpretation is naturally ambiguous, for the confused stresses on this man and this woman in love are shown with both ironic detachment and human sympathy and understanding. Troilus inevitably brings to his private love that sense of 'honour' which he applies so naïvely, as we have seen, to the public, political world in which he must live; it proves equally inappropriate, and for the same reason, because 'honour' means something far less, something more suspect, to others than to him. Cressida has her 'honour' too, but for her it is only a self-protective adaptation to the nature of Troilus; 'honour' for Troilus is absolute, for Cressida conditional. So both are caught in their human dilemmas – Troilus in the end has to try to reconcile his 'honour' with his love for a woman who has shown that she understands nothing of it; Cressida is left with a certain feeling of guilt at betraying Troilus, but it was his 'honour', not her own, that she had betrayed. Act 4, Scene 4, is the moment when both the irony and the human truth become inescapable; the compulsion to part, the shortness of time, crystallise the true underlying situation. For an instant, Troilus sees himself as he really is:

> Fear not my truth: the moral of my wit
> Is 'plain and true'; there's all the reach of it.[88]

To be 'plain and true', only that, is to be quite unfitted for Cressida, and for the cunning forces of politics. Cressida, too, is divided in her situation; her protestations in this scene are more restrained than earlier; there is enough feeling of truth in them to jar with our fore-knowledge of her falsity. There is much irony between Troilus's nature and Cressida's, between each of these natures and the world around them;[89] yet the human quality of these two, as they exist within their inescapable discords, is strong enough to soften that irony almost into tenderness, for a brief moment. There is no such tenderness in the political and martial world, and it will not recur even for the lovers in the rest of the play. When Troilus later, in 5.2 sees the symbolic faithlessness of Cressida's gift of his token to Diomedes, the struggle within him moves close to the edge of madness; two incompatibles are 'facts' established in his heart and mind, and he must attempt to reconcile the irreconcilable: as he says:

> This she? No; this is Diomed's Cressida.
> If beauty have a soul, this is not she;
> If souls guide vows, if vows be sanctimonies,
> If sanctimony be the gods' delight,
> If there be rule in unity itself,
> This was not she. O madness of discourse,
> That cause sets up with and against itself!
> Bifold authority! where reason can revolt
> Without perdition, and loss assume all reason
> Without revolt: this is, and is not, Cressid.
> Within my soul there doth conduce a fight
> Of this strange nature, that a thing inseparate
> Divides more wider than the sky and earth.[90]

This is the deadlock between irrational 'faith' and logical reason which appears in so much of Shakespeare's presentation of Man's nature, which brings Lear and Othello to madness and near-madness, and Macbeth to self-torture and self-destruction. But the simplicity of Troilus is not the stuff of which great tragedy is made, at least in this context; he is too fully involved in his political setting (which itself avoids the conflict of 'ideals' and facts by ignoring it), too characteristic of its underlying futility, to be thought of in tragic terms. He 'solves' his insoluble dilemma by reverting to something of what he has always been, the simple gallant fighter, but now his gallantry has been affected by his world; his courage is now marred by despair, and his faith in honour has been cheapened into a thirst for revenge. Meanwhile the war, with its empty rhetoric and mean scheming, continues; we know that it continues beyond the end of the play; it seems likely to last for ever – indeed, in a sense, it is still dragging on.

This play, in which the outcome of the love story of Troilus and Cressida has been shown as a kind of incidental, pathetic byproduct of the confusion and death caused by the limited minds of 'great ones', is given a final comment by Pandarus's last speech, the 'Epilogue'. This can be seen, of course, as merely an occasion for masculine sexual laughter designed to send the audience away happy, although, throughout the ages to our own time, but especially for Elizabethans, laughter at sexual disease has always contained an edge of uneasiness and fear. But what is the deeper point of such an ending to such a play, its part in the final effect upon us? Whatever its comic appeal, it also adds a further dimension to impressions which the play has already produced. Man has been shown as painfully and ineffectually struggling within his nature, failing to reconcile his rational view of life and his fantasies of himself as 'hero' and 'statesman', 'lover' and 'man of honour'; against this display of the disturbing truths of Man's ironically mixed nature, both angel and beast, is finally set, in this 'Epilogue', an everyday common fact of the tangled motives of life; as Pandarus says after Troilus has cursed him:

> O world! world! world! thus is the poor agent despis'd!
> O traitors and bawds, how earnestly are you set a work, and
> how ill requited! Why should our endeavour be so lov'd,
> and the performance so loath'd?.

Here we are reminded of the role in the play of Thersites, a development of that of the earlier Apemantus in a far slighter play. The latter had stressed Man's pretensions as conflicting with his beast-like folly; Thersites's similar comments are closely attached to the wider theme of the making of history, and to particular examples of those who make history. The final words of Pandarus, joined to the many savagely ironic 'footnotes' of Thersites, remind us that the harsh, disgusting and yet moving realities of human nature are the core of the play, and that they are both particular and universal, as true in Elizabethan London as in far-off Troy.

With *Coriolanus* we seem to enter a different world, but we shall see that it is not so different after all. In its tone and shaping it is far more direct and conclusive than *Troilus and Cressida*, nearer in this respect to *Julius Caesar*, and, like the latter, much more 'modern' both in the kind of history which it portrays and in the social problems that it undoubtedly presents.

Those who attended a performance of *Coriolanus* soon after its completion in about 1608 (assuming that such a performance took place, for there is no contemporary record of one) would have been prepared by publicity to see 'The Tragedy of Coriolanus', as the First Folio calls it; at least they knew, before seeing the play, that Coriolanus was a tragic figure. Some of them would also have known, perhaps from reading North's Plutarch, that he had been a great warrior-defender of Rome, who nevertheless went over to Rome's enemies, but was finally persuaded by his mother to save his native city, although he died for doing so. Plutarch had described the man's pride, his passionate tendency to anger and loss of self-control, and his patrician contempt for the common people of Rome, but had seen him, above all, as a fine man sadly turned traitor. Shakespeare of course adopts the historical matter; the story has obvious moments of crisis which are most suitable for dramatisation – the Corioli victory of Marcius which makes him the hero of Rome, his refusal to undergo the procedure by which his martial fame could bring him political power, his consequent move from Rome to help her enemies, the final overthrow of his purpose by his mother, and his death at the hands of the Volscians. These incidents, merely as 'plot', are enough to provide the movement of an exciting play. Shakespeare also had a protagonist who was both a key historical figure and a strangely divided individual. To place the main emphasis on the political action would have been to follow the way of *Julius Caesar*, and the human quality of Coriolanus was too marked and too well established to be thus minimised. To concentrate upon the conflict within him would have been to use the method of *Macbeth*, and Shakespeare's material (unlike that of *Macbeth*) was too firmly rooted in known historical-political fact to allow this. Shakespeare, in fact, succeeded in striking a unique balance between the two emphases, almost a synthesis of the two. *Coriolanus* becomes a play in which political motives and historical events are fully interwoven with personal human conflict, and the interaction never ceases. Here can be seen the final stage of the approaches to 'man-in-history' of Shakespeare's earlier history plays, of which it is the finest example. Although *Antony and Cleopatra*, as we shall see, shows a similar combination of 'public' and 'private' struggles, this is not as closely worked as in *Coriolanus*, and it develops finally, and amazingly, into something far different from a history play.

So Shakespeare, following his given story, but with his own interpretative emphases, presents us first with the political world in which Coriolanus must live, or cease to be the man he is. His pride, of course, is stressed within the opening moments of the play; it is linked to the patrician class to which he belongs, and the citizens' hostility to that class is established. In this opening, almost casually, is inserted a comment that is a pointer to the direction of the play; the Second Citizen, trying to reason with the First Citizen's obstinate dislike of Caius Marcius, says: 'What he cannot help in his nature you account a vice in him'.[91] The essence of Coriolanus's downfall and its causes is indicated in these few words; his pride is shown, as the play unfolds, to be indeed what makes him the man he is at first, and what later destroys that man. It is suggested here that this pride is uncontrollable; the conflict between private, irrational, passionate pride and the rational self-control required of a successful public man, marks the difference between his success as a soldier and his failure as a politician.

In this opening scene, after the citizens' anger and sense of grievance against the ruling class, comes Marcius's outburst against the common people.[92] It is more than an especially arrogant individual's reaction to the pressure of the commoners; the details of his scorn are worth noting. Twice he says that they cannot be trusted; moreover, they dislike fighting but become proud when there is no danger; they are fickle in their admiration; they will support a wrongdoer, and hate the law when it corrects him; they oppose their superiors, and presume to meddle in their affairs. Marcius, in fact, is expressing the bases of many an Elizabethan's fear of the mob. As an individual, the common man could be amusing, deserving, even admirable in his native shrewdnes, as many of Shakespeare's plays had already shown him. In the mass, commoners were always best treated with caution, and kept under firm control by those in authority, who understood the human and political advantages to society of good order.[93] The fact that there was ample economic and social reason for the commoners' anger and rebelliousness, like most facts of social conflict, probably did not do much to modify an established attitude.

So, early in the play, the basic human qualities of Marcius's nature and of the nature of his associates, are already clearly shown as points of departure; in addition, the world into which he will be drawn, the political arena of patricians and plebs, itself subject to pressures, is firmly suggested. This political setting becomes much more important in this play than it was in *Julius Caesar*, even though the latter play is so plainly political. The reason is that Brutus is never really part of the political game, and so his political failure does nothing to weaken his belief in his own rightness: Coriolanus, on the contrary, finds that his nature, although alien in many ways to the political world, ironically thrusts him into that world; his ill-controlled and violent self-confidence makes him the political hero of Rome and, at the same time, in the existing conditions, proves him unfit for the political role which it has won, through war, in Rome. That city is shown as divided by class-enmity between patricians and plebs, and Coriolanus, by his nature, is unable to accept the cautious, temporising tactics which a Menenius can use, and which are the patricians' safest way of dealing with the threat of the mob. The traditional view of Coriolanus had seen him as a 'proud' man;

Shakespeare shows him as proud, but not merely in and for himself; he has a curiously 'English public school' modesty about himself, but a fierce pride, even arrogance, as a patrician faced with the threat of the mob. The last scene of Act 1 is indirectly an important comment on this Coriolanus, one that can easily be overlooked if not sufficiently emphasised in production. The key lines, spoken by Aufidius, are:

> Mine emulation
> Hath not that honour in't it had; for where
> I thought to crush him [Coriolanus] in an equal force,
> True sword to sword, I'll potch at him some way,
> Or wrath or craft may get him. . . .
> Where I find him, were it
> At home, upon my brother's guard, even there,
> Against the hospitable canon, would I
> Wash my fierce hands in's heart.[94]

Here is a man who, like Coriolanus, is a fighter, but there the kinship ends. His valour is political, patriotic, rather than personal like that of his opponent; his hatred of his enemy Coriolanus is entirely pragmatic, and he is prepared to put aside honour and social decency, use any means, to destroy him. The contrast with Coriolanus suggests how remote he is from his fellows, even at this early stage of the action, and how vulnerable he is in his ignorance of the fact. This is the Aufidius to whom Coriolanus later commits himself to comfort his injured pride and honour – one thinks of the naïvety and innocence of Troilus in a stupid and yet cunning world, or Antony's simple belief that the calculating power-seeker Octavius would risk everything in personal combat with him.

The second phase of the play moves through Acts 2 and 3 and the first two scenes of Act 4; it takes up nearly half the play, working out to a climax the suggestions of Act 1, and preparing the final outcome of the play. The long prose opening of Act 2, Scene 1, acts as an introduction to this phase. Menenius talks frankly to the Tribunes, points to the irony that two such proud men should attack Coriolanus's pride, and constantly shows his dislike of them. Yet, as a practical politician, he is prepared if necessary to treat with those he despises: his enmity is well under control, and, as the following scenes show, he is forced to respect the Tribunes' power, even if not the Tribunes. Menenius is a match for them, but Coriolanus is an obvious danger to the patrician cause, although, and because, he is their hero. At the end of the scene the Tribunes discuss him, and decide that, if provoked, he can be relied upon to harm the patrician cause by showing his scorn for the people. Coriolanus finally forces himself to canvass personally the support of the citizens for his Consulship; they are shown as muddled and easily swayed, giving their vote to the hero and then being talked into withdrawing it by the Tribunes. These actually get them to agree to pretend that they are acting against their advice. Here, in the middle of the play, is displayed the cynicism and calculated dishonesty of political power-seekers; the patricians are no better, although somewhat less frank, and the supreme irony, later, is that the 'noble' Volumnia herself can use a similar cunning in persuading her son to spare Rome. The central point of the play, the contrast between the political world and the nature of Coriolanus, has been made clear, and it leads logically, in human terms, to the rest of the play.

Act 3, as so often in Shakespeare, is the 'watershed' of the action, the point of no return. Act 3, Scene 1, the longest scene in the play, shows Coriolanus drawn into the political debate so alien to his nature, and in the process the social-political situation is further explored. The argument in which Coriolanus is so passionately involved is essentially about where power in the state should reside; there can surely be no doubt that the dramatist is consciously using his material to place this problem (as urgent today as then) before his audience in a way which speaks to the anxiety of many of them. Coriolanus, as one would expect, expresses an uncompromising patrician view: he has no doubt that to hold the power is the natural right of the 'upper', more traditional, better-educated and better-bred class; that any gift of power to the 'lower' class is unmerited, and an act of folly; that any sharing of power leads to confusion and the rule of ignorance. There are echoes of Ulysses' fear of disorder in society, the reason—unreason form of human conflict, and the same irony is present; in Rome as in Troy, the reason on which order depends is merely the 'lower reason' of self-seeking and cunning. The Tribunes, in all their suspect integrity, give the other side of the argument; the crux of the social problem is given in a brief passage after Menenius has asked 'good Sicinius' to placate the people:

SICIN.   (to Citizens) You are at point to lose your liberties.
                      Marcius would have all from you; Marcius
                      Whom late you have nam'd for consul.

MENENIUS   Fie, fie, fie!

This is the way to kindle, not to quench.

FIRST SEN.   To unbuild the city, and to lay all flat.

SICIN.   What is the city but the people?

PLEBIANS   True,

The people are the city.[95]

Consider this in conjuction with Coriolanus's patrician views on the inability of the plebians to rule even themselves: the 'struggle' of reason—unreason links to that of the 'private' man seeking to be the 'public' man (ironically, it is Coriolanus's own problem), and the insoluble difficulty of Rome is manifest — how is the natural right of every member of a society to take his part in running that society, to be reconciled with the various degrees of fitness for that task of the members of the society? This is the question that, of course, is never settled in the play, and is still unsettled today. Similarly, in *Troilus and Cressida* the validity of 'honour' and 'order' is examined but not decided, and in *Julius Caesar* the concept of 'liberty' is presented and then disappears in the turmoil of civil war. Here, in *Coriolanus*, the social argument is followed by uproar and a return to naked fear and expediency:

COMINIUS   But now 'tis odds beyond arithmetic
           And manhood is call'd foolery when it stands
           Against a falling fabric.[96]

Coriolanus is now the awkward ally of patricians who are concerned, not with abstract questions of rights, but solely with controlling the mob, through their equally pragmatic Tribunes, and thus restoring order, and their own power. So after Coriolanus has been sent away, the scene ends with a practical arrangement between patricians and Tribunes to disperse the mob and leave Menenius to effect a working compromise (how modern it all sounds!).

Such a compromise depends on persuading Coriolanus to modify (at least outwardly) his emphatic convictions, and Act 3, Scene 2, shows how this is done, in the only possible way, by psychological trickery. The essence of the method is shown in the following passages, where the patricians' last hope, Volumnia, has been brought in:

COR   I muse my mother
      Does not approve me further, who was wont
      To call them [the plebs] woollen vassals, things created
      To buy and sell with groats; to show bare heads

131

In congregations, to yawn, be still, and wonder,
When one but of my ordinance stood up
To speak of peace or war.
Enter Volumnia
     I talk of you:
Why did you wish me milder? Would you have me
False to my nature? Rather say I play
The man I am.

VOL.   O sir, sir, sir,
I would have had you put your power well on
Before you had worn it out [openly].[97]
 . . .

MENEN.(to COR.)
 Come, come, you have been too rough, something too
rough;
You must return and mend it.

1 SEN.   There's no remedy,
Unless, by not so doing, our good city
Cleave in the midst and perish.

VOL.   Pray be counsell'd;
I have a heart as little apt as yours,
But yet a brain that leads my use of anger
To better vantage.[98]

Volumnia then proceeds to persuade her son by means which many
Elizabethans would have recognised, uneasily, as basically
'Machiavellian', the use (as they saw it) of the cold disregard of
human beliefs in order to achieve political ends. She points out that
in war (an appeal to something dear and well-known to her son) he
must often have pretended in order to deceive the enemy, and done
so without loss of honour; so now she is urging him to speak to the
citizens, not as he truly feels, but in a humble tone put on to please
them and avert the danger of conflict in Rome – to do this is to use
mere words, not to betray his honour.[99] When Coriolanus remains
doubtful, she plays her strongest card, a feint of refusing to lower
herself to beg of him, with a hint of fatal consequences to herself, an
emotional blackmail which she uses 'successfully' again at the end of
the play. Coriolanus reverts (as he does later) to the obedient son; he
promises to face the plebians once more, and treat them 'mildly'.
Volumnia's persuasion of her son in this scene constitutes, in fact, a
psychological betrayal which anticipates and prepares for the political betrayal of Rome by Coriolanus which soon follows. She had

132

reared her son (as Shakespeare has plainly shown) to recognise fixed standards; the acceptance of courage, pride and honour as the only criteria of worthy action had created the Coriolanus who had proved so successful a hero, yet so intransigent, so unequal to the political demands of Rome's situation. Now she has told him that these fixed standards should be manipulated to suit the exigencies of the political situation – no wonder that his mother's authority can persuade him for a moment, but that, in the next scene, he returns to the man he really is, the man that in fact Volumnia had made him (such is the irony of human motives). In this play Shakespeare is displaying the forces of human incongruity both within the protagonist (the special feature of the major tragedies) and also as embodied in interacting representatives of human qualities. Coriolanus shows the struggle between unreason (anger and ideals) and reason within himself, but equally effective dramatically, in this case, is the working of the same struggle in the body politic, with the proud unreason of Coriolanus set against the unthinking passion of the mob, and both these set against the selfish 'rational' drives of ambition and fear of the patricians and the Tribunes, and of Aufidius.

This central part of the play, after the banishment of Coriolanus, ends with Act 4, Scene 1, his farewell to his mother (with its ironic promise to continue to be 'what is like me formerly'), and Act 4, Scene 2, where Sicinius and Brutus are shown as satisfied with their use of their power, but still cautious regarding the patricians.

The third phase of the play occupies the remaining five scenes of Act 4. It deals with Coriolanus's offer of himself to Aufidius as leader of the Volscian campaign against Rome that has already begun, Aufidius's acceptance, and the reaction to this in Rome. Thus it is largely concerned with the events that link Coriolanus's departure from Rome to his triumphant but ill-fated return. But Shakespeare continues to show, by the occasional self-revelations, the inner human nature still at work behind, and determining, the events. Thus we see, from Coriolanus's soliloquy in Act 4, Scene 4, that he is strangely unchanged from what he was before his banishment; like Brutus in *Julius Caesar*, his self-assurance is unshaken by the disturbance he has helped to cause, and the drastic action to which he is proceeding. He comments almost naïvely on the 'slippery turns' of the world, as though the social upheaval in Rome, and particularly his own transfer of loyalty from Rome to Antium, have been caused 'by some chance,[100] /Some trick not worth an egg'. In his offer of himself to Aufidius, in Act 4, Scene 5, he sees his banishment as caused only by 'The cruelty and envy of the people,/Permitted by our dastard nobles', and as a 'misery' of which Aufidius should take advantage. His simple, limited view of himself and his situation has marked the man throughout; it has been shaken for a moment by Volumnia in Act 3, Scene 2, and will again be affected, finally and fatally, by her last 'success' in Act 5, Scene 3, but the Coriolanus with which the play ends is the Marcius of the opening. In contrast to this, the politicians of Rome, patricians and Tribunes, are shown in Act 4, Scene 6, in all the fear, confusion and recrimination caused by the news of Coriolanus's defection, with a background of terrified citizens beginning to protest that they had not really wanted to banish the hero. Finally, in Act 4, Scene 7, we see again (as in 1.10) an Aufidius fixed in his hatred of Coriolanus, but now this hatred is joined with a cold political cunning that will not destroy the man until he has been useful to the Volscians. His description of Coriolanus's nature, of the effects of his pride, or of his failure to seize the chance of power, or of his inability to adapt himself to circumstances, is shrewdly true to what we have seen of Coriolanus; indeed, he recognises the worth of the man, but like the equally pragmatic, worldly Ulysses,[101] he recognises the littleness of the wordly fame of such as Coriolanus:

> So our virtues
> Lie in th'interpretation of the time;
> And power, unto itself most commendable,
> Hath not a tomb so evident as a chair
> T'extol what it hath done.[102],[103]

This is the voice of ordinary, practical reason stripping away the hopes and convictions of idealistic faith; it echoes Ulysses, but it also points to the Enobarbus whose common sense about war was finally overwhelmed by a recognition that Antony's dreams were greater than commonsense.

We come to the fourth and final phase of the play, the contents of Act 5. The first two scenes take us back to the frightened Romans of 4.6; Cominius and Menenius both fail to change Coriolanus's determination to lead the Volscians into Rome; the last hope is the effort which Volumnia intends to make. At the beginning of Act 5, Scene 3, for a few moments, there is a tone almost of pleading, of self-justification, in Coriolanus's defence to Aufidius of his friendly treatment of Menenius; it is strangely akin to his tone to Volumnia, as though Aufidius had taken on something of her dominance. The basic human conflict in Coriolanus still persists, and this fundamental struggle within him between his inborn emotions and ideals and the pressure of practical reason is now beginning to enter its last stage. The final crucial forces of his mother's second pleading with him are preceded by a passage that needs the fullest consideration:

COR.   . . . fresh embassies and suits,
         Nor from the state nor private friends, hereafter
         Will I lend ear to. (*Shout within*) Ha! what shout is this?
         Shall I be tempted to infringe my vow
         In the same time 'tis made? I will not.
         *Enter, in mourning habits, Virgilia, Volumnia, Valeria
         young Marcius, with Attendants.*
         My wife comes foremost, than the honour'd mould
         Wherein this trunk was fram'd, and in her hand
         The grandchild to her blood. But out, affection!
         All bond and privilege of nature, break!
         Let it be virtuous to be obstinate.
         What is that curtsy worth? or those doves' eyes,
         Which can make gods forsworn? I melt, and am not
         Of stronger earth than others. My mother bows,
         As if Olympus to a molehill should
         In supplication nod; and my young boy
         Hath an aspect of intercession which
         Great nature cries 'Deny not'. Let the Volsces
         Plough Rome and harrow Italy; I'll never
         Be such a gosling to obey instinct, but stand
         As if a man were author of himself
         And knew no other kin.[104]

This is the man shown instant by instant in the grip of the alternating forces striving within him; it is a striking example of Shakespeare's unique awareness of, and ability to use dramatically, such forces. First Coriolanus firmly states his rational resolve to allow no more appeals to him – then he betrays a doubt of his decision, then reaffirms it. His mother and his family enter, and at once he expresses the special power over him of Volumnia: she is the 'honour'd mould' in which he was made, his son is not so much his son as 'The grandchild to her blood'. Then he tries to oust 'affection' (which, we note, he equates with 'nature' – he sees himself as striving against 'nature', as, in a deeper sense, he is), and, most unlike himself, he then seeks to defend his obstinacy, his earlier determin-ation. Immediately after, he hints at the power over him of emotional appeals, which subdue even gods, and then come the words which mark the passing of the old Coriolanus: 'I melt, and am not/Of stronger earth than others'. This is the final recognition of himself as he really is, the point reached by so many other Shakespearean characters, in a range from Parolles to Hamlet. With this recognition the inner human conflict of Coriolanus, in effect, is finished. One cannot say that the struggle has been truly resolved, for so much of the Coriolanus we have seen throughout the play has been merely rejected, not assimilated into a new resolution of his whole nature. The realisation of his own ordinary weak humanity is both necessary and salutary in its recognition of the truth, as it is in Othello, but, unlike Othello, Coriolanus achieves this only by an inner treachery to himself, in human terms a far more terrible treachery than the 'political' treachery to the Volscians to which it soon leads. Of course, this speech ends, after another significant reference to 'Great nature', with a last desperate affirmation of his resolve to stand out against 'instinct', but there is an almost conscious irony in his talk of acting as if a man could be only 'himself', untouched by all that has made him what he is.

So the man's conflict, as we have said, is over. The pleading of Volumnia, ending (as in 3.2) with more than a hint of emotional blackmail, pursues its relentless course, and has its inevitable result. When at last Coriolanus gives way to his mother, or more truly, to his mother in himself, he speaks of the gods laughing at 'this unnatural scene'. There are few words in Shakespeare (and it is his addition to Plutarch) which hold such a complex of irony and ambiguity as this 'unnatural'. Does it refer to the sight of a fully-grown man, a great warrior, obeying his mother like a little child (but we have seen that tradition saw him as right to do so)? Does it point to the unnatural quality of Volumnia's 'victory', by which she has saved Rome and destroyed her son (as his following words suggest)? Does it also remind us that Coriolanus is going against his nature as a man, by not going against his nature as a son? Does it even glance, in passing, at the highly-contrived theatricality of this last great dramatic moment of the play? These are not mere idle speculations; they express the doubts, the questionings, the glimpses of truth which are presented to us.

Little remains to complete the final working-out of all that has gone before. In Act 5, Scenes 4 and 5, Rome is shown acting in its characteristic political way, its spokesmen concerned only with their own fate and that of their groups, patricians and plebians. After

Volumnia's 'success', they are not worried about the Coriolanus who is now no longer a threat; Menenius's description of the man who refused to yield to his pleas tells rather of his own wounded vanity than of the Coriolanus we know – the iron-minded, immovable tiger that he portrays is at most the Coriolanus who might have been.

Act 5, Scene 6, shows how the Coriolanus of the end of 5.3 inevitably moves to his last position. He has been reduced step by step to the final isolation that marks such tragic figures as Othello and Macbeth. He has been rejected by the Romans and of course by the Volscians, and he himself has rejected his own true self – he has nowhere to go in this world, he belongs nowhere – his return to the Volscians is in fact an admission of this, a kind of suicide. Aufidius has no further need to delay his long-cherished revenge; Coriolanus has helped Aufidius by destroying himself. In Aufidius's simple view of the matter, Coriolanus has set his 'mercy and . . . honour/At difference' in himself, and Aufidius has only to act. In 5.6 he does so. It is significant that, of course from his own standpoint, he adds a final interpretation of the fatal incongruity within Coriolanus when he deserted Rome and joined the Volscians:

AUF.   . . . I rais'd him, and I pawn'd
Mine honour for his truth; who being so heighten'd,
He watered his new plants with dews of flattery,
Seducing so my friends; and to this end
He bow'd his nature, never known before
But to be rough, unswayable, and free.[105]

The last three lines, although without true understanding, nevertheless describe at least part of what has happened to Coriolanus, the ironical fact that, at the end, to remain himself he had to cease to be himself, both in supporting the Volscians and following his mother's wishes. So Coriolanus returns to Corioli, now as the defeated champion not the conqueror (however much he claims success), and for the last time with a flash of his former predictable proud nature, he reacts as expected to the taunts of 'traitor' and 'boy'; he reminds the Volscians of his former success against them, and to the roar of the enraged mob, the waiting assassins do their work. The final comment returns him to the traditional simple view of him:

SECOND LORD   . . . His own impatience
Takes from Aufidius a great part of blame.[106]

This is a dubious half-truth. Impatience could certainly be seen as his continuing and obvious weakness, and many Elizabethans, and later critics of the play, may have been satisfied with that easy explanation of his downfall, but the dramatist has been at pains to display the complex forces of human incongruity which, in fact, by making him what he at first was, made him what he finally became.

Tragedies

In this section I shall examine what most people would agree are the six main Shakespearean tragedies: *Romeo and Juliet* (*c*1595), his earliest full tragedy, and the sequence of plays (*Hamlet, Othello, Lear, Macbeth* and *Antony and Cleopatra*) which probably appeared in this order in the period 1600 to 1607 which also produced the three 'near-tragedies' *Troilus and Cressida, All's Well that Ends Well* and *Measure for Measure*.

In *Romeo and Juliet*, Shakespeare is still making a play largely in the tradition of the sixteenth-century English 'moral' play; the moral tone of his source is still present within the play, and the component parts of the warring nature of Man exist mainly in separate characters. Thus the stresses of human nature are shown in the conflicts of purpose between individuals or groups, rarely within the individuals themselves. It follows that (as in the English history plays, except *Richard II*, and in the earlier comedies) the struggles within the individual, the 'personal' conflict, is portrayed through 'social' conflict, where the needs of individuals clash with those of others, or of society as a whole.

In the other five tragedies there is a different method of presenting in drama the contrasting pressures of human nature. Certain forms of these pressures are shown as present, and in conflict, within the main individual especially, but often too within secondary characters, where they relate to the forces working within the main figure. Thus the emphasis is now on 'inner' conflict rather than on 'outer' conflict. But of course this is a matter where the primary interest in the main character involves a secondary interest in other characters; 'inner' conflict is revealed and expressed, in dramatic terms, only through the workings of 'external' conflict. The protagonist, as in life, starts in the play by existing in a situation ('given' by the dramatist) involving other characters; the play then unfolds by showing how the natures of these other characters affect and reveal the nature of the protagonist; by the nature of the protagonist thus affected and revealed, the nature of the other characters is affected – and so on in a constant and complex chain-reaction. Characters, of course, exist only in situations, amid events, themselves usually determined by the characters causing or involved in them, and so the movements of the plot are part of this chain-reaction.

In these five tragedies, the source-material of the plot gives at least some suggestion of the kinds of stresses which are at work in shaping the nature and actions of the characters to the final form and outcome of the story. As his stories are well known to many of his audience, Shakespeare must work to some extent within this pattern, but the pattern is so strangely and richly interpreted that, in the end, we realise that the story has been transformed. The dramatist has done this by exploring the forms of human conflict implicit, dormant, within the story, and by doing so in detail, and with a truth recognised and accepted by the audience's shared human nature, and over a range of characters who are at once different from, and like, each other. Thus through his awareness and understanding of Man's inner strife (which is both personal and universal), he creates in the play as a whole, as experienced on the stage or in the study, the truth of each character and its life in the play, and also a timeless, placeless truth which is the essential quality of great tragedy.

In achieving this overall effect, because the play is, as always, created with a craftsman's awareness of the contemporary requirements of his stage, his actors and his audience, Shakespeare in these tragedies often alters the emphases of his source, and with these the details of the action, by omissions, developments or additions of incidents, and by changes of time-scale and settings, and adds the theatrical attractions of vigorous stage-action, stage-pageantry, comedy, and the verbal entertainment of description, rhetoric and wit.

These last two will remind us that in conveying on the Elizabethan stage, for the Elizabethan audience, the full sense of personal and universal human incongruity, Shakespeare's essential tool is the heard language of his drama, the blank verse, rhymed verse and prose which, in their endless variety and combinations, alone can express the inner nuances of character-in-situation, the subtle yet inescapable tone and effects of human struggle. Hence arises the amazing wealth of cross-references, 'echoes', symbols, ironies and psychological insights which have intrigued and delighted so many generations of play-goers and critics. So with the shaping of characters and plot must always be associated the wide range of images and rhythms, of subconscious connections between words, ideas and especially emotions, of the infinite fashionings of language to move and convince; all these becoming part of the audience's sense of Shakespeare's purposes in building the whole conception and achievement of the play, and all on a certain day at the Globe or Blackfriars, together create a microcosm, a psychological equivalent in miniature of the striving, diverse world outside, to which the audience must return at the end of the play, thanks to the dramatist with a new understanding of it, and of themselves in it.

Romeo and Juliet

Shakespeare's major source for this play is Arthur Brooke's *The Tragicall Historye of Romeus and Juliet* (1562). Brooke's version in poetry of a tale taken from a French collection of stories from Bandello, is an indication of the public taste for such Italian tales in English in the 1560s and 1570s, and later.[107] When one reads these English accounts of the violent and passionate behaviour of Italian men and women, constantly glossed by English moral comments on such wickedness, one must suspect that Brooke, Fenton and the others knew that they were profiting both ways: they were purveying scandalous stories which found a ready English readership, and at the same time were able to profess continually a moral purpose in providing vivid warnings of the consequences of evil living, of which Italy was held to offer the most awful (and thrilling) examples.[108] The delightfully horrific stage tragedies of the 1590s and 1600s reaped a similar double harvest of popular enjoyment and moral pretensions, as the poetical satirists of the 1590s had, before the censorship deterred them.

It is not surprising, therefore, that in Brooke's address *To the Reader* we find his ostensible moral intention emphatically stated:

> . . . The glorious triumphe of the continent man upon the
> lustes of wanton fleshe, incourageth men to honest [decent]
> restraynt of wyld affections, the shamefull and wretched
> endes of such, as have yelded their libertie thrall to
> fowle desires, teache men to withholde them selves from the
> hedlong fall of loose dishonestie. So, to lyke effect, by
> sundry meanes, the good mans exaumple byddeth men to be
> good, and the evill mans mischefe, warneth men not to be
> evyll. To this good ende, serve all ill endes, of yll

begynnynges. And to this ende (good Reader) is this tragicall matter written.[109]

For Brooke and his many readers (his work had at least three editions up to 1587) the story of Romeus and Juliet, then, not only provided narrative excitement but also the pleasurable shocks of pity and of moral disapproval (that greatest satisfaction of the hopefully virtuous). The chief lesson offered by Brooke is the common Elizabethan one, that to let one's irrational, especially physical-sexual desires over-rule one's reason is the sure path to worldly and moral disaster. Brooke's Friar Lawrence, seeking to change Romeus's wild desperation after hearing of his banishment, makes the point clearly: 'If thou wilt master quite, the troubles that thee spill [harm]/ Endevor first by reasons help, to master witless will [passion without reason].[110] The same lesson is even plainer, and more frequent, in Fenton's comments on his stories; for him,

> ... love is but a rage or humour [obsession] of frantic folly, derived of ourselves, and converted to our own harm by the indiscretion that is in us, so the next [nearest] remedy to withstand that fury is to encounter him under the ensign of reason.[111]

Shakespeare's play, then, derives closely from a story which is an example of a popular form of entertainment combining narrative interest with moral implications. Even if Shakespeare's material were unknown, it would be obvious that the play is driven by the physical passion of the young lovers, and that the dominant theme throughout is of unreason against reason. The lovers' sexual hunger for each other is set alongside the Montague–Capulet feud, the protagonists of which are themselves as irrational and impatient, as deaf to reason, as the lovers. In addition, as part of the background of these two irrational groups, there is the world of elegant young men moving within a framework of verbal make-believe and the supremely irrational ethos of personal physical courage in the duel; Mercutio's 'Queen Mab' speech is a flight of wonderful fancy rising beyond everyday reason, and his courage against Tybalt, for an average Elizabethan, is a moving example of tragic folly. These centres of youthful and elderly unreason and prejudice are shown existing in a normal society where rational law is designed to control human passions when they threaten disorder in the city. The opening

141

scene epitomises this situation: for an Elizabethan, Shakespeare's Verona is dangerously disordered by impulsive and unreasoning enmities, like much of Elizabethan life, and Prince Escalus's nicely dramatic and authoritative entrance is an assurance that the law will restore the rule of reason. Before it ultimately does so, however, human nature has to learn the dangers, in this world, of the obstinate pursuit of its desires; even then, the uncomprehending stupidity of the Montague–Capulet feud is finally dissolved, not by any rational power, but by love. As Brooke says conerning the Montagues and Capulets, at the end of his tale:

> . . . with their emptyed teares, theyr coler and theyr rage,
> Was emptied quite, and they whose wrath no wisdom could
> asswage
> Nor threatening of the prince, ne mind (memory) of murthers
> donne,
> At length, (so mighty Jove it would) by pitye they are wonne.[112]

The point is an important one, as we shall see, for an understanding of Shakespeare's use of reason–unreason in *Romeo and Juliet* and in the other major tragedies: he shows the various effects of this contradiction, and especially the dangers of an imbalance between these human qualities within the individual and within society, but always the final redeeming quality of his tragedy is one of feeling, not of rational logic; there are emotions which rise above the pragmatic rightness of mere reason, as is shown, supremely, in *Antony and Cleopatra*.

We have seen that the passions are at odds with reason in Verona, and that disorder and personal disaster are therefore to be expected. In Shakespeare's dramatic treatment, what sharpens this potential danger, and makes it increasingly certain to end in tragedy, is his use of time. There is no other Shakespeare drama in which the time-element is so stressed and so important; the speed with which one situation leads to another is the essence of the developing tragedy, and is a function of the passions in their flight from reason. There can be no doubt that Shakespeare is deliberately emphasising throughout most of the play this sense of unthinking haste; from the beginning of the main action in 1.2 to its end in 4.5, repeated and explicit time-references in the text keep us aware of the rapid passage of time, adding to the sense of urgency with which the dominant passions are pursued. The Capulet party starts on a Sunday evening (1.2/1.3); Romeo arrives late, when supper is over (1.4), and meets Juliet (1.5). It is late on the Sunday night, after the party, when

Romeo woos Juliet at her window, and tells her to send to him tomorrow (Monday) (2.2). In 2.3 Romeo arrives at Friar Lawrence's cell at dawn (on Monday), having obviously come straight from Juliet, and insists on marriage 'to-day'. In 2.4 the Nurse is told to warn Juliet to come to be married 'this afternoon', in 2.5 Juliet, after impatiently awaiting the Nurse's return for three hours, receives her message at noon, and in 2.6 the Friar marries the lovers soon after on the Monday afternoon, less than twenty-four hours after they had first met. In 3.1 the fights in which Mercutio and Tybalt are killed take place one hour after Romeo's secret marriage, and in 3.2 Juliet, three hours after her marriage, is impatient for its consummation when Romeo will come 'at night'. In 3.3 Romeo, before going to Juliet, hears of his banishment, and realises that he must leave her very early if he is to escape. In 3.4 'very late' on the same day (Monday), Lady Capulet is told to tell Juliet that she will be married to Paris on Thursday. In 3.5, near daybreak on Tuesday, the lovers part after their brief wedding-night, and Juliet is told of her Thursday marriage. In 4.1, Paris tells the Friar of his coming marriage to Juliet; the Friar says to Juliet that 'Wednesday is to-morrow', and gives her the potion to take 'To-morrow night'. In 4.2 Juliet returns home (it is still Tuesday), and her father puts her marriage forward to 'to-morrow' (Wednesday). Therefore in the next scene (4.3), late on Tuesday night, Juliet takes the potion; in 4.4 Capulet is busy at three o'clock on the Wednesday morning preparing for the marriage, and a little later, in 4.5, Juliet is discovered 'dead'. After this point in the action, there is a necessarily vague passage of time during which Balthazar learns of Juliet's 'death', and goes to Mantua and tells Romeo (the truth, of course, with Shakespeare acting as 'chance', has failed to reach him from Friar Lawrence). However, Shakespeare makes the Friar curiously precise about the period of Juliet's 'death' – she will awaken after 'two and forty hours'.[113] If one accepts this, the time-scale is quite consistent; Juliet should revive on Thursday night, and Friar Lawrence, Romeo and the rest should reach the Capulet monument about then. Thus the lovers first meet and fall in love, on a Sunday night, are married on the Monday afternoon, spend part of Monday night together in bed (for the first and last time), and are both dead before the end of Thursday.[114] The married life of Othello and Desdemona is almost as brief, but with a time-scale deliberately, and necessarily, less precisely established, and for different reasons.

Thus the play shows the very human domination of the young lovers by their Italianate hot-blooded passion, and the older generation of the Montagues and Capulets, especially the latter, governed by their equally human pride and impatience. Prince Escalus stands for the reason necessary in life. So the human struggles (not within but between individuals) are seen as the lovers against Old Capulet and the Prince, Juliet and Capulet against each other, and Romeo against the Prince's authority.

But where is Friar Lawrence's place in these human conflicts? As an Italian priest, he is naturally a suspect figure to the Elizabethan audience.[115] He is also the kind of sententious would-be-shaper of events that Friar Francis represents in *Much Ado*. Curiously enough, he is also the only character in the play who shows some conflict within himself. He believes in the need for caution and reason, and urges the lovers to see the need, yet he performs the secret marriage, and with the haste demanded by those lovers. The fact is that a crucial part of the emotional effect of the whole play arises from the personal confusion of the Friar's nature: he represents, at the heart of the play, the point where the lovers' only possible source of rational, understanding advice fails them at a vital moment. The character who might have been merely the stock agent necessary for an important development of the plot, becomes more than this, a very human figure in his muddleheaded way. From his elaborate devices, his ironic self-justification that he had meant to end the Montague–Capulet feud, only disaster follows (although the disaster does indeed end the feud); by the end of the play he has become an almost pathetic apologist, a dreadful (but still obstinately self-satisfied) example of the dangers of ineffectual good intentions.

But the play as a whole is a tragedy of good intentions, the only Shakespeare tragedy where no deliberate evil is at work. Does this mean that, as the 'star-cross'd lovers' of the Prologue to Act I suggests, this is a play where Fate determines the lives and actions of the main characters? Our answer will deeply affect our view of Shakespearean tragedy as a whole, not only of this play.

To begin with, let us be clear that Shakespearean tragedy does not arise from the so-called 'fatal flaw', in any absolute sense; the tragic protagonist is not an otherwise 'noble' person brought down to disaster by a special weakness. The tragedies especially show that, as in life, people are made up of the conflicting qualities (not always or necessarily conflicting) which constitute their particular forms of inner struggle, and that the degree to which they succeed in dealing with their life depends on how well those qualities can cope with the various pressures of that life. It follows that, in Shakespeare, the inner struggle is always shown at work through 'character-in-situation'; no Shakespearean character, major or secondary, can be understood fully, or described, in its weaknesses or strengths in absolute terms, but only and always in relation to the circumstances in which it operates. Shakespeare can be seen as 'fate' only in so far as he is the obvious agent by which a certain group of characters are placed in a situation at the beginning of a play. Thereafter the dilemmas of each character, as it naturally and endlessly strives towards some resolution of its disparate impulses and desires, is shown dramatically to create their own developing situation in what I have called a 'chain-reaction'. If there is any sense of inevitability, it is not caused by over-riding forces outside and 'above' the character; it is not the result even of a simple determinism by which the end of a character comes solely from what he is in himself. It is a more profound and moving human inevitability than this, springing from the knowledge, which the dramatist himself stimulates in the audience identifying with the characters, that we must always wrestle with the incongruities within ourselves, for this is the process of living. We know of course, as I have said, that the dramatist is making a play in which characters must act out the plot, but we are made to feel that these characters are human beings who must go on living (unless they choose the ultimate failure of suicide). Even where the supernatural enters a Shakespeare tragedy, as in *Macbeth*, it is shown (as Elizabethans believed) that it can affect Man and his end only if his nature accepts and co-operates with it.

This is the only 'fate' at work in this tragedy, but now chance must be distinguished from fate, for *Romeo and Juliet* gives good examples of the difference. Within the first act, Shakespeare establishes the primary situation of the drama, and the basic natures of the characters in that situation. From then on, the passionate, impulsive hunger of Romeo and Juliet for each other, the unashamed promptings of their extreme youth, and their consequent lack of mature judgement, in conflict with the pressure of elderly parental pride and obstinacy, and all this within the controls of Veronese society – these have their own inevitability. That the lovers bitterly feel themselves to be driven by fate, that Romeo can call himself 'fortune's fool', are shown to be ironic comments on their natural lack of understanding of themselves and their situation. But chance is another matter; this is purely the result of Shakespeare's necessary manipulation, from outside the characters, of certain essential movements of the plot. The fact that Old Capulet suddenly (in 4.2) puts forward by a day the marriage of Juliet to Paris (with all its consequences, given the nature of Juliet) is the outcome not of blind fate or of chance, but of the very quality of Juliet, as affected by her situation, and of the quality of Capulet, as affected by his. She has returned home armed by Friar Lawrence with the potion which will prevent her marriage to Paris, and being a young, self-willed girl fighting for Romeo, she delights her father by a sudden show of quiet obedience. Old Capulet, being an obstinate, authoritarian father, equally self-willed, reacts to this unexpected docility by taking immediate advantage of it to hasten the Paris marriage. All this is fully and yet ironically acceptable in terms of human nature in its situation; like many such twists of circumstances in real life, it seems like fate, in retrospect, only because those concerned do not understand their own nature – indeed, many of the audience may have seen fate at work, for the same reason. On the other hand, there are of course moments in the play where the dramatist is devising chance as part of his plot; it is 'chance' in this sense which gives Romeo an opportunity to read the invitations to Capulet's ball, but when he has seen that Rosaline is invited, it is Romeo's nature in that situation, together with Benvolio's, that makes him decide to go uninvited. Once he is there, it is because he is as he is, and Juliet is as she is, that they fall in love so suddenly. The most important example of 'chance' in the play is obviously the unforeseen reason why Friar John fails to warn Romeo in time that Juliet's 'death' is not real; such chances, with disastrous results, do happen in real life, but here Shakespeare, the plot-contriver, is 'chance'. The consequences of the delay, however, are natural human developments arising from everything that we have already learnt about the youthful impatience, the wild impulses, the readiness to despair, of the lovers.

We have now seen something of the way in which, in this early tragedy, Shakespeare has begun to explore, and portray on the stage, the mixed pressures of human motives, and so to create the tragic figure in the tragic situation. Although he has not given that full presentation of the complexities of Man's nature which distinguishes the later tragedies, he has certainly made a play that has never failed to move audiences deeply over the centuries. We should consider why this acted story has evoked emotion, and the quality of that emotion. *Romeo and Juliet* is a tragedy of human suffering; this is true of all tragedy, but in the greatest tragedy death adds little to the suffering already endured. In *Romeo and Juliet* this is not so. The difference may be expressed like this: many Elizabethans could and would have seen the fate of the lovers as something to be feared if passions were given free reign, if children deceived their parents (and parents bullied their children),[116] and if private factions brought disorder to society. Nevertheless, they would certainly have pitied the unhappy lovers and their foolish parents; they would have recognised the folly, yet deplored the consequence. It is the consequence that constitutes the total effect of the play; the death of the lovers is all-important, for without it the play would have been a tale of suffering redeemed and transfigured by a happy ending. The tragedy of *Hamlet* could not be affected like that, nor that of *Othello* or *Lear*, but, as we shall see, *Antony and Cleopatra* is akin to *Romeo and Juliet* in making death the final crucial development of the play – yet in its own unique fashion. So the end of Romeo and Juliet produces a final depth of pity, the culmination of all the pity felt before, but there is something deeper, even universal, in its relevance to the whole of life.

Shakespeare, by the truth to humanity of his characters, has suggested that reason is a useful and prudent quality in man and woman, yes, but not the only one necessary for the finest experience of life. Desire and love are important for self-fulfilment, and although his audience knows that we need some reason to control our irrational urges, it is better, more human, to be naturally passionate and irrational than to be unnaturally passionless and rational (like Iago). So the audience ends the experience of *Romeo and Juliet* with a fresh awareness of the dangers of thoughtless and uncontrolled desire, certainly, but with this awareness, amplified and enriched by the dramatist's magic of poetry and imagination, there is created in us a wonder at the way in which the rational world of Verona (or anyone's home town) can be transfigured in two young people by that desire: indeed, we feel that the private love-world of the lovers lies complete within ·their embraces, and yet, as an imaginative creation, stretches far beyond Verona to our own dreams and desires. Emotion is evoked and then universalised. We, the audience, have had our own human strife suggested, even if not fully explored. We have been reminded of the many stresses in ourselves which arise from our mixed nature, and we realise again that life is always a narrow path between joy and disaster. Yet we have seen the lovers running along this knife-edge as though it were a broad and shining highway to heaven, fearful at times, but always determined in their youthful unawareness of their inadequacy for the workaday world around them. Herein lies the perennial pity of them and their acted story. Our final sense of wonder that human nature can be so foolishly right in its passionate commitment, so bravely ignorant of its own self-destruction; our realisation that youth has been destroyed for lack of mature wisdom, but would have also ceased to be youth if it had had that wisdom; in short, the recognition that, in this tragedy, youth and age can resolve their incongruities only in death, and yet that death is here, in a vital double sense the waste of good: all these perceptions crowd in upon us at the end of this play, and, because the dramatist has offered no deeper resolution of them, we must accommodate them mainly with an embracing pity, not with the full tragic and universal insight (including pity) which makes the truly tragic experience.

Hamlet, Prince of Denmark

Writers on Shakespeare have been and are so often mixed in their reactions to the plays, rightly and properly so, for the very complexity of their own personal awarenesses of human contradictions (itself a source of Man's constant confusion and strife in the business of living), as it responds to Shakespeare's rich awareness of his own and his audience's contradictions, can be expressed only in an intricate body of reactions which can never be completely contained, if at all, in any neat or merely logical exposition. Any such attempt to experience and display the full force of a Shakespeare play is doomed to failure if it seeks to work only in terms of 'analysing' the play or describing its 'meaning'. True, any expositor of Shakespeare's work has at least to attempt to present understandable propositions, in reasonably clear language, in a sequence that can be followed without confusion of the reader's mind, but he must always be aware that a play is not a logical argument, that a Shakespeare play is expressed in poetry that often ranges far beyond logic, in prose that, even at its most banal, conveys more than factual information, and in action that, even when most commonplace, springs from motives and urgencies only partly rational.

Thus no simple contrast between *Romeo and Juliet* and *Hamlet* will fully express the change of tone and effect that one feels in moving from one to the other. It is necessary and important (if somewhat obvious) to note the striking and immediate differences between these plays, but we must remember that, in the works of Man's experience and imagination, differences are like the divergent directions of the spokes of a wheel, significant chiefly because they

148

indicate that the spokes start from a common centre, and are finally contained within a common limit.

What, then, are one's impressions in coming from the world of Romeo and Juliet to that of Hamlet? Certainly one is sure that one is still within an area of grief, of human effort culminating in worldly failure: the Capulet–Montague, Verona milieu is less prestigious than the royal court of Denmark, but for those confined within it no less constrictive; in terms of human feeling portrayed in drama, both the young lovers and the Prince of Denmark are living beings caught in a situation which, to begin with, is not of their making, but which they thereafter constantly attempt to master, given the limitations of their natures. One sees this kinship of the two plays, but immediately one realises that there is a deep difference between them. The difference between *Hamlet* and, indeed, any other play of Shakespeare's, is generally agreed among all students of the play, but it must be realised as a difference of manner and of tone, ultimately of Shakespeare's attitude and approach, rather than as a fundamental difference. The Shakespeare of *Hamlet* is the Shakespeare of *Romeo and Juliet*, but some six years of crowded professional experience and the process of living lie between the two. It is natural to speak of Shakespeare's 'growth to maturity' as a dramatist, but to do so is to employ a kind of 'pathetic fallacy', to think of him as if he were a tree: our knowledge of ourselves and others suggests that human beings, even abnormally gifted ones, do not grow in stature quite like that. In those six years Shakespeare must have experienced a great deal, and learnt from that experience; in that period he had written (and tried out on audiences, noting and profiting from their responses) a series of popular English history plays, two appealing love-comedies, and an effective dramatisation of a well-known story from Roman history. He had also made, in this same busy time, an attractive poetic love-fantasy, and a rambling farce of bourgeois escapades, and two 'comedies' in which, as we have seen, human nature appears as at once amusing and disturbing. This is a period of wide-ranging drama in popular modes of theatre, all the plays employing those two main demands of the audience, an interesting, developing story and human nature revealing itself in action. Increasingly the story is presented as the continuous result of the interaction of the characters involved in it; for the most part these characters seem each to embody a fairly coherent set of qualities, so that the interesting and essentially dramatic conflicts lie between characters rather than within characters.

Romeo and Juliet certainly, as we have noted, displayed this kind of conflict, so that even the protagonists have something of the quality of the older sixteenth-century moral dramatic types. With *Hamlet* there is a significant difference, seen chiefly in the Prince, and there in an almost exaggerated form. One cannot doubt the singleminded impulse that drives the lovers in the earlier play, or the equally simple attitudes of the families that oppose them. In *Hamlet* the protagonist permeates the play,[117] and the struggles of his inner nature, expressed primarily through the frequent and calculated use of soliloquies, form a 'psychological drama' woven into, and shaping the design of, the outer drama of the motives and actions of the other characters.

This leads to two other striking differences between these two plays, the differences in tempo and in length, not always or necessarily related, but here certainly so. In the earlier play, speed of action is the essence of the drama, and it is speed of external action, events in the story not within the characters, but activated by the inner passions of the two main figures hurrying to a goal unchecked by reason. In *Hamlet* there is no such effect. The full text is roughly a third longer than that of *Romeo and Juliet*, but the play seems far longer than this, and far slower. Tempo is not a matter of quantity of text – *Richard III* is not much shorter than the full *Hamlet* (about 300 lines less), and yet it seems almost as quick-moving as *Romeo and Juliet*. The unfolding of *Hamlet* appears unusually slow and weighty; the crucial first act, in which are shown Hamlet's preliminary nature, the situation in which he starts, and the 'primary impulse' of the play (the Ghost's revelation of murder, and his son's vow of revenge) takes up almost the first quarter of the play. We are nearly halfway through the play when the testing of the King's guilt by 'The Mousetrap' takes place, and when we reach the turning-point of the killing of Polonius, and the consequent decision by Claudius to send Hamlet to England to be disposed of, some seventy per cent of the drama is over. Yet so far Hamlet's only material action to avenge his father has been this mistaken killing of the 'wretched, rash, intruding fool', and, as all the world knows, he kills the King in the very last moments of the tragedy. In *Hamlet*, then, we feel that the dramatist's concern is not so much with what happens in the plot, the 'events' of the play, not even with why things happen (as in his other tragedies), but with why they do not happen. In other words, Shakespeare's chief interest seems to be in showing us the 'interior action' of the play, what is going on in the minds of the characters, above all in the mind of Hamlet; the slow and feeling exploration of the Prince's nature is the mode and motive-force of the play.

The tragedy, then, is built around Hamlet's inner reactions to the 'duty' of revenge, the killing of his father's murderer; in fact, the text was registered with the Stationers' Company in July, 1602, as 'A booke (text) called the Revenge of Hamlett Prince of Denmarke'. For an Elizabethan, revenge was felt as a form of the reason–unreason problem which could evoke dangerously conflicting responses: an early example of this view is Painter's comment in his story of a man planning revenge upon a virtuous lady who had repulsed his advances:

> Do wee not see, that after Reason giueth place
> to desired reuenge of wrong thought to be receiued,
> man dispoyleth himself of that, which appertayneth
> to the kinde [nature] of man, to put on the fierce
> nature of the moste brute and cruell beastes, to runne
> headlonge without reason toward the place wher the
> disordinate appetite of affections [emotions], doth
> conduct him?[118]

Yet a moralising versifier (and composer) some forty years later, a year or two after the appearance of *Hamlet*, shows another view of revenge:

> Revenge of things uniust a vertue is,
> That both subdue oppression, force, and wrong;
> All obscure acts which leade men farre amisse,
> She doth repell; be neuer they so strong.
>   It doth defend the pure and innocent;
>   And chastice those that in transgression went.[119]

So for an Elizabethan, revenge could be a regrettable lapse from reason into passion which brought man down to the level of beasts, or a rational social virtue supporting the innocent against the guilty. As we have seen in Part 2(b) (pp.50 and 55) the drama of Shakespeare's lifetime reflects each view, and even the combination of them. *The Spanish Tragedy* exploits for popular entertainment the wild passions and brutal violence arising from the desire for revenge (justified, in some measure, in Leighton's terms), and this melodramatic and exciting approach continues, with increased sophistication, in the passionate welter of such plays as Marston's *Antonio's Revenge* (c1600) and Tourneur's *The Revenger's Tragedy* (c1606). On the other hand, Chapman explores and stresses the other attitude, in which the man of reason seeks to resist the merely passionate impulse to revenge, so that in his *The Revenge of Bussy d'Ambois* (*c*1610) Clermont makes his revenge an unimpassioned and necessary act of justice of which Leighton would have approved, and then commits suicide equally calmly and rationally. From these plays alone, it is clear that the revenge-theme could produce, broadly speaking, two types of dramatic entertainment: an emphasis on passionate revenge gave the audience the popular delights of vigorous and bloody action, with the appropriate rhetorical and highly coloured language, while the portrayal of rational revenge produced a play of less violent action, less vivid language, but with a more 'philosophical' tone almost as appealing to other tastes of the Elizabethan audience.

As we shall see, the special psychological complexity, the curiously indeterminate yet powerful overall effect, of *Hamlet* arise from the fåct that the dramatist in this play is showing that both attitudes to revenge can exist within the divided nature of an exceptional revenger, and the inner conflicts, and final tragedy, which result.

Other plays of the time also show, in their different ways, the ambiguous nature of revenge. Heywood's *A Woman Killed with Kindness* (1603) suggests the doubtful mercy that results when a husband refuses to exercise his conventional passionate right to revenge himself on a guilty wife: similarly, Tourneur's *The Atheist's Tragedy* (*c*1609), perhaps affected by *Hamlet*, seems to question the very need for revenge, for the ghost of the murdered man in fact tells his son not to take vengeance. In Webster's *The Duchess of Malfi* (*c*1614) the validity of revenge is questioned and complicated still further; the 'guilty' Duchess is shown as the victim of an excessive and callous retribution, and, as in *Romeo and Juliet*, the 'reason' of the heart becomes finally far more important, far more moving and convincing, than the rational savagery of social conventions. In fact, Painter's simple and unquestioning view of reason and passion in revenge has been subjected to the moral pressures of a complex, yet deeply true, situation where now it is 'reason' which can transform men into beasts.

It is with an apparently straightforward, popular 'situation-for-revenge' that *Hamlet* begins. An atmosphere of darkness, cold and foreboding surrounds in 1.1 the appearance of the ghost of Hamlet's father; suddenly the matter of fact world of soldiers on guard duty is disturbed by a second incursion of the irrational, the incomprehensible; even the scholar Horatio is unable to understand. This opening sets the tone of the whole play, with emotional confusion and doubt beginning to break up the rational order of everyday life. We are then taken straight into the contrasting Court-world of the new King of Denmark, where apparently formality and order prevail, and Claudius has much to say about the proper reasonable attitude to bereavement: there is a pointed ironic contrast between his rational assumption that death must be accepted as an unfortunate common fact, and our suspicion that the old King's death is already beyond such bland commonplaces, and cannot be brushed aside thus. In this reasonable, 'political' setting where Claudius is obviously in full control (he is dealing efficiently and speedily with the problem of young Fortinbras), there is, however, the figure of Hamlet. Directly he speaks, with disturbing passion, a discordant tone breaks into the scene. For an Elizabethan audience, it is obvious that he is the outsider, a 'witty' man playing upon 'kin' and 'kind', a man of quick reason yet also possessed by an inner grief at his father's death which sets him apart from the everyday world, and makes him an implicit reproach to those around him. When he is left alone, and speaks his first soliloquy, the full passion of his separation from normal life is clear. He is in the grip of that inner pressure of which, as we have seen, the Elizabethans were fully aware, as we are, the conflict between the emotional impact of an individual death and the rational awareness that death is inevitable. But Hamlet has introduced a new dimension into this common feeling; through his grief, and his own special nature, he is possessed by a sense of the worthlessness, the animality, of the common world, arising directly from the eagerness with which his mother has remarried. Shakespeare presents a man obviously intelligent, part of an established rational society, suddenly made aware, in his own blood, how passion can debase human values; thence he is sickened by his own share of physical humanity, and wishes to escape from living. This is the man who very soon afterwards is confronted by the news of his father's ghost, and the suggestion of foul play, of evil even greater than sexual passion.

The next scene (1.3), while of course laying the groundwork for future plot-development, presents the contrast of ordinary life. Laertes is a very normal young man, and Polonius a typical wordy old man, and they are both naturally concerned that the innocent Ophelia should be warned against the possible dangers of Hamlet's interest in her. Such a situation, such advice, are commonplaces of the age. This glimpse of a very ordinary family group, nicely entertaining for the audience, has been insterted between the Hamlet tone of the previous scene and the further strangeness and passion of the next. The contrast is dramatically effective in itself, but it also strengthens the theme of reason–unreason which is now beginning to emerge as the core of the play.

The next two scenes (1.4 and 1.5) form one developing sequence in which Hamlet moves from the apparently 'normal' world of the Court to the secret world which only he and his father's ghost can share. In 1.4 there is the first of those 'semi-soliloquies' in which Hamlet reveals to Horatio, and to the audience, his personal attitudes to his situation; by making the eminently rational Horatio a part of these self-explorations by Hamlet, the dramatist is able to sharpen by contrast, at intervals throughout the play, the special quality of the Prince's inner struggles. Here Hamlet's musings to Horatio, after an entertainingly topical reference to the drunkenness of the Danish court (which also has its bearing on Hamlet's nature), develop into the expression of his fear that a 'complexion', an obsessive emotion, can break down 'the pales and forts of reason'. This was a common Elizabethan concern, and the audience has already seen enough of the unusual inner passion of Hamlet to realise how easily he could run that risk. Following this, the Ghost appears and leads the Prince away for the revelations of 1.5, the beginning of Hamlet's tragic conflict. These revelations are as terrible a justification for revenge as Hieronymo's in *The Spanish Tragedy* (and as melodramatic, too), but complicated by the ghost's warning that Claudius must be punished without harm to Hamlet's mother; Hamlet's 'duty' has been made a clear but peculiarly complex obligation. Hamlet's second soliloquy shows his first passionate response to what he has heard, an almost wild resolve to obey the 'commandment' of his father. His final comment suggests much of the conflict that will grow within him:

> The time is out of joint. O cursed spite,
> That ever I was born to set it right!

This is the end of the first act; the remaining three-quarters of the play must develop from what the Elizabethan audience has seen, and felt, so far. Lacking the advantages, and perhaps distractions, of some three hundred years of comment and speculation about this play (including the present work, of course), most of them would have enjoyed the exciting prospect of seeing the nature and process of Hamlet's revenge, possibly further villainy by Claudius, but certainly his well-deserved punishment by the end of the drama. Hamlet, no doubt, would die, like most revengers, when his task had been accomplished. But some might have wondered whether a 'modern' revenge-play would be quite as straightforward as this; they would have noted the reluctance to act stressed in the final couplet of Act 1, and wondered how the over-sensitive young Prince, rational and passionate, would react to the urgent, bloody killing suddenly thrust upon him.

We, too, must be concerned with Hamlet's response, and with the reasons for his response. We have the complex character broadly defined, and firmly set in his situation; we know his role, but we have yet to learn how, or indeed if, he can fulfil that role. Of all Shakespeare's tragic protagonists, Hamlet is the most 'private'; he is a man of inner thoughts, inner emotions, a personal inner world involved in an insensitive and bustling outer world, and has been placed, by Shakespeare, in a situation where his inner nature forces him to act in that outer world, and yet must render such action peculiarly difficult. Moreover, this intensely 'private' man has been born Prince of Denmark, with the inescapable 'public' responsibilities which make him part of the court world of Claudius: this contrast of the 'private' man and the 'public' man is a further essential factor in that struggle within Hamlet in his situation which is the driving-force of the play. Hamlet, basically, is the man of feeling faced with an emotional need to act, but, as we shall see, also anxious to justify his action, and perform it, rationally. He must keep his passionate urge to revenge, but carry that revenge out with the rational cunning and coolness which alone will be effective in the world of Claudius.

The portrayal of this complex problem of Hamlet requires an exploration of character-in-situation of a scope and subtlety quite new to Shakespeare's drama. His earlier plays had shown something of human conflicts but usually between characters; now the struggles are, essentially, within the protagonist (although Claudius and Laertes have their moments of inner conflict), and all concern the problem of making decisions regarding the proper way in which to carry out the duty imposed on him. The special quality of *Hamlet* suggests that Shakespeare was aware that he was attempting a re-interpretation of an old and popular revenge formula in terms congenial to the new and special popular interest in human responses, under stress, to a worldly situation. The unusual length and complexity of the play arises from this; it is a dramatic tale of revenge enlarged by what one might call a 'running commentary' on the implications of the action for the Hamlet character, and inevitably the commentary becomes more important than the simple plot. In the practical theatre for which Shakespeare was writing, the length of *Hamlet* would not have been a dangerous indulgence; the 'running commentary' would largely have been cut if a normal performance of about two hours' length was essential; the play thus shortened[120] would not have been 'our' *Hamlet*, but it would still have been an acceptable Elizabethan tragedy in performance – indeed, many of the audience might have preferred it to the full version.

After Act 1, then, begins the process of Hamlet's attempt to cope with his situation. To display this is the business of the play, so naturally Hamlet is the centre of the dramatic action, and to him everything is related: he is physically absent from the court of Denmark or its neighbourhood for only three scenes,[121] and in two of these he is the continuing centre of interest.

The next four scenes show the first tentative contacts in the contest between Hamlet and the King, culminating in Claudius's reaction to the play within the play, a reaction which does not prove his guilt beyond question, although Hamlet's rational side needs such definite proof. The King responds to Hamlet's strange behaviour by trying to find the reason for it, using both the willing cunning of Rosencrantz and Guildenstern and the loving innocence of Ophelia; cunning will ultimately lead Rosencrantz and his partner to their deaths, but Ophelia's love and innocence equally leads to her final madness and suicide. All Shakespeare's major tragedies have what may be called a secondary tragic victim, a character caught up by the main tragic current and destroyed, as it were, in passing; such a figure must not be given a full tragic effect to compete with that of the protagonist, but the deep pathos of Ophelia's end needs only a touch, even, of universality to make it almost as tragic as Hamlet's.

Hamlet's encounter with Rosencrantz and Guildenstern in 2.2 evokes another of his self-revelations which throughout the play add to our understanding of the full complex nature of this would-be revenger:

> What a piece of work is a man! How noble in reason!
> how infinite in faculties! in form and moving, how express
> and admirable! in action, how like an angel! in
> apprehension, how like a god! the beauty of the world!

the paragon of animals! And yet, to me, what is this
quintessence of dust?[122]

The essence of the Renaissance revelation is here, and with it, part of
it, the very core of that form of human conflict of which the age was
so often and so painfully aware – the sense of being at once potential
angel and potential brute, of being immortal in aspiration and, in
sorry truth, doomed to death and decay (see Part 1, Sections (b) and
(c), pp.2–5). But Hamlet's words are far more than a moving
comment on us all; the universal, as so often in Shakespeare, is linked
to the particular, the words give yet another insight into the nature of
the speaker. This Prince committed to requite killing with killing is
aware of the infinite possible greatness of man, but his commitment
has nothing of the angel or the god in it, merely anticipates and
stresses man's mortality. His words to Ophelia in 3.1 are a further
comment on the same theme, this time marking the littleness of Man
as Hamlet experiences it in himself:

I am myself indifferent honest, but yet I could
accuse me of such things that it were better my mother
had not borne me. I am very proud, revengeful, ambitious;
with more offences at my beck than I have thoughts to
put them in, imagination to give them shape, or time
to act them in. What should such fellows as I do
crawling between earth and heaven? We are arrant knaves,
all; believe none of us.[123]

This feeling man, caught up in an evil world, which threatens to
entrap his passionate imagination into its own mould, for a moment
swings to that pessimism regarding Mankind which lies in wait for
every human being poised between angel and beast. His reaction to
his mother's marriage, in the soliloquy at the end of 1.2, had shown
largely a personal, 'family' disgust at a mother who could forget his
father and love another man; by now the personal has moved out
into the world around; that world's evil is pressing upon him, but
Shakespeare makes him still see it for what it is, and express what he
sees.

Before he confronts Ophelia in 3.1, we have already been shown a
great deal of what has been happening both within and outside the
Prince since the end of Act 1. Shakespeare's way is to reveal both the
inner and the outer worlds continually overlapping and interacting
with a complexity which is exceptional, compared even with his

other tragedies. The first hint of this form of incongruity which all Mankind knows, the strange contrast between one's secret life and the outward life of one's fellows, is present in Hamlet's first words in the play, where he contrasts the inner grief and the outward conventions of grief; it is a commonplace, of course, but common because so often true, and fundamental to our existence. And so in 2.2, even as Hamlet is expressing that inner vision of the 'quintessence of dust', he is parrying the probing of the King's agents, and within a few minutes he is greeting his friends the Players.

As an experienced dramatist, Shakespeare knew that, once the serious human concerns of a tragedy have been firmly established, nothing in life seems irrelevant; the paradox is that the business of living, in a proper context, can be felt simultaneously as amusing and true, and deeply serious, deeply part of a wider tragedy. In bringing Hamlet and the Players together at this moment, on the surface the dramatist is of course both amusing his audience and preparing for the crucial 'Mousetrap' scene (3.2). But the Players also reinforce that sense of 'within' and 'without' to which I have just referred. The 'Pyrrhus' passage is not merely an audition for the coming play, not just a contemporary parody of popular acting; it also and at the same time becomes yet another comment on Hamlet's conflict.[124]

Hamlet's practical problem is that, to be the effective revenger, he must learn to translate his inner emotional need to revenge into the rational cunning needed for killing an established and wily King; inner turmoil must emerge into outer, ordered expression in action. This is why Hamlet sees in the professionally controlled passion of the 'Pyrrhus' speech a paradigm, as it were, of his own need to combine passion and reason. His fourth soliloquy, which ends 2.2, expresses the complexity of his awareness of this, and it is perhaps the most important self-revelation in the play. For the first time in this process of trying to understand his own nature in relation to the demands upon it of his situation, he begins to show a realisation of his true difficulty. The speech itself is a wonderful example of the unique power of great poetry to suggest rather than define, at moments when only such suggestion can show the intricate inter-action of overtones of thought and feeling. The soliloquy shows a passion of reaction to the Player's example, but around that passion, and now consciously trying to control it, is a realisation of the need for reason: it is futile merely to feel genuine passion against Claudius – emotion, however sincere, is not enough in a world where only action counts. Hamlet sees that his instinctive belief in the truth of the Ghost's message must be logically tested; he must not trust the emotional effect on him of a ghost which, as the Elizabethan audience would have agreed, might have been the agent of the Devil, a product of his own brooding imagination, or even a messenger from God. So he must use 'The Murder of Gonzago' to prove Claudius's guilt, as a necessary and rational prelude to revenge. Very right and proper, of course, but such reasoning seems strangely foreign to the Prince's nature as it has been shown up to now; we wonder whether a 'guilty' reaction by the King to the play will in fact have the power to move Hamlet's grief into bloody action – passion, if it is strong enough, unhampered by a desire to act rationally, does not need the support of logical proof. And, of course, the King's reaction to the play can never be convincing, logical proof – we know him to be a man who would never blurt out a frank confession in public, for he is essentially the 'public' man who can control emotion. When later (in 3.2) Claudius in fact breaks off the play, calls for lights, and hurries away, he admits nothing; when Hamlet appeals to Horatio, always his touchstone of reality, to confirm that this sudden reaction is proof of the King's guilt, Horatio's reply is entirely non-committal, however convinced Hamlet may be.

In the next scene (3.1), in which Ophelia is made a trap for the Prince's true feelings, we realise that it is as important for Claudius to know whether his stepson is merely love-sick or a dangerous malcontent, as it is for Hamlet to be sure that the King is guilty; the Ophelia test is equivalent to the 'Mousetrap' test in this deadly game of suspicion. The King, in an 'aside' on Polonius's sententiousness about innocence used as a cover for guilt, for the first time admits guilt, but not yet explicitly the guilt of a brother's murder.

When Hamlet speaks his fourth soliloquy,[125] something further is added to the slow exploration of the character. The opening of it, so well known and so admired over the centuries, is in fact hardly a deep or truly 'philosophical' insight into life and death; the Elizabethan audience would have accepted it almost as a commonplace, however movingly expressed. Its real significance (the significance of all Hamlet's 'philosophical' comments) is its relevance to his inner struggle, and the fact that it leads on to:

> Thus conscience does make cowards of us all;
> And thus the native hue of resolution
> Is sicklied o'er with the pale cast of thought,
> And enterprises of great pitch and moment,

> With this regard, their currents turn awry
> And lose the name of action.[126]

Certainly Hamlet is still thinking almost longingly, as in his first soliloquy, of suicide, the certain end to all the perplexities of human struggle, but more important is what follows this glance at suicide, this wish to escape from his situation: the suggestion is that he is growing impatient with thinking, is feeling hampered by his attempt to be the rational man. A foreign writer, translated some years before, had neatly summed up and anticipated Hamlet's quandary, and, indeed, the very nature of his slowness to act which is the essence of the play:

> It is very good that we goe about to doo all thinges
> with reason, and it is good that we doo guide all our
> enterprises in order: but yet in this there falles out
> to be great difficulties. For wise and staid men in
> perfourming their affaires, doo consider, resolue &
> compasse with such diligence those inconveniences that
> may spring in ye same, that they neuer almost determine
> to resolue upon any finall end.[127]

The next scene (3.2) returns to Hamlet's problem. His well-known advice to the Players is more than the amusement of a playwright's edged comments on what bad acting can do to a play. Behind this topical criticism lies a repeated suggestion that in acting even the portrayal of passion must be controlled by the reason; good art is the balanced combination of feeling and thinking, precisely what Hamlet is trying to seek. Soon after this, Hamlet's praise of Horatio is significant:

> Since my dear soul was mistress of her choice
> And could of men distinguish her election,
> Sh'hath seal'd thee for herself; for thou hast been
> As one, in suff'ring all, that suffers nothing;
> A man that Fortune's buffets and rewards
> Hast ta'en with equal thanks; and blest are those
> Whose blood and judgment are so well comeddled
> That they are not a pipe for Fortune's finger
> To sound what stop she pleases.[128] Give me that man
> That is not passion's slave, and I will wear him
> In my heart's core, ay, in my heart of heart,
> As I do thee.[129]

The young Prince's frequent testing of his fitness for his situation against the firm wisdom of Horatio (this speech ends by asking his judgement) is here explained and emphasised. Hamlet's ideal, at this moment, seems to be near to the 'Senecan man' who, in the hands of Chapman above all, introduced into the old revenge play concept (as we have seen) a radically different approach to the revenger's role. Hamlet's respect for such a man, for the wise balance of 'blood' (passion) and judgement which keeps him, in spite of 'fortune', in control of his human incongruity, clarifies what the play has already suggested about his awareness of his own unfitness for his situation. The Prince was shown at the beginning as a son shocked by the realisation of the human frailty of both his father and his mother – a father can die, a mother can so soon forget and love elsewhere – and reacting to the Ghost with both passionate commitment and regret at the burden of his task. From then until now, Shakespeare has shown him struggling with the need to adapt his nature to his obligation to revenge; in some way he must control feeling with the higher reason which seeks truth, something far different from the lower reason of the 'political' world around him, which is merely the expedient cunning of selfish or subservient men. Hamlet, in fact, has too much respect and desire for wisdom to be an Hieronymo, too much depth of feeling to be the 'Senecan man', and he must seek the balance between these two. Here Hamlet, I am sure, represents the dilemma in real life of many Elizabethans in their growing sophistication and self-awareness. It is surely not only a desire to thrill the groundlings (poor wretches blamed for so much that is considered 'unworthy' of Shakespeare) that makes the dramatist, so soon after the speech to Horatio, give us the almost Hieronymo tone of the fifth soliloquy's opening:

> 'Tis now the very witching time of night,
> When churchyards yawn, and hell itself breathes out
> Contagion to this world. Now could I drink hot blood,
> And do such bitter business as the day
> Would quake to look on.[130]

Here is passion ready for violence, the straightforward road to revenge which, for an instant, Hamlet seems tempted to take, but immediately afterwards we see yet another complexity in the struggling Hamlet – feeling is not merely poised against reason, but feeling itself is divided between love for his father and love for his mother.

As a transition from this soliloquy to the next decisive point in the play (3.4), there is the irony of 3.3, a scene in which Shakespeare seems to wish us to smile wryly at the mistaken scrupulousness (or is it merely indecision?) of the would-be wise revenger. Before considering this main part of the scene, we should note the effect of its opening. We are over halfway through the play, and constantly, parallel to the difficulties of Hamlet, there has been displayed the contrasting world of Claudius and his courtiers, a 'political' world, where an appreciation of 'the art of the possible', far from Hamlet's quest for an ideal, has been the mark of the King. While Hamlet has been wrestling with his nature, Claudius has been shown as an efficient ruler fully aware of what has to be done, and skilful in doing it; the 'villain' of the new revenge tragedy is now not simply villainous, but has his own complexity of nature; his evil is not wholly evil in its own context, and can be explained (if not justified) by the selfish but accepted pragmatism of the world in which he operates. The King has by 2.2 settled the potential danger of Fortinbras broached in 1.2, and has acted with proper caution against the difficult behaviour of the Prince; now he is arranging to get Hamlet out of Denmark, so far with no murderous intent. One of the many human ironies of this play is that Hamlet's confusion of purpose and consequent delay is seen to evoke an equivalent 'waiting game' on the part of his opponent, but one deliberately chosen, and for entirely different reasons.

In this same opening of 3.3 Shakespeare chooses to give the audience a typical Elizabethan comment on the people's dependence, for their own safety, on the safety of their King. This part of Rosencrantz's speech is especially interesting:

> The single and peculiar life is bound
> With all the strength and armour of the mind
> To keep itself from noyance; but much more
> That spirit upon whose weal depends and rests
> The lives of many.[131]

The 'private' man has the duty to use his reason to protect himself from trouble (as Hamlet is trying to do), but the 'public' man, the man in authority, has a far greater duty to do so, not only for his own sake, but for that of the common people whose safety is bound up with his. This is an Elizabethan commonplace which has a surprising irony in this particular context – the dramatist seems determined at least to touch on every dimension of the Claudius–Hamlet situation. It suggests that Claudius, as King, has the duty to defend himself against any danger from Hamlet, and it even implies that Hamlet, as revenger, may be a danger to society. Certainly the simpler motives and situations of the older revenge tragedy have here taken on an astonishing complexity.

But the most striking irony of this scene arises, of course, from Hamlet's response to his one obvious chance to carry out an immediate revenge on Claudius. The King's soliloquy is his first and only explicit admission that he killed his brother; if Hamlet had overheard it (here again is Shakespeare playing 'chance'), it would have settled what was still, rationally, the strong likelihood of Claudius's guilt, and as far as Hamlet's conscience was concerned, would have justified the immediate killing of the King. Yet Hamlet's problem is not exactly one of conscience; it is rather a doubt as to the right way to obey his conscience. But now the emphasis is rather on the King: for a moment Shakespeare enters deeply into the humanity of Claudius, so that never again can he be merely the simple villain of the play – we realise that he too, even like Hamlet, is trapped within his own character-in-situation. His is the traditional dilemma known to every member of any (even nominally) Christian society, that between desiring to repent and the true full act of repentance.[132] Hamlet, for his part, has had time to consider action against the King, and, characteristically, has found a reason to control his emotional impulse – the opposite will be shown, very shortly, in his killing of Polonius.

The next scene (3.4) is the turning-point of the play. It has scarcely begun before the Queen, frightened by her son's vehemence, cries for help, Polonius stirs behind the wall-hanging, and Hamlet immediately lunges with his sword – and says 'Is it the King?'. There is no better example in Shakespeare of the highly effective piece of stage-action which is also a vital insight into character.[133] This Prince whose only concern, in the play so far, has been to achieve action fully justified by emotion and by reason, has now killed on impulse, without any thought, with only the subconscious hope that he may have reached his goal in spite of himself. Suddenly it is plain that, for such a man as the Hamlet we know, this is the only way in which he will ever act violently and decisively, and the rest of the drama proves the point. Equally important is the fact that, with the killing of Polonius, the terms of the rest of the play will be different. Hamlet has now been moved further into the world of the King; the Hamlet who had been so apart from the alien society around him is now deeply involved with that society on its own terms; now, he is the murderer of Polonius; the revenger has become the legitimate object of revenge, and Hamlet is now a kind of Claudius. Of course, Hamlet can never be reduced to the level of the King's cold villainy (that would be to write a different play – perhaps a very interesting one that might be offered to a modern dramatist), but the simple contrast between Claudius's evil and Hamlet's fineness has already been blurred by the recent insight into the King's desire for repentance, and now the killing of Polonius has confused it still further. Not so much the killing, perhaps, as Hamlet's reaction to it; on one level this may be seen as Elizabethan comic relief in an 'antic humour', but Polonius has been made too human a figure, even in his stupid worldly cunning, to end easily as merely a 'wretched, rash, intruding fool', ignored the next moment, and his corpse later made the subject of verbal sparring between Hamlet and the King. This offhand callousness contrasts with Hamlet's later regret expressed to Laertes, but it has a kind of wild desperation beneath it which matches the tone of Hamlet's talk with his mother in the rest of the scene.

His tirade against his mother, his pleading with her to control her passion, however magnificently dramatic on the stage, is itself ironically an outburst of uncontrolled passion, a reversion to that condition where 'reason panders will' (reason ignobly serves emotional need). The Ghost, certainly the acted, visible ghost which the Elizabethans enjoyed, reminds Hamlet of his 'blunted purpose' and of the need to spare his mother, and the two things are in fact connected; to him, his mother represents the passion in himself – to pour out his agony of reproach to her, and to try to force her to share it, is really an emotional self-indulgence which is still diverting him from his main aim of balanced action. Here is one of the many examples of the fruitful ambiguity that now, in Shakespeare's greater tragedies, is arising from his use of complete, human, detailed character-creations within a framework of theatrical plot-construction. The protagonist here has all the complexities of motive of true human incongruity, complexities which in real life, as we all know, often prevent clearcut action; Shakespeare seems now to accept and indeed exploit the consequences of this, not to simplify Hamlet to fit a neat plot, but to shape the plot to the truth of Hamlet. By now it is clear that this Hamlet is scarcely the man to make a carefully contrived plan to murder the King, and carry it out with controlled fervour; he is much more likely to kill, if at all, on impulse, and to do so would be to relinquish that ideal of the wise man which he had praised in Horatio.

In the next three scenes (4.1, 4.2 and 4.3), Shakespeare turns to the practical 'political' results of the killing of Polonius. The King who was shown in 3.3 as torn for a moment between worldly desires and personal guilt, has now resolved or suppressed his dangerous human conflict, and is ready to meet the rational demands of his situation. Now that Hamlet, once only a strange, brooding misfit in Claudius's world, has shown that he can kill an eavesdropper, he has become an active danger to the King. But Claudius's nature is well fitted to deal with such a practical crisis by practical means; as he says:

> How dangerous is it that this man (Hamlet) goes loose!
> Yet must not we put the strong law on him:
> He's lov'd of the distracted multitude,
> Who like not in their judgement but their eyes;
> And where 'tis so, th'offender's scourge is weigh'd,
> But never the offence.[134] To bear all smooth and even,
> This sudden sending him away must seem
> Deliberate pause. Diseases desperate grown
> By desperate appliance are reliev'd,
> Or not at all.[135]

By the end of the scene, he has decided to send Hamlet to England with secret letters arranging for his immediate execution.

In the following scene (4.4) Hamlet appears for the last time before his physical absence from the play for some twenty-five minutes of acting-time. It contains his last full soliloquy, in which the dramatist shows the problem of Hamlet's character-in-situation as it exists at this moment. He is still the same man on whom the Player's speech had had such an effect in 2.2 as a lesson from the ordinary world outside him. Here again the dramatist has brought him into sudden contact with the 'normal' world (while also neatly linking to the Fortinbras affair of 2.2). Once more Hamlet encounters the every-day life in which men do their job, not from carefully established personal principle, but like most ordinary people, from a mixture of desire and accepted convention. The Captain whom he meets is just a soldier who carries out his role, and risks his life for his country's 'honour' without further thought. Hamlet's reaction to this example is characteristically complex: first he sees this meeting as another reminder of his lack of revengeful purpose; then immediately he returns to his constant sense of the importance of reason, but now it seems to be reason as the power of 'looking before and after', of planning action; from this he goes on to see himself as either entirely thoughtless (like an animal), or else swayed by reason which is merely the caution of a coward; finally he returns to the shame that even common soldiers, 'Examples gross as earth', can show him (and here is the significant turn of his thought) that one should act instinctively, especially if one's impulse is strong, and his conclusion is:

> O, from this time forth,
> My thoughts be bloody, or be nothing worth!

Here he feels for a moment the relief of imagining passionate, violent revenge unchecked by reason; it is a return to the mood of the opening lines of his fifth soliloquy (3.2).

Now Shakespeare puts Hamlet into the background for a while, and takes us into the world of Claudius. Of course, what happens in that world in Hamlet's absence prepares for the final outcome of the play; the plot-mechanism is clear, and dramatically satisfying and effective. But within this 'bridging' action are placed touches of human nature which must relate to the Prince, for though he is isolated throughout the play, his inner problem is in fact a heightened form of what all his fellow humans must feel in their own situations. Thus the Queen in 4.5 expresses perfectly the over-anxious suspicion of the guilty, wherein the emotion of fear finally destroys the power of reason. Thus, too, Ophelia's madness in 4.5 shows us the deep and sorrowful beauty that can arise from the flight from reason, the sense of wasted youth and beauty, and love too simple and frail to survive the shock of encountering the complexity of life, the moving danger of emotion without full understanding; Ophelia must die as Desdemona must die. The King's comment:

> poor Ophelia
> Divided from herself and her fair judgement,
> Without the which we are pictures, or mere beasts[136]

reminds us once again of the constant theme of the importance of reason as the only thing which prevents Mankind from being mere appearances 'pictures' of humanity, or even beasts. Yet when Laertes enters, wild for revenge for his father's murder, the ordinary Elizabethan must see in him a revenger easier to understand, closer to the natural, instinctive breaking-out of a bereaved son's passion, than the over-thoughtful, complex Hamlet. Laertes's emotion is beyond all rational argument; every thought of danger in this world or damnation in the next, is swept away by it. When in 4.7 Claudius asks him what he is prepared to do to avenge his father, his reply is: 'To cut his throat i' th' church', and we remember that other avenging son who failed to kill his father's murderer at prayer. The King's cunning working upon Laertes in 4.7 (an ironic example of how 'lower' reason can control emotion), also has its relevance to the main theme; he warns him that passion can soon exhaust itself, that it must be expressed in action quickly, before the opportunity passes, and his words are strangely applicable to Hamlet's problem:

> That we would do,
> We should do when we would; for this 'would' changes,
> And hath abatements and delays as many
> As there are tongues, are hands, are accidents;
> And then this 'should' is like a spendthrift's sigh
> That hurts by easing.[137]

Claudius also speaks of Hamlet directly; in contriving the plot to kill him with an 'unbated' (unbuttoned) foil, he says:

> He, being remiss,
> Most generous (gentlemanly), and free from all contriving,
> Will not peruse the foils.[138]

Here there is much in the overtones of 'remiss'. The Elizabethan senses of the word[139] were mainly associated with failing to do one's duty, being too lenient, lacking violence and energy, and mild rather than intense and strong; so the king's remark is a nicely ambiguous and ironic description of a Hamlet who, from Claudius's practical viewpoint, is too ineffectual to be aggressive and too naïve to know how to plot – the rational man is blind to the power of the irrational – we remember Iago and Emilia.

Hamlet returns to the stage in the churchyard scene (5.1), a large and obvious part of which is entertainment of a popular Elizabethan type. Death is the natural professional preoccupation of grave-diggers; yet the contrast between Man's brief life and his inevitable end is intensely painful and paradoxical – it can seem to him at once amusingly ironical and tragic. At first we feel the irony, the wry amusement, but the detached comments of the gravediggers, of Hamlet and Horatio, come nearer home with 'poor Yorick', and finally Ophelia's burial as a suicide shows an almost symbolic swing in Hamlet from 'philosophy' to the sudden grief of another bereavement; to throw off restraint and vie with the wild passion of Laertes seems a welcome release for Hamlet.

As the final scene of the play (5.2) opens, Hamlet, as always when speaking to Horatio, is quietly serious – the contrast with the emotional Prince of a few moments before is both theatrically and psychologically effective. In telling Horatio of his journey towards England, and of how he condemned Rosencrantz and Guildenstern to death, he says:

> Rashly,
> And prais'd be rashness for it – let us know
> Our indiscretion sometime serves us well,
> When our deep plots do pall; and that should learn us
> There's a divinity that shapes our ends,
> Rough-hew them how we will.[140]

The Hamlet who has returned to Denmark is apparently the Hamlet of 4.4, impatient of rational planning, eager to follow his impulses without thought. His view of rashness (with which, for once, Horatio agrees) expresses the same belief in impromptu action without 'deep plots', but with a significant development which anticipates his final position – he is suggesting that a man need not struggle (as he has) to control and plan his actions, for there is a greater power which over-rides all his efforts. When he tells Horatio how he tricked his two companions into death, however, he is eager to justify his action; apparently he acted quickly and ruthlessly against them, with no more pause for reflection, and less compunction, than when he killed Polonius. He still needs rational support in his problem of revenge on Claudius, and again appeals to Horatio:

> Does it not, think thee, stand me now upon –
> He that hath kill'd my king and whor'd my mother;
> Popp'd in between th'election and my hopes;
> Thrown out his angle for my proper [own] life,
> And with such coz'nage – is't not perfect conscience
> To quit him with this arm? And is't not to be damn'd
> To let this canker of our nature come
> In further evil?[141]

We are back with the earlier Hamlet, struggling to find a rational justification for the action to which his emotions have always impelled him. Horatio's reply is again non-committal, but practical:

> It must shortly known to him from England
> What is the issue of the business there.

It leads directly to Hamlet's reply:

It will be short; the interim is mine.
And a man's life's no more than to say 'one'.[142]

Shakespeare has here pointed to a new factor, but one linked to the killing of Rosencrantz and Guildenstern – the killing of the King is no longer a problem, but an immediate necessity for self-preservation. Hamlet's comment that he has enough time, for killing takes only a moment, has a moving and tragic irony, for we know of the plot to murder Hamlet shortly. After a long and slowly-developing play, a sudden time-urgency is tightening the action, as so often in a Shakespeare tragedy towards its close.

Yet, at this very moment of gathering speed and tension, the dramatist has the skilled professional audacity, the precise knowledge of how long one can safely distract an audience on the very brink of climax, to introduce the conversation with the egregious Osric, more than a hundred lines of very effective and popular contemporary satire. Such social satire, of course, always tends to take the audience from the world of the play into the real world outside the theatre, and it could be disastrous if too lengthily or clumsily done; when expertly timed and executed, as here, it increases the tension which follows.

But first we have Hamlet's last important self-revelation in the play. When Horatio, uneasy at Hamlet's mood, offers to stop the fencing-match, he replies:

Not a whit, we defy augury: there is a special providence
in the fall of a sparrow. If it be now, 'tis not to come;
if it be not to come, it will be now; if it be not now,
yet it will come – the readiness is all. Since no man
owes of [owns] aught he leaves, what is't to leave betimes?
Let be.[143]

'Let be'. . . . Here, at last, is a Hamlet who can contemplate death with the true rational control of emotion (here the fear of death) which he has been seeking throughout the play; with a strange and moving irony, 'the readiness is all' seems to relate to both killing and dying, and, yet again ironically, it is a readiness to act as providence determines. We are at the very heart of the complexity of human conflict, where, in achieving knowledge of one's self, one accepts that this self is subject to greater, unknown powers, and the conflict ends with that acceptance. At this point, all that remains to be done is to finish the action neatly and effectively, and add the traditional final comment.

The last phase of *Hamlet* is swift, marvellous visual stage-excitement greatly to the Elizabethan taste, as melodramtic as anything in contemporary or earlier revenge tragedy. This quick ending, with much sudden decisive action, killings, must inevitably seem strange as the ending of a play in which inaction was the essence of the effect. In fact Shakespeare, in fully satisfying his audience's natural expectation of some appropriate punishment for the King and Laertes, if not for the Queen, has also created a superb contrast, at once dramatic and full of an irony typical of the whole of the play.

The careful rational plotting of Claudius and Laertes is destroyed in a moment by 'chance', and Hamlet is subjected to sudden pressure, the only situation in which, as we have been shown, he can act instinctively and without thought. Thus Hamlet at last, at very last, kills the King, with a certain fine excess of double killing by sword and poison – yet this killing is not the final success of an ordinary revenge tragedy; in Hamlet's case, it marks the final failure of his long attempt to be the rational revenger, the last intrusion of passion. Perhaps he realises and regrets this, and perhaps this is what Shakespeare makes him refer to in his dying words to Horatio:

> O God! Horatio, what a wounded name,
> Things standing thus unknown, shall live behind me!

And so to the last, inevitable irony, seen in *Henry V* and *Julius Caesaer* and in all the main tragedies except, significantly, *Antony and Cleopatra*. The final comments are made, and suddenly the intensely personal struggles of the protagonist (and minor figures) are seen against the wider background of the continuing ordinary life of Mankind. So Hamlet, for all his efforts towards wisdom, Claudius, for all his scheming ambition, the Queen with all her passion and regret, Laertes, passionate too yet repentant, go from the world to join Ophelia, Polonius and the others – and what is the final result of all their grief and scheming and struggles? The state of Denmark remains much as it was, with its new King Fortinbras, who thus, despite himself, avenges Old Hamlet's killing of his father, the last irony of the play.

What, then, is the total effect of *Hamlet*? It is, of course, a play at two levels, both linked and interwoven with a complexity and skill unique even in Shakespeare. On the 'surface' level it has a great many constant theatrical excitements: a ghost, killings, madness assumed and real, a play within the play, moments of suspense and tension, contemporary satirical comment, and intriguing battles of words – in fact, the play is almost a complete compendium of the stage effects and dramatic techniques (especially methods of plot-manipulation) used by Shakespeare and his fellow dramatists. Presented directly in the Elizabethan manner, unhampered by elaborate scenery, the long intervals so profitable to a modern management, and the (to me) intrusive quirks of some modern producers, it moves steadily and excitingly to its end: Shakespeare's professional skill creates a constant sense of movement, curiosity and anticipation which makes even this long play seem far from prolix or boring. The dramatic verse is often rich with thought, not so much with emotion (in this respect *Hamlet* is the opposite of *Othello*), and a vast variety of prose, from the most formal to the most colloquial, sustains our sense of the presence of ordinary humanity, of many kinds, throughout the play. Accompanying, deepening and transforming this 'surface' appeal, is the 'inner' level of the drama, the deliberate, constant presentation, centred on Hamlet, of those personal and social inner doubts and conflicts which shape and colour the lives of us all in all ages. This tension, as we have seen, is not the product of human nature in isolation; it springs from the contact of that nature with the world and with the life of Man; so the world in which Hamlet lives, and his inner struggles, depend and react on each other, and by showing this in words and in actions, Shakespeare also achieves that wonderful interweaving of 'surface' and 'inner' worlds to which I have just referred.

When we experience such interweaving, something strange and memorable happens to us. We identify with the special human quality of Hamlet, the uniqueness of his nature, and so we are reminded that each of us, too, is unique in his own self. Yet we also realise that he is enduring the conflicts of human existence which assail us, and like us is striving to resolve those conflicts. All this takes place within the world of the 'surface' level, a world theatrically heightened but still, in all its essentials, recognisably our own world.

Thus we find ourselves constantly and simultaneously realising, in thought and feeling, both our true inner and outer self, set in the world we inhabit, and also the special, exotic and yet familiar Hamlet in his far-off but so near world of Elsinore. These two human beings, these two private and public worlds, intermingle within us; we each become ourselves and Hamlet, and, through these, all

171

Mankind – in a curious way (yet it is a common experience in the theatre), by leaving our self in order to feel and think more closely with Hamlet and the human nature he represents, we are finally brought back more deeply within our self, with a new awareness of that self and a disturbing yet exhilarating sense of having begun to 'take upon's the mystery of things'.

So the fact that *Hamlet*, like all Shakespeare's tragedies, is a story of failure in this world, in itself does not matter; it is the quality and ultimate importance of that failure which counts in our final impression. Indeed, in this respect *Hamlet* can be called 'positive' tragedy contrasted with *Macbeth* as 'negative' tragedy, for Hamlet fails in spite of his continual attempts to be something greater than the mere bloody revenger which his situation seems to demand, and he never gives in to that demand. Therefore, at the end of the play, the exhilaration which I have noted is enriched by a sense of the wonderful, stubborn, valiant determination which a mere man (one of the race of men to which we too belong) can show in pursuing his finer vision. Beside such determination, worldly failure has no real significance, and death is ultimately irrelevant.

Othello, the Moor of Venice

Othello (c1604) is a tragedy of jealousy within marriage, and therefore implicitly it is as concerned with sexual passion as *Romeo and Juliet*, to which (like *Antony and Cleopatra*) it is a kind of companion-piece: *Romeo and Juliet* showed the immediate results of passionate, ill-considered love and marriage; *Othello*, as we shall see, displays more fully and deeply a passionate, unthinking jealously arising largely from the weaknesses inherent in a hasty and unsuitable marriage in which there is yet great and genuine love. The difference between *Hamlet* and *Othello*, on the other hand, seems obvious at first sight: *Hamlet* has continuing emotion, but sexual passion plays only a small part in it; it is a slow-moving, long play, whereas *Othello*, only about 600 lines shorter, moves far more quickly and decisively, especially after the crucial 3.3. But there is a deep affinity between these two plays: both are concerned with a basic form of human conflict, that of feeling and reason, the irrational and the rational, and both in this context display and explore the human problem of revenge – in *Hamlet* throughout, and in *Othello* from 3.3. In both, revenge is the battleground of feeling and reason; in both, revenge is an intensely personal matter, in the former an almost secret quandary, in the latter a passionate, fully-revealed explosion within the nature of Othello.

The Elizabethan conception of jealousy in marriage was a most widely accepted part of their awareness of human dilemma. Inevitably, in a man's world, it was seen mainly from the man's point of view, and although *Othello* itself expresses the attitude to it of two contrasting wives, the major emphasis of the play is obviously on the man. The characteristic Elizabethan reaction to jealousy is expressed in a comment by William Painter in his very popular collection of stories, which Shakespeare knew and used for dramatic material:

> Yet will I not prayse, but rather accuse aboue al faulty men, those that be so fondly [foolishly and lovingly] Jealous, as eche thinge troubling their mindes, be affrayde of the Flyes very shadowe that buzze about their Faces. For by payning and molestinge theymselues with a thinge that so little doth please and content them, vntill manifest, and euident proofe appeare, they display the folly of their minde's imperfection, and the weaknesse of their Fantasy [fancy]. But where the fault is knowne, and the Vyce discouered, where the husbande seeth himselfe to receyue Damage in the soundest part of his moueable goods, reason is that he therein be aduised by timely deliberation and sage foresight, rather than with headlong fury, and raging rashnesse to hazard the losse of his honour, and the ruine of his life and goods.[144]

To this should be added comments in another well-known collection of stories, Sir Geoffrey Fenton's *Certain Tragical Discourses*:

> For what is he so ignorant in the passions of love
> that will not confess that jealousy is an evil exceeding
> all the torments of the world, supplanting oftentimes both
> wit and reason in the most wise that be. . . .
> In like sort, what greater sign or argument can a man
> give of his own folly, than to believe that to be true, which
> is but doubtful, and yielding rashly to the resolution
> and sentence of his own conceits [fancies], thinks his wife
> as light of the sear [easily tempted] and apt to deceive him,
> as he is ready to admit sinister suspicion; which proceeds
> but of an imperfection in himself, judging the disposition

of another by his own complexion [temperament].[145]

For an Elizabethan, jealousy not only creates a situation where passion will inevitably war against reason, and trouble will arise if reason is not in control of passion, but it may also cause an entirely imaginary situation, the product of dangerous fancies. If jealousy is proved to be well-based, it can affect a man's public reputation as well as his private life, if the matter is not handled with wisdom. It is a common danger to both the private and the public man. Obviously, as so many Elizabethan tales of jealousy show us, it is linked to the contemporary male view of love as both desired and feared, of woman as possible bliss and possible purgatory,[146] of marriage as perhaps desirable, but also as a burdensome way of satisfying desire.[147] All these anxieties are forms of personal discord in any age.

Thus for Elizabethan men, and women, jealousy was a very serious matter, but not so much in England, they felt, as in Italy, where husbands were notoriously quick to suspect their wives, and infamously brutal in punishing them. All the popular Elizabethan tales of passionate love and jealousy were set, like *Othello*, in Italy. Yet in the Italianate English passion-drama of Shakespeare's time, married jealousy, as such, is rare; indeed, *Othello* is the only Elizabethan-Jacobean tragedy specifically and entirely devoted to this subject, apart from the special case of *A Woman Killed With Kindness* (1603), where the husband's jealous revenge is important only by its absence.

Like all forms of human incongruity which are common and feared, marital jealousy was often laughed at by Elizabethans; seen from the outside as the mark of the cuckold, it was of course a popular material for jokes. Jonson's Kitely is the best example early in Shakespeare's career of the comic 'type' of the jealous husband; Shakespeare's Ford, in *The Merry Wives of Windsor*, because he is more humanly presented than Kitely, is less purely funny, and at times almost moving. The comic potential of marital jealousy should be remembered even in considering *Othello* (especially 4.1); all the greatest Shakespearean tragedy derives some of its deepest effect from the latent possibility of comedy, for the same struggle that produces tragedy could evoke comedy if viewed differently, and comedy, too, has its latent tragedy.

It is against this background of Elizabethan conceptions of love, jealousy, tragedy and comedy, that *Othello* must be considered, and in some detail.

174

A tragedy of jealousy in marriage is a tragedy of marriage, and it is important to appreciate how closely, in the preparatory part of this play, Shakespeare deals with the nature of the Othello–Desdemona marriage. It is significant that in Shakespeare's main source for *Othello*, Disdemona says to the Ensign's wife (i.e. Emilia), when the jealous Moor begins to change towards her:

> I fear greatly that I shall be a warning to young
> girls not to marry against their parents' wishes; and
> Italian ladies will learn by my example not to tie
> themselves to a man whom Nature, Heaven, and manner of
> life separate from us.[148]

This almost seems to suggest the clear and precise indication that the dramatist gives of those qualities of the marriage which most members of his audience would recognise as dangerously weakening its stability, making it peculiarly vulnerable to jealousy and collapse.[149] To begin with, the marriage is between a black man and a white woman: Iago uses the fact to rouse Brabantio in the first scene of the play; his calculated emphasis on the bestial quality of such a coupling, and Brabantio's repeated references to the unnaturalness of it, certainly express the response of many of the Elizabethan audience. With this are associated further facts which shock the father: Desdemona has married without his knowledge or consent, and, in addition, has gone outside her class (indeed, outside her race); moreover, she is young and Othello is much older, and Shakespeare does not ignore the sexual implications of the fact. When Desdemona is urging the Venetian Duke and Senators to let her go to Cyprus with her husband, she says:

> That I did love the Moor to live with him,
> My downright violence and storm of fortunes
> May trumpet to the world. My heart's subdu'd
> Even to the very quality of my lord:
> I saw Othello's visage in his mind;
> And to his honours and his valiant parts
> Did I my soul and fortunes consecrate.
> So that, dear lords, if I be left behind,
> A moth of peace, and he go to the war,
> The rites for why I love him are bereft me,
> And I a heavy interim shall support
> By his dear absence. Let me go with him.[150]

The speech has several significant indications of her attitude to the marriage. The first sentence connects 'the Moor' with her own active and disturbing flouting of 'the world', her open display of her wish to be with him; the following lines imply a defence of Othello's blackness by stressing that for her his real self is 'in his mind' (as indeed the play shows), and claim, with tragic irony, that she married him to serve his 'honours and his valiant parts' as a soldier; finally she returns to her first point, that, if separated from him, she will not be sharing his life, and will miss him. Without undue emphasis on 'The rites for why I love him are bereft me',[151] it is clear that the passage as a whole expresses a young girl's need to be with the admired and beloved husband whom she has just married; I cannot believe that any normally human audience, certainly not an Elizabethan one, would not understand that part of that need is sexual. Certainly Othello, supporting her plea, immediately seeks to reassure the Duke and Senators on that very point, but with regard to himself:

> Let her have your voice.
> Vouch with me, heaven, I therefore beg it not
> To please the palate of my appetite;
> Nor to comply with heat [desire] – the young affects
> In me defunct – and proper satisfaction;
> But to be free and bounteous to her mind.[152]

He goes on to deny emphatically that 'light-wing'd toys/Of feather'd Cupid' can ever, should ever, divert him from his serious professional duties. Apart from the deep tragic irony of his last claim (but this whole scene before the Senate is packed with such ironies), the tone of both Othello and Desdemona must cause doubt of the firm basis of a marriage in which the girl is young, idealistic and sexually passionate, and the man is no longer young, disclaims any great sexual need, and despises any man who would put the demands of marriage before those of his profession. This disturbing difference of attitudes between husband and wife has already been suggested, in another form, in Othello's account of how he and Desdemona came to love (when he was a trusted guest in her father's house, as an Elizabethan would have noted):

> She wish'd she had not heard it; yet she wish'd
> That heaven had made her such a man. She thank'd me;
> And bade me, if I had a friend that lov'd her,
> I should but teach him how to tell my story,

176

> And that would woo her. Upon this hint I spake;
> She lov'd me for the dangers I had pass'd;
> And I lov'd her that she did pity them.[153]

The simple, protected girl had, in fact, proposed to this exciting stranger (as Miranda does to Ferdinand) – the audience would have seen the provocative ambiguity of 'she wish'd/That heaven had made her such a man' – and Othello had taken the plain hint. The last two lines also suggest the very human, but fragile, basis of Othello's love, in origin at least a surprised and gratified response to being so plainly loved by this beautiful young patrician. The professional foreign soldier's inexperience of young, Venetian 'society' girls, suggested here and directly used by Iago in 3.3, is linked to the soldier's natural attitude to marriage. It is expressed first to Iago in 1.2.:

> For know, Iago,
> But that I love the gentle Desdemona,
> I would not my unhoused free condition
> Put into circumscription and confine
> For the sea's worth.[154]

This is one professional soldier talking to another, expressing their common difficulty, the male's conflict between the fear of the loss of freedom and the joy of loving, and especially the essential male independence of the solider as against the gentle influence of love which Othello condemned to the Venetian Senate. When later, in 3.3, Othello is reacting passionately to the feeling that Desdemona may be false, is false, the dramatist gives him a magnificently stirring (yet tragically naïve) description of the glories of martial life as a born soldier sees them.

Thus, by the end of Act 1, Shakespeare has presented in quite exceptional detail the human incongruity which is for the moment dormant within the marriage. There is no tragedy yet, merely the carefully formed suggestion that the conditions for possible tragedy exist side by side with the potential goodness of the obvious love of these two; always in Shakespearean tragedy there is the sense that human nature is open both to good and to evil influences, and 'the pity of it' that in a particular case the evil influences are able, largely if not finally, to affect that human nature.

In *Othello* the possibly evil influence, and its nature, is also established by the end of Act 1, as an essential part of the preparation for later tragedy. The secular development of moral tragedy has by now taught both Shakespeare and his audience that in real life the Devil does not appear in person, an embodied 'pure' evil, to encourage the evil sides of Man's nature against the good. Iago is certainly nearer to portraying the moral essence of the old stage devil than any other Shakespearean villain, but he nevertheless represents evil from within human nature, not from outside. He is not inhuman; his malignity is not motiveless (*pace* Coleridge), except in the sense that even simple beings, and Iago is far from simple, rarely find clear logical reasons for their impulses towards evil – or towards good. The potentialities for evil of Iago are being suggested in Act 1 side by side with those susceptibilities in Othello and Desdemona (separately and in marriage) upon which evil may work successfully. Iago's early appearance in 1.1 shows him, at first, as a type of man known to Elizabethans and to every age since, an experienced professional soldier rightly angry at losing promotion in favour of a gentleman soldier. A contemporary writer shows that Iago's sense of unfair treatment was not uncommon or unjustified:

> But in England we neuer consider, neyther of his
> [a soldier's] actions, nor of his knowledge and
> experience: but most commonly our Captaines are
> chosen, more for fauour then for knowledge: more for
> freendship, then for experience: for if they have a
> good opinion of him, they neuer consider his desert,
> whether he be a man able to discharge his place or no.[155]

Shakespeare shows Iago frankly admitting his hatred of his leader, the 'Moor' which he is hiding for his own ends. Already he is plainly not a nice man; the Elizabethan will have begun to suspect that he is a 'malcontent', a human type now becoming a popular excitement in drama, the man who delights in destroying social and personal harmony;[156] within a few minutes, in fact, he is ending for ever Brabantio's complacent trust in his daughter. Further touches to Iago's duplicity and cynicism are added as Act 1 proceeds, but the essence of his nature, his attitude to life, is made clear at the end of 1.3 in his lecturing of Roderigo (where he seems as sincere as he can be); it follows the Venetian Senate's expedient favouring of Othello, and its brushing aside of Brabantio's heart-break. 'I never found a man that knew how to love himself . . .' he says, and later:

> Virtue? A fig! 'Tis in ourselves that we are thus or thus.
> Our bodies are our gardens to the which our wills are

gardeners ... the power and corrigible authority of this [of how to rule our action] lies in our wills. If the balance of our lives had not one scale of reason to poise [balance] another of sensuality, the blood and baseness of our natures would conduct us to most preposterous [illogical] conclusions. But we have reason to cool our raging motions, our carnal stings, our unbitted lusts; whereof I take this that you call love to be a sect or scion.

ROD. It cannot be.

IAGO It is merely a lust of the blood and a permission of the will.

Here, it seems at first, is a moral view with which every decent Elizabethan must agree – of course one should control one's sensuality by one's reason. But it becomes suspect when Iago goes on to apply it to Roderigo's genuine, but foolish, love for Desdemona (and the actor should show how deeply it shocks him). If Iago can see love as nothing but lust, indistinguishable from lust, he is a man of reason without feeling, far more dangerous to others than a man of passion without reason. Such a man, today, might be admired as an 'enlightened realist', but few Elizabethans would see him as other than an aberration from the human norm, a being not only cut off from human feeling, but one whose reason, cold, arrogant and calculating, sought to reduce virtue, love, human goodness, to its own cynical level – a kind of Machiavelli of private life. Here, for Elizabethans, is the ultimate perversion of the divine power of reason which raised Man above the beasts. Most Shakespearean villains have some passion and some cunning – one might say that they are reasonably beastly – but Iago uses reason to make himself, in the end, worse than a beast, a would-be rational machine deliberately seeking to cut itself off from humanity, and choosing evil. Predictably, as we shall see, Iago is finally entrapped and destroyed by his own lack of human feeling.

So it is this Iago, with his scorn of love and, indeed, of all emotion, who intrudes into a marriage built on unreason and incompatibility yet also on love, creating a situation in which true and complete love is the only possible protection. All the play after Act 1 is a steady dramatic exploration of how this marriage fares against Iago (and, in a sense, against Othello and Desdemona themselves), and of the inevitable question whether he can destroy this soldier-lover and the love which he despises. Iago's first soliloquy, at the end of 1.3, is essential to the dramatist's exposition. On one level, it is the soliloquy as 'villainous self-display', popular from the old Vice onwards, but now more subtle. On another level, it finally establishes the nature of Iago as we must know him for the rest of the play. That nature is shown functionally rather than descriptively; if the play is to have its effective logic of human behaviour (the foundation of Shakespeare's method), it is important for us to feel what kind of Iago is postulated, but even more important to know how such an Iago, because he is such, sees those he will attack, for his attack, and its result, will be determined by his view of them. Shortly before this soliloquy, Iago has described Desdemona, as he sees her, to Roderigo, in order of course to encourage his hopes of seducing her, and benefit from them, but we feel that the Iago we are beginning to know would see her like this — as no more than a mere woman caught in sexual passion, who will soon choose a younger man. In his soliloquy, Iago describes Cassio as just a lady's man who will make an ideal suspect for a jealous Othello. And this Othello? A suggestible, naïve fool who trusts everyone's honesty, an easy victim for a really intelligent rational man. Very effectively, the dramatist is making Iago not only display, but betray himself; we already know that Othello and his wife are not wholly like this. Through the rest of the play we shall continue to realise how true, and yet how deeply false, is Iago's conception of his victims, and a main irony of the play will increasingly spring from this. In so far as Othello and Desdemona are indeed foolish and simple, hopelessly ill-equipped against Iago, the play is potentially a cruel 'comedy' of human inadequacy and self-ignorance, akin to *Troilus and Cressida*; in so far as they show, through the very suffering their weaknesses entail, that human beings can be admirable in failure (perhaps most truly admirable only then) they give the play, finally, the tragic effect of that obstinate hope which is a saving grace of our human condition.

In the next scene (2.1) we begin to see the consequences of everything established in Act 1. The action has been transferred to Cyprus, starting that claustrophobic sense of wide human concerns trapped inside a closed physical setting which gives the play part of its special quality. Cassio shows himself a typical fashionable gentleman (one can understand Iago's earlier irritation); we note the respect shown to the black Governor of the island. There is the contrast between Othello and Desdemona as newly-weds, very concerned with their love, and the bitter worldly cynicism of a still outwardly respectful Iago which is also a conventional source of laughter almost in the Thersites vein. The opposing forces of fine unreason (love, trust, hope) are ranged against the forces of narrow, destructive reason (the strength of Iago's limited view of life), and the balance is a delicate one. Shakespeare has certainly enlisted our sympathy for the lovers, but Iago is far from unbelievable – his evil now begins to grow the more impressive because it is the misuse of a reasoning which we must acknowledge. Iago, paradoxically, is often a great exponent of the power of truth, as we shall see, but always it is truth used falsely, out of its context, and therefore more dangerous than plain lying. Logically, for Iago's narrow reason, it is likely that the Moor and the young white girl will be divorced by the more natural appeal of Cassio to her – Iago is using the actual weaknesses of the marriage as we have seen them, but with his own distortion. By the end of the scene, Iago has formed the outline of his plan. Cassio is to be used to create jealousy in the Moor, and that jealousy will depend on the fact that he is 'A most dear husband' to Desdemona (the ambiguity grows with the play). The power of jealousy springs from the power of the love from which it derives, and which it seeks to destroy; Iago's passing references to suspicions of his wife's infidelity with Othello or Cassio are a casual self-justification with no suggestion of real love for Emilia – the man of 'pure' reason cannot love, and so is not truly jealous. The scene ends with Iago's second soliloquy, the final words of which offer an insight into his future method of evil:

> 'Tis here, but yet confus'd:
> Knavery's plain face is never seen till us'd.

Again, through the obvious, old-fashioned appeal of the self-conscious villain, there emerges a further ambiguity. The very strength of Iago's evil is that its 'plain face' is not seen by the victims when in use, but only by the audience; but the audience is both within Othello and Desdemona, sharing their innocent blindness, and outside them, observing and fully aware of Iago's destructive purpose. These lines also suggest the curious fact about Iago, that he is perhaps the greatest improviser of all Shakespeare's villains. As we have just seen, he adopts a general strategy in which to work, but time and again his tactics are to develop opportunities, to respond to sudden chances. In other words, he encourages and helps his victims to destroy themselves, and succeeds because he continually adapts his methods to the nature of the victim.

Between 2.1 and the turning-point of the play in 3.3, four scenes show the first step in Iago's plan, the necessary preparation for his direct assault on Othello's trust in Desdemona. Act 2, Scene 3, is by far the longest and the most important of these four. When Othello and his bride have gone to bed, Cassio's weak head for drink proves just the kind of human weakness on which Iago thrives. Iago seizes upon it, telling us in his third soliloquy how he can use it, with Roderigo's blind help, against Cassio. Iago well knows the human weaknesses of others, and, with only a little assistance from him, Cassio in fact acts quite indefensibly for a senior officer in charge at night of a community at war. Othello and Desdemona are aroused from their first night of marriage, and his reaction (fuelled by Iago's characteristic selective use of truth and suggestion) is just what Iago knew it would be,[157] a passionate mixture of the professional soldier's disgust at Cassio's weakness, and the husband's anger at having his bride disturbed. It is ironic that the General who rightly punishes Cassio's failure to control himself, should himself suggest that he, too, is allowing his reason to falter:

> Now, by heaven,
> My blood begins my safer guides to rule;
> And passion, having my best judgment collied [affected]
> Assays to lead the way.[158]

From this point onwards, even if not before, we are aware that part of Othello's vulnerable inner confusion is the conflict between his nature as 'private' man and his role as 'public' man. I shall concentrate attention on more important conflicts in him, but we are always conscious of the presence of this stress. In this connection we must realise the importance, in production, of emphasising Othello's physical 'presence' as the great leader, however strange it may later appear; if this is not made clear, the final destruction of the dominant 'public' man by the inner 'private' man will lose much of its proper force.

He deals with Cassio summarily, depending of course on Iago's 'honesty' for an understanding of what has happened. It is typical of Iago that soon after he can easily persuade the shocked and ashamed Cassio to seek help from Desdemona to change her husband's decision; he has only to use Cassio's emotions, directing them in the required path; in doing so, he can make very sound comments on 'reputation', just as later the most noble opposite sentiments about 'good name' when the manipulation of Othello requires them.[159]

When Cassio goes out, Iago comes down-stage to confide in the audience in his fourth soliloquy. His evil is now gathering momentum towards the point early in 3.3 when he will begin to attack Othello directly; it is only some ten minutes' acting-time away as Iago begins the soliloquy, and this is the essential display, before that, of the moral nature of his evil. At the core of the speech lie the following lines, once again old-fashioned in their naïve sudden switch to the audience's external moral standards, but the pivot of deeper truth around which the whole speech turns:

> Divinity of hell!
> When devils will their blackest sins put on,
> They do suggest at first with heavenly shows,
> As I do now.[160]

To an Elizabethan audience especially, the main dreadful point of the speech is that it shows Iago preparing to use what in traditional Christian terms is an ultimate form of evil, the deliberate perversion of the good. Good advice has been used for evil ends; now the generous nature of Desdemona is to be an instrument of evil:

> And by how much she strives to do him good
> She shall undo her credit with the Moor.
> So will I turn her virtue into pitch; — *into black*
> And out of her own goodness make the net
> That shall enmesh them all.[161]

Iago, characteristically, sees himself as the manipulator working 'by wit', cold intelligence, on these innocent, loving[162] (and therefore vulnerable) ordinary human beings; here is the near-megalomania, the contemptuous arrogance, of the amoral rational man untouched by feeling; today, perhaps we feel the danger and evil of it even more deeply than the Elizabethans, in social and political contexts undreamt-of by them.

There follows a fourth display of Iago's cunning control over Roderigo, a final comment by Iago on how he will get Othello to see Cassio asking Desdemona's aid, and the scene ends. Then there are two scenes (3.1 and 3.2) in which Cassio moves towards the innocent, but fatal, plea to Desdemona (with the broad 'comic' moment of the musicians and the clown before the turn into tragedy), and the vivid, six-line, final glimpse (3.2) of the old Othello, the capable commander who is about to be disrupted.

Then 3.3 opens, with Desdemona warmly agreeing to help Cassio, as Iago knew she would; Cassio, uneasy and ashamed, naturally

[marginalia: knowing his using honesty in a false manner]

183

leaves quickly when Othello appears with Iago. As he does so, Iago of course quickly uses this innocent reaction; he makes the first, tentative, direct movement against Othello:

IAGO   Ha! I like not that.

OTH.   What dost thou say?

IAGO   Nothing, my lord; or if – I know not what.

OTH.   Was not that Cassio parted from my wife?

IAGO   Cassio, my lord! No, sure, I cannot think it,
            That he would sneak away so guilty-like,
            Seeing your coming.

This is enough for the moment; the 'doubt' around Cassio has been neatly touched on, and will soon be developed. Meanwhile Desdemona, with her impulsive warmth, proceeds to drive even her devoted husband to near-irritation by her insistence that he must see Cassio soon,[163] and in doing so she mentions, not only that Cassio was a go-between in their wooing, but also that he had to defend his friend against her criticism. She has scarcely gone off with Emilia, Othello has only just uttered perhaps the most terrible of Shakespeare's uses of tragic irony:

> Excellent wretch! Perdition catch my soul
> But I do love thee; and when I love thee not
> Chaos is come again

when Iago delicately picks up the weapon that Desdemona has let fall:

IAGO   Did Michael Cassio, when you woo'd my lady,
            Know of your love?

OTH.   He did, from first to last. Why dost thou ask?

IAGO   But for a satisfaction of my thought –
            No further harm.

OTH   Why of thy thought, Iago?

These last five words are the turning-point of the turning-point of the play, in human truth the beginning of the actual tragedy of Othello. We have all met people who must know the whole truth, who cannot 'leave well alone' (J.B. Priestley's 'Dangerous Corner' is built on the dangers of the human error that one can ever know the whole truth about life); Othello, perhaps suitably as a military leader, is given this quality by his creator, and it leads him into Iago's grasp. After this innocent remark, we know that the nature of Othello is exactly right for Iago's purpose, and Iago instantly pursues the line of attack offered him. Othello, by his nature, must see Iago's careful hinting as the 'honest' man's caution, and Iago can actually get Othello to urge him to do precisely what he wishes to do, to give his 'worst of thoughts/The worst of words'. The Elizabethan would see a great leader's subordinate working to convince him that he is a cuckold, and would understand that he must feel his way (I suppose that even in military circles today, Iago would need to be careful). But soon he can be bolder, can even (with his characteristic use of truth) frankly tell Othello that his suspicions are perhaps caused by his own vicious nature, and warn him of the agony he plans for Othello:

> It were not for your quiet nor your good,
> Nor for my manhood, honesty, or wisdom,
> To let you know my thoughts.

Othello's impatience is beginning to rise – he ignores Iago's sententious moralising on 'good name', the mark of course of the 'honest' man:

OTH.   By heaven, I'll know thy thoughts.
IAGO   You cannot, if my heart were in your hand;
        Nor shall not, whilst 'tis in my custody.
OTH.   Ha!

At this moment, the first inkling of the suggested jealousy enters Othello's mind; Iago immediately fixes it there with what sounds like a warning, but is really an exact description of the evil that Othello can no longer avoid:

IAGO   O, beware, my lord, of jealousy;
        It is the green-ey'd monster which doth mock
        The meat it feeds on. That cuckold lives in bliss
        Who, certain of his fate, loves not his wronger;
        But, O, what damned minutes tells he o'er
        Who dotes, yet doubts, suspects, yet strongly loves!
OTH.   O misery!

Othello is now entering the heart of that form of human conflict which we call 'jealousy'. It springs from love, which is irrational, and unless the infidelity is certain, it too must always remain irrational. When Othello proceeds to try to reassure himself by a proud refusal to remain in doubt, and by remembering his wife's many goodnesses, we know the confusion of the man; his reason is at war with his feelings, and he can only demand proof. Iago is again quick to respond to Othello's reaction; of course he has no proof (he can even admit this soon, and turn it to his advantage), but suggestion twisting truth is his way, and equally effective. So he first impresses the innocent Othello with his description of the immorality of Venetian wives, and then reminds him of the fact that his wife, so young a woman, by marrying him deceived her father and revealed the love she had previously hidden from him: the actual weaknesses of the marriage are now proving effective material for Iago. For a moment or two he enjoys his victim's agony (he even comments on it to the victim: 'I see this hath a little dash'd your spirits'), and then Othello gives the cue he can use, with his usual deadly quickness of mind, to emphasise the marriage further:

OTH.	And yet, how nature erring from itself –
IAGO	Ay, there's the point: as – to be bold with you –
	Not to affect [like] many proposed matches
	Of her own clime, complexion, and degree,
	Whereto we see in all things nature tends –
	Foh! one may smell in such a will [desire] most rank,
	Foul disproportion, thoughts unnatural.
	But pardon me – I do not in position
	Distinctly speak of her; though I may fear
	Her will, recoiling to her better judgment,
	May fall to match you with her country forms,
	And happily [haply, perhaps] repent.

Shortly after this, Iago leaves Othello alone, inevitably to explore this agony which has invaded his being. Thus he speaks his first soliloquy. It is symptomatic of the man and his situation that it is made up of attempts at reasonable thinking mingled with feeling. He takes as a fact Iago's honesty, accepts as true his own blackness, lack of social charm, and even his age, but with this he shows passion against this possibly uncontrollable creature, his wife; he despairs at his loss of her, is disgusted at the mystery of women's hidden desires, and recoils from the idea of physically sharing his wife with another man. All these are common signs of the disease, but his soliloquy ends on something peculiar to himself; he seems to grasp at a kind of pride that, as a great man, he is more susceptible to the pains of jealousy (great ones feel greatly), more a target for destiny – but of course as Shakespeare's tragedies always show, the only 'destiny' is the nature of such a man in such a situation.

Then comes the essential 'break' in 3.3, a brief movement away from the contest of Othello and Iago; it gives a reminder to Othello, and to the audience, of the real Desdemona, it starts the handkerchief theme (again, Shakespeare as 'chance'), and finally it suggests time passes before Othello returns to Iago, time in which jealousy has worked further into him. It helps to make this long scene one of the dramatist's finest pieces of stage-craft.

As Othello enters at the rear of the Elizabethan stage, Iago is standing at the front, and comments as the Moor slowly approaches him, coming down-stage:

> Look where he comes! Not poppy, nor mandragora,
> Nor all the drowsy syrups of the world,
> Shall ever medicine thee to that sweet sleep
> Which thou owed'st [owned'st] yesterday.

These four lines exemplify the secret of the dramatist's power over his audience, a power springing from deep within our awareness of the paradoxes of life; in them are fused two opposites, our sense of Man's unique gift of cruelty (for Iago describes his victim's suffering with a terrible detached callousness), and our wonder at the quiet glory that Man can create from 'mere' words and rhythms.

When Othello speaks once more to Iago, he shows at once that he has reached what, for Iago, is a dangerous stage in this creeping sickness of jealousy so minutely presented by the dramatist. His agony is at the point where he will grasp at any relief from doubt, even an acceptance of his cuckoldry. Iago for once speaks sincerely when he says: 'I am sorry to hear this'; a victim who accepts his position is no victim for Iago; he cannot create disaster around a man who (like Iago himself) tolerates the possibility of a faithless wife. But Othello, of course, is not an Iago; he loves Desdemona, and immediately his pain swings into a fresh area of suffering: in his marriage there has been, from the beginning, the incompatibility between the soldier's successful professional career, and the narrower world of matrimony, and now the conflict of jealousy seizes upon this. The lines beginning 'O now for ever/Farewell the tranquil mind' say it all. Othello looks at his former life, the calmly routine, excitingly active, professional soldier's life; all the glory and honour of his martial skills, his assured position among duties which this essentially simple man can understand and handle, are now confronted with himself as the confused and contemptible cuckold, outwitted and mocked: if this is true, certainly 'Othello's occupation's gone'.

Now comes the last twist of human truth in this closely packed scene. Othello moves into the last stage, the final madness, of jealousy, in which the passion of anger joins with the absurd 'reason' of a demand for proof. A good actor should show a subtle relaxation, a quick touch of relief in Iago when Othello threatens him and demands certain evidence of his wife's infidelity: it tells him that he is fast in the trap, blind to real reason. Iago responds perfectly. First a great parade of his 'honesty', so that now he boldly sets Othello's trust in this 'honesty' against his trust in Desdemona's, and knows that, by the reversed values he has established, his 'honesty' will prevail. Then a quiet display of the final deadend into which he has led Othello, the ultimate logical madness of reason—unreason in jealousy, the fact that, rationally, the only sure proof that a man can have of his wife's infidelity is to see her copulating with her lover, the one proof that, emotionally, even jealousy, when it springs from true love, cannot contemplate.[164] So Iago, for the first time in this scene, can use complete falsehood to offer Othello a less terrible 'proof' which he is only too ready to accept: the pitiably thin account of Cassio talking in his sleep, the offhand reference to seeing Cassio with Desdemona's handkerchief, are quite enough, now, to send Othello into wildly passionate conviction of her falsity. As poor worldly-wise Emilia says in the next scene (3.4) about 'jealous souls':

> They are not ever jealous for the cause,
> But jealous for they are jealous.[165]

So this great scene ends at last with (Othello fully possessed by jealousy – and by Iago.) The final words, Iago's 'I am your own for ever', suggest a deep and disturbing human truth; as Dostoievsky's Raskolnikov discovered, the aggressor, by the very act of aggression, becomes inescapably bound to his victim; from now almost to the end, Iago and Othello are to be as closely dependent upon each other as if they were lovers – indeed, evil is a perverse mirror-image of love.

So much, for the moment, for the establishing and growth of Othello's jealousy. In the next scene (3.4) the Moor has a passage of effectively dramatic, mounting anger with Desdemona, but it is to her that our main attention is directed. Shakespeare must show her reaction to the changed nature of Othello; to understand the third member of the trio, the innocent centre of the storm, is vital to a complete grasp of the situation. In *The Winter's Tale*, the wrongfully suspected wife is of a different calibre from Desdemona, a more mature heroine well able to understand the danger and to protest her innocence – this is a far simpler, even melodramatic, jealousy situation. In *Othello* Desdemona has been shown from the beginning as the loving young girl, sincerely devoted to her Moor; but her very innocence and love broke her father's heart, and now her almost complete inability to understand or complain of her husband must be displayed as an ironic factor in Iago's success, and finally in her own death. Her qualities are a vital part of her tragic significance in the play. This is a tragedy in which the great Commander is ultimately brought to murder, at least partly by his incongruous inability to judge correctly the characters of his close companion and of his wife, his lack of rational control over his passions, and his ignorance of the realities of true love (towards the end of the play 'noble' Othello becomes as ironic as 'honest' Iago). Desdemona's innocence matches his, and reinforces its tragic effect; it strengthens our growing feeling of the play as showing an almost childlike goodness systematically destroyed by a calculating evil. Shakespeare runs a serious risk here; his age, his audience, enjoy innocent victims, but to make her and Othello simpletons rather than simple would be disaster; there is no tragedy (although perhaps much pathos) where evil has merely puppets to play with.

In 3.4, then, Shakespeare goes as far as he dares in showing Desdemona's incomprehension of her situation; he wisely shows also that she can respond, if only partly, to the realistic judgements of more worldly people, including of course Iago himself. The contrast between her and Emilia is nicely effective in emphasising both her kinship with ordinary life and her remoteness from it, in fact her strange likeness to Othello.

In 4.1 Iago is at work again on Othello; he cannot allow the jealousy to cool, and he has to prepare and execute the 'handkerchief trick' on his victim. The disintegration of Othello's nature is continuing, and here it reaches a pitch of confused passion that is near to actual insanity. The Elizabethans knew, as we do, that the opposing forces within our being are always capable, if in great enough conflict, of driving us to that ultimate incongruity (yet escape from incongruity) which is madness. Othello has now for some time been trying to reconcile irreconcilables: the great Captain and the ignoble cuckold, the admired husband and the deceived fool, the innocent Desdemona and the lustful cheat; the need to kill the cheat and the horror of killing a Desdemona. Othello does not at this point find the refuge of madness, as Lear does, but later, as we shall see, he is very close to doing so. For the moment, when Iago, as if annoyed that his victim has dared to forget the handkerchief, increases his agony by a reminder of the physical implications of infidelity, Othello obtains a brief release in unconsciousness. This of course, like so many such examples of the dramatist's technique, is both psychologically true in itself, and technically necessary, for Iago has to prepare the talk with Cassio. Othello recovers, and Iago is now so sure of his mastery that he can dare to say to him reprovingly:

> Whilst you were here o'erwhelmed with your grief –
> A passion most unsuiting such a man –.[166]

So the curious episode of Othello observing, but not hearing completely, the conversation between Iago and Cassio takes place. Iago can now further convince Othello's jealousy by the ludicrous 'proof' of a sequence which is intended by the dramatist, I believe, to come near to farce, and which should be played at moments for laughter. It is obvious, but clever and entertaining theatre, but when we see the 'noble' Moor crouching in the background, moving at Iago's gesture, thrown into passion by an innocent laugh, and finally completely convinced by this charade, we feel the full force of Othello's decline, and laughter and tragic sorrow are mingled in a special paradox which lies at the root of all our lives. There follows another phase of the Moor's path to murder; his inner struggle again shows itself. One part of Othello is passionately moved to thoughts of killing his wife, yet another is still lingering over the reality of her gentle, womanly ways. Once more, Iago must turn the Moor from these dangerously loving feelings:

OTH.	Hang her! I do but say what she is: so delicate with her needle, an admirable musician – O, she will sing the savageness out of a bear! – of so high and plenteous wit and invention.
IAGO	She's the worse for all this.
OTH.	O, a thousand, a thousand times – and then of so gentle a condition.
IAGO	Ay, too gentle.
OTH.	Nay, that's certain. But yet the pity of it, Iago! O, Iago, the pity of it, Iago!
IAGO	If you be so fond [foolish and loving] over her iniquity, give her

                    patent to offend, for, if it touch not you, it
                    comes near nobody.
OTH.   I will chop her into messes. Cuckold me![167]

Now that Desdemona's evil has become a 'fact', on it Iago can
quickly base a distorted image of her in which, by perverted logic,
Iago's reason manipulating Othello's emotion, true goodnesses are
become additional forms of evil. Othello moves on to plans of actual
murder 'this night' – the tragic process is beginning to quicken
towards its end.

The outside world, the 'political' scene in which the Moor is still
outwardly an important figure, has been latent for what seems a long
time, with only a brief poignant reference to it in Othello's 'farewell'
speech. Now 4.1 ends with the entry of Lodovico bringing letters
from Venice, and the episode in which the Moor, having learnt that
he is to return, leaving Cassio in his place as Governor of Cyprus,
suddenly loses publicly his self-control at an innocently ambiguous
remark from Desdemona, and publicly strikes her. A modern audience sees this action as a brutal sign of how far Iago has developed
the passionate savagery of Othello, and (I hope) feels outraged. The
Elizabethan audience would certainly feel this, but also something
more. A writer of one of the popular contemporary books of
'packaged wisdom' had recently offered aphorisms on 'The Husband's dutie to his wife', among which appeared:

> 3. As it is meere folly for a Husband to praise and
> commend his wife in company: So it is as dangerous to
> checke and reproue her before witnesse.[168]

This feeling that Othello is very unwise as well as cruel to hit his wife,
is of course accompanied by the shock of seeing a man in authority
unable to control himself in public. As another 'moral philosopher'
said in a well-known book of the time:

> ... Secondly, a Generall must be a man of authoritie,
> by reason that γ nothing is more available [useful] in   γ cic pro
> the ordering of battels, then authority. Thirdly, he   lege Maneli
> ought to be temperate: for how can he gouerne others,
> that cannot rule his own affections [feelings]?[169]

An Elizabethan would have well understood the Venetian envoy's
surprise, and his final remark (after Iago's dark hints at worse
faults): 'I am sorry that I am deceiv'd in him'. The disruption of the

'private' man has now spread out to the 'public' man; Othello is now almost destroyed as a military leader no less than as a husband.

There follows a scene (4.2) which is essentially an amplification of the significance of that physical striking of Desdemona. The feelings of Othello are rapidly coarsening under the many ugly suggestions of Iago. More than this, Othello is now seeking desperately to have his view of his wife's cheapness confirmed by her own confession (how ironic that, as we have seen, he is a man who cannot bear half the truth!). There is still, too, a lingering doubt in him, part of that sense of her loveliness that he cannot lose. This will come to a head just before he kills her; for the present, he tries to convince himself by creating the fantasy of Desdemona as a whore in a brothel, so that her beauty becomes a degradation, and both her and Emilia's protests can be brushed aside as tricks of the trade. He must find a way to end the inner deadlock between his love and his jealousy; one way is to corrupt the love until it matches and merits the corruption of jealousy. One speech stands out here among all his passionate appeals (for that is what they really are) to his wife:

> Had it pleas'd heaven
> To try me with affliction; had they rain'd
> All kinds of sores and shames on my bare head,
> Steep'd me in poverty to the very lips,
> Given to captivity me and my utmost hopes,
> I should have found in some place of my soul
> A drop of patience; but, alas, to make me
> The fixed figure for the time of scorn
> To point his slow unmoving finger at! – O,O!
> Yet I could bear that too; well, very well;
> But there, where I have garner'd up my heart,
> Where either I must live or bear no life,
> The fountain from the which my current runs,
> Or else dries up – to be discarded thence!
> Or keep it as a cistern for foul toads
> To knot and gender in! Turn thy complexion there,
> Patience, thou young and rose-lipp'd cherubin –
> Ay, here, look grim as hell.[170]

Poetry of this special kind has been rare in Shakespeare up to now; there is something akin to it in Hamlet's outburst against his mother.[171] The dramatist-poet has found a way of expressing the speaker's emotions through imagery which directly creates the emotion in us. Here poetry is emotion, not the description of emotion; it is near to the direct effect of 'romantic' music.

When Othello leaves, Desdemona remains, as dazed as if she had again been hit. She too has her inner conflict, irreconcilables to reconcile, but in her case love is simple, complete and uncomplicated; she can quickly acknowledge, and then accept once and for ever, the discrepancy between the Othello she loves and the Othello who strikes and insults her. The dramatist now, in the final phases of action and reaction before the end, is creating the sense that her love is a love that exists in its own right, unaffected by ordinary worldly reason – all Shakespeare's portrayals of true love have this quality. As we shall see, the final meeting between her love and Othello's jealousy will be the inevitable last encounter of two irrationals, the glory of real love and the evil madness of distrust. The second half of the scene sets this love of Desdemona's against the common experience of Emilia; Shakespeare almost lets Emilia disturb the fine balance between 'real' and 'imagined' time in the play, but his daring succeeds, for it is associated with a preliminary hint of Emilia's later realisation that the 'outrageous knave' who alone could destroy a marriage in a few days, must be Iago. With a brief necessary conversation between Iago and Roderigo, in which the young dupe's doubts of Iago are quickly changed to his uneasily agreeing to kill Cassio, the scene ends.

The last three scenes of the tragedy are an impressive example of Shakespeare's mature skill in dramatic orchestration, with tempo and mood contrasting in 4.3 and 5.1, and finally mingling in resolution in the two phases of the final scene (5.2).

The 'willow scene' (4.3.) is made to create an atmosphere of fragile peace, of a momentary pause before the final sweep towards disaster – it is like the apparent hesitation of a waterfall before it plunges down. Its slow poignancy owes much to the contrast of the 'human incongruity' embodied in these two women. Each is a wife, each has suffered from the traditional dominance of a husband: Desdemona has instinctively taken refuge in an inviolate world of emotion, Emilia sturdily faces up to the facts of the everyday existence of such as herself – these are two opposite ways in which human beings may deal with life. But Shakespeare, with his regard for complete truth (and its unerring effect on the audience), also shows a Desdemona half-intrigued by the other world of Emilia, while entirely uncomprehending. The 'willow song' itself, like many such songs of common experience, has the irony of its theme of human longing and human frailty, human idealism and its opposite, as an accompaniment to the contrast of the two women; even the fact that a boy acting a woman, a male-female, sings the song, adds to the irony. There is, moreover, the further ironic effect of the general 'domestic' tone of the scene; for the first and last time in the play we see Desdemona as a married woman preparing for bed, like so many Elizabethan married ladies, with quiet lazy gossip and inevitable talk about husbands.

This peaceful scene is followed, immediately on the Elizabethan stage, by the complete contrast of 5.1, a scurrying dark confusion of sudden violence; Iago is at the centre of the mêlée, partly controlling, partly taking quick advantages of it (as when he secretly stabs Roderigo). Othello for a moment looks on 'at a distance'; the 'noble' Moor, who has already shown himself quite ready to lurk ignobly in the background to spy on the Iago–Cassio meeting (4.1.), now watches again and is glad when his 'cuckolder' Cassio is apparently assassinated by Iago; for a moment he reaches a depth where there is little to choose between him and the 'villain'. The tone of the scene is one of hurried, partly improvised, almost desperate savagery: Iago's soliloquy near the beginning suggests that the calm deliberation with which he proceeded against Othello earlier is now breaking up as his time grows short. Everything is being driven into a final narrowing impasse – the end is near, not only for Othello and Desdemona, but, with the inescapable 'logic of violence',[172] for Iago's other victims and for himself. The scene ends with Iago's aside:

> This is the night
> That either makes me or fordoes me quite'.

Emilia has just been sent by him to tell Othello what has happened, and she arrives as Othello is finishing the murder of his wife – events are now snapping together like the jaws of a trap.

The action moves (5.2) to Othello as he enters his marriage bedroom; he has witnessed, he believes, the killing of Cassio, and now he has to kill his wife. As Shakespeare shows, all the human conflicts inherent in the Moor, his marriage and his jealousy, so carefully portrayed throughout the play, now crystallize to a point in the five minutes or so between Othello's entrance and his wife's dying words. Othello's first speech shows this final stage of his inner conflict. The dramatist has shown him gradually pushed, by Iago's promptings, down between the opposing pressures of his own nature; the differences of age, colour, birth, sexual desire, vocation, between himself and his bride, have been forced into opposition with the emotional truth of his love for Desdemona and hers for him. The resulting conflict of the emotions of jealousy and love cannot be resolved, by an Othello, as it is; it represents the typical incompatibility of two powerful drives each felt as equally valid, under the weight and pain of which the sufferer is destroyed unless he can resolve them, or escape into a fantasy outside the incompatibility. This is the moment when Othello, by such a fantasy, temporarily resolves his conflicts, or attempts to do so. As he moves towards the sleeping Desdemona, he sees himself, in effect, as an imaginary Othello in an imaginary situation, and as such, once more 'noble' and 'just'. He is no longer a wretched black General destroyed for ever by a lustful girl, nor a fine soldier blessed by a love shared with his beautiful and talented wife: he is now, in fantasy, the suffering but majestic agent of Justice acting as such, not from passion, mere personal desire for revenge. Thus he can love the criminal and detest and punish the crime, almost like God himself, and the slow, stately march of Shakespeare's blank verse has all the appropriate dignity and weight:

> It is the cause, it is the cause, my soul –
> Let me not name it to you, you chaste stars –
> It is the cause. Yet I'll not shed her blood,
> Nor scar that whiter skin of hers than snow,
> And smooth as monumental alabaster.
> Yet she must die, else she'll betray more men.

Then, as he kisses her:

> O balmy breath, that dost almost persuade
> Justice to break her sword!

But such fantasy is more fragile than the madness to which it is akin, and Othello's lasts only a moment. To maintain it, not only must Othello see Desdemona as a pitiable sinner, but she must act her part; she must repent and confess if he is to be the justified minister of Justice. Of course, Desdemona insists on her innocence, and so, innocently as ever, instantly destroys his fantasy, as she did in 4.2:

> By heaven, I saw my handkerchief in's hand.
> O perjur'd woman! Thou dost stone my heart,
> And mak'st me call what I intend to do
> A murder, which I thought a sacrifice.

Desdemona has made him feel himself suddenly reduced to a mere cuckold, driven to find 'reasons' for murdering his wife, and when she dares, in her simplicity, to weep at Cassio's 'death', thus missing her last chance to vindicate herself, Othello murders her in passion, not with the judicial coolness he had tried to assume.[173]

Then comes Emilia's knocking at the door, an intrusion of the outside world upon the narrow room of murder as effective here as in *Macbeth*, and with it Othello's swing from fantasy to reality, a stark realisation of what he has done. For the first time since the beginning of 3.3, he begins to see the real Desdemona, and he can try to escape the realisation only by clinging to his jealousy: in response to Desdemona's last naïvely loving attempt to defend him, and Emilia's horror at the deed, he can do nothing but maintain his wife's falseness and his own justification:

> Cassio did top her; ask thy husband else.
> O, I were damn'd beneath all depth in hell
> But that I did proceed upon just grounds
> To this extremity. Thy husband knew it all.

At this point the elaborate fabric of Iago's plotting, and with it the world of specious 'fact' in which Othello had come to exist, begin to crumble. It is ironically apt that the coldly rational Iago, in the previous scene, could foresee that either Cassio or Roderigo, if allowed to live, could so easily betray his cunning to Othello, but could not, by his very nature, foresee or even understand that Emilia's love for her mistress could be equally fatal to him. As the scene progresses, as Othello is painfully thrust slowly forward into reality, it is this love which proves stronger than Iago; although he finally kills his wife, it is only after both he and Othello, linked in falsehood nearly to the end, are stripped to the bare truth of their natures − 'honest' Iago an unrepentant man of evil (there is no repentance without feeling), and the 'noble' Moor, despite his fine and moving regret, still the victim of his inability to control his imagination and passion by common reason, more fatally inadequate for his situation than even poor silly young Roderigo.

Yet Shakespeare's fashioning of the play has made it impossible for us to leave *Othello* with such a cursory judgement − it has taken us far beyond this mere rational appearance of the story. Othello, as he has been formed and presented by the dramatist, cannot be seen as only another fool of a husband; true, he shared the passions and conflicts, the errors, of common men, as Shakespeare has fairly shown, but the dramatist has also taken great care to present his human struggles as charged with a unique power of wide implications.

From the first, Shakespeare has made Othello not only important 'politically', but also a strange, curiously lonely figure in the world he dominates. Thus, even when he is reduced by Iago, he still retains our feeling of his authority, his special quality, and with this a sense of the universal grief at greatness brought low. Moreover, his downfall is contrived by an enemy equally exceptional in his special hostility, one who by his nature is himself set apart from ordinary men; in him we feel a power of evil which, although active in a limited setting, suggests a principle affecting all Mankind. So Othello, too, while guilty of the human frailties of jealousy and revenge, suffers and struggles, in a situation of special human complexity and unusually wide relevance, with a passion heightened beyond normal feeling and expression; thus both situation and passion become significant beyond Othello himself, and take on a larger, almost symbolic, quality.

But above all, however foolish, by ordinary rational standards, Othello's jealousy and need for revenge may appear (indeed, have been made to appear at one level), all Shakespeare's poetic and imaginative power has been used to make the audience feel his situation rather than judge it logically; as in life, emotional understanding, human empathy, are felt in the end as stronger than cold reason. In fact, Iago becomes the supreme warning against this cold reason, and it is through his example that the dramatist can lead us finally to the emotional acceptance of Othello's tragic stature.

All this suggests, perhaps, how the effect of this tragedy, and of every full Shakespeare tragedy, is ultimately formed within us. Our minds note the events and situations as they interweave, interact, and move toward the climax of the last act: side by side with this, however, our hearts and imaginations are constantly being worked upon by Shakespeare's creation and display of emotions in conflict both at the simplest personal level and at the level where the personal hints at the universal. So, at the end of the play, our final emotional state is complex, yet richly rewarding because so complex. We have identified ourselves with the feelings of many human beings from Othello the great protagonist to Bianca the minor tragic victim, and have felt in them, with them, a reminder of our personal experience of human incongruity. But we have also been reminded, by experiencing that incongruity in 'great ones' and in minor folk, and seeing both kinds against ourselves, that it is both personal and universal, shared by us with our nextdoor neighbour, with our representatives on the stage, and with all mankind. We have been given a fresh and poignant awareness of all the potentialities of our nature for grief and yet final endurance, for recognition of evil and yet assertion of good – we have been taken within ourselves and beyond ourselves, and this experience, the unique gift of grate drama, will have changed us, in some degree, for ever.

King Lear

Shakespeare's treatment of *King Lear* is a good example of his way of employing popular dramatic material to give his audience stage entertainment of the kind which they enjoyed, while at the same time extending their awareness of the results of their own human pressures, a process which they also found absorbing.

Let us consider *King Lear* first, then, as an effective piece of Elizabethan popular 'theatre'. To begin with, it has a special appeal to contemporary views of the obligations of 'great ones' and their far too common inability to fulfil those obligations. For ordinary Elizabethans (as for most of us today), such moral attitudes were delightful in their iconoclastic implications, and uneasily thrilling in their suggestion of the social disaster that might overwhelm all men if their 'betters' did fail. Like the *Leir* play (c1590) and the older-fashioned *Gorboduc* (1562), *Lear* has this political–human interest placed in a remote legendary setting; thus the 'history' itself is unimportant enough to serve merely as a background, and the dramatist can concentrate upon the human emotions which lie within, and help to shape, social and historical events. Shakespeare's opening of the play gives an impressive, eye-catching presentation of the crucial action of Lear's division of his kingdom, from which everything, both inside and outside the characters, results. The consequent events, if only as 'stage happenings', provide good opportunities for theatrical scenes of violent action, horrible cruelty, madness, suspense and extreme pathos. Throughout the play the theme of parents and children, good and bad, runs in two obvious, but effective, interwoven exemplary tales, and permeating the whole drama is the dramatic display of the traditional struggle between good and evil; at the end, evil is seen to be properly punished with death, and decent order is restored to the state. Even if the good Cordelia and much-tried Lear are sacrificed, this provides at least popular pathos; there is much common sympathy to be created around these two and the figure of Gloucester, while 4.7 goes far beyond the pathos of, say, little Arthur in *King John*, to the edge of tragedy. In addition, of course, there is the magnificent popular theatre of the two great 'heath' scenes (3.2. and 3.4.), where tragic but exciting madness and topical satiric wit support each other in a complex appeal to Elizabethan hearts and minds. Indeed, the Fool, as the traditional voice of shrewd common sense, comments most wittily (in Elizabethan terms) on Lear and his situation throughout the middle third of the play, accompanying his master's change from mere irritation to open insanity; however much moved by Lear's suffering, the contemporary audience would also have enjoyed the Fool. They would have appreciated, too, Edgar's Bedlam beggar, the horrific blinding of Gloucester, Kent's sturdy frankness, and the confiding villainy of Edmund.

All this may suggest an attempt to reduce a great tragedy to the level of popular melodrama. Of course not – it merely emphasises a fact too often forgotten, that every Shakespeare tragedy, at least, is popular stage excitement transfigured by the poet-dramatist's expression of his insight into the deeper significance of the feelings, thoughts and consequent behaviour of men and women akin to his audience. So, like all the tragedies, *King Lear* is viable even at its most obvious level as stage entertainment.

To this must be added that the actual media of the play are also effective for every purpose of the dramatist. The prose works well at all points in the range from the height of colloquial rhetoric to the most striking simplicity, while the variety and power of the blank verse, of course, does much as always to create the tone of the play. This blank verse rarely has the tightness, the compressed depth, of blank verse found in *Hamlet*, *Othello* or *Macbeth*, but its looser, rolling force, especially in the mouth of Lear, becomes the central symbol of the dissipating flood of aged majesty.

In fact, as we begin to examine the play more closely, 'the dissipating flood' may be taken as a preliminary key to an understanding of this tragedy. The essential pattern of the play is of two 'great ones', a King and an Earl, confident even arrogant at the beginning, declining to defeat and death at the end. Elizabethan tragedy, including Shakespeare's, so often deals with the collapse of greatness, but usually the great men decline after constant active effort, and are powerful almost to their end. In *King Lear* the effect is curiously different: all the 'good' react rather than act; they suffer nobly, piteously, but their lives on the stage are a process of decline from power to weakness under the assaults of an active, cunning and aggressive evil. Thus Lear in particular, at his beginning in plain political folly and personal self-delusion, gives one the uneasy feeling that the main prop of the state has already begun to crumble within, that the personal force which should accompany his autocratic manner has started ebbing away even before he speaks his first words. That force continues to waste itself almost wantonly as he presents his pathetic scheme for power without responsibility, and soon after it begins to spread out, weaker and weaker, as it encounters the firm, concentrated opposition. In one sense, *King Lear* is a play of old age, its vulnerability when deprived of respect and the support given by respect, and of weakness, for soon the King's only power lies in his emotions and the strength of the language in which he expresses them. From the end of 1.1 he is a defeated man, and so a defeated king; all the wonderful poetry which Shakespeare continues to give him invests him with a new and different power, but one irrelevant to the struggle for political supremacy which has already passed him by. In this, Lear is somewhat akin to Richard II, and the pathos of their self-pity is similar.

So *King Lear* seems a curiously diffuse play,[174] one of words rather than of action: what physical action there is (notably the blinding of Gloucester in 3.7, his attempted suicide in 4.6, and the Edmund–Edgar fight in the final scene), although very good 'theatre', is strangely pointless action, examples of cruelty, despair and retribution which have no material effect on the inevitable outcome of the plot: the defeat of Cordelia and the French forces is barely suggested on the stage, and is important in personal, not political, terms.

This play, then, shows a different mode of Shakespearean tragedy, significantly different in that it seems to suggest a changed approach to tragedy such as is not seen, in this form, in his other tragedies. It is of course plain that these all reveal a special interest in the conflicts of human incongruity which, in given circumstances, lead to tragic results. In *King Lear*, however, although here too human nature is shown to produce disastrous consequences, the emphasis is almost continuously on the human nature, scarcely on the consequences: it is as if Shakespeare took care to provide the scenes of stage excitement which everyone enjoyed (and these are nicely motivated, linked closely to character), but devoted his chief attention, his most moving and evocative poetry, and deepest perceptions, to displaying the human conflicts within and between the central characters. One can define this emphasis more closely: the major human struggles of the play, in simple terms, are between goodness and evil, and nearly all the detailed exploration of Man's nature is devoted to goodness, however imperfect and ineffectual that goodness may appear. Compared with this exploration, the presentation of evil is almost naïve in its directness and simplicity. Edmund is scarcely more subtle a villain than Richard III, and shows much of his Vice-like delight in divulging his wickedness to the audience; the two 'wicked sisters' (as contrasted with the 'good sister') certainly begin as convincingly human daughters, but they rapidly become almost morality type-figures of Cruelty and Lust. In fact, as we shall see, the full consideration of goodness is limited to Lear and Gloucester, and in each case it is a very flawed goodness. Other good characters such as Edgar and Kent and Albany are far less emphasised; they are established as being on the good 'side', and have a cumulative effect in the play. As for Cordelia, despite the wonderful pathos around her and in her, Shakespeare does little more than state her goodness; even Ophelia is more closely portrayed.

Shakespeare's special emphasis on feelings rather than deeds is connected with the curious atmosphere of remoteness which marks the setting and plot of the play. As I have suggested, this is largely due to the legendary nature of the material used, but as the play proceeds it is increased and given new significance by Shakespeare's treatment. When a play, as here, shows a concern chiefly with the inner conflicts of its protagonist, and relates everything to that, it is freed to some extent from 'local' relevancies of specific time and place and incident, and can take on a kind of universality. Some of the old 'moral plays', and especially *Everyman*, had shown how effectively this could happen, how strongly the presentation of inner struggle in a central figure could thus be given archetypal significance. It is this sense of human nature raised to wider meaning which creates the unique quality of *King Lear*. Shakespeare had used the distancing effect of remote settings and strange stories in a number of his earlier plays; the comedies owe much of their pleasant human truth to the fact that, for example, Benedick and Beatrice have a living reality quite unrelated to Messina and the remote world in which the far-fetched plot takes place. All the other main tragedies have some remoteness of place and time, but their plots are far more important than in *King Lear*, much more essential to the central purpose of the display of human conflict – indeed, in *Othello* and, especially, in *Macbeth*, the plot is the working-out, and the symbol, of the personal inner struggles which lie at the heart of the play.

Bearing in mind these more general considerations, we can now turn to a detailed examination of the nature and effect of *King Lear*. In moving from *Othello* to this play, one notices an immediate difference of dramatic technique. Although Shakespeare carefully postulates the natures and relationship of Othello and Desdemona early in the play, and so creates the roots from which later tragedy will spring, Othello is not confronted with his own human incongruity until 3.3, nearly halfway through the play. In *King Lear*, the fundamental nature of the old King's human incongruity is at once clear to everyone except himself, and he is aware of a conflict which he cannot yet begin to understand; the consequences are already appearing. Even when the play ends, the old man is still unaware of the true meaning and cause of his suffering.

Within moments of Lear's first appearance on the stage, his nature begins to reveal itself, increasingly so as the scene continues. To an Elizabethan there could be little doubt of the dangerous political folly of this ruler's decision to divide his kingdom: the old play of *Gorboduc*, in print as recently as 1590, had shown in emphatic moral tones the disastrous results of such an action, and two comments of Gorboduc's advisers are especially relevant to Lear, the impatient autocrat who will not accept advice:

> When fathers cease to know that they should rule,
> The children cease to know they should obey;
> . . .
> Within one land, one single rule is best:
> Divided reigns do make divided hearts.[175]

Lear, in fact, is plainly a greater fool than Gorboduc. The latter divided his kingdom between his two sons so that they might be prepared for full kingship; Lear's motives are far more stupidly selfish – he wishes to avoid the cares of a ruler while at the same time retaining all the respect and authority of a king. The confusion in his mind about his status runs through his words to Cornwall and Albany:

> I do invest you jointly with my power,
> Pre-eminence, and all the large effects
> That troop with majesty. Ourself, by monthly course,
> With reservation of an hundred knights,
> By you to be sustain'd, shall our abode

202

Make with you by due turn. Only we shall retain
The name, and all th'addition to a king:
The sway, revenue, execution of the rest,
Beloved sons, be yours; which to confirm,
This coronet part between you.[176]

He is giving away 'all the large effects' of 'majesty', while retaining 'all th'addition to a king'; the Dukes are to have his power (or are they?), but be forced to maintain him and a small army; the final gesture of 'This coronet part between you' is almost ludicrously symbolic, for only one head can wear a crown. His intention is autocratic and foolish; his method of carrying it out, linking the division to his daughters' profession of love, takes him from folly into fantasy. Lear is seen in his confusion as split not only between conceptions of himself as both 'private man' and 'public man', both not-King and King, but also between the reality of his public responsibilities as a king, and his private domestic fantasy of himself as the dearly loved and revered old father of three devoted daughters. In this fantasy he tries to make his daughters' private personal love (as assumed by him) fit into a pattern of dubious political statecraft which is itself built on his own personal selfishness. Fact and fantasy, reason and desire, are already at strife in Lear's nature – now they have to come into contact with the natures of the daughters, and of Cordelia's suitors. Of course the personal love of Goneril and Regan for him (if it existed) quickly turns into political love, ambition, and they find it easy to pretend to satisfy his fantasy. Cordelia, whose love is very personal and real, cannot accept it; to Lear, her response is an unbearable intrusion of reality into his private fantasy, akin to the effect on Othello of Desdemona's inability to justify his fantasy just before her death. So there begins the real human struggle within Lear which is to carry him to madness, and beyond madness – the attempt to reconcile the irreconcilable, to make his selfish and arrogant dreams and the unfeeling realities of life, of which he is so innocently ignorant, prove in some way compatible.

This opening scene of *King Lear* sets the tone of the play, and suggests the difficulty inherent in that tone. It is a curiously naïve scene, almost akin to the world of a fairytale; the passionate old King, the selfish hypocritical daughters, the simple good Cordelia, the brave Kent, the mean-spirited Burgundy and the devoted France – how can such storybook figures ever become the stuff of that great tragedy which the play eventually proves to be? After all, here is no conventional framework for romantic comedy such as Shakespeare had used in *As You Like It*, where a usurper duke can suddenly and conveniently repent at the end of the play (although Edmund comes close to this). The difficulty is that which we have seen in many earlier plays, arising from the dramatist's increasing preoccupation with presenting the truth of human nature despite the shallow unreal quality of the plots which so many of his audience enjoyed. Shakespeare's attempt to raise into dramatic life the human truths lying dormant in the old tale of Leir, is a task harder than anything he has yet faced; in *Hamlet* he successfully managed to penetrate to, and display, the eternal truth of the man despite the folktale excitements of the story, but *King Lear* is even harder. The foolish old autocrat of the first scene, apparently impregnably entrenched in his misconceptions, must be shown, little by little, as a human suffering being with whom we can identify and whose conflicts we can find in ourselves, until at the end we experience through our own natures the true magnitude of his struggle.

The opening scene has suggested something of human nature and its confusions which make Lear, finally, the epitome of Mankind, of us all. His conflict is that between reason and unreason which is fundamental in our nature, but which is exacerbated by the circumstances into which Lear is shown to place himself; the major tragic interest of the play, relevant in various degrees to all members of the audience, will be whether, to what extent, Lear's unreason will be modified by reason, and how, if at all, he will be able to emerge from fantasy into truth. This latter step, as we all know in our own experience, is a painful one. Shakespeare had already shown this pain in tragedy, of course, but he also reminds us, in quite different contexts, that this experience can cause laughter or amused pity: in *The Merry Wives of Windsor*, Falstaff had to realise the truth as against the fantasy of his own amorous appeal, but he could shrug off the realisation without difficulty, while in *Twelfth Night* Malvolio was awakened from the dream of Olivia's love with a shock that went deeper and is therefore more moving.

The nature of Lear's fumbling attempt to emerge from fantasy into reason and truth, made without any final full realisation of his real conflict, is deeply affected by the kind of rational world which he encounters around him. In Othello's case, his fantasy was encouraged and fashioned by the 'reason' of Iago; Lear's fantasy springs readymade from himself as he is, but the worldly reason against which he strives is akin to Iago's. Edmund is a more human, more

acceptable 'rationalist' than Iago, but the two are alike; the Edmund
of 2.1 is a livelier, simpler version of his predecessor, with something
of the bravura of Richard III, as I have said, and he soon shows that
he has the quickwitted, unscrupulous opportunism that marked ←
Iago. Edmund's 'world' is shared by Regan and Cornwall, and by
Goneril; it is stubbornly opposed by the 'world' of Cordelia, Kent,
Edgar and Albany, in which selfish 'lower reason' is replaced by the
divine unreason of love and pity. It is thus that the traditional,
storybook conflict of the Lear tale, simple good against simple evil, is
deepened into a revelation, in dramatic terms, of the universal
struggle of Man's nature with itself and its fellows, of human
qualities striving for mastery.

For the Elizabethan, this struggle was exemplified, in particular,
by the incompatibility between following in life unalloyed, calculating reason and allowing one's instinctive emotions to assert human
fellowship. Something of this Elizabethan awareness is suggested by
Albany's words to Goneril in 4.2:

> I fear your disposition:
> That nature which contemns it [its] origin
> Cannot be border'd certain in itself;
> She that herself will sliver and disbranch
> From her material sap perforce must wither
> And come to deadly use.[177]

Goneril has shown herself totally committed to that selfish 'reason'
which admits only cold expediency, and has rejected the natural love
of a daughter for a father. To the average Elizabethan, as to Albany,
she is a human being who has moved out of the ways that make us
human, and so has become non-human, unnatural; as Lear had said
earlier:

> Filial ingratitude!
> Is it not as this mouth should tear this hand
> For lifting food to't?[178]

If human nature can no longer be trusted to act in a human way, it
not only splits away from its roots and perishes, as Albany says, but
the fact that such a thing can happen opens up an appalling prospect
of Mankind falling into disorder, ending the natural order ordained
by God – 'chaos is come again', as Othello said. Reason without
feeling is the danger, and in this context Edmund represented for
many in the audience what may be termed their 'new rationalism',

shocking but exciting to some, evil and dangerous to others, akin to the unfeeling rationality (as Elizabethans saw it) of Machiavelli's advice to his Prince which so impressed the Elizabethan mind that for a generation 'Machiavelli' was a synonym for 'Devil'.[179] Goneril, Regan and Cornwall are less self-aware and explicit than Edmund, and so are more simply 'bad' by traditional standards, selfish, greedy and brutal. Moreover, it is characteristic of the Elizabethan attitude that the rational evil which Edmund represents, being devoid of human feeling, is devoted to causing social and personal disorder amid which the cunning can grasp power. Edmund can sneer with complete conviction at the human, if foolish, beliefs of his father, just as Iago dismisses with contempt the need of ordinary men to excuse their follies: that both of them may be logically correct, does not lessen the dangerous arrogance of their belief in nothing but their reason. This, for many Elizabethans at least, is a rationalism that seeks to destroy those irrationalities (which could be called faith and belief and trust) which had always been part of the distinctive quality of being human. Of all Shakespeare's characters, it is given to Lafeu to suggest what they felt:

> They say miracles are past; and we have our philosophical persons to make modern and familiar, things supernatural and causeless. Hence it is that we make trifles of terrors, ensconcing ourselves into seeming knowledge when we should submit ourselves to an unknown fear.[180]

Some of us today, among the inhuman dangers of this scientific age, would echo his implied warning.

Shakespeare accompanies the course of Lear's struggle by Gloucester's painful progress towards the realisation of the truth about himself and his sons. The parallel is the more effective because of the differences between the two 'great ones' who have to face similar conflicts; yet those differences themselves do much to show the essential nature of each man's struggle. Moreover, as the major emphasis is on Lear, the human pity evoked by Gloucester seems to deepen our sense of Lear's tragic quality by making his sufferings part, as it were, of a universal destiny shared by another and different man.

Gloucester is first presented, briefly but effectively, as the average sensual man, a self-satisfied lord scarcely embarrassed by the presence of his young bastard at Court. An Elizabethan would not have been shocked by a great man's easy acknowledgement of his own sexual fault, nor would he have been surprised when the bastard soon showed that he scorned his legitimate brother and would plot to oust him. After all, bastards were known to have to rely on their own wits rather than on legal rights; Shakespeare had made a great deal of this in portraying the Bastard in *King John* – indeed, Edmund, although scarcely a national hero, has something of Philip's attractive audacity. Gloucester begins as the traditional type of the honest lord devoted to his ill-used King, with a natural goodness similar to Kent's, but like all the characters on Lear's side his goodness is 'old-fashioned', and ineffective against the self-seeking callousness of the King's enemies. This 'public' function of Gloucester is interwoven with his 'private' function as a father (in Lear the two functions are confused). But Gloucester's trust in his bastard son is as much a personal fantasy as Lear's faith in Regan and Goneril, and it runs counter to his natural love of Edgar, like Lear's treatment of Cordelia. In 3.7, amid brutal suffering, Gloucester's fantasy is swept away by the sudden awareness of truth. Thus his progress towards self-knowledge, a tragedy in itself, culminates at the end of Act 3, leaving a third of the play to deal mainly with the final working-out of the tragedy of Lear. The rest of Gloucester's life in the play is used by the dramatist for at least one oddly striking scene, effective in itself, but knit into Shakespeare's main emphasis, on what happens to a man's outlook when all his previous beliefs have led only to pain and disillusionment. His inner battle between fantasy and truth is brought to a violent resolution, with a swing towards the cold logic of despair, and then the balance is achieved through Edgar's pity and love. Gloucester has been shown as brought to the edge[181] of that complete pessimism where Man's life seems futile nonsense: Macbeth was to see it as 'a tale/Told by an idiot' – and die in that belief; Gloucester, through love, moves back into some kind of human trust, if only the resignation of stoic acceptance.

When Gloucester is blinded in 3.7, much has already happened to Lear and within Lear. From the end of 1.1, the process of his striving is shown, stage by stage, in all its inevitability. Once again, as in all Shakespeare's mature drama, but especially in the tragedies, we feel that such a man, in a situation including such other characters, is necessarily drawn towards certain reactions, creating new situations and other reactions, and so on to the end. It is a kind of determinism at work within the contrived world of the play, yet it is not absolute; the creative will of the dramatist can always introduce external modifications. After the crucial action of 1.1, Regan and Goneril begin their counteraction against the foolish conditions which Lear has attached to his 'gift' of power. At this stage, Shakespeare takes care to show that, from the viewpoint of a rational world, the two sisters are hypocritical and selfish, but not yet inhumanly cruel; Regan says that Lear, as we can well believe, 'hath ever but slenderly known himself'[182] (that is the root of his tragedy), and for a time we can almost understand their impatience with the old man. From here on, until the sisters' growing callousness culminates in their abandoning Lear to the storm, Shakespeare is steadily establishing the nature of Lear's personal struggle, but he is also showing the precise kind of cruelty which must provoke it further. Lear's nature needs understanding, tolerance and love – he has put himself into a world where ambition and greed are incapable of acknowledging such emotions. Lear's imagined world to which he still clings for a while (and ironically it is based on moral values which will ultimately prevail in the play) has nothing but words and passion with which to sustain itself. When we experience on the stage or in the study, Lear's first terrible reaction to the unbearable reality of the world around him, those dreadful words uttered by him to his own daughter Goneril, we may even today feel something of the shock of the unnatural which an Elizabethan would have felt – this is the moment when *King Lear* moves unmistakably into tragedy:

> Hear, Nature, hear; dear goddess, hear.
> Suspend thy purpose, if thou didst intend
> To make this creature fruitful.
> Into her womb convey sterility;
> Dry up in her the organs of increase;
> And from her derogate body never spring
> A babe to honour her! If she must teem,
> Create her child of spleen, that it may live
> And be a thwart disnatur'd torment to her.
> Let it stamp wrinkles in her brow of youth,
> With cadent tears fret channels in her cheeks,
> Turn all her mother's pains and benefits
> To laughter and contempt, that she may feel
> How sharper than a serpent's tooth it is
> To have a thankless child.[183]

This is wonderful poetic rhetoric, an immensely dramatic moment, but morally it is wild and inhuman nonsense as addressed to his daughter, and a daughter who has so far, at worst, failed to treat her father with the love and respect which he has taken for granted. Lear is speaking from within his fantasy, unable to see reality, and in his pitiable arrogance he almost takes on the role of the savage pagan goddess to whom he appeals.[184] Behind this near-megalomania lurks the self-pity and petulance of a spoilt child encountering the real world for the first time, as the dramatist also shows in Lear's exclamations in 1.5 and especially in his reaction to Regan in 2.4, but there is the suggestion of more than this in his last speech to Regan in the latter scene. The first few lines of this speech show a momentary new awareness entering Lear's almost closed mind, and they go to the heart of the tragedy:

> Oh reason not the need! Our basest beggars
> Are in the poorest things superfluous.
> Allow not nature more than nature needs,
> Man's life is cheap as beast's.[185]

A moment later, Lear becomes again the intensely moving spectacle of former greatness trying to ignore the unacceptable fact of present weakness, but these four lines suggest the moral direction of the play, and the final outcome. The tragic force of *King Lear* lies in its revelation of the vulnerability of goodness, pity and love in a world of practical, cold reason, and at the same time, the ultimate irrelevance of that reason, and the permanent value of the good. So, as we shall see, the paradoxical essence of the human greatness of Lear, and with him of Cordelia, is their final defeat in this world.

But Lear is now taking refuge from his daughters in the impersonal, and therefore bearable, assaults of the storm to which they have committed him. These heath scenes (3.2, 3.4 and 3.6) are in themselves most effective 'theatre', but they also give us the next important stage in Lear's conflict. Lear's first reaction to the storm, with which 3.2 opens, shows him almost identifying with the wild power around him, as though finding in it the strength he lacks, and yet defying that strength. A little later, he sees the storm as a breakdown of order through which the hidden evils of men will be revealed (and this of course is a theme of the play), but the evils committed against himself are his chief concern, and he can still regard himself as 'a man/More sinned against than sinning'.[186] He is entrapped in his self-centred fantasy of complete rightness, but he is slowly moving outside this, for before the end of this scene he can say to the Fool:

'Poor fool and knave, I have one part in my heart
That's sorry yet for thee'.[187]

For the first time in the play, Lear has shown rather than demanded pity.

In the second heath scene (3.4), Lear's 'human incongruity' comes to a full realisation that he is locked in conflicting, irreconcilable opposites:

> Filial ingratitude!
> Is it not as this mouth should tear this hand
> For lifting food to't? But I will punish home.
> No, I will weep no more. In such a night,
> To shut me out! Pour on; I will endure.
> In such a night as this! O Regan, Goneril!
> Your old kind father, whose frank heart gave all!
> O, that way madness lies; let me shun that;
> No more of that.[188]

Of course our response to such language, the bare vivid truth of Lear's feelings, can only be the immediate pity which Shakespeare intends; we are made to experience within ourselves the dreadful impasse in which the old King is struggling, his impossible dilemma. In a strange way, Shakespeare's characteristic insistence on giving us more than one side of truth has put us, too, in a dilemma at this point in the play. In terms of plain, prosaic fact, we have seen Lear as a foolish autocrat seeking to impose his private imaginings on two unpleasant daughters, and suffering a predictable rejection which would have made an ordinary father 'learn sense'. Yet we have also come to feel, in the equally valid terms of Lear's personal emotions, the essence of the man as he is, that the greater truth of Lear is about uncomprehended suffering. Now that suffering has come to the point of madness, which for Lear, as for so many lesser Lears, is the only present escape from an incongruity unbearable in sanity. In going mad, Lear remakes the bitter world of outer fact into an amenable, acceptable inner world of vivid fantasy; he 'knows' himself to be above all trivial outward pomp, even clothes. For the first time in a pampered life he realises that a man is, finally, no more than what he is in himself; stripped of his status, old and infirm, he can yet see himself now as supremely powerful, able to administer justice to his wicked daughters and to all the evil-doers of society. So even in fantasy grown into madness there is a new kind of wisdom, of understanding, that is leading him towards his acceptance of the essential human condition which he shares with all men – in a true sense, to try to strip himself amid the storm is the 'mad' symbol of a new sanity. With this goes a crucial movement from his old narrow self-pity to a potentially redemptive awareness that a man must face up to the needs of his fellow men before he can be truly sane, that self-pity ceases to be sterile only when it is transformed by a sense of the pity and love that all men need. So he can now say:

> Poor naked wretches, wheresoe'er you are,
> That bide the pelting of this pitiless storm,
> How shall your houseless heads and unfed sides,
> Your loop'd and window'd raggedness, defend you
> From seasons such as these? O, I have ta'en
> Too little care of this! Take physic, pomp;
> Expose thyself to feel what wretches feel,
> That thou mayst shake the superflux to them,
> And show the heavens more just.[189]

This expresses a new insight that a fictional king has been shown to achieve under the pressure of circumstances contrived within a play, but as this fiction is composed entirely of human truth, it stands as truth not only for Lear, but for every member of the audience: the last four lines, especially, reveal more about the moral and social assumptions underlying the Elizabethan conception of charity than any mass of statistical analysis.

There is the third heath scene with the mad Lear, where he is back again in his fantasy of vengeance upon his daughters, and then he leaves the play for about 400 lines,[190] a series of six fairly short scenes in which Gloucester is blinded and taken under the disguised Edgar's protection, Regan and Goneril begin their rivalry for possession of Edmund, and Cordelia comes to Dover with the French forces. Shakespeare is bringing together what one may call the 'practical' elements of the plot, the political struggle between the 'evil group' and the 'good group' and the conflicts of evil within the former group. In the process he is ending the account of the personal conflict of Gloucester, but first he has his last meeting with Lear, in 4.6.

In this scene Gloucester finds a final resolution of his human incongruity in a stoic acceptance, as I have said, of life as it is. His final wisdom is:

> Henceforth I'll bear
> Affliction till it do cry out itself
> 'Enough, enough' and die.[191]

Beside him Lear is still mad, still wrestling with the fact of evil. He shows that he has come to realise that, when he was King, he was insulated by flattery from a true knowledge of himself; he is now very close to accepting that pain of an evil world against which he had reacted so violently earlier, the realisation of which, set against his fantasy, had so disrupted his mind – he has almost reached sanity. Gloucester for a moment is made the understanding commentator; when Lear has poured out his bitter vision of a world of sensual, disgusting confusion, it is Gloucester's comment.

> O ruin'd piece of nature! This great world
> Shall so wear out to naught– [192]

which raises Lear briefly from the particular to the universal, reminding us at the same time of an Elizabethan view of the transience and decay of their world and all its greatness.[193] It is he, too, who voices the essential difference between himself and Lear, his own painful sanity and Lear's madness:

> The King is mad; how stiff is my vile sense,
> That I stand up, and have ingenious feeling
> Of my huge sorrows! Better I were distract;
> So should my thoughts be sever'd from my griefs,
> And woes by wrong imaginations lose
> The knowledge of themselves.[194]

The next scene (4.7) brings Cordelia on the stage with a Lear at last restored to sanity – it is a quiet and moving prelude to the final outcome of the tragedy in 5.3, somewhat similar in its effect to the 'willow song' scene in *Othello*. There is quietness, yes, and obvious pathos here, but beneath them is something almost shocking in its unsparing truth. Lear's words to Cordelia show how impossible it is that he should have changed completely from what he was at the beginning; although he has learnt much about the world and himself, and has gained thereby a new humility, he still believes, as he did in 1.1, that love is something to be paid in return for benefit, for he applies the converse of this to Cordelia; to him still, it seems obvious that, as he has wronged her, she cannot love him; he can only ask her to 'forget and forgive', and of course true love like Cordelia's needs no forgetfulness, sees nothing to forgive.

The stubborn determination to achieve their desires of Edmund, Regan and Goneril is continuing; in all three, even in Edmund, their actions have something of the automatic reflex quality of the violence of the later Macbeth. Only Albany, and Cordelia and the French army, stand against them. The action is highly contrived but, by Elizabethan standards, surprisingly direct and uncomplicated. From the end of 4.7, a mere eighty lines take us through the defeat of the French to the entrance of Lear and Cordelia as Edmund's prisoners (5.3). Cordelia has a brief speech of quiet defiance for herself and grief for her father, her last words in the play, and then, after her realistic acceptance of worldly disaster, comes the contrast of Lear. His words here to Cordelia,[195] create a sense of complex poignancy around the man at this, almost the last stage of his long struggle throughout the play. His nature had sought to escape the conflict of fantasy and fact through the greater fantasy of madness, by creating a world in which he could master and control all evil; he had finally emerged into sanity to find awaiting him Cordelia's love, a true love above any considerations of reward or self-interest. If the play had ended at that point, a moment of love freely offered and humbly received, above the pressures of real life, we should have had a 'happy ending' arbitrarily imposed upon a human story remarkable for its uncompromising presentation of the folly and cruelty of which Man's nature is capable. The discrepancy would have been like, but far more disturbing than, that which we feel at the end of *Measure for Measure*, where Angelo and Isabella move quite easily from the darker agonies of 'human incongruity' into the placid acceptance that all is now well. Such an ending is impossible if Shakespeare is to preserve his insistence on human truth in this tragedy. So in these wonderful lines of Lear at the beginning of the last act, the dramatist merely holds off for a while the inevitable and true end, without in fact modifying the truth of what is happening. The Lear who welcomes life in prison with Cordelia, who knows only that he will never again let himself be parted from the daughter whom he threw away so stupidly, is a Lear who has entered a new world of fantasy, one withdrawn from the brutal reality of life, but this is not a return to the old Lear, for now, we might claim, his belief is founded, not on self-pity or bitterness, but on a newly won and valid faith in the power of love. At this penultimate moment, Shakespeare seems to suggest the final problem of the play; in spite of all that he has shown us of the brutal reality of life (even because of it), can we see Lear's momentary vision as Man's only hope – or do we accept in Lear a human inability to face the evil of life as it is? By the end of the play, we shall realise that we need not choose between these two apparent incompatibles – that the true hope of our existence lies in a resolution of the two.

There follow the winding-up movements of the political action of the play: the appropriate defeat and deaths of Regan and Goneril, the cunning and determined evil of Edmund given its overthrow by the courage of the good Edgar (the traditional but still reassuring methods of the old moral tale), and a most adroit piece of stage-craft by which the audience is teased by the suspense of Edmund's dying repentance, delayed until it cannot save the life of Cordelia, the last turn of the screw. The play is ending with that gathering irony which so often marks the close of Shakespeare's tragedies: the forces of evil have been defeated almost by chance, and there is re-established that good order in the state which, we remember, Lear himself was the first to disturb. Then what might well be the supreme irony – Lear enters with the dead Cordelia in his arms, for a brief, terrible moment utterly sane, yet still with one hope, that his daughter is alive. The comments of the onlookers voice the feelings of the audience:

KENT   Is this the promis'd end?
EDGAR   Or image of that horror?
ALBANY   Fall and cease.

Our own daily struggle between trust in love and goodness and our awareness of life's cruelty and evil, have now been brought by the dramatist into an almost unbearable confrontation; Lear, in his last few moments, becomes the epitome of a universal problem. Lear, at one level in us, embodies here the final height of pathos of the play – wonderful and cleansing for us to experience – but pathos is no answer to what we have been made to realise. That answer lies deeper, in the play as a whole. Throughout the tragedy, and building up to this last phase, Shakespeare has slowly and in detail given a view of our existence in which selfishness and love are inescapably opposed, and that view has been fairly and honestly presented. In the end, evil by its very nature has destroyed the essence of itself; it has ended the life of the good, but not the essential goodness. Evil has been shown as forever dangerous, but also as self-limited, self-destructive and negative, love and goodness as creative and positive even in worldly defeat. So there is, in the end, no cause for pessimism; drama has reached here an inner reality which is both terrible and bracing, and our trust in our human integrity is strengthened, not dismissed. As Milton affirmed at the end of *Samson Agonistes*:

> Nothing is here for tears, nothing to wail
> Or knock the breast; no weakness, no contempt,
> Dispraise or blame; nothing but well and fair

Like the Elizabethans, we leave the theatre shaken and disturbed, but in a strange way re-established in our value as human beings. With Lear, we may be foolish, blind, even morally ineffectual, yet we are still members of that human race which, alone among living creatures, has the privilege of knowing good from evil, and the power, if we wish, of striving for good. The play has reminded us, painfully, that death is waiting whether we win or lose, but the real victory is to have seen the truth of goodness and to have fought for it. To point this out is not sentimental moralising – it is the recognition of how truly Shakespeare has presented in this tragedy the essential reality, and the final hope, of that human nature which we all share.

Macbeth

Macbeth (*c*1606) is by far the shortest of the major tragedies that we are examining. It is very much more closely woven in its construction than the others; even *Othello*, *Hamlet* and *King Lear*, although full of important detail and movement, seem diffuse beside it; *Antony and Cleopatra*, only a little shorter than *King Lear*, is packed with 'outer', political action, with a very slow, even sparse (but all-important) 'inner' action.

Macbeth, to be properly understood, must first be recognised as the climax in the fullest tragedy of all Shakespeare's previous use of historical material for dramatic purposes. In considering his earlier history plays, both classical and English, we have seen how, in *Richard II*, he went for a moment beneath the events of history to suggest the personal human conflict lying within those events, but his other English history plays were chiefly the dramatisation of historical facts. *Julius Caesar* and *Troilus and Cressida*, in very different ways, had shown the human factors at work in the historical plot, the former still with much emphasis on 'outer' happenings, the latter with a wider and more general portrayal of human nature in a political situation. Throughout these earlier plays, one is aware of the growing interest of the dramatist, and of his audience, in the ways in which human conflict in great ones affects the quality and the course of history; now this culminates in *Macbeth*, in which a vivid series of 'historical' events springs from, and is closely and constantly affected by, the complex nature of the protagonist and his wife.

As usual, we must first assess the 'outer' appeal of the play as an exciting tale of political struggle, an immediate appeal to the contemporary taste more melodramatic than tragic, and then consider Shakespeare's portrayal of the 'inner' truths of the protagonists, which raises a brilliant drama of villainy and strife to the level of great, universal tragedy.

The play has obvious and highly effective attractions for an ordinary Elizabethan audience. It starts with mysterious witches, followed by a lively eye-witness account of courage and carnage, and ends with society restored to order after stage-fights, a killing, and finally a wicked tyrant's head presented to the onlookers. Between these points lies an exciting sequence of shocking murders, a ghost at a banquet, and a sleepwalking. These ingredients, in addition to their immediate stage-appeal, contain much of more general, everyday interest to Elizabethan play-goers. Firstly, one can be certain that all of them were concerned about the nature and powers of witches, if in fact such ministers of the Devil existed – that was still debatable, although many poor, defenceless wretches had been destroyed in the conviction that witchcraft did indeed exist, and could damn one's soul. A number of learned and dogmatic works (including one by the new King James himself)[196] had been written to prove the terrible spiritual and physical dangers of witches; Henry Holland, Vicar of St Bride's in London, exemplifies the contemporary strong religious attitude:

(MYSODAEMON) I would gladly be resolved in another doubt, *Theophilus*: most men are wont to seeke after these wise men and cunning women, such as they cal witches, in sicknesse, in losses, and in all extremities: what think ye of this, *Theophilus*?

THEOPHILUS I am assured, *Mysodaemon*, that such miserable people commit a most horrible & dreadful sinne, that they are iustly brought into Sathan's snares, for the contempt of God & his word, that they seeke helpe of the same serpent that stung them, that against the knowen principle of the Gospel they would have Sathan to drive out Sathan.[197]

There were many others who published such views, and notably one who dared to oppose them, Reginald Scot, whose *The discouerie of witchcraft* (1584) still remains (as I have earlier said) a fine sensible and humane argument against belief in witches. On the whole, most of Shakespeare's audience would have taken the witches in *Macbeth* very seriously, especially, as Theophilus suggests, Macbeth's deliberate recourse to them for aid.

Secondly, the general political pattern of this play would have been of great interest to a contemporary audience. It shows a good king, Duncan, who has just quelled rebellion and brought order to his land; he is then murdered, and his throne taken by the usurper; this causes disorder and civil war, and order is restored only when the tyrant is killed by the power of Malcolm the legitimate king. Here is the old theme of 'private' disorder (a man's failure to choose the right) causing 'public' disorder in the state. It had been present in Shakespeare's history plays, and indeed in each of the three tragedies before *Macbeth*; it had been part of the specific lesson of the old *Gorboduc*, and of the teaching of the Homilies against rebellion and disorder. *Sir Thomas More*, acted in London some ten years before *Macbeth*, had stressed this lesson, and particularly the fact that violence begets violence, a major theme of Shakespeare's play; Jonson's *Sejanus*, as recently as 1603, had displayed the rise and fall of a Roman tyrant. Certainly the theme was a popular Elizabethan preoccupation.

In fact, an emphasis upon the special gravity of disorder in the state was added by Shakespeare to the material that he used from Holinshed, in the curiously intrusive discussion of the 'good king' in 4.3 of *Macbeth*. The political view expressed here is that a king may have many private moral weaknesses, and still be acceptable as a ruler, but if he does not love peace and good order, and maintain them in his realm, he is not fit to rule – 'No, not to live!' says Macduff. Hoby's translation of Castiglione's *The Courtier* (1561), a popular[198] Elizabethan book of social teaching, in the person of Lord Octavian had said the same thing at the beginning of Elizabeth's reign:

> Therefore is it also the office of a good Prince so
> to trade [treat] his people and with such lawes and
> statutes, that they may live in rest and peace, without
> daunger and with increase of wealth, and injoy peaceably
> this ende of their practises and actions, which ought to
> be quietnesse.[199]

The Elizabethans who had so often praised the Queen for the years of settled rule which they felt she had given them, and who were now waiting to see how James would use the Kingship by which he set such store, would certainly have had a keen interest in 4.3.

So the goodness of a king was a very practical contemporary concern, and its obverse, the nature of a tyrant, equally so, and perhaps rather more exciting to see on the stage. Nearly two-thirds of *Macbeth* portrays the bloody career of a tyrant (quite different from Holinshed's account), although the true tragic force of Shakespeare's play lies in his revelation of the human being within the tyrant. Earlier Elizabethan comments show an accepted view of the tyrant which is part of Shakespeare's picture. For example, in a play of about 1565, printed in 1571 and 1582, a character says of tyrants:

> So are they never in quiet, but in suspicion still [ever];
> When one is made away, they take occasion another to kill;
> Ever in fear, having no trusty friend, void of all people's love,
> And in their own conscience a continual hell they prove
> [experience].[200]

This could almost be a specific description of Macbeth himself, although the dramatist goes more deeply than this. Again, in Thomas Churchyard's description of violence begetting violence there are lines which could be used as an epigraph for *Macbeth*:

> But who seeks blood[,] in blood shall glotted [glutted] be,
> And his own end by blood shall quickly see.[201]

This is the contemporary background against which the dramatic material and plot of *Macbeth* must be seen; in these terms the play has a number of well-tried popular ingredients, including an opening as effective as anything in Shakespeare. If the dramatist had been content to make this merely a play of vivid, exciting physical action, with a simple and forceful plot, *Macbeth* would still have been a good Elizabethan history play. It is partly such a play, but Shakespeare has transformed its total effect with the disturbing human truth of great tragedy. *Macbeth*, like all his tragedies, was certainly not written to teach moral truths explicitly; it is a long way from the worthy dramas which Bale, for example, wrote for a select audience of believers, or from the narrow range of Chapman's dramatisations of his 'philosophy'. It gives a clearsighted, deeply felt portrayal of human nature as we know and experience it, and must therefore deal with the values by which men live; those values must be moral values, however much some modern attitudes may dislike the term. Thus the importance of *Macbeth*, which makes it especially significant in any age still concerned with the truths of our nature, lies in the presentation of Macbeth himself, and of Lady Macbeth, as they are in their situation, and of the reciprocal effects of their situation and their natures. This is the essence of the tragic quality of the play, and the examination of this is the basis of any full understanding of that quality.

The first movement of the play, from the opening to the discovery of Duncan's murder, occupies over one-third of the text. By the end of 2.3 the tragic root of the drama has been shown and established; the rest of the play follows the personal and political growth from that root to its final consequences.

The 'symbolic' importance of the very brief opening scene of the play can easily be overstressed, to the neglect of its obvious dramatic effect. The witches, of course, instantly suggest that the supernatural is to be a material part of the play, just as the opening of *Hamlet* suggests this, but at a far greater length and with an entirely different tone. For a moment or two there is no explanation of the witches' words or their context, but very soon the second scene, firmly set in the real and violent world, links up to the witches' reference to 'When the battle's lost and won', and the name 'Macbeth' is joined to this – the witches, the battle and Macbeth. This second scene has an especially vivid and bloody description of Macbeth's valour in the winning of the battle just ended. Thus the beginning of the play is a mixture of unexplained supernatural intrusion, bloody killing, and the re-establishing of order and peace, with the rebels dead or to be punished, and Macbeth, the great fighter, rewarded by the grateful King with new and public honour. The 'public' Macbeth is the Macbeth who is first given to us, and in the context, so ironic later, of his violence bringing peace and security to his King and the state.

In 1.3 the witches (already recognised as evil, of course, by the audience) make contact with Macbeth and Banquo. The prophecies to the latter are not of immediate importance, but the first of those to Macbeth, that he is Thane of Cawdor, is quickly proved correct by the King's messengers. Macbeth, whom we knew at the beginning of the scene only as a brave and authorised killer, by the end of the scene has begun to be a much more complex figure. Both he and Banquo are tempted by the possibility that all the prophecies are as true as the first, but at this point their natures diverge. Banquo's reason can control his personal desire to believe in the witches; he sees that Macbeth is attracted by the hope of kingship, but he warns him, and it is part of the essence of the play, that from one 'honest trifle', one minor truth, can proceed a vast betrayal of 'deepest consequence'. Macbeth, on the other hand, has begun to move uncertainly between reason and his own private fantasy; thus he says to himself (and to us):

> This supernatural soliciting
> Cannot be ill; cannot be good. If ill,
> Why hath it given me earnest of success,
> Commencing in a truth? I am Thane of Cawdor.
> If good, why do I yield to that suggestion
> Whose horrid image doth unfix my hair
> And make my seated heart knock at my ribs
> Against the use of nature? Present fears
> Are less than horrible imaginings.
> My thought, whose murder yet is but fantastical,
> Shakes so my single state of man
> That function is smother'd in surmise,
> And nothing is but what is not.[202]

To understand these lines, and the divided human spirit which utters them, is to understand the subsequent course of Macbeth's tragedy, that is, the central 'inner' theme of the play. Shakespeare's words are carefully chosen for the Macbeth he wishes to establish in the minds of his audience; the witches' prophecies are 'supernatural soliciting', and 'soliciting', for an Elizabethan, has a sense of 'offering' with overtones of specious tempting to do evil,[203] so Macbeth starts by seeing the dubious nature of the promises made to him. Immediately following this he assumes that his 'success' must be a good thing, and at once his basic moral confusion (in which his 'single state', his integrity as a person, is shaken) begins to show; 'success' is the 'good' he desires, and yet this 'good' is at once connected with 'horrible imaginings' of murder and evil. The nature of Macbeth has already been led into a state of uncertainty where reason is called upon to deal with fantasy, and is powerless because the terms of the implied contest are ambiguous; 'ill' is both moral evil and failure to achieve 'success', which itself is both the 'good' of kingship and the moral evil by which it is obtained. This is the essence of Man's confusion between personal good and moral evil; this is the 'Foul is fair and fair is foul' which is the vital paradox of the Devil's temptation of Man, and gives the witches their power to trigger the movement to evil of a nature like Macbeth's. A line later, Macbeth in fact says to himself:

> If chance will have me king, why, chance may crown me,
> Without my stir.[204]

He sees, for an instant, the common rational wisdom of a Banquo prepared to accept what fate brings, and not to try to manipulate that fate, but Macbeth, like other Shakespeare tragic figures, has the quality of mere humans trying obstinately to shape their own destinies; Hamlet learnt the folly of this, but nothing can now stop a man like Macbeth from pursuing the fantasy of making sure that the witches' prophecy of kingship is proved correct. It was Banquo who had seen the simple logical fact that if the witches were powerful enough to make all their prophecies come true, they needed no help; if not, their prophecies were pointless, and so was any action.

The next scene (1.4), like so many of the plays, shows the pressure of outside 'chance' (Shakespeare's timing of events), here working upon the nature of Macbeth as we have so far seen it. There is first a thread of irony running through the earlier part of the scene, arising from the contrast between our knowledge of Macbeth's potential evil and the emphasis on the apparent goodness and actual treachery of Cawdor, Macbeth's profession of loyalty to Duncan and the King's trust in that loyalty as he had trusted the defeated traitor. Then, by 'chance', Duncan innocently chooses this moment to state his intention to proclaim Malcolm heir to the throne; at once Macbeth's fantasy, his imagining of possible action for the crown, is forced to meet the challenge of political urgency – obviously he cannot kill Duncan to make Malcolm King; Duncan must die soon, before Malcolm is made the heir. This is made clear in Macbeth's words as he leaves the stage, but what is also made clear, once more, is the discord which is at the centre of his nature:

> The Prince of Cumberland! That is a step,
> On which I must fall down, or else o'er-leap,
> For in my way it lies. Stars, hide your fires;
> Let not light see my black and deep desires.
> The eye wink at the hand; yet let that be
> Which the eye fears, when it is done, to see.[205]

This, at an obvious level, is the popular self-revelation of the villain, but it is also an indication of that contradiction within Macbeth which his wife is to analyse so exactly a few moments later: here is a man now obsessed by the fantasy of a greatness which only evil action can bring; he wants the greatness, yet hopes to ignore the evil.

In the following scene (1.5) we first meet Lady Macbeth, already aware, from her husband's letter, of the promises of the witches and the quick fulfilment of the first of them. Her soliloquy gives full detail to our preliminary sense of Macbeth's divided nature, but it also, in the process, establishes the nature of Lady Macbeth herself. This is important for an understanding of the murder of Duncan, and especially of 1.7, where Macbeth finally decides on the killing. Her soliloquy is plainly expressed; from 'Yet I do fear thy nature' to 'Than wishest should be undone', her words are an almost clinical exposition of the inner conflict of her husband: his reason, quite aware of what taking Duncan's crown implies, is at odds not only with his irrational lust for kingship, but also with an emotional need to feel innocent in spite of sinning. This is a traditional struggle in Man, as old as the moral instinct itself, between desire and reason, between wanting the wrong and knowing, even prizing, the right. To Lady Macbeth, we realise, such a conflict is an unfortunate and foolish weakness of Macbeth's character,[206] one which she is confident that she can remedy by 'the valour of my tongue'. This is her nature, which is to be of terrible significance in Macbeth's actions until Duncan is dead; after that, the Macbeth whom she has helped to fashion passes beyond her to the full consequences of being what he has become. In this scene and beyond the murder of Duncan, she shows herself as singleminded and unable to comprehend or accept the anomalies in Macbeth's nature. She is, in dreadful truth, a simple woman, and a good wife. Having none of that practical knowledge of what killing means of which her husband has too much, she sees murder as merely the practical and sensible way of getting what she knows Macbeth wants (there is no suggestion in the play that she is driving her husband to make her Queen). She never becomes fully aware of evil as evil, merely of the unfortunate messiness of murder, and its regrettable effects on her husband. Her inability to kill an old man who resembled her father, while remaining eager to have him killed, scarcely suggests more than a psychological quirk, certainly not goodness at war with evil, although it shows Shakespeare's insight into pathological states of mind. So she remains a unique figure in Shakespeare's plays, one who encourages evil in another, and shares in that evil, and yet who stays unaware of the moral reality of evil, an 'innocent' in the darker Elizabethan sense of the word. But still the sleepwalking scene fills us with pity for the woman; the essential charity of Shakespeare's display of human nature makes us feel that no-one, not even a woman so fatally amoral, so destructive of good, should suffer like this. Nevertheless, however moved we may be, we must recognise that she is not truly tragic, for there is no true tragedy without self-awareness; she is 'merely' the most pathetic evil-doer ever created in drama, and only Vittoria, Webster's 'White Devil', comes anywhere near the poignancy of her end. To the whispered pity and horror of those watching, she fades out of the play – but the train of bloody and tragic events which she has helped to set in motion goes on to its inevitable end.

We return to a Macbeth still only half-accepting the thought of killing his King, but content, as his wife urges, to hide such impulses and let her welcome Duncan as their guest. In the evening of Duncan's arrival, the unexpected opportunity for murder, Macbeth and his wife meet for the crucial decision. Macbeth's opening soliloquy of 1.7 is a good example of how the charged and vivid imagery of great poetry can be used to show the real nature of the speaker's feelings lying behind the logical sense of his argument. Macbeth's arguments are rational and clear. He would take his chance of spiritual damnation if the murder could end with itself, without further consequences, but violence teaches others how to use violence against the violent; in addition, social pressure forbids the killing of Duncan, for he is Macbeth's kinsman, his lord, and his guest, and so good a king that his murder would cause widespread pity for him, and hatred of the killer. Again, Macbeth recognises that he has no real reason for killing Duncan except simple ambition, well-known as likely to overreach itself. In any case (and now he is addressing his wife), he is admired and respected by all after the King's favours, and will not jeopardise this. These are his surface-reasons for rejecting the idea of murder, but they are expressed in poetry which continually suggests the wider and deeper, even universal, emotional forces which Macbeth is feeling as he speaks. The whole speech, especially as spoken language, carries this undertone, but one can point to such phrases as 'this bank and shoal of time', 'even-handed justice', 'poison'd chalice', 'plead like angels, trumpet-tongu'd, against/The deep damnation of his taking-off'. Both the thinking and the feeling Macbeth are revealed side by side in this passage – surely no murderer was ever more logically and emotionally aware, before he killed, of every reason for not killing. This is where the essential human tragedy of Macbeth is seen to begin, for it is this same man who, some forty-five lines later, says:

> I am settled, and bend up
> Each corporal agent to this terrible feat.[207]

Plainly, what Lady Macbeth has said to him during those forty-five lines has changed his decisions not to murder the King – how has she 'succeeded'? Quite simply, as one would expect from the almost naïve, yet determined, Lady Macbeth we already partly know. In persuading Macbeth, she at once associates his scruples, not with valid moral beliefs (she never suggests that killing Duncan is murder), but with a lack of the manliness which a wife should expect from her husband; there is a sexual overtone here which an Elizabethan would have noted. To her, a real man should have the guts to take what he wants. Macbeth is roused to reply in her terms, to reject indignantly her doubt of his manhood:

> I dare do all that may become a man;
> Who dares do more is none.[208]

There is deep tragic irony here in the latent truth that Macbeth, by daring to be more than the man he had been, became at length far less than that man. Lady Macbeth continues her line of attack; she reminds him of his old ideas of seizing the crown, is disgusted that a real man could throw away such ambitions, especially now when a good opportunity is offered. Still there is no hint of the moral or emotional arguments against murder which Macbeth has been feeling so recently – she has now simplified his complex human struggle into a matter of tactics, and she proceeds to show that the whole plan of the murder is already clear in her mind. So killing Duncan becomes a practical task which it should be easy to carry out, and it seems equally easy to put the blame on others. Moral doubts, for the moment, have been put aside by practical considerations; the question 'Is it right?' has given way to 'Can it be done?'. At this point, Macbeth is convinced, but only that the murder can be done safely; he has been brought to agree to murder although his deeper scruples have not even been touched upon.

Before we come to the murder of Duncan, Macbeth's soliloquy in 2.1 is a salutary reminder that we are dealing with a successful Elizabethan playwright as well as a creative master of human truth. This speech is wonderful, popular melodramatic rhetoric, and if a modern actor should regard a full-throated, full-blooded delivery of these lines as old-fashioned and impossible, so much the worse for his insight into the play as a whole. Although Shakespeare's primary

224

object here is no doubt to give his audience the pleasure of an authentic theatrical shock (and how well he succeeds, if we will let him!), the speech is also an effective prelude to the murder of the next scene, setting the personal side of murder against the universal tradition of the unnaturalness and sinful terror of the deed, so that we see Macbeth, not only as a man disturbed almost beyond sanity, but one rightly so, deserving to be associated with Tarquin, the archetype of the destroyer of innocence through selfish desire.

Then with 2.2, we are brought back into the enclosed, hushed world of the killing of the King, both the physical and psychological effects of which on Macbeth and his wife are the core of the action, while the actual killing, very effectively, is not shown on stage.[209] It is surely unnecessary to stress the immense dramatic power of this scene, the atmosphere of darkness and tension, hurrying and suspense, the sense of the ugly and irreversible nature of slaughter; the words and imagery, the staccato rhythms, the sudden knocking off-stage, all play their part. Behind all these effects upon our senses and imaginations, lies the truth of what is happening to these fumbling sinners, the first fruits of their decision. Lady Macbeth is still consciously and persistently directing the murder, taking care of necessary details and coping as well as she can with a husband who has finally committed, not merely dreamt of, the killing of his King. Nevertheless, it is Macbeth who holds the centre of the stage, his inner conflict shown not only by him, but by his wife's reactions. Against her anxiety for a speedy and complete end to their task, her realisation of the danger of being caught, in terrible truth, red-handed, stands the almost bemused figure of Macbeth, taken in the trap of his own discord: one part of him, which he had ignored in 1.7, is a man aware of the moral and social evil of this murder, the other a naïvely courageous man, yet too weak to fail to respond to his wife's taunts. This is the confused and divided 'hero' of Scotland who says to his wife:

> But wherefore could not I pronounce 'Amen'?
> I had most need of blessing, and 'Amen'
> Stuck in my throat.

Lady Macbeth's simple mind sees the truth, and its dangers:

> These deeds must not be thought
> After these ways: so, it will make us mad.[210]

She is right: to hold together in one mind the act of murder already

225

done and desire for blessing is an incongruity which that mind can escape only by madness or (since the murder is a fact that can never be undone) by losing the will to be blessed, the main moral impulse of one's nature. To put Macbeth's tragic dilemma in other, equally valid, terms, he is a man essentially ill-fitted for the role he has chosen; to be a successful murderer and usurper, a man must have overpowering ambition, complete dedication to his own ends, some courage, and a certain callous common sense; if he is to seize illegally the delights of kingship, and enjoy them, he must not have conflicts within him, and, above all, he must not have a sensitive, feeling imagination. In a sense, Macbeth is Richard II trying to be Richard III.

But Macbeth has committed murder to become the King, even at the cost of suppressing his better part, and so has given himself to a 'rational' course of political expediency in which goodness and mercy are foolish weaknesses. This 'rational' view, which we have seen shared by Iago and Edmund, had been exactly expressed by the villain, Mordred, in a play some twenty years before:

> Weak is the sceptre's hold that seeks but right,
> The care whereof hath danger'd many crowns.
> As much as water differeth from the fire,
> So much man's profit jars from what is just.
> A free recourse to wrong doth oft secure
> The doubtful seat, and plucks down many a foe.
> The sword must seldom cease: a sovereign's hand
> Is scantly safe, but whiles it smites. Let him
> Usurp no crown that likes a guiltless life:
> Aspiring power and justice seld [seldom] agree.[211]

These lines are a comment on Macbeth's path through the rest of the play. His inner struggle has consequences far wider than the personal results. In the political setting into which he has now thrust himself, his human conflict grows more complex; there is now added the struggle between Macbeth the 'private' man and Macbeth the 'public' man, the one who sought power and the one who has to keep it. The very facts of the situation into which he has chosen, with a dreadful simplicity and blindness, to place himself, unfit him to be the happy and successful king he had thought to be. The dramatist's insertion in the play, in 4.3, of that emphasis on disorder as the mark of a bad king which I have already mentioned, is more than a general comment much to Elizabethan taste; it suggests another side of

Macbeth's tragedy. He has committed himself to disorder by the act of regicide through which he took on the public role of king, and from now on the man's efforts to remain the King must inevitably proceed by way of disorder, first within himself, and then spreading out to the whole of the society around him. As a worthy clergyman wrote at this time: 'Evill behaviour in Princes, infecteth as it were the ayre round about'.[212]

In this context of evil and disorder, what is the significance of the supernatural in the play, apart from its obvious appeal to the audience? The effect of the witches' first partly fulfilled prophecies on Macbeth, as has been suggested, was to give an edge, an urgency, to a moral conflict already present in him, but it was his wife's pressure which decided him to kill Duncan, as Shakespeare carefully shows. After the killing of Banquo, the appearance of his ghost in 3.4 is far more than a popular stage excitement, although it is certainly that. This almost pathetic usurper, who had seen his crime (through his wife's prompting) as an easy road to unqestioned kingship, is still relying on the witches' prophetic truth; they had said that Banquo's line would be kings, and Macbeth tries to end that line by other murders. By now Shakespeare has made it clear that this man's nature is ruled by instinctive, emotional responses to supernatural pressures of an emotional and irrational kind; he has been placed in a situation precisely suited to play on his weakness; the supernatural plays an analogous role in *Hamlet*, though with entirely different results. As Macbeth sees Banquo's ghost, he realises, but only briefly, that killing settles nothing, that the path that he has chosen with so much determined self-destruction leads nowhere if the dead still live. Yet he has reached the stage where, emotionally conditioned by evil, he must continue in evil. Indeed, the shock of Banquo's ghost drives him into a further, and decisive, weakening of his original moral sense. He resolves to seek out the witches; originally evil had come to him – now the ultimate point of evil is reached, where a man goes willingly to evil for help. For an Elizabethan, to give way to evil temptation was sinful but human; to go to the evil powers voluntarily, and seek their help for one's own ends, was the special, damnable mark of witchcraft – *Doctor Faustus* is but one contemporary expression of this belief. Macbeth's decision to take this step is shown in all its stupid but tragic obstinacy:

> I will tomorrow,
> And betimes I will to the Weird Sisters:

> More shall they speak; for now I am bent to know
> By the worst means the worst. For mine own good
> All causes shall give way. I am in blood
> Stepp'd in so far that, should I wade no more,
> Returning were as tedious as go o'er.
> Strange things I have in head that will to hand,
> Which must be acted ere they may be scann'd.[213]

This is a man who knows the evil he is about to do, who is choosing to act first and think afterwards, with a self-blinded impatience that must have its way, whatever the evil folly of it. In Elizabethan terms, his will hears wit and rejects it. Then Lady Macbeth, good but uncomprehending wife that she is, says what any wife might say: 'You lack the season of all natures, sleep' and Macbeth, who had once been able to realise that, in a real sense, 'Macbeth shall sleep no more', replies:

> Come, we'll to sleep. My strange and self-abuse
> Is the initiate fear that wants hard use.
> We are yet but young in deed.[214]

After this dreadful half-apology for not being at present callous enough, the pair go to bed.

In 4.1 Macbeth goes to the witches. A few minutes before, in a brief but highly theatrical appearance, Hecate has anticipated the only direction that such a man can now take:

> He shall spurn fate, scorn death, and bear
> His hopes 'bove wisdom, grace and fear;
> And you all know security
> Is mortals' chiefest enemy.[215]

There is a nice ambiguity here; 'security', in the sense of Macbeth's trust in the witches, will be fatal to him – equally, his need to have the security of assured success is damning him. The witches, at this second meeting, give him, he wrongly believes, the security he seeks, but this merely confirms, does not create, the hubris which has already begun to possess him. At the end of a wonderfully effective and spectacular stage-scene, when he hears of Macduff's escape to England, he can think only of immediate bloody action, however pointless and politically foolish it may be.

When Macbeth appears on the stage again, more than a fifth of the play has intervened. Much has happened outside his narrow personal world: the slaughter of Lady Macduff and her children is a frankly pathetic appeal to the sensibilities of his Elizabethan audience (and, one hopes, to ours), but the fate of these 'secondary victims' of tragedy leads directly and inevitably to the shocked reaction of her husband and his predictable determination to destroy the monster Macbeth, and thence to the approach of Macbeth's enemies towards Dunsinane. As Malcolm says in 4.3:

> Macbeth
> Is ripe for shaking, and the pow'rs above
> Put on their instruments.[216]

An Elizabethan might take 'the pow'rs above' as Fate, even as God, but the dramatist shows throughout this play (as so often elsewhere) that human beings are their own Fate. Indeed, in 5.1, just before Macbeth's return to the stage, Shakespeare has shown in the sleep-walking scene the dreadful, poignant truth of how a human being, once so blindly self-assured, can be finally destroyed from within by her own unrealised nature – a brief but terrible anticipation of the 'Fate' awaiting her husband.

To 5.3, then, to Macbeth in his castle awaiting attack. All the emphasis of the scene is upon him, especially upon the social isolation to which his nature has brought him; it is a characteristic of Shakespeare's tragic figures that, while they seek to cope with human society, shape and are shaped by their situation within it, they are never, ultimately, fully a part of it. Macbeth is shown here as the fighter faced with the prospect of a hard battle, and to that extent he is still partly involved in the world, the world of his beginning in the play, but within him his nature sees itself as cut off from the normal life of men; this is the man, we realise, who at the start desired so much 'Golden opinions from all sorts of people',[217] and who has now brought himself to the point where:

> ... that which should accompany old age,
> As honour, love, obedience, troops of friends,
> I must not look to have.[218]

Now his disruption has reached almost its final stage; the logic of his emotions has brought him to the self-destructive state where emotion itself can feel no meaning in living. Yet he still has his courage, and he still clings to what seems the witches' promise of his assured victory. The once successful soldier is now waiting like a child for the realisation of a fantasy, and with tragic irony he brushes aside the Doctor's warning that the sick mind must cure itself. As the scene ends, he can continue to find assurance in Birnam Wood.

A moment later, in 5.4, we learn that the Wood will move to Dunsinane. Equally important is Malcolm's comment that Macbeth's 'main hope' is to remain within his castle and resist a siege. This is the solid common sense of military tactics, and Siward's words:

> Thoughts speculative their unsure hopes relate,
> But certain issue strokes must arbitrate;[219]

define the difference between Macbeth's world of hopes and fears, and the reality which confronts him.

The next scene brings us back to Macbeth again, and his first speech links to what Malcolm has said; he sees that his proper policy is to rely on the strength of his castle, and for an instant we can see the rational, practical soldier that he must once have been. But then he hears of the death of Lady Macbeth, and emotion, his deep-seated tendency to feel life rather than to understand it, sweeps over him. He had earlier begun to see the futility of his life; now it overwhelms him, and is expressed in lines so well-known, so often discussed, that a critic might hesitate to comment on them yet again. But they mark the virtual extremity of Macbeth's inner strife, the substance of the play, and they cannot be ignored:

SEYTON   The Queen, my lord, is dead.
MACBETH   She should have died hereafter.
            There would have been a time for such a word.
            To-morrow, and to-morrow, and to-morrow,
            Creeps in this petty pace from day to day
            To the last syllable of recorded time,
            And all our yesterdays have lighted fools
            The way to dusty death. Out, out, brief candle!
            Life's but a walking shadow, a poor player,
            That struts and frets his hour upon the stage,
            And then is heard no more; it is a tale
            Told by an idiot, full of sound and fury,
            Signifying nothing.[220]

Of immediate importance is the complex effect of this passage directly upon the audience. There is the slow, regular rhythm of the

230

lines, wherein consonants echo each other, and vowels ring, like the reverberations of a tolling bell. Carried upon these sounds is the 'meaning', the emotional pressure; first Macbeth's realisation, not so much that his wife has gone, but that he has now no time to mourn her, or, more terribly, no emotion to spare for her; then comes the immediate spreading outwards of all the bitterness at the final futility of his life which we have seen gathering within him. Here, as always in Shakespeare's tragedies, the particular becomes the universal, quite explicitly for once; Macbeth is voicing for us, then and now, a vision of life which we all glimpse, I suppose, at some time in our lives, even if, hopefully, we are not bound within it as Macbeth is. For he is a man who has knowingly (in a way) confined himself to a world of conflicting fears and desires, blind unreason and fantasy; now he can do nothing but rely passively upon the witches' promises, and even if he should act, no action will restore his wife, or give him the quiet kingship which his own deeds have made impossible from the start. The business of his life, his motives for existing, have no further point or goal; living is just the empty pretence of 'a poor player', mere transitory nonsense. To see one's life like this is to be virtually dead – none of the other tragic protagonists in Shakespeare reaches this position of negative despair, for they all end still believing that there is some meaning in life.

A moment after this speech, Macbeth learns that the first of the final prophecies was a false 'truth', and as half his last foundation is suddenly removed, he returns to the only power left in him, that stubborn courage which made him Thane of Cawdor and so started his tragedy. His sudden wild decision to leave his castle and rush upon his enemies, as Shakespeare has already shown, is a fatal tactical error, merely passionate and irrational however gallant it may seem. So the great fighter whose valour, in the beginning, had saved Duncan's throne, goes out now like a blind bear to fight against Duncan's heir, with only one witches' promise on which to rely. He kills Young Siward almost in passing, and then, face to face with Macduff, his last foothold on supernatural 'truth' crumbles – Macduff was not (technically) 'born of woman'. The world of fantasy which Macbeth chose to enter, and in which he has fought with reality throughout the play, clashes with the hard fact of the real, and vanishes as the witches themselves vanished. For a long moment, it seems that Macbeth, now indeed completely without hope, will refuse to fight. But Shakespeare knows the truth of the Macbeth he has created – and the dramatic potential of the situation; Macbeth the soldier suddenly falls back upon the only solid power which he has had throughout all his inner struggles, the only force which can resolve them, even if too late: he finds his courage, and dies fighting. Order is restored to the state once more – long misery and suffering for all, a man's self-destruction, the deaths of many, and Scotland returns to where she was when the first traitor Cawdor was killed.

These last moments of the play have fine dramatic power and great human truth, as have all the endings of Shakespeare's major tragedies, and these tragedies, too, leave questions in our minds, make us re-examine Man's life, our lives, with a new awareness of the eternal problems of our divided nature. This is true of *Macbeth*, but, again like the other tragedies, it has its own special quality or tone. It is important, therefore, to consider both our general reactions to the play, and its special effect upon us.

To begin with, it is worth noting that *Macbeth* is the only one of these main tragedies in which the essential primary inner struggle of the protagonist is over early in the play, following the murder of Duncan in 2.2, after which it changes. In *Hamlet* the pressures of 'human incongruity' begin early, and last almost to the end, as they do in *Romeo and Juliet* and in *King Lear*; in *Othello* they do not begin (although anticipated) until nearly the middle of the play, and then they last to the end of the play. In *Antony and Cleopatra*, in many ways a very special case, human conflict is a political rather than a personal force until near the end, when suddenly it becomes wholly and powerfully personal, and then, as suddenly, is resolved in strange magnificence. To return to *Macbeth*, the nature of his human incongruity, as often, does not lie entirely within himself; the witches and Lady Macbeth represent (like Iago) outside forces which awaken the conflict latent within the protagonist, and start it working, and that incongruity is resolved in 2.2 because (again like Iago) they confuse good and evil in his mind. Thus far it seems that Shakespeare is presenting a traditional moral conflict between good and evil in Macbeth, but in fact little true sense of good and evil is shown in him: he seems to feel none of Banquo's moral fear of the witches as evil; when in 1.7. he decides at first not to kill Duncan, his conscious arguments against murder are mainly matters of expediency, almost of convention – above all else, he wants to be 'good Macbeth' because he fears to be known to have done evil. Thus Lady Macbeth's simple amorality has little difficulty in turning her husband to evil action; she has only to convince him that he can seize the throne without guilt, that is, without being publicly known to be guilty, to make him accept that public 'morality' supersedes private morality. So by the end of 2.2 Shakespeare has evoked in his audience their horror of the powers of evil and of murder, and this sense of horror will be progressively increased throughout the rest of the play. Yet there is no such lasting horror in Macbeth himself. The intensity of inner struggle which makes the early Macbeth so memorable, embodies and accepts, in fact, the human truth that, as we all know, a man can fear evil for both moral and selfish reasons, and then commit it only for selfish ends, having finished his conflict by ignoring the moral pressure.

Here is the root of our main final two-fold response to Macbeth and his tragedy. Up to his first act of murder, we have been led to feel pity for the man mixed with horror at his deed, but already that pity and horror have been set within the traditional universal sense of the struggle between good and evil, with its pity for every sinner and horror for his sin. After the murder of Duncan, this double view of Macbeth is gradually intensified by Shakespeare even in the necessary process, at the 'plot-level', of presenting exciting 'political' action leading to a satisfying and dramatic ending. We are given more insights into the spreading confusion and strife in Macbeth and realise that these now arise from his obstinate and irrational clinging to a kingship which is a fantasy of what in fact he had never possessed; his conflict has finally lost any moral basis it might have had. Perhaps this is partly the reason, this blind fantasy, why we still feel pity for the man, and it is extended by our pity for his wife, who shared his fantasy of kingship. Their failure to understand their original situation, their consequent inability to understand their suffering, the uncomprehended perversity with which they used married love and trust as means to evil, these move us to mercy rather than judgement. But all this is taking place within a sequence of 'political' events which is forcing us to see that the evil of murder and violence is spreading out from Macbeth into the whole of society; suffering and death reach those who are entirely innocent, like Banquo and, especially, Lady Macduff and her children. As the play continues, our sorrow that Macbeth and his wife cannot feel the nature of their evil, and the torment that it brings to others as well as themselves, becomes involved with a sense of the universal consequences of evil, consequences seen as spreading from the evil of the 'private' man into the evil of the 'public' man, and so beyond into human society.

Thus, by the end of the play, we have been brought to realise so many inter-related personal and social truths, so much of the effects of 'human incongruity' on individuals and the world, that a complex of emotions and perceptions is at work within us. Certainly we have enjoyed an exciting and dramatic story – that is the immediate fact. Beneath that enjoyment, what else do we experience? Most people in the audience, I believe, are left possessed mainly by that mingled pity and horror to which I have referred, and, created with them, that response which is one of the marks of great tragedy, the sense of having understood ourselves more clearly, and, because of that, of having risen for a moment above our narrow personal view of life into a wider vision of Mankind.

In addition to all this, from this particular play, forming its special quality, there grows in us a disturbing yet salutary awareness of the real nature of violence. Something of this is implicit from the beginning, first in the account of the battle in which Macbeth routed Duncan's enemies (shortly to be seen as so full of ironies), and later, especially, in the callous killing by Macbeth of Duncan's two 'grooms'. But it is when Macbeth, at the end of 4.1., instantly decides to kill Lady Macduff and her children that we fully recognise the awful 'logic of violence' in which he is trapped, and which gives this play its distinctive effect. This 'logic of violence' is not only mere brutal self-assertion that establishes nothing, and solves no problem, but also, by its very nature, it cannot exist except by perpetuating itself. It is the 'argument' that bypasses reason, and can never return to that road; it must continue, as in Macbeth, as a sterile kind of conditioned reflex, with always the same automatic and bloody response to any challenge. At that moment in 4.1., Macbeth shows that he has finally lost that rational control of his unreason which he had so painfully struggled to be rid of before and during the murder of Duncan. With that 'success', achieved only by suppressing the best of himself, destroying the balance of his nature, he had begun to leave the human company which, ironically, he prized so much; now he finally enters the lonely wilderness of the man who lives by violence and, at last, like Macbeth, dies by it. The Elizabethans had reason, in their often brutal and stormy age, to know and fear this 'logic of violence'; in *Macbeth* Shakespeare has completely and truthfully displayed to them the workings of it, just as it is, without moralising. For us today, in a world perverted and debased by the threat of far greater violence, this is an even more disturbing, yet even more necessary, part of the play's total effect on us; this, for us, is the unique quality of *Macbeth*.

Antony and Cleopatra

The immediate appeal of this play for an Elizabethan audience is plain; it shows in exciting detail that political strife between Roman 'great ones' which *Julius Caesar* had dramatised some seven years before. The earlier play had been comparatively restricted in range, with the main action simple, and taking place chiefly in Rome. In the present play, the Antony who had out-manoeuvred Brutus and Cassius is older, more complex, and his opponent a younger man, Octavius Caesar, a more calculating political figure than even Antony had ever been: the action moves widely throughout the Roman world of power-seeking, and the prize of victory is supreme control of that world. So the struggle has something of the historical dramatic appeal that the dramatist had used earlier, in *Richard II* for example, but here the history is wider, more varied, and has the traditional grandeur and importance always associated in Elizabethan minds with the great names and events of far-off classical times.

But there is an important addition, the presence of Cleopatra as an integral part of the play. The power-struggle between Caesar and Antony had always been very closely associated with the love-story of Antony and Cleopatra, and that love-story had been seen, from Plutarch down to Shakespeare's time, as a special example of the power of love to change the course of history. The Elizabethans had inherited conflicting views of Cleopatra's part in the story; she was seen as both a wily sensualist who entrapped Antony and brought him to ruin, and as the martyr to love that Chaucer had presented in *The Legend of Good Women*, a woman 'good' in her devotion to her love for Antony. For example, a serious-minded writer on true nobility said with some scorn in 1563:

> Conquered not *Cleopatra Caesar*, so valeant conqueror?
> Maryed not *Antonius* the selfe same minyon [darling], thoughe
> a common harlot?.[221]

While a popular writer, praising 'Virtuous Ladies' in 1599, had taken the opposite view:

> Some will say women are unconstant; but I say not all:
> for Penelope, and Cleopatra, Lucretia, with divers more too

long to rehearse, shall stand for examples of such constancie,
as no man (ever) more constant.[222]

Whichever attitude one adopted (or even if one managed to accept
both), the story certainly carried a moral lesson acceptable to
Shakespeare's age: we have seen earlier the very human Elizabethan
interest in Woman as temptation, a prominent part of a man's
struggle with his human incongruity of passion and reason, his need
to control his animal passion by the use of reason. This conflict, as
we have seen, had already been present in a number of Shakespeare's
plays.

This old and well-known story of the loves of Antony and
Cleopatra culminated in their suicide. The usual Elizabethan view of
suicide was the traditional Christian one, as expressed in a very
popular religious work of 1600:

> Abridge the time [the length of our life] we may not,
> we ought not, for all the afflictions that may betide
> the sonnes of man. The lawes of nations have forbid in this
> case the benefit of decent buriall, to terrifie men from
> this shamefull fact [act] of casting away themselves
> desperatelie.[223]

Whilst no doubt accepting this view as part of their religion, many
members of Shakespeare's audience would also be aware of the quite
different classical opinion, the Stoic teaching that suicide was the
supreme symbol of a wise man's ability to be the sole arbiter of his
own fate. Thus in Chapman's *Caesar and Pompey*, written about
1605, shortly before *Antony and Cleopatra* (*c*1607), Cato is the only
man in the play strong enought to be true to himself and end his life
when he thinks fit. Brutus, of course, had similarly found in suicide a
personal victory in the face of political defeat. Indeed, Mary Herbert,
Countess of Pembroke, in her 1595 translation of Robert Garnier's
Marc Antoine, had helped to pass on this Stoic conviction; in her
version of Garnier's work, *The Tragedie of Antonie*, the Chorus at
the end of Act 3 sums up this view of suicide in relation to Antony:

> Who freely can himselfe dispose
> Of that last hower which all must close,
>   And leave this life at pleasure:
> This noble freedome more esteemes,
> And in his heart more precious deemes,
>   Then [than] crowne and kinglie treasure.
> . . . .

> How abject him, how base thinke I,
> Who wanting courage can not dye
>   When need him thereto calleth?
> . . . .
> O *Antony* with thy dear mate
> Both in misfortunes fortunate!
>   Whose thoughts to death aspiring
> Shall you protect from victors rage,
> Who on each side doth you encage,
>   To triumph much desiring.
> That Caesar may you not offend
> Nought else but death can you defend,
>   Which his weak force derideth.[224]

Thus, for Elizabethans, suicide was a typical symbol of the human dilemma, whether this was between a man's desperation and his fear of death, or between that fear and a rational belief in Man's autonomy. The story of Antony and Cleopatra which Shakespeare took from North's translation of Plutarch's *Lives* of course portrays Antony similarly, as regarding suicide as a final test of courage and manhood, whereas Cleopatra, in Plutarch's account, kills herself to escape from Caesar to Antony. But Shakespeare, as we shall see, changes the nature of these deaths in altering the atmosphere around them.

Thus, for Shakespeare's audience *Antony and Cleopatra* was, at the least, a vivid and exciting historical story joined with a famous love-story, the whole giving perhaps some warning of the dangers of ambition, but certainly showing how 'great ones' can fail in the world through enslavement to passion. The pattern of part of the play clearly emphasises this last point. In the body of the play Antony is shown as moving between reason (the ability to concentrate rationally on the best way of defeating Caesar) and passion (mainly, of course, his need of Cleopatra, but also of the whole life of unRoman fantasy and desire which she enriches with her love). The play opens with the contrast between Antony's infatuation with Cleopatra, and the shocked reaction of Demetrius and Philo; in 1.4. Caesar is also shocked, but rather for personal political reasons than morally; Antony his partner could do what he liked if he were the only sufferer, but to Caeser it is childish to destroy by self-indulgence not only his own but his associate's power in the political game. Already Antony and Caesar are established as representing contrary attitudes to life, the fundamental opposition between the rational and the irrational which had earlier been illustrated by Shakespeare's historical drama in, for example, the contrast of Worcester and Hotspur. The Elizabethan audience was quite aware of this; it was of course a feature of the traditional story, the moral overtones of which are well shown in a French writer's comment translated in 1595:

> *Antonie* and *Cleopatra*, who spent three or foure hundred thousand French crownes at a banquet in one day, were vanquished by *Octavius*, who was sober, and contented himselfe with common meats, eating and drinking but little.[225]

But Antony breaks away from Cleopatra on hearing of his wife's death, and returns to Rome, where in Act 2 he marries Octavia. For the moment he has moved to a hardheaded acceptance and use of political pressures, but Enobarbus, who knows his Antony, foresees that this strictly rational mood will not last long: in Act 3 the Antony–Octavia marriage breaks up, and Antony, falling again under the power of his irrational desires, returns to Cleopatra. Then comes the turning-point of the play, the defeat at Actium, the very symbol of sound political tactics overthrown by the weakness (in military terms) of feminine impulse affecting even a soldier like Antony. This disaster swings him back to a new attempt at a rational opposition to Caesar, but Cleopatra and their love still influence him, and in 4.2. the Egyptian forces again destroy his political chances. From this moment, the whole world of Antony and Cleopatra moves into a final phase where defeat, although accepted as a fact, is transformed into a new kind of victory in death.

This is the obvious effect of the play, then and now, upon an audience, but this is little more than the bare story as told by Plutarch and used as a dramatic framework by Shakespeare, a basic pattern of the struggle of Antony with his human weakness. In fact, the play is far more complex than this in its methods and effects, as a closer analysis will show.

To begin with, the play does not present merely a bald contrast between the world of Caesar and the world of Antony. There are three 'worlds', three attitudes to life, displayed and working within the play. First there is the political world of power-seeking, in which rational cunning (the 'lower' reason) and tactical skill are the only effective weapons, and emotion, apart from the controlled use of anger and indignation, is a handicap. It is the world of Caesar, Antony and Pompey, but Antony is not wholly of it, and Pompey is weakened by quite unsuitable moral doubts; it is the world in which Richard III is at first so successful, which Bolingbroke-Henry IV largely accepts, which Macbeth destroys himself by entering, which Antony (in *Julius Caesar*) once knew so well, and for which Brutus was so plainly unfitted. It is epitomised in Menas's bitter comment on Pompey's scruples in 2.7 about the possible assassination of his rivals:

> For this,
> I'll never follow thy pall'd fortunes more.
> Who seeks, and will not take when once 'tis offered,
> Shall never find it more.[226]

This is akin to Lady Macbeth's attitude to Macbeth, the voice of amoral practical reason.

Accompanying this world, there is the world of heroic courage, where the ideal of honour and the desire for personal glory are dominant. Ambition is its characteristic, and ambition, in such a context, is scarcely a rational impulse. Caesar has political ambition, but in him it is a form of hard, calculating pride; in Antony, the older Antony, ambition and honour, the desire for power and success, are fluctuating emotions closely linked to the powerful and irrational sexual needs which are themselves part of the heroic personality. In Garnier's *The Tragedie of Antonie* (in the Mary Herbert version) Antonie expresses exactly the full heroic, passionate position with its sexual overtones:

> So fervent this desire to commaund:
> Such jealousie it kindleth in our hearts,
> *Sooner will men permit another should*
> *Love her they love, then weare the crowne they weare.*
> All lawes it breakes, turnes all things upside downe:
> Amitie, kindred, nought so holy is
> But it defiles. A monarchie to gaine
> None cares which way, so he may it obtain.[227]

The Elizabethan audience of *Antony and Cleopatra* would remember the recent real-life example of such heroic, disruptive ambition, the pathetically incompetent and hopeless Essex revolt of 1601, speedily crushed with the full weight of the law. Essex was thought of as a sort of gallant fool; more than this, I feel certain that in the years following the Essex débâcle, amongst thoughtful people in London there was an increased sense of the futility, and social danger, of such heroic but ineffectual ambition. Beyond doubt there was a general fear of the public effects of such personal ambition, a fear nourished by both religion and the 'Homilies'. It is interesting that in Samuel Daniel's 'classical' closet-drama *The Tragedie of Cleopatra* (1599 edition), the Chorus deplores 'Opinion', and the desire for fame, as:

> O mindes tormentor, bodies wracke,
> Vain promiser of that sweete rest,
> Which never any yet possest.[228]

and that this play ends on the following words:

> Is greatnesse of this sort,
> That greatnesse greatnesse marres,
> And wrackes it selfe, selfe driven
> On Rockes of her own might?
> Doth Order order so
> Disorders overthrow?[229]

This serves to remind us that many of Shakespeare's audience would have regarded his play, no matter how exciting an entertainment, as also the story of how warring ambitions created a struggle in which disorder spread through the Roman world and Romans fought against Romans (just as Essex, if he had succeeded, might well have started a civil war), and all through ambition and, in Antony's case, heroic pride. Indeed, at about this time Shakespeare was writing *Coriolanus*, where, as we have seen, the protagonists's obstinate yet heroic arrogance leads him, in his particular situation, to betray his country and almost destroy it. Thus the Antony–Caesar conflict has overtones of universal application to Man's political behaviour in general, but with, of course, particular relevance to one man's, Antony's, human conflict. This conflict is clearly shown, not just as the contest of two ambitious leaders, but also as an exposition of two contrasting ways in which the 'private' man (the personal ego) can attempt to take on successfuly the burden of becoming a 'public' man. We have seen before how this is a common difficulty of the human spirit of which Elizabethans were well aware, and which Shakespeare often demonstrates in his plays. In the present play, the problem is given a deliberately ironic and unusual treatment inspired by the material. On the face of it, Caesar is shown, following accepted history, as fitted for the role of successful politician and conqueror, while Antony is plainly unfitted. But by the end of the play, the dramatist has created such depth of emotional sympathy with Antony that Caesar's worldly success is no longer impressive; the major emphasis has shifted to Antony and to that special factor intruding into political struggle, Cleopatra.

She is, in fact, unique among Shakespeare's women-in-politics, both in herself and in her function in the play. Lady Macbeth, a little earlier, and Volumnia, a little later, are shown to be examples of the crucial effect that women's emotional power over men can have on the struggle for power, but neither has anything of the quality of Cleopatra. She has throughout the true heroic, 'larger than life' tone which, ironically, Antony himself, for all his talk of courage and honour, barely achieves fully by the end of the play. Her peculiar gift, her supreme fitness for her complex role, consists in what is hinted at in Enobarbus's reference to 'Her infinite variety'.[230] She is of course the centre of the third 'world' of the play, the realm of sexual passion, but she is also completely at home, and effective, in the other two worlds of the play. Something of this is certainly present in Plutarch's account, but it is Shakespeare who uses it as the central irony of his drama. In Shakespeare's presentation of her, she is far more than either the woman-as-seducer or the woman-as-love-martyr of traditional views. In Roman history she had figured as a great ruler, the political equal of Caesar, and as a woman whose territory was an essential prize for any such would-be master of the Roman world. The play shows this quite clearly: Cleopatra is a woman, and therefore, an Elizabethan would assume, probably unfitted for the strategies of political struggle, but she is shown in fact as able to take a place in the arena of international power-seeking, temporise with the superior might of Caesar, and, finally, outwit him in at least part of his political designs. She is also the partner of the 'political' Antony, and shares with him the handling (or mis-handling) of his struggle with Caesar. Moreover, she is part of the heroic, grandiloquent world of honour of the other Antony; indeed, at the end of the play she transforms that world until it overshadows all the 'real' world, but long before that she is shown sharing, or reflecting, all Antony's aspirations to glory and honour, without, it is true, blinding herself to their limitations, as Antony does. Finally, especially and obviously, she is the centre and essence of that third world of sexuality which shapes and colours every moment of Antony's success or failure in the play. Her personality permeates the drama, even when she is not on the stage, and she links together every theme in it, modifying the otherwise dominant masculine quality of the play.[231] I wonder, in passing, if any members of Shakespeare's audience thought of that other super-woman who had spent her life using both her feminine strengths (perhaps even her sexual wiles) and her masculine mind to achieve and hold political power in a man's world for herself and her English subjects – and who had been succeeded by an inept king who possessed weaknesses of both sexes.

If one turns from Cleopatra to the only other major woman character in the play, Octavia, the contrast emphasises the special quality of Cleopatra. Octavia is indeed the 'good woman', as the condescending sentimentality of men has always seen the type. Her role in the play is that of the decent, caring woman thrown into the midst of political manoeuvring of which she has no comprehension; she is used as a piece in the game between Caesar and Antony. Plutarch says that Antony's treatment of her in leaving this worthy, respectable wife for the delights of Cleopatra, was one of the reasons why popular feeling in Rome turned against their former idol;[232] Shakespeare shows that it certainly gave Caesar good acceptable grounds for pursuing Antony to his final defeat.

The part of Enobarbus in the total effect of the play now requires some detailed consideration, for he helps to shape our realisation of Antony and his situation in the main body of the drama, and in himself is a moving example of the effects of human conflict. It seems obvious that up to 4.2 (after which he leaves Antony) his reaction to events is a recurring reminder to the audience of the ordinary, practical soldier's attitude to the growing danger of Antony's folly. But it also becomes clear that this apparently sensible soldier, like his master, has his own inner struggles. In the earlier part of the play, he changes from his normal, characteristically male view of women as negligible in the man's world of fighting, with predictable heavy irony about Cleopatra's sufferings,[233] to an awareness of her special greatness. Thus we are shown how this ordinary professional soldier becomes divided between his common reason and an irrational appreciation of the 'heroic' world of love and honour in which Antony increasingly exists: in 2.2 there is subtle self-revelation in his glowing description of Cleopatra in the barge (which Shakespeare took from Plutarch but gave to Enobarbus), in his almost admiring description of her strange and enduring feminine attraction, and then in his admission that marriage to Octavia can never keep Antony from her. His personal problem later goes deeper than this. In 3.10, after the crucial defeat at Actium, there is the first clear indication of this dilemma which is eventually to bring him to a miserable death. Canidius, a worldly-wise man, sees that his leader is

doomed to failure, and decides to go over to Caesar with his men, but
Enobarbus can now say:

> I'll yet follow
> The wounded chance of Antony, though my reason
> Sits in the wind against me.[234]

Shortly afterwards, in 3.13, he sees very clearly the 'heroic' folly of
Antony's offer to fight Caesar in single combat, but again his
irrational devotion to him prevails:

> Mine honesty and I begin to square.
> The loyalty well held to fools does make
> Our faith mere folly. Yet he that can endure
> To follow with allegiance a fall'n lord
> Does conquer him that did his master conquer,
> And earns a place i' th' story.[235]

Yet only a few minutes later he sees how Cleopatra is trying to keep
in favour with Caesar, and comments bitterly on Antony:

> Sir, sir, thou art so leaky
> That we must leave thee to thy sinking, for
> Thy dearest quit thee.[236]

It is Antony's behaviour in the rest of the scene that finally makes
Enobarbus decide to leave his master: Antony first blames both
Cleopatra and his loss of his 'good stars' for his failure; then he turns
on the unfortunate envoy Thyreus and in uncontrolled passion has
him whipped; finally he swings over to a desperate 'heroic' optimism
in which he returns to his love for Cleopatra and foresees a magnificent victory over Caesar. As seen by Enobarbus, his leader has lost all
rational judgement, and has ceased to be worthy of leadership:

> Now he'll outstare the lightning. To be furious,
> Is to be frighted out of fear, and in that mood
> The dove will peck the estridge; and I see still [always]
> A diminution in our captain's brain
> Restores his heart. When valour preys on reason,
> It eats the sword it fights with. I will seek
> Some way to leave him.[237]

Although shortly afterwards, in 4.2, he is moved by Antony's speech
to his servants, in 4.5 we learn that he has finally left him, and that
Antony, with a fine gesture, has sent his treasure after him. This

generosity is what, ironically, destroys Enobarbus. His dispassionate realisation of his leader's obvious inadequacy is swept away by the other side of him, irrational but powerful; gratitude and loyalty cannot be argued for logically, but they represent the emotional ideal of life which he shares at last with his leader. So in 4.9 he leaves the play overwhelmed by the guilt of his desertion of Antony, and his dying words show how completely his original wordly common sense has been swept aside by an emotion stronger than reason:

> O Antony,
> Nobler than my revolt is infamous,
> Forgive me in thine own particular,
> But let the world rank me in register
> A master-leaver and a fugitive!
> O Antony! O Antony![238]

So the clash between everyday reason and the special unreason of 'noble' fantasy has destroyed Enobarbus as it will, in one sense, finally destroy Antony, but the fact that the hardheaded soldier was thus changed is a significant indication (elaborated from Plutarch's brief mention of Domitius) of what is now happening to the tone of the play. With the death of Enobarbus, the final transformation of the normal definitions of the rational and the irrational has begun to appear; the world of Antony, and of those attached to him, is becoming one where emotional heroic greatness rises above the level of mere reason, the common cunning of power-seeking. Hotspur, long before, had been an example of how such heroic spirit can leave the world unconquered; now we are about to experience, through Shakespeare's deeper use of his creative imagination and technique, a far greater, far more complex and moving development of this human truth.

To realise something of the nature of this 'transformation' with which the play ends, we must go back at least as far as 4.14. At this point the two opposite sides of Antony's nature have both suffered; his belief in himself as a political leader has been undermined by Caesar's superiority in war, and his confidence in his honour as the gallant lover has been diminished by Cleopatra's betrayal, as he believes. This lies behind his talk with Eros with which the scene opens: like Hamlet demonstrating the compliant subservience of Polonius,[239] Antony speaks of the changing forms of clouds, but now their evanescence symbolises Antony's feeling of what has happened to his nature:

> My good knave Eros, now thy captain is
> Even such a body. Here I am Antony;
> Yet cannot hold this visible shape.[240]

Both sides of his being have been weakened, and for a moment he has lost that sense of identity without which one cannot live as a person, a 'persona'. But shortly after he is again struggling with the inescapable facts of Caesar's triumph and Cleopatra's 'betrayal', when Mardian tells him of her 'death' for love of Antony. The belief that Cleopatra is dead resolves the conflict within him, as the death of a loved one often does.[241] Cleopatra's love for him has been vindicated, her suicide shows her courage and honour, and the way in which he can end his situation. Suicide, the Senecan supreme act of self-assertion against the trials of the world,[242] will do for him all that he needs: it will prove his heroic love and valour, unite him with Cleopatra, and render Caesar's victory meaningless. It is now that Antony gives the first example of the creation of an atmosphere which will grow in power from here until the end:

> I come, my queen. . . . Stay for me;
> Where souls do couch on flowers, we'll hand in hand,
> And with our sprightly port make the ghosts gaze.
> Dido and her Aeneas shall want troops,
> And all the haunt be ours.[243]

Up to now the play has been largely an account of worldly struggle in which the heroic mood was futile (as in Antony's personal challenge to Caesar), and love was merely self-indulgence and political folly. Now Antony, and later Cleopatra, are shown as beginning to move from that everyday world of successful cunning and brute force, into an area where the emotion of love, firing their imagination, raises the lovers above the level of reason or, more exactly, creates its own special kind of reason which makes love and death the only rational and valid course, one to be followed willingly and with passion. Shakespeare, much earlier, had shown a similar process at work in Romeo and Juliet, but he had made this younger and simpler pair transform the mundane world instinctively through their love, and stumble, as it were, upon their solution. In contrast, he gives the mature Cleopatra, at least, a more consciously sought and achieved, more imaginatively compelling, answer to the incongruity between this world and such love, such love and death. There is pathos in the fate of Romeo and Juliet – one can scarcely dare to pity the end of Cleopatra, or even of Antony.

But the full change of Caesar's world into the new world of Antony and Cleopatra is as yet only suggested. After Antony's suicide, ironically bungled (but for dramatic reasons, of course, and following Plutarch), and the news that Cleopatra is not dead, the dying hero is brought to her side, and their last meeting begins the end of the play. Antony is at first back in Caesar's 'world', anxious that Cleopatra shall protect herself against him, but he dies in 'the high Roman fashion' (the phrase is Cleopatra's), remembering the greatness that was once his, and glad that only Antony could defeat Antony. This is the fine heroic mood, and in it he has found the resolution of all his inner conflicts, but where is the full apotheosis of love which he had glimpsed earlier in the lines quoted above? The fact is that Shakespeare transfers this vision of transformed and ennobled love to Cleopatra, and that in her it will develop into the full glory of the end.

Here, around Antony's death, this transference is beginning, marked by that special use of the 'universal phrase' (already used briefly by Antony) which distinguishes Shakespeare's poetry at the height of his insight into the wider implications of life, both in his drama and in the Sonnets.[244] When Cleopatra first sees the dying Antony, the dramatist gives her this special tone of speech, this imagery particularly, which she has never had before:

> O sun,
> Burn the great sphere thou mov'st in! Darkling stand
> The varying shore o' th' world.[245]

and soon she is lamenting his death in poetic terms which continue to create the new world of heightened feeling in which she is to die:

> The crown o' th' earth doth melt. My Lord!
> O, wither'd is the garland of the war,
> The soldier's pole is fall'n! Young boys and girls
> Are level now with men. The odds is gone,
> And there is nothing left remarkable
> Beneath the visiting moon.[246]

This is the very tone of the conversion of everyday truth into the strange new imagined 'truth' whereby all the established values of reason and unreason amid which the bulk of the play has taken place, will be finally superseded. It is this special poetry, that is reserved for Cleopatra in the last scene of the drama and which will modify our conception of the play as a whole, that works this new creation. Shakespeare is conveying emotion, not logical thought, and the emotion derives from the earlier, private world of passion in which the lovers had sometimes lived apart from the ordinary, rational, political world. We are reminded of the similar use of specially emotive poetic imagery, 'colour' and tone, to form the fairy world of *A Midsummer Night's Dream*, the passionate, impulsive world of the love of Romeo and Juliet, and, more darkly, the perverted world of Othello's jealous imaginings. But here the poetry has its own unique quality, and its effect grows through crucial passages from here to the end. This effect is obtained, to begin with, by Shakespeare's choice of words (usually quite ordinary in themselves) which in their context carry overtones of suggestion far beyond individual 'meaning'. To this extent, the dramatist is using language in the way known to many of his contemporaries, from poets to preachers, who were primarily seeking to arouse men's imagination and feeling, and of course to many later creative writers. But the special effect which he obtains in this last phase of the play springs from the fact that the cumulative suggestion carried by the words is one of striking incongruity resolved in unexpected harmony, where 'the odds' are linked with 'the visiting moon', 'delights' with 'dolphin-like', 'fire and air' with 'the last warmth of my lips', and this harmony is felt to be constantly formed of the 'local' and the 'universal'. So we are led to experience the ending of the play, not just as the final struggles and peace of certain historical characters, but as a new vision of human beings, even ourselves, as an essential part of the pattern of the universe. This is not the result of Shakespeare's creative poetic art alone; he is a poet-dramatist, and his poetry never works in isolation; the total effect is achieved because the poetry is designed to be heightened, in its music and in its implications, by the skilled voice of actors, their gestures and facial expressions, their dramatic timing of words and movements. In the last two scenes of the play, we are made aware in this complex way of Shakespeare's shaping of the final impression, the fading of factual standards and, rising up through them, an emotional modification of our normal judgement of life: Enobarbus, in his simpler manner, had had the same experience before he died.

In 5.1 the dramatist is bold enough to remind us of the cunning political manoeuvring of Caesar in his desire to keep Cleopatra alive long enough to ennoble his triumph in Rome. This last glimpse of the 'real' world before Cleopatra's death, not only shows Shakespeare's confidence in his ability to create the final effect. The typical

self-assurance of Caesar, against which Cleopatra's apparent submission to his will is felt as a hint of her ultimate power, itself helps to
increase the significance of that power; Shakespeare must know that
he will soon persuade us, deep within us, that the physical might of a
great conqueror can be made irrelevant by the glory of an emotional
vision.

The final scene (5.2) brings the completion of that glory. It starts
with a further step towards it in Cleopatra's opening words:

> My desolation does begin to make
> A better life. 'Tis paltry to be Caesar:
> Not being Fortune, he's but Fortune's knave,
> A minister to her will; and it is great
> To do that thing that ends all other deeds,
> Which shackles accidents and bolts up change,
> Which sleeps, and never palates more the dug [teat],
> The beggar's nurse and Caesar's.

The passage begins with the paradoxical truth, quite against ordinary reason, that her very sense of loss is in fact the source of
something finer, as her sorrow itself forces her to adopt a new view of
life. Then, in some six lines, there comes to us the realisation that
Caesar, after all, is no greater than the beggar when he reaches the
earthly finality of death. This is Hamlet's Elizabethan commonplace,[247] but the quality of the poetry lifts us into a vivid 'universal'
experience of the final unimportance of all Mankind's material
desires, strangely but effectively echoing something of the age-old
'De Contemptu' view of the littleness and greatness of us all.

The scene continues with Cleopatra's temporising with Caesar's
emissary, Proculeius, leading to her capture on the Monument, and a
fine tempestuous outburst by the Queen that reminds us of the
special vigour and royal arrogance which had always marked her.
Then Dolabella enters, and a moment later there occurs a passage in
their conversation which is essential to our appreciation of the
'transformation' now taking place:

CLEO.   I dreamt there was an Emperor Antony –
　　　　O, such another sleep, that I might see
　　　　But such another man!
DOL.　　　　　　　　　　　　　If it might please ye—
CLEO.   His face was as the heav'ns, and therein stuck
　　　　A sun and moon, which kept their course and lighted
　　　　The little O, the earth.

DOL.   Most sovereign creature –
CLEO.   His legs bestrid the ocean; his rear'd arm
          Crested the world. His voice was propertied
          As all the tuned spheres, and that to friends;
          But when he meant to quail and shake the orb,
          He was as rattling thunder. For his bounty,
          There was no winter in't; an autumn 'twas
          That grew the more by reaping. His delights
          Were dolphin-like: they show'd his back above
          The element they liv'd in. In his livery
          Walk'd crowns and crownets; realms and islands were
          As plates dropp'd from his pocket.
DOL.   Cleopatra – [248]

This is the apotheosis of Antony into a cosmic power raised far above the common world of men's struggles in which the play has moved so far, and which is still represented by the presence of Dolabella – it is almost symbolic that he cannot make himself heard against Cleopatra's soaring vision. Then the dramatist takes us into the heart of the matter:

CLEO.   Think you there was or might be such a man
          As this I dreamt of?
DOL.   Gentle madam, no.
CLEO   You lie, up to the hearing of the gods.
          But if there be nor ever were one such,
          It's past the size of dreaming. Nature wants stuff
          To vie strange forms with fancy; yet t'imagine
          An Antony were nature's piece 'gainst fancy,
          Condemning shadows quite.[249]

Here Shakespeare, with that persistent concern to present full human truth which is his most enduring greatness, dares to make us examine the validity of that power of imagination on which his final effect must rest. The last six lines present, but do not argue philosophically, a truth that he can leave us to recognise within ourselves: there is a point at which the power of human vision goes beyond mere dreaming, mere imagination; it creates a new kind of 'reality' which the ordinary reality of Nature cannot equal, yet, as this power is given us by Nature, it can be seen as Nature excelling herself in ways beyond the reach of simple fancy.[250] Thus the ordinary reality of a warring world in which the play, and its source-material, had been set is now being left behind; it is replaced by a realm of poetic creation born from love and the triumphant assertion of the power of emotion, one in which Antony and Cleopatra are recreated beyond the reach of earthly struggle, and Caesar and everything he represents – the 'lower' reason, ambition, cunning – are finally reduced to irrelevance.

And so to Cleopatra's dying speech, set against the down-to-earth realism of the Clown:

> Give me my robe, put on my crown; I have
> Immortal longings in me. Now no more
> The juice of Egypt's grape shall moist this lip.
> Yare, yare, good Iras; quick. Methinks I hear
> Antony call. I see him rouse himself
> To praise my noble act. I hear him mock
> The luck of Caesar, which the gods give men
> To excuse their after wrath. Husband, I come.
> Now to that name my courage prove my title!
> I am fire and air; my other elements
> I give to baser life. So, have you done? [to the asp]
> Come then and take the last warmth of my lips.
> Farewell, kind Charmian, Iras, long farewell.
> (*Kisses them. Iras falls and dies*).
> Have I the aspic in my lips? Dost fall?
> If thou and nature can so gently part,
> The stroke of death is as a lover's pinch,
> Which hurts and is desir'd. Dost thou lie still?
> If thus thou vanishest, thou tell'st the world
> It is not worth leave-taking.[251]

Cleopatra here rises into that queenly fire and majesty, the warm pride, which makes her the fitting consort in another world of the noble Antony, that lord of life whose image she herself had created; sexual desire is part, as ever, of her inspiration, and can transfigure death itself into a love-caress. Then the final moment:

CHAR.   O Eastern star!
CLEO.   Peace, peace!
        Dost thou not see my baby at my breast
        That sucks the nurse asleep?
CHAR.   O break! O break!
CLEO.   As sweet as balm, as soft as air, as gentle–
        O Antony! Nay, I will have thee too: (*Applying another asp*)

250

> What should I stay – (*Dies*)
> CHAR.   In this vile world?.[252]

Shakespeare here reaches almost the limit of the power of subconscious word-association in his audience, which experiences a sudden shock and conflict within its own human nature. At one instant we are feeling within us that we are the longing Queen reaching up for her Antony; at the next, the phrase 'Eastern star' and 'my baby at my breast' make us experience her, from outside, almost as Mary with Jesus. The very incongruity, near-blasphemy, of the two perceptions, scarcely realised or admitted consciously in the theatre, surround her with such a width of reference that she takes on as she dies something of the universality of the individual woman who is also all Womankind, just as Antony became, in her vision, the warrior-hero who was also the immortal archetype of all triûmphant Mankind.

The play ends, and, as always, we step back into the ordinary world of contemporary living, as we had to after the deaths of Romeo and Juliet, Hamlet, Othello, Lear and Macbeth. Each of these tragedies had offered a different setting, different conflicts, yet always something relevant to ourselves, a chance to see our lives in a wider context. *Antony and Cleopatra* at first seemed mainly an exciting and moving account of human beings making history, succeeding or failing in their attempts to fill the roles of greatness which their natures led them to play. Antony's struggle with Caesar and thereby with his own nature, took up nearly four-fifths of the play. After Antony's death the 'historical' play seemed almost over, with only Cleopatra's last contest with Caesar left to finish the story. Then something happened to change the nature of what had appeared to be a classical history play. *Troilus and Cressida* had shown us how love can be cheapened and dismissed by the political talkers, *Coriolanus* how heroic gallantry and courage can blindly become the victims of political expediency. Such salutary but miserable truths seem to have been repeated in the defeat of Antony and Cleopatra. Then suddenly they are shifted to being merely the background to a new vision of the old situation. The world of worldly reason, of common prudence and acceptance of things as they are, is no longer reaffirmed, even regretfully; it is set aside in our imaginations by the triumphant claim that love can create a greater world above all the rational compromises of ordinary life. Shakespeare must have sensed that this outcome was latent in, particularly, the Cleopatra of his source, requiring only the imaginative power of his dramatic technique and his poetry to release it into

251

our hearts and minds. True, after the play, as we walk out into our world, the common 'reason' by which we have to live may come flooding back, and even reduce these lovers to mere self-deluders – yet the vision persists as long as these created characters continue to live on the stage.

Antony and Cleopatra remains the final point of Shakespeare's movement from 'plays of plot' to 'plays of character-in-situation', when a play based closely on the events of history has ended by rising above those events into the private and personal world of the two main characters. We have seen earlier examples of how discrepancies could arise when the dramatist's presentation of characters grew too humanly real for the story in which they were placed. Now the discrepancies have been deliberately emphasised, yet finally transmuted; the possible unease has changed into the triumphant assertion of an unsuspected glory more real than everyday reality. Certainly *Antony and Cleopatra* belongs, in traditional terms, among the great tragedies, but the disturbed yet persisting hope for Mankind which Shakespeare's other tragedies, even *Macbeth*, leave with us at the end, has become something more than hope; the cruelties, the stupid self-assertions, the constant efforts of our mixed human quality, have been suddenly shown as insignificant in the presence of the power of imaginative, creative truth. The traditional defeats of tragedy (of which Enobarbus is a better example than the protagonists themselves) are now important only because they form the conditions necessary for the final transmutation of despair into glory. No other play has shown more clearly the unconquerable strength of the human spirit, and it is characteristic of Shakespeare that here this strength is shown to spring from human love: thus, in a strange but very true sense, *Antony and Cleopatra* is religious in the real meaning of the word, and a special manifestation of the tragic spirit.

Retrospect

As we now approach a consideration of the last products of Shakespeare's career as a dramatist, we can usefully pause for a short review of the main modes of his approach to drama as we have seen them up to this point. If the idea of development is not rigidly attached to the sequence of his plays, if we realise that the dramatist's methods and purposes are related chiefly to the type of play which he is writing, so that *All's Well* can be produced a year or two after *Hamlet* and yet appear less 'mature' than its predecessor – in short, if we look briefly at Shakespeare's work again, as a whole, up to the time when *Coriolanus* and *Antony and Cleopatra* have just been completed, we shall distinguish the overall movement in the manner and tone of that work, and by doing so we shall understand better the relationship of the last four plays to all that has gone before.

The first important characteristic of this movement derives from the basic nature of his drama, and indeed, of the traditional drama before him. Shakespeare, like his contemporaries, inevitably constructs a play on the framework of a plot, a story of events, and in doing so creates characters whose primary function is to act out those events. But his plays, for many years up to now, have shown him as frequently varying the relative emphasis between plot and characters.[253]

His plays based mainly on 'fact', that history of which his audience was at least partly aware, of course place the major emphasis on plot, and character is displayed, and even explored (as in *Richard II*), in direct relation to that plot. *Julius Caesar*, however, shows Shakespeare almost equally concerned with history and with the human inner conflicts which produce history, and in *Troilus and Cressida*, *Coriolanus* and, above all, *Antony and Cleopatra*, the interest in character is very strong, and modifies significantly the nature of the plays; the personal struggles of the characters grow out of and above the plot, and their human struggle is felt to be the essence of the plays.

Shakespeare's comedies are a series of 'happy-ending' plays ranging in their effects from simple amusement (but amusement is never really simple) to the complex impressions of the later 'conflict-comedies' where laughter is never care-free, and the final pleasure is rather a sense of relief when human disaster has been approached but at last avoided. Here in the comedies there is, of course, more freedom from the control of a known plot than in the history plays; the balance between plot and character can vary more subtly, and often have wider and deeper effects, and ultimately it does. The early comedies, *The Comedy of Errors* and *The Two Gentlemen of Verona*, are plainly plays where plot is paramount, and the characters exist amost entirely to serve plot. *Love's Labour's Lost*, *A Midsummer Night's Dream* and *The Merry Wives of Windsor* still have a fundamental emphasis on plot, but now the human quality of the characters is more stressed, and the plot is starting to seem to be the creation of the characters themselves. In *As You Like It* and

Twelth Night this process is carried as far as it can be taken within the nature of happy comedy; these two plays delight and impress us chiefly because of the vivid and memorable characters, and of the human truth of the reactions within and between those characters; the incidents of the plot are required as direct and effective entertainment, but they have an added importance as the outcome of human nature in action. In *The Merchant of Venice, Much Ado, All's Well* and *Measure for Measure*, the emphasis on character goes even further; they are 'comedies' only in the technical sense that they end without actual plot-disaster (there are no deaths, in fact), but they are 'conflict-comedies' because Shakespeare (and the taste of the time agrees) seems now much more interested in exploring and displaying human nature and its stuggles; there is even a marked increase in this emphasis on character within the group, from *The Merchant of Venice* (the earliest) to *Measure for Measure* (the latest). The plot is now certainly felt to proceed from the characters.

When we come to the tragedies, we are reminded that the very nature of tragedy encourages, requires, an even fuller and deeper emphasis on the nature of the characters and their efforts within it. We have seen how, throughout the history of English drama to the time of Shakespeare, there was the sense that drama was most impressively used when it portrayed the inner conflicts of men and women in a serious, tragic or potentially tragic way; however interesting the plot, ultimately it existed for its human implications. The earlier drama usually embodied the incongruous elements of Man's nature in separate characters.[254] Shakespeare, outstandingly among his contemporaries, learnt to display the complexities within each of certain dominant figures, and also to show the conflicts between such characters. Thus, as we have seen, in Shakespeare's tragedies the character reaches its fullest truth, and interest, as character-in-situation, and the plot, while still entertaining in its own right, remains in one's total impression of the play chiefly a succession of moments at which the crises of psychological stress are shown; we remember all too keenly the blinding of Gloucester as a terrible but exciting event in the stage action of *King Lear*, yet we realise that his physical suffering is only part of a far more disturbing reminder of the evils and follies of which human nature is capable.

This shift of emphasis from plot to character is one tendency in Shakespeare's drama up to this point. Another feature of his career as a dramatist is allied to this, but is much closer to the essence of his work. It is his awareness, shared by his audience, of human incongruity, and his use of it in his plays; this has already been shown in discussing individual works, but now it is necessary to examine his main general approach in this matter. To begin with, the essence of Man's life, for Shakespeare and his public, is that Man is a divided creature, divided first against himself; that he is also divided from his fellows, and in society is partly of it, partly not of it. Moreover, the root cause of this division within Man, and between Man and his world, is the fact that he is composed of both rational and irrational elements, is drawn towards rational thought and order and, usually more strongly, towards personal irrational feelings of many kinds. It is true to say, therefore, that Shakespeare's plays always show at least something of this basic human conflict between reason and the variety of forms of unreason, while, of course, often showing other effects of inner conflicts of a different sort; in early Shakespeare plays the struggle is merely indicated and used for direct entertainment; in later plays it is shown in detail, and Elizabethans found a deeper, more lasting interest in recognising, in themselves as on the stage, the unsettling yet moving effects of human dichotomy on both personal and social life.

As I have already shown, for Elizabethans love was the supreme irrationality, always likely to disturb rational life, to throw decent order into disorder, even to bring one to disaster. Yet it was an inescapable part of human nature, and it could raise one to heights of ecstasy unknown to the rule of reason: it could be laughable or terrible, but always it was essentially and dramatically the way of normal human life; the only kind of person whom Shakespeare and his audience seem to have feared instinctively was the inhuman creature ruled only by a narrow, selfish reason and entirely untouched by emotion – Iago, of course, is the prime example. So Shakespeare's course as a thinking and feeling dramatist can to a large extent be followed by understanding his growing range of exploration, in dramatic terms, of love (including lust and jealousy).

First come the comedies. In the earlier ones, love is just a part of the nature of youth, accepted, as traditional drama had always shown, as something liable to cause complications in life, and therefore natural dramatic material. Later, in *As You Like It* and *Twelfth Night*, love is more fully shown in its inner complexity; Shakespeare's imaginative feeling, working through increasing dramatic and poetic power, is showing how love can transfigure (and also mislead) both the lover and the beloved. Love is coming to be felt as a special form of fantasy, very human, very precious, which can be justified in and for itself. These two comedies show both the glory and the humour of love, but Elizabethan comedy always has its common sense, and Shakespeare's Touchstone and Malvolio are there to remind us that 'love' can be casual desire or even the silly yet painful result of vanity, self-love. In *Much Ado About Nothing* a childish but savage jealousy is finally rendered irrelevant compared with the wonderfully human, deliberate unreason of the love of Benedick and Beatrice. Then, in three 'conflict-comedies' within four years, the man–woman passion is explored still more deeply, and the dramatist takes his audience into darker areas, more questionable situations, of love. *Troilus and Cressida* has a lover who is akin to Orlando in his simple devotion, a romantic love which goes with his Hotspur-like sense of martial honour, but this becomes almost a futility under the pressure of the 'real' world of expediency and acceptance of the second-best, in love as in politics, and ends as an empty, sad gesture. In *All's Well That Ends Well* the plot is romantically popular in its combinations of appealing situations and exciting developments, but the love is treated far more realistically, with disturbing effects; the whole play rests on Helena's love for Bertram, and this is shown as frankly selfish and calculating. Earlier, Shakespeare had mingled the true tenderness of love with touches of unsentimental realism; now the love itself is suspect, and the weaknesses of human nature are shown almost brutally – Helena, Bertram and Parolles are uncomfortably akin. *Measure for Measure* scarcely pretends to admit love at all, although the disruptive force of lust is portrayed in vivid and ruthless detail; yet this lust remains the only genuine and instinctive emotion in the play, and nothing replaces it in the second half of the drama, where 'success' in life is shown as the product of what is reasonable and socially acceptable. These plays seem to transfer love from a happy world of romance, with its own wise truth to life, into a setting with a far more cynical and worldly truth, where the finer reality of love becomes an anomaly.

Yet if one turns to Shakespeare's two great love-tragedies, *Romeo and Juliet* and *Antony and Cleopatra*, appearing some eleven years apart, one sees that before and after the 'conflict-comedies' he was presenting the true importance of love in a world far more real than that of those comedies. In the earlier tragedy, love is portrayed in a simple and traditionally romantic way, yet with realism enough to have the special poignancy of human truth. No other play has expressed more frankly and movingly the real nature of young love, in which falling in love is a sudden conversion to an overwhelming faith, and being in love transfigures all everyday values by passionate need. Yet those mundane values still surround love and exert their blind pressure; although the lovers retreat into a realm where, for them, their emotion is the only reality, they at last have to face another reality, death. Even so, death proves to be their happy resolution of the painful stresses between the supreme fantasy of love and the 'reality' of normal life; only the 'real' world outside, the world of uncomprehending parents and friends is left to mourn. Certainly *Romeo and Juliet* should be a compulsory study for all parents of teenagers today! *Antony and Cleopatra* is the complement to this. Here the love is less sudden, but equally an expression, finally, of complete conversion, which changes worldly-wise, middle-aged political figures into devout visionaries. The world of political expediency, of Roman power-seeking and ambition, exercises a far more cunning and powerful influence than the Montague–Capulet world; the lovers themselves are part of that political world, and their own worldly wisdom is an internal enemy to their love, and part of their struggle between reason and emotion. The inevitable end for them, as for Romeo and Juliet, is worldly failure and death, but death is now not merely a resolution, but the setting for a new heightened love-fantasy which creates a new form of reason.

The last plays[255]

It is against this background that we must now consider the last four plays of Shakespeare, remembering that behind them lie many busy years in which he had been a practical man of the theatre of his age, successful because he had given his various audiences, at the Globe, the Blackfriars, and at Court, not only the direct entertainment of exciting stage-action, but with that, increasingly, the very Elizabethan satisfaction of exploring and seeking to understand the human nature of themselves and of their fellows, as seen in the process of living shown in the plays. By the time of *Pericles* the tastes of the audience had not radically altered, it seems (in essence they are very similar today, in fact), but one can see a more 'sophisticated' desire for plots cleverly contrived to provide novel situations in which the workings of human incongruity give the pleasure rather than the challenge of realising human truth: the emphasis, in fact, is on plot rather than on character-in-situation.

The first impression of *Pericles, Prince of Tyre*, indeed, is that it is a return to a largely plot-determined type of play such as Shakespeare had written as long before as *The Comedy of Errors*, for example.[256] A Chorus directing the plot throughout the play was somewhat old-fashioned, and Shakespeare had never before used it in this mechanical way; it is needed because the play depends on telling a long and complex story only the salient episodes of which can be shown on the stage. This is 'romance' of the highly complicated kind which Sidney's *Arcadia* had made popular earlier, but current stage romance, typified by Beaumont and Fletcher's *Philaster*, largely avoided such detail and long complexity. The result is that *Pericles*, overburdened with plot-events, has little of that interest in the deeper workings of human nature in which Shakespeare, as we have seen, had shown himself greatly involved. The last speech of Gower (the Epilogue in fact) explains this; in it the audience is virtually told to treat the play as a 'moral' drama in which the characters are to be taken as examples of stock virtues and vices (compare *Timon of Athens*). Antiochus and his daughter stand for lust, Cleon and his wife for murderous intent, Cerimon for 'learned charity', Helicanus for truth, faith and loyalty and, of course, Pericles, Thaisa and Marina for virtue preserved from destruction and finally made happy. So the plot and characters are intended to be exciting in themselves and salutary as moral examples in action. With such clearcut 'type' characters and largely fortuitous events, there is little likelihood of that display of conflict within characters, and events arising from such conflict, which had marked so much of Shakespeare's work. The struggles of Man's nature are shown, as in the old morality plays, in simplified form in the conflicts between characters (Dionyza, for example, against Marina), each representing a virtue or vice, not within characters. The main emphasis of the play is on the bare morality theme of lust (including incest) confronting purity, from which the audience, no doubt, derived more excitement than true edification. Shakespeare's insight into humanity, and his practised skills of language, give Marina something of an appealing truth in the brothel sequence, but compare with this the subtle search for the human realities of 'the pure woman' in Isabella in *Measure for Measure*, and Marina is seen, at best, as a dramatic sketch in keeping with the general psychological superficiality of the play as a whole. Similarly, the theme of 'the lost found', the final reunion of Pericles, Thaisa and Marina, is little more than a pleasant storybook ending requiring merely conventional responses; *The Winter's Tale* will show the same theme used with far deeper and more moving effect.

Cymbeline follows. Here, compared with *Pericles*, Shakespeare is much closer (if that was his purpose) to interpreting the popular 'romance' features of contemporary plays in terms of his former interest in the complexities of human nature. The plot emphasis is still strong, and the manipulation of this plot to produce 'strong situations' is to the current taste – the dramatist, of course, had known how to contrive such effects since the early days of *The Two Gentlemen of Verona*. But *Cymbeline* does show Shakespeare using such situations, at least partly, to present people suffering the reality of their inner struggles; the plot gives the easy pleasure of remote times and places, of court intrigue and sylvan innocence, of startling violence and cunning slander, but the two central figures, Posthumus and Imogen, are near enough to the truth of human beings to lift the play far above the storybook characters of *Pericles*. We have considered plays in Shakespeare's earlier career where he dared to put three-dimensional, complex characters into readymade stories which could scarcely contain them, and we have seen the consequent difficulties. In *Cymbeline* Shakespeare does not stress too deeply or too long the emotional truth of Posthumus and Imogen, and a somewhat precarious balance with the story is achieved. The rest of the characters are basically the acceptable types of romance, but Cloten seems to break the mould; he is portrayed with such verbal richness of psychological imagery that he grows beyond a mere type of stupid lust and evil into a living person of appalling human truth. The story is far-fetched, the themes conventional (including again the 'lost–found' theme), but above these ordinary qualities, made less ordinary by Shakespeare's dramatic skill and his poetry, there stands out the human truth with which he endows the equally ordinary story of Posthumus's jealousy and Imogen's loving loyalty. Even so, the living quality of Imogen (and, much later, of Posthumus) has to emerge through 'theatrical' effects which, however popular they may be, almost obscure it. Indeed, it is only the strength of Shakespeare's conception of Imogen, and the precise emotional force of the language in which he expresses that conception, that enable our sense of her human reality to survive the spectacle of her grieving over the headless body of Cloten, in a situation contrived with the popular effrontery worthy of a far worse dramatist. But Posthumus and Imogen are made to offer us much of the truth of human love surviving errors and strains, and that truth is still the life-blood of the play.

The Winter's Tale, too, gives us a story of human love and jealousy, but now the pressure of plot, overwhelming in *Pericles* and scarcely more manageable in *Cymbeline*, is relaxed. The story of the play is a romantic one set in a typically remote world and an unspecified period, but Shakespeare now adopts a bold method of handling a plot which, depending on an interval of many years, might have been as long-drawn-out as that of *Pericles*. The play is divided into two parts, the first linked quite deliberately, even mechanically, to the second, and ultimately completely transformed by it. Shakespeare very carefully leaves the 'death' of Hermione unquestioned at the end of the first part, and throughout most of the second; in fact, he sacrifices some possibly good 'theatre' (the recognition of Perdita by Leontes, relegated to an eye-witness account) and reserves the living Hermione until the final moments, in order to obtain the fullest effect from the 'resurrection' of Hermione, a *tour de force* carried off with great appeal and expert timing. All this is a new use of an old Shakespearean method; it gives the audience the romance incidents and the stage effects which it enjoyed, while at the same time creating enough room to portray the reality of human nature far more deeply than had been possible in the previous two plays. Thus this play achieves the difficult overall impression of real characters growing in substance within a 'storybook' framework, yet without any sense of serious anomalies. The time-break in the middle of the play might have caused a fatal disruption of the characters, but the fact is that, by the end of the first part, their inner truth (even of secondary figures like Camillo) has been firmly established; they are strong enough to continue to live in the changed world of the second part, and the dramatist, in the highly artificial final scene, can even risk drawing attention to the fact that real-life heroines look older with the passing of the years:

LEON.   But yet, Paulina,
        Hermione was not so much wrinkled, nothing
        So aged as this seems.
POL.   O, not by much!
PAUL.   So much the more our carver's excellence,
        Which lets go by some sixteen years and makes her
        As she liv'd now.

Here the romance world of Paulina's elaborate deception and the real world of husbands and ageing wives are quietly and movingly combined – it is a symbol of the play as a whole.

So everything in this play depends on Shakespeare's ability to convince us that, although the storyline is delightfully unrealistic, the characters are basically living beings like ourselves, an ability which had created much of the enduring quality of his previous plays. Yet his success must not be exaggerated; Leontes is no second Othello, nor are Florizel and Perdita as near to full humanity as Romeo and Juliet. The deeper truth of these later characters, in a romance happy-ending play, can be effectively suggested and shown, but not pursued to the point where the quality of the play would be changed.

The main inner theme, the human truth, of the play lies in love of different kinds; loyal married love, jealousy that can doubt it and then return to repentant love, and young love that lives on impulse and emotion, and yet is pathetically eager to use the older wisdom in which it places so much innocent trust. So age and youth is a theme that accompanies the theme of love, and counterpoints it. In fact, as so often before, Shakespeare is evoking the most powerful parts of our human make-up – in this case, our constant awareness of the passing of our life, while unwilling to accept our inevitable death, and with this our sense of the beauty of youthful love conflicting with our knowledge that it is always in danger from our folly and passion, and from the tooth of time. These tensions are awakened very gently, however, and are placed in a setting where death, for once, is not suffered but used, used to affirm the power of love and forgiveness, and even for comedy, in the special stage-treat of the bear. We are reminded firmly of our divided humanity, but also of the beauty and joy of which that humanity is capable. The end of *The Winter's Tale* is a romance 'happy ending' that has acquired a new reality and truth because we have been shown our human conflict within the play, and have been brought to recognise it without serious disturbance.

The Tempest moves even further along the path opened up by the previous play. It is an experimental drama, and the experiment succeeds against the odds. Shakespeare, in effect, has taken as his framework the long story of how a Duke of Milan failed to carry out his responsibilities because of the incompatibility between the 'private' man and the 'public' man, was usurped by his brother, was saved from death, was committed to live with his young daughter on a desert island, overcame all perils by his magic arts, and then at last had the chance to take vengeance on his wicked brother or forgive him. Like *The Winter's Tale*, this story could have become another *Pericles*, but the dramatist has chosen to give us only the last act of such a play, with a mere report (nicely devised to avoid the obvious danger of boredom) of all that has happened in the first four acts. So he is not burdened with plot; his play becomes a 'situation' play, in which everything evolves directly from the given facts of Prospero's past life, and his present nature. Of course the dramatist fills the play with comic, exciting and tender incidents, but these do not form a plot in the normal sense, for they are all within the ultimate control of Prospero at their centre, and are indications of this final situation. Within the compass of this short play, Shakespeare provides, as it were in miniature, all the standard amusements of romance drama: there is a most exciting opening, presented without explanation for the moment (as in *Hamlet*), there are a majestic, good magician, his beautiful young daughter, a spirit, a monster, noble, evil and funny courtiers, satire, a transformation scene and a brief 'masque' – something for everyone. Beneath this outer diversity lies the inner process of the play, by which within the natures of the characters, their feelings at the opening of the play are changed to their finer feelings at the end. This is the main point of the play, but even here Shakespeare remains true to life as it is. Early in the last scene, Prospero publicly forgives his 'unnatural', murderous brother Antonio, yet the latter expresses no remorse as the play ends, no reaction at all (at least Sebastian and Caliban are afraid, if not repentant), although of course there is a wide field of interpretation still open to the actor as he stands silent, except for one colourless remark, gazing at the general sorrow and joy around him. The suggestion seems to be that human nature does not always accept mercy and love, but they must be offered, whatever the response. *The Tempest* is certainly a moral play, but one with a quiet and persuasive emphasis far different from the naïve and aggressive moral quality of *Pericles*. At the core of *The Tempest* is the affirmation of the endless struggle in Man between the power to harm and the need to bless, and of the unifying ability of love to resolve this struggle, as the Epilogue confirms in its unusually explicit Christian message.

It is dangerously easy to see the last work of any great writer as a climax, the final crystallisation of his 'purpose'. In fact, as I have insisted earlier, artists rarely 'develop' thus, seldom lend themselves so neatly to our urge to fit human nature into a rational sequence. Of course Shakespeare's career reveals a fluctuating growth in his technical skills, and an increasing tendency to show deeper insights into human truth, but the stage-craft of *The Tempest* is no more assured than that of *Twelfth Night*, and its poetry has a mastery of effect achieved years before. But there is a quality in the play that is indeed new. It seems that the dramatist is employing old ideas and effects in a fresh and individual combination; it is as though he were bringing together, in a brief play, something of the sylvan atmosphere of young love of *As You Like It*, a touch of the sense of Man's evil felt in *Macbeth*, and a gentle suggestion of that awareness of the mixed greatness and littleness of Man which had permeated *Hamlet*. With *The Tempest*, in short, plot, character and Hamlet's 'mirror up to nature'[257] (the essential truth of life) work together, fuse together, in an epitome of much that has marked the special quality of Shakespeare's approach to drama throughout most of his career, and given the plays that deeper effect by which they still live.

Before considering this deeper effect of this play as a whole, I think it fair to give a warning example of the need always to judge such 'deeper effects' with caution. The case in point is what is probably the best known, most quoted, speech of the play, that by Prospero beginning 'Our revels now are ended'.[258] It begins as a gentle comforting of Ferdinand and Miranda, disturbed by the sudden breaking-off of the masque. Then Prospero, through Shakespeare's poetry, moves within a few lines from the transient nature of his spirits and the visions they present, to the equally transient nature of all stage spectacle, and then to the transience of life itself, and of ourselves as actors in that brief 'pageant': thus

> We are such stuff
> As dreams are made on; and our little life
> Is rounded with a sleep.[259]

This is the 'accepted' interpretation of this speech, but it is one which needs closer examination. Every Shakespeare play has it own 'logic of effect', a certain overall consistency of tone and outlook, and if one takes this speech as a comment, finally, on the actual life of Mankind, one renders almost pointless Shakespeare's portrayal in this play, as in so many earlier plays, how in this world Man struggles with his human dilemma and tries to resolve the conflict. A Prospero who can suggest that our life is a mere passing show ending in oblivion, and that his creator is a dramatist ending his career in a mood of bland nihilism, makes nonsense both of this play and of the career.

The comparison of our life to a part played on the stage is of course a common Renaissance and Elizabethan thought. It is found not only in the theatre (used with conscious irony), but also widely outside, from Cicero[260] and Erasmus[261] to, for example, a much later religious writer who declared, in the old typical 'De Contemptu Mundi' tone:

> We shall bee forgotten with all our pompe, as the
> traveller is that tarrieth but a night, our honour shall
> come to an end, as the players part upon the stage; our
> doings, sayings, lookes, gestures, states and maiesties,
> shall be rowled up as a scroule, and cast into the
> office [place] of forgetfulness, where nothng can be
> found againe.[262]

But such comparisons were not intended to suggest that life itself is without meaning, a dream ending in a sleep; on the contrary, Cicero was asserting that we should choose the most fitting role in life, and play it well; Erasmus was emphasising the many parts that one has to take in life; Babington was insisting that life is transitory, and the pursuit of earthly honours irrelevant, but only as compared with the eternal state of the soul. None of these writers would have believed that life is a mere fantasy, nor indeed would Shakespeare and his audience, in such a context as *The Tempest*, accept such a view, even when expressed with all the beauty of great poetry. Only once had the dramatist given a character a truly nihilistic vision of life, in Macbeth's 'To-morrow and to-morrow and to-morrow' speech. In that context, the speech voiced a truly human, but entirely non-religious, emotion, one that a man may well feel, but only, as in Macbeth's case, when evil has perverted his existence and brought him, like Dr Faustus, to a despair beyond reason and even beyond grace. But *The Tempest*, and especially Prospero, stand at the opposite pole of human experience from Macbeth.

I would suggest a not over-ingenious interpretation that is simpler and more consistent. The passage begins with a reference to spirits who have been actors in 'revels' on the stage which are over; now these actors and their setting, like the world itself one day, shall melt away. Then come the key words already quoted: 'We are such stuff. . . .'. I can see Prospero, at this moment, turning not to the audience but to his fellow actors, Ferdinand and Miranda, and with a slight emphasis on 'We' stressing the ironic yet moving truth that all actors exist to create dreams, exist only in the dreams that they create, and that there must always come the moment when they must step outside these dreams into the 'real' world in which a day's acting ends in sleep, and a life of acting in death.[263] This reading of the speech may lack the fine universality of the older interpretation, may even seem sadly matter of fact, but it would have been appreciated by the audience, and at least it makes its own wry comment on the actors's life; above all, it does not jar with the implicit tone and meaning of the play as a whole.

What is this implicit 'meaning' of the play, the deeper impression of the truth of life which underlies the obvious surface entertainment that it offers? After the purely theatrical impact of the opening scene, with its nicely calculated tantalising of the audience, the second scene places Prospero at the centre of the drama, and he remains its dominant figure until the last line of the Epilogue. Throughout he is the source and controller of the action, and it is understandable that many have seen him as related to the dramatist himself, his magic as Shakespeare's art as poet-dramatist, and Ariel as the scarcely amenable but essential inspiration of the artist. Certainly he is the master of a microcosm of human fears, passions and greeds, confusion and ignorance, a figure who would be seen by an Elizabethan as like God, allowing these struggles to take place as part of his own ultimately wise and loving plan for their final resolution. From this viewpoint, the play has a special quality quite different from anything to be found in the rest of Shakespeare's plays, something akin to that of the old specifically religious dramas, in which, whatever the confusions of human nature, they were felt to be contained within the inescapable purpose of God. Thus the ambitious greed and cynical violence of Antonio and Sebastian, the savage hatred of Caliban touched with a dawning wisdom, the childish appetites of Stephano and Trinculo, the guilt and sorrow of Alonso, are in themselves vivid, true, and exciting expressions of Man's struggles, but they are increasingly felt as irrelevant (pathetically so in the case of Caliban) in view of Prospero's power. Even Miranda has her touch of human conflict, the result of a simple struggle between love and duty, but her disobedience to her father seems only a passing incident, made innocent and tender by the goodness of the lovers and Prospero's beneficent wisdom.

If this were the whole truth of the play, it would seem that in the play Shakespeare has presented merely a sequence of vignettes of human effort set within the framework of a 'romance' world where evil is powerless, and the happy ending is inevitable. But of course the impression made upon us is more complex than this, more disturbing in its progress to the final resolution of conflict. The reason lies in the nature of Prospero as the dramatist has shown it.

To begin with, his earlier history as told to Miranda in 1.2,[264] is significant, and plainly stressed by Shakespeare. He had been a ruler apparently akin to so many of those whom the dramatist had portrayed in previous plays, a duke who in the 'public' world of rulership had tried to remain the 'private' man devoted to his personal desires; so he had become unfitted for his public role, and the easy victim of a usurper. But at once one notices a difference from the usual pattern of a fall of rulers; Prospero's personal commitment had been to wisdom, not to the 'lower reason' that makes most men cling to power. Yet Shakespeare makes it plain that Prospero through much of the play is not perfectly wise; what transforms the play is the dramatist's demonstration that Prospero himself is a central example of the struggles of human nature that all the other characters display in their several ways. He has come from a dukedom to a microcosm of power; the outside world of human striving has been concentrated into a closed pattern of that striving, a kingdom where the ruler, for most of the play, has yet to learn the full wisdom of rulership, of oneself and others, that lies in the control of one's own discords. He is not master of himself, at first, and therefore is not fully master of all his 'subjects'; he is impatient with Ariel, and deeply disturbed by the savagery of Caliban that has remained unaffected by authority imposed without true understanding. His magic, taking advantage of the proximity of the 'ship-party' (Shakespeare as 'Fate'), can bring them within his control, but thereafter for much of the play Prospero is using his physical power merely to impose his will upon them. The implied suggestion is that magic gives only mastery over material things, not that inner moral power that Prospero must finally achieve to justify his true pre-eminence. At length, in 4.1, he can say to Ariel:

> At this hour
> Lies at my mercy all mine enemies.

At this point, more than four-fifths of the play are over, and the phrase 'at my mercy' is still ambiguous. But already in 4.1 there has been an indication of the possibly higher quality of Prospero's wisdom. Ferdinand and Miranda, of course, are at one level only the ideal lovers of the romance tradition, yet in this episode of Prospero's gentle warning to Ferdinand, and his reply, one can feel how the play is beginning to modulate towards its close. Earlier, in 3.3, Ariel's speech to Alonso, Antonio and Sebastian had stressed their guilt and their complete subjugation, and had threatened them with 'ling'ring perdition' unless they showed true penitence followed by reformation of their lives. But now Prospero is not just using his power to impose goodness upon Ferdinand; his greater wisdom is used to evoke a genuine response from the young lover, a sincere resolution of one traditional form of human conflict, an acknowledgement that true love is found only when physical passion is subject to reason. Goodness comes from within, is not imposed by force from without.

This is the position at the beginning of 5.1, the long last scene of the play. Prospero can now deal with his enemies, indeed, with everyone on the island, as he wishes; he is controlled only from within himself. The crucial question is how he will choose, finally, to use his power. Almost immediately the question is answered when Prospero says:

> Though with their high wrongs I am struck to th' quick,
> Yet with my nobler reason 'gainst my fury
> Do I take part; the rarer action is
> In virtue than in vengeance; they being penitent,
> The sole drift of my purpose doth extend
> Not a frown further.

These lines contain the epitome of *The Tempest*; Prospero might have exacted a vengeance fully justified by the 'lower' reason of the world; instead, his 'nobler reason' has resolved his human conflict between 'virtue' and 'vengeance' by the choice of mercy.[265] Suddenly and decisively the course of the rest of the play is determined – in fact, the play is over, and the remainder of Act 5 is an admirable example of the dramatist's technical skill in contriving a satisfying close (through some three hundred lines!) when nothing essentially new or unexpected remains to be offered.[266]

In this speech Shakespeare expresses, through Prospero his creation, the heart of the problem of inner human strife which, as we have seen, had been the interest of himself and his audience for so much of his dramatic career. When we have appreciated the point of the speech, and later come to the Epilogue's plain echo of the central Christian teaching, we cannot fail to recognise how much more this play is than an entertaining and exciting 'romance' play. The normal response to *The Tempest*, in the Elizabethan age or ours, must be to feel that, through a contrived situation and the truth of human nature within that situation, the Shakespearean combination of life and art, the play has quietly but unmistakably suggested that this human nature is marked by passion, greed, cruelty and many other such evils constantly at war within itself with wisdom, that is, reason enriched by love and understanding, and that these virtues can prevail, can resolve all problems, and bring peace at last.

How, then, do these last plays compare with the body of dramatic work that precedes them? Certainly they show a natural and predictable kinship with those interests and emphases which, as I have shown in the previous section, have run through all Shakespeare's plays; that is to say that his plays from first to last, while always primarily stage entertainment, are also, and therefore, concerned with the varieties of human experience, and so with the basic oppositions within that human experience.

Yet these last four plays, seen as a chronological group, create a curious impression. Although, as has just been said, they are firmly linked to the rest of Shakespeare's plays by their continuing human interest, they show a strangely wide diversity of dramatic effect concentrated within a relatively short period of about four years.

Pericles, appearing just after *Timon of Athens* and *Coriolanus*, has none of the psychological complexity of the latter, and is constructed quite differently from either, although in its 'morality-play' naïvety it does remind one of the former. Of course, *Pericles* is probably Shakespeare's development of another dramatist's unfinished play, yet Shakespeare is responsible for the play as finished, and that play remains an anomaly. Experienced resources of dramatic language and skilled stage-craft are used for a total effect surprisingly crude, and largely lacking the deeper insight into human nature characteristic of the main Shakespeare plays of the previous ten years or so. This fact offers that temptation to indulge in speculations, which assails all writers on Shakespeare, but which should be at least resisted: we know virtually nothing of the professional stresses on him or of his relations with his colleagues, little of the practical demands of the dramatic group for which he wrote, (although much more of the theatrical tastes of his audience). But we do know how Shakespeare at his best had presented certain attitudes to life in moving detail and richness, in well constructed and wonderfully expressed dramatic entertainments, over many years, and against that record *Pericles* can only be judged a second-rate Shakespeare play, though no doubt popular enough in its time, and one not very much more impressive than *Timon*.

When we come to *Cymbeline*, we find a stage-craft in individual scenes, an overall control of unwieldy material, and an effective use of superb dramatic poetry, equal in themselves to anything found earlier in Shakespeare, but the play nevertheless lacks the coherent 'purpose' that so many of his dramas had suggested. Although *Cymbeline*, as a whole, is a far more interesting play than *Pericles*, with at least something of the dramatist's old concern with the natures of people, it still remains a 'plot-play', dominated by the requirements of a complicated and far-fetched story in a way that had not been seen for years before *Timon* and *Pericles*. Of the two attractions for his audience of most of his plays, an interesting story and living, complex human characters, here Shakespeare seems to have been emphasising chiefly the former.

The Winter's Tale also shows the dramatist taking great care in his handling of an extraordinary story, but now it appears that he has returned to something of the balance of (say) *Twelfth Night* or *Macbeth*; the story, interesting in itself, is also made the occasion for the portrayal of the ways in which characters, felt as living representatives of ourselves, encounter and struggle with their human nature. Well-known forms of human conflict are strong and moving, but not finally disruptive, in this play, and it becomes far more than a mere theatrical amusement.

With *The Tempest*, the movement of the previous three plays (one cannot claim it as a conscious process) reaches its final stage. The aggressive 'moral' tone, and pedestrian and involved plot, of *Pericles* had changed to the almost equally complicated events of *Cymbeline*, through which appeared human truth more subtle and convincing, although often put aside for the more obvious appeal of 'romance' characters of simply stated goodness or evil. Then *The Winter's Tale* had shown a shift towards a much firmer emphasis upon the inner life of the characters, and for the first time in this group 'human incongruity' had begun to be felt, as in earlier plays, as shaping the pattern of events. After this, *The Tempest* comes as a solution of the difficulty beginning to appear in *Cymbeline* and *The Winter's Tale*: how to offer the audience a type of plot-entertainment that they enjoyed, and within it truths of human behaviour which they also found interesting, yet without burdening the play with a grave and disturbing exploration of human nature unsuited to the plot. The 'conflict-comedies' had shown the anomalies and the confusion of tone that could result when the human truth was too directly unsettling for the type of plot in which it was embodied. The answer of *The Tempest* lay (as so often in the theatre) in a return to dramatic essentials, in a new brevity, and a fresh development of the possibilities of the 'romance' story. As I said, *The Tempest* has a situation rather than a plot, and that situation is carefully controlled and limited, providing exciting stage entertainment within which Shakespeare can also show, gently but as truly as ever, the mistakes and final wisdom, the struggle and its resolution, of typical human beings living in their situation. The result is that Shakespeare creates a play which on the surface seems far simpler, even more naïve, than most of his major works, but which carries in it a special quality, something of the basic reality of our human condition that speaks to us all in the great parables or in *Everyman*.

APPENDIX ONE

Marlowe's Doctor Faustus *(c1590)*

On the surface, *Doctor Faustus* is a powerful and extremely effective dramatic entertainment made for the Elizabethan stage, with many of the popular traditional elements which earlier English drama had evolved: an exciting story, the constant use of stage-effects, anti-Pope satire, farcical episodes and, equally attractive to the contemporary audience, that high-sounding, evocative theatre poetry which Marlowe had already used so impressively in the two *Tamburlaine* plays. Moreover, the obvious theme of the play, the 'story', carries a plain warning against the consequences of enlisting the help of the Devil to gain personal advantages; thus it expresses a current attitude to magic, and offers a widely acceptable moral lesson. At this level, the play harks back to the older 'moral' plays that were concerned primarily with a dramatic display of the Christian need to fight constantly against the powers of evil which could destroy the soul, plays often containing, like *Doctor Faustus*, a good deal of popular farcical amusement.

But *Doctor Faustus* has long been seen as something much more than this, as many Elizabethans would have recognised; this is partly because it contains magnificent moments of pure Marlovian poetic beauty and dramatic power, especially at the end, which have no equal in earlier non-Marlovian drama. It is perhaps almost unfortunate that so many have been deeply impressed, and rightly so, by these special moments; critics and audiences alike have therefore tended to see the play as an unfortunate marriage of popular, crude stage-craft and superb dramatic poetry, with a queer, old-fashioned religion officiating dimly in the background. To take such a view is, in fact, to emphasise means rather than ends, and to miss the full human and religious tragic effect that the play offers when properly experienced.

Doctor Faustus is a moral play, but in a far deeper sense than as a mere warning against the results of magic. The apparently simple

Appendix 1

pattern of the action (Faustus sells his soul to Lucifer, later regrets it, and is finally taken to hell and eternal damnation) is in Marlowe's treatment made to suggest matters which, as we have seen from Shakespeare's plays, were of great interest to Elizabethans. They largely accepted the teaching that Man should rule his life by reason, but reason was traditionally of two kinds, working at two levels: there was the practical, everyday reason of the world (a 'lower' reason) which was often merely the selfish cleverness by which a man might gain personal ends, and there was the 'higher' reason, wisdom, that was essential if a man were to lead a good Christian life and reach Heaven.[1] These two were obviously at odds in Man's nature, especially since the higher wisdom included faith, a gift of God beyond reason, and it is from this conflict in the nature of Faustus that the deeper tragic force of the play is created.

The beginning of the play shows the true nature of the desire that drives Faustus to seek through magic the aid of Lucifer. His lower reason seeks vast knowledge, not so much for itself as for the power that such knowledge brings. He has already rejected other forms of learning as leading nowhere, but he sees magic as offering the only knowledge that gives supreme earthly power; as he says:

> Oh, what a world of profit and delight,
> Of power, of honour, of omnipotence
> Is promis'd to the studious artisan [sc. of magic]!
> All things that move between the quiet poles
> Shall be at my command.[2]

All Marlowe's other major plays are concerned with power of various kinds in different contexts in the world, how to acquire or keep it, and how to use it successfully, but *Doctor Faustus* is his only play in which the urge for power has implications reaching beyond the material world. In *Tamburlaine*, as in this play, the special Marlovian 'enthusiasm' of the sweeping blank verse cannot disguise the real nature of this urge, of which a well-known Tamburlaine speech is the most characteristic expression:

> Nature, that fram'd us of four elements
> Warring within our breasts for regiment,
> Doth teach us all to have aspiring minds:
> Our souls, whose faculties can comprehend
> The wondrous architecture of the world,
> And measure every wandering planet's course,

> Still climbing after knowledge infinite,
> And always moving as the restless spheres,
> Will us to wear ourselves, and never rest,
> Until we reach the ripest fruit of all,
> That perfect bliss and sole felicity,
> The sweet fruition of an earthly crown.[3]

Here a recognition of Man's discord, the 'warring within our breasts', is not a preliminary to seeking to resolve that struggle, but a symbol of the need to strive constantly for supreme earthly power gained from 'knowledge infinite'. The rapture and force of the first nine lines create an effect of almost spiritual aspiration, but against this the last line has the sudden hollow ring of anticlimax, bringing an inspiring assertion of the limitless reach of men's 'souls' down to the level of mere self-aggrandisement. Something of the same greed for power, for knowledge now seen as the road to riches as well as power, appears in an early speech where Faustus is following the lead of the Evil Angel:

E.ANG. Go forward, Faustus, in that famous art
      [sc. of magic]
     Wherein all Nature's treasure is contain'd:
     Be thou on earth as Jove is in the sky,
     Lord and commander of these elements.

(*Exeunt Angels*)

FAUST. How I am glutted with conceit of this!
     Shall I make spirits fetch me what I please,
     Resolve me of all ambiguities,
     Perform what desperate enterprise I will?
     I'll have them fly to India for gold,
     Ransack the ocean for orient pearl,
     And search all corners of the new-found world
     For pleasant fruits and princely delicates;
     I'll have them read me strange philosophy,
     And tell the secrets of all foreign kings;
      . . .
     I'll have them fill the public schools with silk,
     Wherein the students shall be bravely clad;
     I'll levy soldiers with the coin they bring,
     And chase the Prince of Parma from our land,
     And reign sole king of all our provinces;[4]

Faustus speaks with a fine exaltation akin to Tamburlaine's, but his ringing aspirations are merely a desire for wealth, privilege and power; when, just after this speech, Valdes and Cornelius encourage Faustus to use magic, the results they offer him are also power and wealth. All that he seeks throughout most of the rest of the play until the last phase (that is, about three-quarters of the whole) is the knowledge and its special power that magic seems to promise, but it is a central and dreadful irony of *Doctor Faustus* that this knowledge and power for which he gives his soul are shown to be ludicrously petty and limited. He can use his new information about the physical world to impress his fellow academics (always a desirable achievement, certainly), and his dearly bought power over things to humiliate a rude knight and a horse-dealer, to please a pregnant Duchess, and even to call up the appearance (not the reality) of Helen of Troy, but these feats are all typical of the limitations of magic as well as its powers; it can only manipulate Nature mechanically, it can give no understanding or control of the ultimate nature and causes of Creation. Thus all the buffoonery of the play, however amusing at first, especially to an Elizabethan audience, comes to be felt as an essential part of the graver theme, adding to the tragedy of Faustus. These clever, superficial tricks played with the physical things of the world represent the 'power' for which he has damned himself; the comedy of such episodes contains both the tragic irony of the empty kingship that repaid Macbeth's commitment to evil, and the pathos of the little personal triumphs for which (as most Elizabethans believed) old women in English villages were giving themselves to damnation, unless saved by repentance and God's mercy.

The folly of Faustus's bargain with Lucifer is made clear early in the play. Soon after he has signed away his soul, we are shown his curiously limited conception of the knowledge he has bought. When Mephistopheles, with the candour which marks him (as also Iago) in so many of his dealings with the victim, describes Hell to Faustus:

> Hell hath no limits, nor is circumscrib'd
> In one self place; for where we are is hell,
> And where hell is, must we ever be:
> And, to conclude, when all the world dissolves,
> And every creature shall be purified,
> All place shall be hell that is not heaven.

This is deeply and truly theological, at the root of contemporary Christian belief, but Faustus can only reply: 'Come, I think hell's a fable'. When, a moment later, Mephistopheles assures him that he,

Faustus, is damned, Faustus insists: 'Tush, these are trifles and mere old wives' tales'. Then follows the most revealing exchange:

MEPH.   But, Faustus, I am an instance to prove the contrary,
        For I am damn'd, and am now in hell.

FAUST. How! now in hell! Nay, an this be hell, I'll willingly
        be damn'd here: What! walking, disputing, etc.[5]

This is the Faustus who earlier had laughed arrogantly at Mephistopheles's awful sense of loss expressed in the lines beginning 'Why, this is hell, nor am I out of it'.[6] His 'lower reason' is confined, as one would expect, to material meanings, and he lacks the sensitive imagination needed to feel the metaphysical and human truth of what Mephistopheles has said. Soon after, Faustus seeks more knowledge, concerning 'divine astrology', but his mentor gives him only physical description, some of which he already knows, and when for once he asks for more than material facts, for the ultimate maker of the world, Mephistopheles flatly refuses to tell him. The point is a theological one that many of the audience would have appreciated: Mephistopheles exists in the denial of God and His almighty power, and this fact carries its own logical and inevitable restrictions (which are now shared by Faustus); by the very nature of this commitment, he is unable to acknowledge, still less discuss, the Creator and His works, just as Faustus cannot be allowed even to utter the name of God.

Faustus, indeed, is constantly shown to be foolish, fatally foolish like so many other tragic protagonists, and the implication is that his foolishness is an intrinsic part of the limitations imposed on his mind and spirit by the nature and working of his apparently grand aspirations; he wants, and can be given by Mephistopheles, only knowledge of the material world (what we call today 'scientific knowledge'), and thereby he is confined within the closed limits, however wide or exciting, of such knowledge. True wisdom, true understanding of the nature of Man and of the universe he inhabits, demands insights, imagination, feeling, spiritual perceptions, necessarily beyond the reach of knowledge of this kind.[7] Marlowe has, in fact, chosen a protagonist who, in the terms of the crude source-material and its popular appeal, must be shown as a foolish–clever man, for contemporaries considered it Man's greatest folly to turn deliberately from God's supreme power and love to try to find satisfaction in the Devil's limited power under God and hatred of God and Man. The greatness of Marlowe's use of this material is that, while he exploits the popular idea of the traditional Faustus, he also offers a far deeper conception; he reveals the living man within the 'moral' folk-puppet, showing his 'lower' reason in conflict with the 'higher' reason which he at times recognises partly, but can never fully accept.

Throughout the long middle part of the play, from Faustus's compact with Lucifer to the appearance of the Old Man, this conflict is shown at intervals. At first he is prepared, in his 'lower' understanding, to accept as fact that he is damned.[8] Some two hundred lines later, he is moved by the sight of the heavens to say that he repents of his bargain, and he even echoes the Good Angel: 'Ay, God will pity me, if I repent'. But his 'higher' understanding has been able to express this vital truth only for a moment, and almost immediately he swings back to: 'My heart's so harden'd, I cannot repent' and from this to:

> And long ere this I should have slain myself,
> Had not sweet pleasure conquer'd deep despair.

Ironically, this pleasure proceeds from the mere illusions that magic can create, yet it is enough to bring him, a few lines later, to:

> Why should I die, then, or basely despair?
> I am resolv'd Faustus shall ne'er repent.
> Come, Mephistopheles, let us dispute again.[9]

Less than a hundred lines later, the Good Angel's urging brings Faustus, in spite of the Evil Angel, to the edge of repentance, it seems, but his cry –

> Ah, Christ my Saviour,
> Seek to save distressed Faustus' soul! –

reveals neither true faith nor true repentance. It is merely the tortured appeal of a frightened man; Lucifer has only to resort to that 'logic of justice' which marks Faustus's 'lower' reason – 'Christ cannot save thy soul, for he is just' –[10] and he is soon vowing never to look to God.[11] Finally, just before 'an Old Man' enters to begin the last struggle for Faustus's soul, he has one more moment when repentance might reach his mind

> What art thou,
> Faustus, but a man condemn'd to die?,

he says, but, once again, this is only a brief return of blind despair, and he falls back into a vague hope that Christ may save him, as He did the thief upon the Cross.[12]

Here is the struggle of despair and faith ('lower' and 'higher' reason) which, in Marlowe's treatment, becomes more than a theological truism shown in earlier religious plays; it is transformed into a dramatic exposition of the deepest human conflict, present and working within Faustus. Around this is gathered all the more facile entertainment of the play, and from Faustus's failure to resolve this incongruity Marlowe creates, in human rather than theological terms, the full tragic force of the ending. It is this ending, its nature and effect, that must now be considered.

Throughout the play it is increasingly clear that Faustus's nature, having created his situation, is then, within that situation, responsible for the final outcome. At the human level, Marlowe anticipates Shakespeare in his ability to suggest that Man's nature, in his situation, is Man's fate, not in a rigid deterministic sense, but because the personal conflicts of each man inevitably shape the course of his life. Marlowe's *Edward the Second*, which he wrote at about the same time as *Doctor Faustus*, is far nearer to Shakespeare's use of Man's inner struggles than the latter, because, like all Shakespeare's plays, it deals only with the life of this world; the Faustus story requires Marlowe to show the theological implications which are part of his dilemma, implications which Shakespeare never pursues, not even in *Macbeth*. But the ending of *Doctor Faustus* makes this play unique in that it is tragic in combined human and religious terms; the theological assumptions and the human realities are both essential to its tragic effect – indeed, all through the play it is implied that Man's spiritual nature and his worldly nature together compose his complete nature, living and dying, a commonplace of Christian teaching already seen in the earliest English drama.

For the average Elizabethan, two accepted Christian truths were that one could be damned by committing sin, and yet that one would not be lost if one truly repented and had faith in Christ's mercy. But the opening of the play makes it plain that Faustus is a difficult case. His nature is shown as already formed, and still conditioned, by the lower reason of purely materialistic, intellectual desires; although in the course of the play, as we have seen, he reveals in moments of doubt and fear that something of the 'higher' reason is present in him, striving against his lower reason, towards the end it becomes obvious that only a final and complete resolution of his struggle, through the victory of his 'higher' reason, could enable him to experience faith in

Christ's mercy, and hence that mercy, which is beyond all Man's logic. His ultimate tragic dilemma is of course inherent in the terms of the play; he has given himself to his 'lower' reason, and the next logical step is to give to Lucifer, in return for the limited pleasures of the 'lower' reason, that soul of his that is beyond the understanding of the 'lower' reason. A modern reaction to this would perhaps be to feel that Faustus's primary move in going to Lucifer is a dreadful error rather than a sin – can a man be damned for being a fool? But this is a Christian play, and intended for Elizabethans who would know that such a question, for Christians, is mistaken. The point is that Faustus is damned, not as punishment for being a fool (otherwise, who would be saved?), but because, first, he is one by his own deliberate choice, through an intellectual arrogance akin to that 'aspiring pride and insolence' that caused Lucifer's fall, as Mephistopheles tells him,[13] and second, because, being this kind of fool, he must of necessity find it impossible (except through repentance and grace) to follow his 'higher' reason and so be able to receive the faith and mercy which alone can save him. A man may be a wicked fool, yet 'Between the stirrup and the ground' he can find mercy – but he must first seek it, even in the last second, through repentance and faith.

The 'Old Man' is plainly intended as an essential part of the display of Faustus's final struggle. He is presented as simple enough to be able to trust himself solely to faith in Christ, and Mephistopheles has to admit that he 'cannot touch his soul'.[14] But Faustus, for all his talk of repentance and his mounting fear of damnation, cannot learn from the example; he has long ago lost the kind of simplicity which can have faith intuitively without reasoning. When the Old Man urges him to 'call for mercy and avoid despair', it is significant that Faustus only asks him to 'Leave me awhile to ponder on my sins';[15] an Elizabethan would have believed that thinking of one's sins may bring contrition, but not necessarily the true repentance and faith in the mercy of Christ that Faustus needs. In fact, only a moment later Faustus says: 'I do repent, and yet I do despair'.[16] This hopeless cry, in a sense, epitomises his problem, torn as he is between the higher reason and faith that can bring repentance, and the lower reason that offers only despair. It also shows his tragic confusion, his inability to realise his true difficulty; if he were able to repent, he could ask for mercy, and despair would be impossible. Perhaps the most tragically ironic expression of Faustus's mental state comes in the midst of his last frenzied appeals against damnation:

Oh God,
If thou wilt not have mercy on my soul,
Yet for Christ's sake, whose blood hath ransom'd me,
Impose some end to my incessant pain [sc. in Hell].[17]

Here he acknowledges, as indeed he had a little earlier (before fear of 'the heavy wrath of God' swept over him), the saving power of Christ; only a step separates him from a direct appeal to Christ's mercy, but he cannot take that step; he can only see his damnation as inevitable, and beg for mitigation rather than pardon. Faustus, in his moments of fear and near-penitence, always reverts to his merely rational, legalistic conception of sin and forgiveness, a view of justice which cannot even conceive the irrational nature of mercy – Shakespeare later showed the effects of this encounter of justice and mercy in *The Merchant of Venice*, and so let near-tragedy enter his 'comedy'. Faustus falls into the final Christian sin of despair (the failure to believe that Christ's mercy can always save) because his 'lower' reason cannot contain the paradoxical truth that Christ forgives a man precisely because he is guilty and truly repentant, not because he is guiltless. Early in the play, the Good Angel had told Faustus that 'Contrition, prayer, repentance' could bring him to Heaven; the Evil Angel had called these

Rather illusions, fruits of lunacy,
That makes men foolish that do trust them most.(456–7),

and Faustus had turned again to the power of Mephistopheles, and the honour and wealth that the Evil Angel offered.[18] The dismissal of the Christian hope as madness, and the immediate acceptance of this by Faustus, are typical of the rationalism that began his tragedy and holds him until the end, where it lies beneath his growing desperation as his mind, possessed only by the fear that precludes faith, darts hopelessly around in the closing time-trap.

About fifteen years before *Doctor Faustus*, a far less impressive minor English play had presented the final situation of Faustus in the person of Judas; the contrast will show the special complex quality of Marlowe's conception of his protagonist. Near the end of his play, Judas says:

I did see Christes miracles and heard his predication
                                              [preaching]:
Oh that I had had grace to be with the rest in salvation.
I wanted Gods grace and his especiall fauour,

Whereby I hanged my selfe and dyed in despaire.
And nowe the time is past anie mercie to craue,
One halfe houre to liue I would desire but to haue.
Well it will not be, nothing will helpe me nowe,
Where euer I do go Damnation doeth me followe.
Wo worth [be to] that money, that euer it was made
By which occasion my master was betrayed.
But had I had grace to haue asked mercie therefore
And repented my faulte as Peter did before,
I should haue bene pardoned as other sinners be,
And accounted no sinner, God will haue mercy,
So that [if] they aske mercie so long as they do liue,
All which time he is readie their sinnes to forguie.
Wo therefore to me, and to all that haue so dyed,
For without remedie nowe I am for euer damned.[19]

This is a plain and pedestrian reminder to the audience of the Christian doctrine of mercy; despite a touch of pathos, it seems dull indeed beside the last speech of Faustus, where all the power of Marlowe's exceptional poetic-dramatic imagination is used to evoke an urgent human agony rather than a doctrinal truth: but Marlowe has already shown this doctrinal truth which now underlies the agony, and the terrible irony of the destruction brought upon a man by his own inner nature that itself bars his way to salvation.

In short, an awareness of the religious assumptions contained in *Doctor Faustus* is essential to a true grasp of the tragic effects of Faustus's human conflict, and therefore of the total impact made upon an Elizabethan audience by the play as Marlowe conceived it. Much of this impact may now be missed, therefore, by many in a modern audience. That is why a production today may give the impression that, at the end of *Doctor Faustus*, it is enough to show merely a wicked man, naturally quite scared, waiting for the Devil to claim him. Marlowe, and his play, deserve more understanding than this, the recognition that *Doctor Faustus*, while unique in the nature and implications of its subject-matter and treatment, is also, like Shakespeare's great tragedies, made for its age and for all ages. Indeed, I would regard it as an allegory for our age in particular.

APPENDIX TWO

Comedy and tragedy in drama

Comedy on the stage works through humour and wit. Humour evokes in us a new and delighted awareness of the oddity, the many incongruities, of our common human nature: this awareness springs from perceiving the universal in the particular, in recognising in a certain character's attitude to life, expressed verbally and/or in action or in situation arising from that attitude, something which we too have felt, or which we might well do or encounter in our own lives. Laughter or a smile, of course, is the outer sign that this process is at work in our consciousness; it shows the pleasure caused us by the confirmation of our kinship with our fellow human beings, and by the ability for a time to recognise and accept, without conflict or guilt, our own irrationalities as revealed with special dramatic emphasis in another person. Thus humour is the outcome of human truth experienced emotionally, and it is often deeply instinctive. But following this immediate response, I believe, there is always a more intellectual sequel, in which, as a performance develops the humour of a character and its wider implications, we form and explore a conception of that humour which embraces both the character and our self, and sets the combination consciously against the background of Mankind in general, our Mankind which, with all its incongruities, has been given self-awareness and the miraculous power of laughter at ourselves.

Wit involves a similar process, but one mediated to us through the mind rather than the heart. It gives us the pleasurable shock of the sudden realisation of a logical connection, novel yet strangely valid, between ideas usually thought of as dissimilar; it uses words and ideas, and is often in the form of a pun or paradox, or of the deliberate and even shocking re-presentation of an accepted idea – it makes us realise suddenly the deeper reality of Wilde's epigram, 'Truth is never pure, and rarely simple', itself the essence of wit. So, just as humour can disturb our emotions, even if pleasantly, wit can shake up our ideas, and both humour and wit can modify our views of life.

Appendix 2

Tragedy, however different its effect upon us, is akin to humour. Like humour, it influences us chiefly through our feelings, or through ideas coloured by feelings; like humour, too, it works by arousing in us, through the vivid representation of the inner discords of the tragic figure on the stage, speaking and acting in its situation, a new realisation of our own inner discords. But tragedy reminds us of the painful, even disastrous, potentialities of these discords, of which humour suggests only the milder possibilities. Such incongruities in ourselves we already know only too well (perhaps, being human, we have tried to brush aside their darker forms), but now, through the prompting of tragedy, we feel them and their possible consequences with all the wider, universal connotations which the tragic character (at once a stage figure, even a symbol, and also a human being who is in essence our very self) creates within us. The experience of tragedy, in fact, displays a central paradox of our nature – it produces in us exaltation in and through the act of suffering (no less acute, often, for being vicarious). The reason is that human beings seem to have an essential desire to experience every potentiality of their natures. This desire is not necessarily satisfied by (to use a somewhat suspect phrase) 'living life to the full'; drama especially, and with it much creative art, can make us briefly become, in our sympathies, a far more suffering, discordant personality than we shall ever be, I hope, in 'real' life. It is often said that at a performance of *Othello* we can 'enjoy' all the agonies of jealousy, and still be able to leave the theatre without having murdered our wife. But this, no matter how true in a limited sense, strikes me as a curiously narrow, even clinical, conception of tragedy. Tragedy is, of course, a psychological tonic or safety-valve (these scientific metaphors are deliberately and appropriately mixed), but it is something far more important, especially in terms of human *caritas*, than merely the psychiatrist's apprentice. Of course, through self-identification with Othello (a figure already felt and experienced by the dramatist in the process of creation) we do feel and learn the possible follies and dangers of our human incongruity. But tragedy does something much more than this, something that reminds us of its origin from religion. It creates and explores, not merely Man's suffering, but the causes and inevitable process of that suffering; through the tragic protagonist, and through ourselves when in full empathy with the protagonist, it makes us feel not just Othello's agony and its relation to ourselves, but the very nature of human agony, the essence of suffering as it exists throughout Mankind. To have truly and fully experienced *Macbeth*, is to have moved closer to a full understanding of the human reality behind Belsen, behind every evil and agony of which human beings, we ourselves, are capable. Even so (and this is the last stage of the paradox mentioned above), tragedy is never wholly pessimistic. In the process of realising Man's potential for evil and suffering, we can become aware that that potential is not of absolute force, that the evil and suffering are not inevitable or final. Thus one can benefit in the theatre from experiencing the extremes of evil and its accompanying pain, as long as one knows that good is present: I would claim that all the greatest tragedy, even the starkest Greek tragedy, always suggests that good, something positive as against the negative nature of evil, does exist in the midst of evil and torment, even if it is no more than the assertion of Man's courage, his power of stoic acceptance. Indeed, the fact that drama can make us feel the strength of evil, proves that we recognise its opposite, and cherish it in spite of all – otherwise there would be no agony – evil exists only in the knowledge of good.

Tragedy, then, has a very wide range of effect upon us (far wider than the range of comedy); it operates all the way from the near-pathetic to what we must regard as the truest and greatest tragedy, an experience which is so powerful, so charged with universal and permanent overtones, that it can scarcely be understood in merely rational terms, and needs all the imaginative resources of the finest verbal media, the best stage-craft, the most sensitive and inspired acting, even to suggest something of its full nature and scope.

Thus both comedy and tragedy in drama depend ultimately for their different effects upon the same human quality present both in ourselves and, vicariously, in the created figures upon the stage – that is, the awareness within us which I have called 'human conflict' or an equivalent. Knowing the incongruities reacting in our natures, our continual struggles to reconcile or avoid them, we are as thankful for the happy relief that comedy gives us, as for the painful yet salutary new understanding, perhaps the renewed courage, offered by tragedy. Through the imaginative empathy to which drama persuades us, which it finally demands of us, we can relate the full sense of the dramatic character's joys and sufferings to our own. Then we can leave the theatre (where our experience has been heightened and universalised by knowing that it has been shared by those other human beings around us) with the feeling, either that our own discords can be laughed at (at least once in a while) or, on the other hand, that we have realised in time to what despair Mankind's, our, more terrible inner conflicts can lead us. In fact, we may even depart with a strange mixture of these two feelings, for in drama, as in ourselves, comedy and tragedy can be very close to each other.

Notes

Introduction

1   As shown in Part 2(a), social conflicts are often present in the
    sixteenth-century English 'moral' plays in their emphasis on the social
    implications of Man's inner struggles. Bale's *John, King of England*
    (*c*1538), the anonymous *Respublica* (1553) and Lupton's *All for
    Money, Plainly representing the maners of men, and fashions of the
    world noweadayes* (*c*1577) are examples (see pp.40, 42–3, 38–9
    above). In the first two, social conflicts are the obvious concern,
    although shown in terms of personal conflicts; in the third, while
    individual struggles provide the main entertainment of the play, the
    general theme (as the full title suggests) is social. In effect, such plays
    show how an interest in human conflict can lead to the treatment of
    social stresses, and, conversely, how a social awareness demands some
    attention, at least, to personal tensions. Shakespeare, in fact, while
    primarily intent on individuals and their inner discords, also shows
    the social and 'universal' relevancies.

Part 1 Forms of human conflict

1   Throughout this work I have used 'Man' and 'man' to denote
    respectively Mankind and a human being (irrespective of sex).
2   Erasmus (1534, 8 edn 1545–76) *Enchiridion militis christiani* (trans.
    perhaps William Tyndale), Anne M. O'Donnell (ed.) (1981) *Early
    English Text Society* Oxford: Oxford University Press, pp. 60–1. Refs.
    to dates, editions, etc. of non-dramatic texts are from texts on *Short Title
    Catalogue* (Pollard and Redgrave)
3   John Boys (1616) *An Exposition of the proper psalmes. The first part*,
    p. 33. The sermon was delivered some time before publication. Cf.
    Henry Lok (1597) *Sundry Christian Passions*; Sonnet XXVI, where
    Cain and Abel are made the symbol of the 'ancient hatred' between the
    body (Cain) and the soul (Abel). A.B. Grosart (ed.) 1871 *Miscellanies
    of Fuller's Worthies' Library*, vol. 2 (P.P.).
4   *Christ's Teares over Ierusalem*, L4. R.B. McKerrow (ed.) (1958)
    Works (rev. F.B. Wilson), vol. 2. Oxford University Press.

285

5   George Webbe (1610) *A Posie of Spiritual Flowers*, pp. 106–07.

6   *A Demonstration of God*, p.29. More was a religious man, and an important public figure under Elizabeth I and James I.

7   *Nosce Teipsum* 1599 (six editions by 1622); 'Of Humane Knowledge': last three stanzas. A.B. Grosart (ed.) (1869) *Collected Poems of Sir John Davies* Fuller's Worthies Library, vol.1, pp.23–4.

8   See p.5, and note 1:4.

9   T.R. (Thomas Rogers) (1576) *A philosophicall discourse . . . the Anatomie of the Minde*, (A_{iii}^r).

10   *The anathomie of sinne (the genealogie of vertue)*, (C_7)^v.

11   William Painter, *The Palace of Pleasure*, Tome 1, Novel 46. D. Nutt (ed.) (1890) Jacob's edition (3 vols) (published in 3 vols 1966). The whole work had at least five editions between 1566 and (1580?); vol.2 at least two editions, in 1567 and (1580?).

12   See below, Part 1, section (h) (pp.18–24).

13   *The thre books of Tullyes offyces . . . translated by Roberte Whytinton* (1553, 1544, (a_6r).

14   *MARCUS Ciceroes thre bookes of duties*, (trans. Nicholas Grimalde), 1553.

15   Cf. [Reason], thou art the soules bright Genius

   . . . .

   Thou the soules, bodies Queenes allie most neere.
   The first Prince of her blood, and chiefest peere,
   Nay, her protector in nonage, whilst she
   Liues in this bodies weake minoritie.

   (Everard Guilpin (1598) *Skialethia*, D_8^r) (G.B. Harrison (ed.) (1931) *Shakespeare Association Fac. No. 2*. Oxford: Oxford University Press

   and:

   Nay, man within himself hath self *debate*,
   His *soule* and *body* are at deadly feede [feud],
   Yet *man* himselfe is a publike state,
   And *reason* Prince seems so to sway that steede [place],
        As foule *concupiscence* that sowes her seed
        In fleshlie furrowes to corrupt the soule,
        Should not prevaile, but have her due controule.

   (John Norden (1600) *Vicissitudo Rerum*, stanza 102) D.C. Collins (ed.) (1931) *Shakespeare Association Fac. No.4*. Oxford: Oxford University Press. (cf. also: Donne's 'great prince' in *The Ectacy*).

16   *Thomas Tuke* (1607) *The Trve Trial and Turning of a Sinner*, pp.6–7.

17   Loc.cit. (A_{vi})$^{r-v}$ (cf. Grimalde, p.10 above).

18   Loc.cit. 2^r.

19 As we shall see, Shakespeare and his audience disliked the inhuman use of cold reason in human affairs. This dislike is implied in the Elizabethan attacks on Machiavelli's *The Prince*, beginning as early as John Jones (1579) *The Arte and Science of preseruing Bodie and Soule*, p.90, where Machiavelli is seen as setting aside in that work all religious and human considerations in order to achieve political ends. (cf. pp.205–6 below, and Part 3, note 179).

20 Edward Topsell (the author of popular works on animals and serpents), *Times lamentation*, p.85.

21 *A Dyall for dainty Darlings*, (F$_{iv}$)^v.

22 *A pettie Pallace of Pettie his pleasure*, 1576 (and at least 4 more editions up to 1603); Israel Gollancz (ed.) (1908) *King's Classics*, vol.2, London: Chatto, pp.32–4.

23 Loc.cit. p.27.

24 For example, Donne's *The Ectacy*.

25 *The Praise of Folly* (1549) (trans. Sir Thomas Chaloner). C.H. Miller (ed.) (1965) *E.E.T.S.* Oxford: Oxford University Press, E$_4$^{v}.

26 Reginald Scot's humane and sensible refusal to see anything more than very human folly and frailty, without any intervention of the Devil, in the so-called 'witches', stands virtually alone in the Elizabethan age (see his *The discouerie of witchcraft*, 1584).

27 Sir George More, loc.cit. p.50.

28 Cf. Richard Hooker: *Of the lawes of ecclesiasticall politie*, 1594–97:

> It is both commonly said, and truly, that the best men
> otherwise are not always the best in regard of society.
> The reason whereof is, for that the law of men's actions
> is one, if they be respected only as men; and another,
> when they are considered as parts of a politic body. Many
> men there are, than whom nothing is more commendable when
> they are singled [taken separately]; and yet in society
> with others none less fit to answer the duties which are
> looked for at their hands.

(Book 1, Ch. xvi, 6; John Keble (ed.) (1845) *Works*, 3rd edn, vol.1, Oxford: Oxford University, Press, p.282)

29 Everyman Library edn. London: Dent, pp.224–25.

30 (William Fulke), *A Godly and Learned Sermon*, p.15.

31 Loc.cit. p.118.

32 Loc.cit. p.119.

33 'By the example of the ruler, the whole world is arranged'; a variation of Claudian's 'Componitur orbis/Regis ad exemplum', which continues: 'nec sic inflectere sensus/Humanos edicta valent, quam vita regis' (nor are edicts as powerful to change human feelings as the life

of the man who rules). Cf. the Elizabethan proverb 'Like King [prince], like people'; in M.P. Tilley (1950) *A Dictionary of the Proverbs in England in the sixteenth and seventeenth centuries.* University of Michigan Press, K.70.

34 Radford Mavericke (1596) *Saint Peters Chaine*, p.95.

35 Also the compiler of *A Treatise of morall phylosophie*, (1547) (see above, p.8).

36 William Baldwin (1559) *Myrroure A for Magistrates*, C$_{ii}$^{v}.

37 Ibid. A$_i$^{r} (follows C$_{iii}$).

38 Loc.cit. p.120. Elyot's wide influence is suggested by the fact that Baldwin and Paulfreyman quote this translation from Claudian in full (with acknowledgement) in their section 'Of Kings, Rulers, and Gouernours, & how they should rule their subiectes' in *A Treatise of morall phylosophie*, (1587).

39 *A Defensatiue*, A$_{ij}$^{4}.

40 William Barlow (1607) *A Brand*, (C$_4$)^r.

41 For example Horace, *Epodes*, ii.1 ('Beatus ille').

42 *Eglogs, Epytaphes & Sonettes* 1563, Arber reprint, London, 1871, pp.84–5.

43 For examples see G.G. Emmison (1970) *Elizabethan Life: Disorder,* and (1975) *Elizabethan Life: Morals and the Church Courts*, Essex County Council.

44 *The mirror of mans lyfe* (trans. H. Kerton): at least four Elizabethan editions (1576 (twice), 1577, 1586). It had an influence on the more pessimistic attitudes to life in Elizabethan times; for example, George Gascoigne's *The Droome of Doomes day* (1576 and 1586) has a strong 'De Contemptu' tone.

45 *The Tudor Regime* (1979) Oxford: Clarendon Press, pp. 403–04.

46 Cf. the Elizabethan proverb, current from the 1540s to the early 1600s and after: 'A multitude of people is a beast of many heads' (Tilley, M 1308).

47 For example, 'Sermons, or Homilies, appointed to be Read in Churches in the time of Queen Elizabeth of famous memory' (1824). London: The Prayer-Book and Homily Society (from which my quotations and the titles in note 48 are taken).

48 Homily X (Book 1) *An Exhortation concerning good order and obedience to rulers and magistrates* and Homily XXXIII (Book 2) *Against disobedience & wilful rebellion*; also Homily VII (Book I) *Against swearing and perjury*, Homily XII (Book I) *Against contention and brawling*, Homily XVI (Book 2) *Of good works*, Homily XVII (Book 2) *Against gluttony and drunkenness*, Homily XVIII (Book 2) *Against excess of apparel*, and Homily XXI (Book 2) *Against idleness.*

49 Cf. Richard Hooker, *Of the lawes of ecclesiasticall politie*, 1594–97:

For we see the whole world and each part thereof so
compacted, that as long as each thing performeth only that
work which is natural unto it, it thereby preserveth both
other things and also itself. Contrariwise, let any principal
thing, as the sun, the moon, any one of the heavens or
elements, but once cease or fail, or swerve, and who doth
not easily conceive that the sequel thereof would be ruin
both to itself and whatsoever dependeth on it? And is it
possible, that Man being not only the noblest creature in
the world, but even a very world in himself, his
transgressing the Law of his Nature should draw
no manner of harm after it?

(Book I. Ch.ix.l. John Keble (ed.) (1845) *Works*, 3rd edn, vol.1,
Oxford: Oxford University Press, p.237).

50   This point is crucial to an understanding of *Doctor Faustus* (see
     Appendix 1).
51   Cf. the Elizabethan proverbs: 'Pardon makes offenders' (Tilley, p.50)
     and 'Foolish [peevish] pity mars a city' (Tilley, p.366). Cf. also 'for
     iustice without mercy, will soone proue extremity, and mercy without
     iustice, will as quickely prooue but foolish pittie, that marres many a
     Cittie' Thomas Sparke, 'Pastor of Blechley' (1593) *A Sermon
     Preached at Whaddon*, p.47.

Part 2

1   The approximate or definite dates given to dramatic works in Parts
    2(a) and 2(b) and Part 3 are based on: Alfred Harbage (1964) *Annals
    of English Drama, 974–1700* (rev. S. Schoenbaum) (with
    supplements). London: Methuen.
2   Mark Eccles (ed.) (1969) *The Macro Plays* E.E.T.S. Oxford: Oxford
    University Press. *The Castle of Perseverance*, 11.14–26.
3   See above, p.13, concerning the old view of women as inferior to men.
4   *The Macro Plays*, (loc.cit), *Mankind*, 11.194–204.
5   Ibid. 11.226–28. 'The life of man is a warfare on earth.'
6   See *Wisdom* (*The Macro Plays*, loc.cit.), 11.133–60, where Wisdom
    refers to the higher reason, by which Man knows God and therefore
    serves and loves Him, and the 'neyther' (lower) reason, by means of
    which Man can rule his earthly life (see also *Wisdom*, 11.293–300).
    The distinction is important for an understanding of *Doctor Faustus*
    (see Appendix 1).
7   The two parts of *Nature* each contain about 1500 lines; the whole
    play is thus nearly as long as the full version of *Hamlet*.
8   Cf. Part 1(a).

9   J.S. Farmer (ed.) (1966) '*Lost*' *Tudor Plays*, Guildford: Traylen (1907), p.48.

10 Cf. the passage from Erasmus, *The Praise of Folly*, on pp.16 above.

11 J.S. Farmer (loc.cit.), p.49.

12 See Appendix 1.

13 These provincial performances, however, had little direct relevance to the new drama developing chiefly in London after about 1570 (see Part 2(b) below).

14 The sixteenth-century English concern about education is well-known; a contemporary proverb is 'Better unborne, then [than] untaught' (Tilley, U.1 and U.9), quoted by Thomas Rogers in 1576 (*The Anatomie of the Minde*, 70ᵛ).

15 I suggest that this means '[I] refer to you [the listener] as a proof', in other words, 'You know I'm right' (see *O.E.D.* s.v. 'report').

16 J.S. Farmer (ed.) (1966) *The Dramatic Writings of Richard Wever and Thomas Ingeland*, Guildford: Traylen (1905), p.32.

17 This human dilemma had been expressed long before, in Horace's 'Naturam expelles furca: tamen usque recurret' (*Epistles* 1.x.24). (You may drive Nature out with a fork, yet always it will return.)

18 Cf. Part 1, Section (h) (pp.18–24).

19 J.S. Farmer (ed.) (1966) *Six Anonymous Plays (Second Series)*, Guildford: Traylen (1906), p.287.

20 Ibid. pp.126–29 (continued in a shorter passage on pp.130–31).

21 Ibid. pp.131–32.

22 J.S. Farmer (1966) '*Lost*' *Tudor Plays*, Guildford: Traylen (1907), pp.183–84. Avarice tells the audience that Respublica (the state) is cheated by many forms of dishonesty (which he specifies), so why shouldn't he take a little? She will never miss it. The attitude seems strangely modern.

23 *The Four Ps* (*c*1520), *Johan Johan* (*c*1520), *Thersites* (1537), *Ralph Roister Doister* (*c*1552), *Gammer Gurton's Needle* (*c*1553), *Jack Juggler* (*c*1555) and *Tom Tyler and his wife* (*c*1560) are the main examples.

24 Most were acted about 1538 at St Stephen's, Canterbury, although some were later revised (see Alfred Harbage, loc.cit.).

25 An example is *Johan the Evangelist* (*c*1520-57) (author unknown), a short play of some 500 lines: it tells of the sudden conversion of two very worldly men, Actio and Eugenio, by a brief sermon by St John. The emphasis is on the evils of this world and the need for humble awareness of one's sinfulness.

26 J.S. Farmer (ed.) (1966) *The Dramatic Writings of John Bale*, Traylen 1907, pp.132–33.

27 See the first section of Giles Fletcher (the youngers)'s *Christ's victorie and triumph*, 1610.

28 W. Haughton (1598) *Englishmen for my Money: Or, A Woman will have her Will*. The sub-title shows that the play deals with another form of human conflict, Woman regarded as the possibly disruptive, yet all too lovable, epitome of unreason working against reason (see Part 1(f), pp.12–16).

29 Contrast *Misogonus* (p.37 above): in Haughton's play the sympathy of the audience is asked for the disobedient children, not the father, who is a bad man rightly ignored.

30 Philip Massinger (before 1625) *A New Way to Pay Old Debts*.

31 That is, those most obviously continuing, but in a more sophisticated manner, the popular entertainment of, say, *Johan Johan* and similar plays (see note 23 above). I am thinking of such plays as *The Two Angry Women of Abingdon* (c1588), *The Shoemakers' Holiday* (1599), *The Merry Devil of Edmonton* (c1602), *The Knight of the Burning Pestle* (c1607), *The Roaring Girl* (c1608) and *Greene's Tu Quoque* (1611).

32 W. Hazlitt (1875) *Dodsley's Old Plays*, vol.1. London: Reeves & Turner, pp.199–200.

33 Ibid. p.241.

34 Ibid. p.271.

35 Probably by Shakespeare and Fletcher (with perhaps some help from Beaumont) (see Alfred Harbage, loc.cit.). The story and its psychological situations are from Chaucer's *The Knight's Tale*.

36 C.F. Tucker Brooker (ed.) (1908) *The Shakespeare Apocrypha*. Oxford: Clarendon Press, p.256. The same form of human incongruity is movingly expressed in Fulke Greville's lines:

Oh wearisome Condition of Humanity!
Borne vnder one Law, to another bound:
Vainely begot, and yet forbidden vanity,
Created sicke, commanded to be sound:
What meaneth Nature by these diuerse Lawes?
Passion and Reason, selfe-diuision cause:
Is it the marke, or Maiestie of Power
To make offences that it may forguie?
Nature herselfe, doth her owne selfe defloure,
To hate those errors she her selfe doth giue.
For how should man thinke that, he may not doe
If Nature did not faile, and punish too?

(*Chorus Sacerdotvm*, at the end of *The Tragedy of Mustapha*, 1609. G. Bullough (ed.) (1939) *The Poems and Dramas of Fulke Greville*, vol.2. London: Oliver & Boyd, p.136).

37 In considering such tragedies of the period (roughly) from the 1590s to the 1620s, I shall avoid labels like 'revenge tragedy'; to me,

obviously, all these plays are tragedies mainly of reason–unreason, whatever plot-form the conflict may take.

38 G.K. Hunter (ed.) (1965) *Regents Renaissance Drama Series.* London: Edward Arnold, pp. 83.4. Hunter in his Introduction (p.xiv) refers to these contradictions in Feliche and Andrugio.

39 H. Harvey Wood (ed.) (1934) *Works of J. Marston*, vol.1. London: Oliver & Boyd. Earlier religious and moral drama had shown the belief that Man could see and obey the need to control himself from 'breaking out'; now there seems to be some acceptance of the pessimistic, even cynical, view that Man is unable to control his unreason. (cf. Webster below).

40 See Part 1, section (h). The story of the Duchess of Malfi is in Painter's *The Palace of Pleasure* loc.cit. (Tome 2, 23rd Novel). He criticises the Duchess at some length, eg. 'a woman being as it were the image of sweetness, curtesie and shamefastnesse, so soone as she steppeth out of the right tract, and abandoneth the sweete smel of hir duety and modesty, besides the denigration of hir honour, thrusteth her selfe into infinite troubles, causeth ruine of sutch whych should bee honoured and praysed, if Women's Allurements solicited theym not to Folly.' Here there is something also of the old tradition of seeing Woman as the primal seducer of Man.

41 Cf. in Part 3, the treatment by Shakespeare of a similar theme in *Love's Labour's Lost* and, more disturbingly, in *Measure for Measure*.

42 Act 2, Scene 1 (final couplet) (orig. text). This is Ovid's 'Video meliora, proboque/Deteriora sequor' (Metamorphoses, vii.20): 'I see and approve better things – I follow the worse things'. Cf. the quotation from *A Yorkshire Tragedy* on p.47–8 (above).

43 See Part 3, pp.222–3.

44 *The Gentleman Usher* (c1602), *Bussy d'Ambois* (c1604), and *The Revenge of Bussy d'Ambois* (c1610), *Caesar and Pompey* (c1605), *The Conspiracy and Tragedy of Charles, Duke of Byron* (two plays) (1608), and *Chabot, Admiral of France*, (c1622); revised by James Shirley 1635).

45 *Bussy d'Ambois*, 5. 4, 12–14. T.M. Parrot (ed.) (1910) *Tragedies of G. Chapman*. London: Routledge.

46 *The Tragedy of Charles, Duke of Byron*, 5. 4, 245–52 (ibid).

47 See 2, 1, 83–94 (ibid).

48 See Ronca's description of him in 1, 1, 59–82 of *The Conspiracy* (ibid.).

49 *Chabot*, 2. 2, 53–7 (ibid.).

50 As T.M. Parrott (1914) points out in his introduction to *An Humourous Day's Mirth* (1597), (*Comedies of G. Chapman*, vol.1. London: Routledge), this play is a Jonsonian 'comedy of humours'

appearing more than a year before *Every Man in his Humour* (1598);
he also adds, 'Chapman and Jonson were for some years at least
intimately associated' (see pp.687–88 loc.cit.). Jonson's Roman
tragedy *Cataline his conspiracy* (1611) shows a very Chapmanesque
(and 'classical') attitude to passion and reason, when Cataline's selfish
and wild lust for power is contrasted with the calm foresight and
patience of Cicero.

51 2. 1. Everyman edn (1910/46) *Complete Plays of Ben Jonson*, vol.1.
London: Dent, p.577.

52 5. 1. Ibid., p.28.

53 See the final 30 lines of Pope's *The Dunciad* (1743) (cf. also 11.63 *et
seq.* of Chapman's Hymnus in Noctem (in *The Shadow of Night*
1594) where the author deplores 'A . . . Night of mind' and 'blindness
of mind'. *The Works of G. Chapman: Poems (etc)* (1904) (New edn).
London: Chatto & Windus, pp.4–5.

54 *The Nicomachean Ethics*, Book 5, Chap. 1. (Trans. J.A.K. Thomson
(1953). London: Allen & Unwin, p.123).

55 See pp.39–41 (above) for earlier examples of the use in drama of the
themes of disorder, the danger of the state of passion in 'great ones',
and the importance of goodness in the ruler. Cf. also Part 1, section (i)
(pp.24–6).

56 C.F. Tucker Brooke (ed.) (1908) *The Shakespeare Apocrypha*:
Oxford: Clarendon Press. 2. 4, 100–07, p.394. *Sir Thomas More* is a
play of unknown authorship, extant in a ms of about 1593–1601:
More's speech to the rebels may be by Shakespeare (see Tucker
Brooke's Introduction).

57 *Certain Devises and Shewes presented to her Majestie by the
Gentlemen of Grayes-Inne* (etc). It was written mainly by Thomas
Hughes, helped by eight other 'gentlemen' students of law.

58 W. Hazlitt (1874) *Dodsley's Old Plays*, London: Reeves & Turner,
vol.IV, p.283.

Part 3 Human conflict in Shakespeare

1 For a fuller treatment of this see Appendix 2, 'Comedy and tragedy in
drama'.

2 See Part 2(b), pp.52–3 (above).

3 5.2.843–45. All specific references to the text of Shakespeare's plays
are to that edited by Peter Alexander (1951) London: Collins (repr.
1979). Throughout Part 3, in my text and notes, I have used (for
example) 2.1.23–4 to denote Act 2, Scene 1, lines 23–4. Play lengths
are based on E.K. Chambers, *William Shakespeare* (Oxford,
Clarendon Press, 1930), vol.2, App. It.

4 See 2.1.128 *et seq.*

5 4.1.30–3.

6 See, for example, *Much Ado About Nothing* and *Measure for Measure* (below).

7 This is akin to Berowne's expression of the human dilemma of being in love, in 3.1 of *Love's Labour's Lost* (see p.70 above), but whereas Proteus is speaking as part of the plot, Berowne also shows the situation, the inner conflict, of all such young men, outside as well as inside the play.

8 3.1.130–33.

9 See Part 1, section (g) (pp.16–18). When used for full satire, as in Jonson's comedies, reason can expose and demolish the more foolish and selfish fantasies of men, but only, of course, if reason (the 'lower' reason of worldly commonsense) is accepted by the audience as the sole criterion to be used in such satire.

10 5.2.47.

11 This uneasiness is like that which some Elizabethans, at least, may have felt at the pairing-off of the Duke and Isabella at the end of *Measure for Measure*, but in the later play, as we shall see, Shakespeare has to pay something for enclosing deep human reality in a 'romance' framework.

12 3.1.148–9.

13 2.5.146–9.

14 5.1.365.

15 Compare 'romance' love in the very popular *Mucedorus* (*c*1590) and the much more realistic treatment of lovers in *Fair Em* (*c*1590): see also Part 1, section (f) (pp.12–16) and Part 2(b), pp.47–9 (above).

16 Sir John Ferne (1586) *The Blazon of Gentrie*, p.73.

17 There is some anti-Puritan satire in the discussion of usury in 1.3, where Shylock gives the example of Jacob tricking Laban by manipulating the 'natural' increase of the flock, and applauds his cunning. The puritan attacks on usury saw natural increase as the only permissible form of 'usury'; Shylock's example points to a loophole in this, and Antonio is shocked. The satire is derived from the reason–fantasy form of 'human incongruity' (where fantasy is represented by a kind of 'honour' or 'convention').

18 1.3. (*ad finem*).

19 3.2.149–75.

20 From this Elizabethan delight in considering rationally the irrational emotion love, seems to me to have developed the earlier Restoration comedy's use of love as a matter of fact subject for wit and cynicism, and as an activator of clever, complex plots in which reason is dominant. When, with Congreve and his audience later, lovers begin to feel rather than to think rationally, the original Restoration comedy is finished.

21 Thomas Draxe (1608) 'Minister of the word of God'. *The Worldes Resurrection*: The Epistle Dedicatorie (to 'Lady Lucie Countess of Bedford'), p.3.

22 *Claudio* (to *Don Pedro*): 'Hath Leonato any son, my lord?'. Don Pedro sees the point and replies, 'No child but Hero; she's his only heir' (1.1.256–7).

23 'No; not to be so odd and from all fashions,/As Beatrice is, cannot be commendable' (3.1.72–3).

24 In 4.3.18–20 and 67–72, Shakespeare gives a kind of Chorus commenting on the unhappy nature of Bertram's 'human incongruity' and its relevance for all of us:

> SECOND LORD   Now, God delay our rebellion! As we are ourselves, what things we are!
> FIRST LORD   Merely our own traitors . . .
> SECOND LORD   The web of our life is of a mingled yarn, good and ill together . . . our virtues . . . our crimes.

25 'All's Well That Ends Well. Still [always] the fine's [end's] the crown, Whate'er the course, the end is the renown' (4,4.35–6).

26 See, for example, Sir John Ferne's *The Blazen of Gentrie* (1586) and W. Jones's translation (1595 and 1600) of Giovanni Battista Nenna's *Nennio, or a treatise of nobility.*

27 2.3.133–35.

28 *Lafeu* (to Parolles) 'you are more saucy with lords and honourable personages than the commission of your birth and valour gives you heraldry (2.3.255–7).

29 4.1.28–30.

30 4.3.276–8.

31 4.3.307–11.

32 4.1.41–2.

33 Thomas Churchyard (1593) *Churchyards Challenge*, p.48.

34 Boccaccio, *Decameron* (Day 3, Story 9) via Painter's *Palace of Pleasure.*

35 Gerald Cinthio's (1583) dramatisation (*Epitia*) of his story of 1565, itself dramatised in the English play *Promos and Cassandra* (two parts, 1578) by George Whetstone.

36 G. Bullough (1958) *Narrative and Dramatic Sources of Shakespeare*, vol.2. London: Routledge & Kegan Paul, p.443.

37 Bullough, loc.cit. p.341 (Bullough's summary).

38 1.2.120–24. This is a good early example of Shakespeare's ability to raise poetically a personal human conflict to the universal level of Mankind's inner struggles. Such moments of insight add much to his greater plays, especially the tragedies. As we have seen in Part 1, Elizabethans were fond of such 'philosophical' comments, a taste

deriving largely from the popularising of Classical philosophers and, of course, the influence of the Bible.

39 1.4.79–83. This is the simple human reaction, typical of Lucio, to the complex problem of justice–mercy.

40 Cf. the Elizabethan proverb 'Pardon makes offenders' (Tilley, p.50) related (see pp.27–8 above) to the Homily teaching of the disciplinary side of 'charity'.

41 A well-known religious writer, William Perkins, a few years after *Measure for Measure*, gives the best Elizabethan indication I have yet found of the place of 'will' (ie. intention, resolve) in Man's actions: 'this is the order whereby our actions are produced: first the minde thinketh; then that thought delighteth the affection [feeling, desire], and from that commeth consent of will; after consent of will, commeth execution of the action' *(A Treatise of Man's Imagination*, 1607; p.173). Thus without consent of the will, action cannot take place; until Angelo has the will to act towards Isabella, his desire cannot move into performance – in other words, for an Elizabethan will is a vital part of the display in action of human inner conflict, here in the form of will against reason.

42 2.4.132–3.

43 See Part 1(b).

44 W.A. Armstrong (ed.) (1965) *Elizabethan History Plays* (OUP World Classics). Oxford: Oxford University Press, pp.149–50. The play dates from the early 1590s, and it has been suggested that Shakespeare may have had a hand in it (see Armstrong's Introduction, p.x).

45 3.1.119–33.

46 The Duke in the final scene quotes 'Measure for Measure' as the equivalent of 'tit for tat', 'an eye for an eye', yet the actual ending of the play does not follow this Old Dispensation of strict justice, but the New Dispensation of mercy. The fact is that in Elizabethan English the title of the play was nicely ambiguous; it could mean both 'action for action' and 'moderation for moderation'.

47 Barnadine's reaction to the threat of death is of course a contrast to that of Claudio, although not necessarily or chiefly the moral one suggested by the bogus Friar's comment on the former: 'Unfit to live or die, O gravel heart!' (4.3.60). Although Shakespeare gives Barnadine little to say, no active part in the play, he has made him a memorable odd human being, and one important in relation to Claudio and the play as a whole. Claudio's breach of the law brings him, under Angelo, to a serious human dilemma, the unwilling recognition of the reality of death; however exceptionally expressed, this is the normal human reaction. Barnadine, like Claudio, has broken the law, and has been finally sentenced to execution only because Angelo came to power (see 4.2.125 *et seq*.); but his response is exceptional, and quite unlike Claudio's. Barnadine is shown as a man

who does not fear death, as one who regards it, in fact, as a mere intrusion upon his stubborn independence, and prefers to ignore it. He is a non-conformist, then, almost of the school of Falstaff, and humorous (however briefly) in the same way. But he also represents an effective ironic comment upon the vast perturbation that the thought of death evokes from Claudio, and from most of us; almost casually, between drink and sleep, he has resolved a common and terrible human difficulty, and achieved a calm detachment; it is fitting that when he is cursorily reprieved at the end, he should have nothing to say. In short, in their contrast Claudio and Barnadine can be seen as symbols of the two 'halves' of the play to which I refer; Claudio represents the intensely human conflicts of the first 'half', Barnadine the way in which such conflicts are almost ignored, and finally brushed aside, in the second 'half'.

48   Part 1, sections (h) and (i) relate of course, to all Shakespeare's history plays, both English and Classical.

49   *Richard III* and *King John*, and *Richard II* (c1595), *Henry IV, Parts 1 and 2* (c1597) and *Henry V* (1599).

50   1.1.196–8.

51   Even in *Othello* and the other main tragedies, of course, the world of the protagonist is not wholly 'private'; there are always and essentially historical and/or social relevancies, the use of what I have termed 'social conflicts' (see Introduction, note 1), supra-personal truths that derive from the common humanity that all men, kings and commoners, share with the protagonists.

52   2.1.27–8.

53   2.1.113–4.

54   3.2.23–6.

55   3.2.54–62.

56   In *Macbeth*, where Shakespeare puts far more dramatic emphasis on the protagonist's divided self, the usurper is 'hampered' by having something of Richard's vivid imagination and emotion, and has to suppress this better part of himself in order to 'succeed' in his desire to become King.

57   Such sequences as Hotspur's learning of setbacks in *1 Henry IV* 4.1 and Regan's and Goneril's successive reductions of Lear's followers (2.4).

58   3.2.174–7.

59   3.3.136–9.

60   4.1.247–252.

61   5.5.32–8.

62   See Part 1, section (g) (p.16–18).

63   Cf. the Prologue to *Henry V* and the Prologue and the Chorus to Act 2 of Dekker's *Old Fortunatus* (of the same approximate date as *Henry V*).

64 *2. Henry IV* 3.1.4–31. Cf. Part 1, section (h) (pp.18–24).

65 *Henry V*, 4.1.226–80.

66 *Julius Caesar* (*c*1599), *Troilus and Cressida* (*c*1602) and *Coriolanus* (*c*1608).

67 The modern interest in such 'Jacobean' plays suggests how close many people are today (at least in recurring moods of cynicism and depression) to one mood of that age.

68 4.3.298–9.

69 John Carr, *The Ruinous fal of Prodigalitie*, E^{r-v}.

70 Lodowick Lloyd, *The Consent of Time*, p.536–7.

71 T.R (Thomas Rogers), *The Anatomie of the Minde*, 204^v.

72 George Whetstone, *The Censure of a loyall Subiect*: J.P. Collier (1966) *Illustrations of Early English Popular Literature* (orig. edn 1863), vol.1. New York: Blom, p.45.

73 For example, in the anonymous *The Rare Triumphs of Love and Fortune* (perhaps by A. Munday) (1582) (W. Hazlitt (1874) *Dodsley's Old Plays*, vol.VI. London: Reeves & Turner) 'the show of Troilus and Cressida' is introduced in Act 1 by Mercury with the words: 'Behold how Troilus and Cressida/Cries out in love, that framed their decay' (this is in a sequence where 'romantic' and 'heroic' examples are being held up to crude ridicule).

74 Loc.cit. Tome 1, Fourth Novel.

75 Sir George More (1597) *A Declaration of God*, pp.153–54. Cf. Geffrey Whitney (1586) *A Choice of Emblems*, p.110:

With these, by right comes *Coriolanus* in,
Whose cruell minde did make his countrie smarte;
Till mothers teares, and wiues, did pittie winne.

76 Thomas Floyd (1600) loc.cit. p.8.

77 *The Lives of the Noble Grecians and Romans* (1579 etc) (trans. from French T. North).

78 Lines 63–9. This passage should belong to *Macbeth*, where (as we shall see) it would have had a wonderful tragic point. Brutus and Macbeth are alike in believing that killing ends with itself, and in learning that the dead live on. But Brutus seems unaffected by the grim irony of 'the spirit of Caesar', whereas Macbeth's final inner destruction begins with the ghost of Banquo.

79 5.5.68–72.

80 Cf.

When as *Brutus* and *Cassius* tooke vpon them to recouer their auncient libertie, whereof they were vniustlie depriued by the ambition of *Iulius Caesar*; who would not haue thought that such an enterprise should haue had a prosperous end?

notwithstanding this action of theirs, did breede more
mischiefe in their countrie, then [than] all the former
warres.

Jean de L'Espine (1592) *A VERY EXCELLENT AND LEARNED
DISCOURSE*. Newly translated into English by Ed. Smyth, 131ʳ.

81   Geoffrey Fenton's translation (via the French) of Bandello's (1567,
     1579) stories (*Certain tragicall discourses*) is a good example of this
     attitude; each of the tragic, violent love-stories is accompanied by
     moral warnings to young men and women, and their parents, of the
     dangers of uncontrolled passion.
82   This realisation is akin to that Websterian despair concerning human
     nature to which I have linked the mood of *Timon of Athens* (see
     pp.150–1 above); *Troilus and Cressida* also has something of this
     mood in it.
83   1.3.116–24.
84   Cf. Claudio's comment on the sexual equivalent of this (p.93 above).
85   2.2.163–93.
86   2.2.195–8.
87   Cf. *Antony and Cleopatra* which, in this respect, is a companion-piece
     to *Troilus and Cressida* as well as to *Romeo and Juliet*.
88   4.4.106–7.
89   Part of this irony is that the Trojans and Greeks, in their pride and
     'honour', are committed to fight for a faithless woman, Helen, whilst
     all the traditional and conventional disgust is directed against another
     no more faithless (indeed, less faithless) woman Cressida.
90   5.2.135–47.
91   1.1.39–40.
92   1.1.165–94.
93   Compare the somewhat idealised presentation of commoners in *The
     Shoemaker's Holiday* (1599) with the paternal attitude to the mob
     shown in *Sir Thomas More* (*c*1595), and the more frightened tone of
     The Life and Death of Jack Straw (*c*1591). One can also contrast
     Shakespeare's Dogberry and the mob shown reacting in violence (as in
     the source) after Antony's funeral oration (*Julius Caesar*, 3.3).
94   1.10.12–16, 24–7.
95   3.1.194–200.
96   3.1.245–7. Cf. Enobarbus's final reason for leaving Antony (p.243
     below).
97   3.2.7–18.
98   3.2.25–31.
99   At this point 'honour' (the essence of Coriolanus's human conflict),
     begins to take on a suspect tone which, for the rest of the play,
     underlies the pressures of that conflict. There is a similarity to Troilus
     and his 'honour' in a world where 'honour' is ambiguous.

100 Shakespeare is showing, as so often, that 'chance' ('fate') is really an uncomprehending term for the effects of human discord, a means by which men avoid the realisation of their own responsibility.
101 *Coriolanus* is one of the best examples of the way in which Shakespeare can relate human struggles closely to social struggles.
102 Cf. Ulysses speaking of fame to Achilles (*Troilus and Cressida*, 3.3 145 *et seq.*)
103 4.7.49–53.
104 5.3.17–37.
105 5.6.21–6.
106 5.6.145–6.
107 Sir George Fenton's (1567, 1579) *Certain tragicall discourses*, William Painter's *The Palace of Pleasure* (vol.1 1566, 1569, 1575; vol.2 1567, (1580?)) and George Pettie's 1576; later edns to 1613 *A petite Pallace of Pettie his pleasure* are examples of popular collections of such tales.
108 The effect of such comments on Italian life was of course reinforced by the horror of Machiavelli, and by preachers' attacks on the enormities of Italian Roman Catholicism.
109 G. Bullough (1957), loc.cit. vol.1, pp.284.
110 *The Tragicall Historye of Romeus and Juliet*, 11.1399–1400 (Bullough loc.cit.).
111 Loc.cit. Hugh Harris's (ed.) (n.d.) *Broadway Translations*, London: Routledge, p.156.
112 *Romeus and Juliet* (loc.cit.) 3007–10.
113 See 4.1.105–6.
114 Few members of the audience, seeing the play for the first time, would note the full details of the sequence of time-references, but all would feel the general sense of urgency.
115 Brooke, in his *To the Reader* (Bullough, loc.cit. p.284) says that the lovers' principal advisers are 'dronken gossyppes, and superstitious friers (the naturally fitte instrumentes of unchastitie)'.
116 In *A petite Pallace* (vol.1), Pettie, in a moral comment on his story of *Icilius and Virginia*, advises his gentlewomen readers, if parents seek to marry them to rich old men, to 'Dutifully tell them that such pressiness [pressure] of parents brought . . . Romeo and Julietta to untimely death'. (Israel Gollancz (ed.) (1908) *King's Classics*. London: Chatto, p.168).
117 He speaks about 40 per cent of the text, appears in 13 of the 20 scenes of the play, and is the main centre of discussion in 6 other scenes. The only scene in which he does not appear and also is barely mentioned is 4.5, in which the chief emphasis is on Ophelia's madness.
118 Loc.cit. Tome 1, Novel 41, pp.205–6.
119 Sir William Leighton (1603) *Virtue Triumphant* stanza 174.
120 It is probably represented by Q_1 (1603).

121 4. 5, 6, 7 (about 10 per cent of the play).

122 2.2.306–8.

123 3.1.122–9.

124 One of the many 'possibilities' of this complex play is the relevance of this speech to Hamlet's actual situation. Paris, the well-known stealer of another man's wife, in one version had killed Achilles, Pyrrhus's father, and was the son of Priam. Pyrrhus's slaughter of Priam and his family (but not Paris) was a classical example of an unbridled, brutal act of filial revenge. (See *Lemprière's Classical Dictionary* s.v. Neoptolemus, Paris, Priam and Pyrrhus).

125 3.1.56–88.

126 3.1.83–8.

127 Francesco Sansovino (1590) *The Quintessence of Wit* (trans. R. Hitchcock), p.134.

128 This is the metaphor with which Hamlet, in the next scene (3.3.354 *et seq.*) is to react angrily against the cunning prying of Guildenstern, and assert his ability to defend his independence.

129 3.2.61–72.

130 3.2.378–82.

131 3.3.11–15.

132 Marlowe's *Doctor Faustus* (*c*1590) is the only Elizabethan play which presents fully this specifically Christian 'human incongruity', its origins, and results (see Appendix 1).

133 Othello's public striking of Desdemona is another example.

134 Coriolanus is given by Shakespeare almost exactly the same view of the common people (*Coriolanus* 1.1.172–4).

135 4.3.2–11. A writer on travel, a few years after *Hamlet*, perhaps adds further light on how the Elizabethan audience might have interpreted Claudius's care not to upset the Danish people:

> Such in times past were the people of *Denmark*: whose force was their law, in so much that their Prince [ruler] held his royaltie at their *placitum* [pleasure]. For, if at any time they misliked any of his actions he was instantly deposed, and an other set in his place.

(Sir Thomas Palmer (1606) *An Essay of the Meanes how to make our Trauailes . . . the more profitable*, p.70).

136 4.5.81–3.

137 4.7.118–23.

138 4.7.134–36.

139 See *OED*, s.v. 'remiss'; 2, 3b, 4 and 4b.

140 5.2.6–11.

141 5.2.63–70.

142 5.2.71–4.

143 5.2.211–17.

144 Loc.cit., vol.2. Painter's introduction to the 33rd Novel ('The Lords of Nocera').

145 Loc.cit. The introduction to Fenton's fourth story, of an Albanian captain (which may be connected with *Othello*) and p.199: (see G. Bullough, loc.cit. vol.7, pp.202–5).

146 Cf. Iago's expression of popular cynicism about women (*Othello*, 2.1). Shakespeare had recently displayed dramatically the 'sexual war' between men and women in *Troilus and Cressida, All's Well* and *Measure for Measure*.

147 Cf. Touchstone's comic frankness about Audrey (*As You Like It* 3.3 and 5.4), the voice of reality ('lower' reason) against 'romance' fantasy (in which Orlando, Rosalind and Celia also join Touchstone).

148 Cinthio's (1566) *Gli Hecatommithi*, Third Decade, Story 7 (Bullough, loc.cit., p.248).

149 Cf. *Cymbeline*, where the jealousy of Posthumus is part of an ultimately happy 'romance' plot, and a realistic analysis of his marriage, as in *Othello*, would be unsuitable.

150 1.3.248–59.

151 By now, perhaps, sufficient critical effort has been spent on the possible meaning of 'rites' (or 'rights?').

152 1.3.260–5.

153 1.3.162–8.

154 1.2.24–8.

155 Giles Clayton (1591) *The Approoued order of Martiall discipline . . . To the Reader*.

156 In connection with Iago, it is interesting that Marston's (and Webster's) *The Malcontent*, appearing at about the same time as *Othello*, shows how the 'malcontent' points to the weakness of ordinary folk. In a tragic sense, Iago can also be seen partly as serving this function, but ironically.

157 Cf. the way in which the Tribunes, and Aufidius, used Coriolanus's predictable and inevitable reactions.

158 2.3.196–9.

159 See 3.3.159 *et seq*. It is one of the incidental pleasures of studying *Othello* to remember how often these later lines have been quoted with approval (as, in themselves, they should be) without any reference to their purpose or context.

160 2.3.339–42.

161 2.3.347–51.

162 'Even as her appetite shall play the god/With his weak function' (336/337) picks up the earlier suggestion of Othello's weakened sexual desire, and makes that another cynical element of Iago's view of Desdemona's love, a view sound in worldly reason but blind to the truth.

163 From Desdemona's references to 'to-morrow night, or Tuesday morn,/On Tuesday noon or night, on Wednesday morn' (61–2), one can work out a possible 'plot-time' of the play's action in Cyprus of only a few days: in *Othello*, Shakespeare is combining an exciting 'time pressure' with the need to suggest that Othello's jealousy has time to grow, so the 'plot-time' must not be as explicit or exact as in *Romeo and Juliet*. In this connection, I should stress the fact that Othello's closing comment on himself as 'one not easily jealous, but, being wrought,/Perplexed in the extreme' (5.2.348–9) cannot mean that he was not quick to suspect Desdemona (obviously, and by his very nature under Iago's influence, he was), but that jealousy for him (unlike Iago) was a profound and painful experience, which he could 'not easily' suffer.

164 In Ford's (1632?) *Love's Sacrifice*, greatly influenced by *Othello*, D'Avolo (the Iago figure) offers to show the jealous Duke his actual cuckolding, but even the later and more permissive audience has to be content with the Duke's surprising Bianca, in night attire, kissing and trying to seduce Fernando.

165 3.4.161–2.

166 4.1.76–7.

167 4.1.182–96.

168 Robert Cawdrey (1600) *A Treatise or Storehouse of Similies*, p.400. Cf. another writer, in 1603: 'The duty of a Husband towarde his wife, must bee confirmed. . . . Fourthlye, in not vsing her roughlie or iniuriouslye before others. . . . Seauenthly, in striking her neuer' (Anon, *The anathomie of sinne (The genealogie of vertue)*, D5^v).

169 William Vaughan (1600, 1608) *The Golden Grove* Dd3^v.

170 4.2.48–65.

171 *Hamlet*, 3.4.53–88.

172 *Macbeth* is Shakespeare's major presentation of this 'logic of violence' (see pp.234–5 below).

173 Cf. the final position of Hamlet, killing Claudius at last in haste and passion, without the rational control that he had for so long tried to bring to his revenge (see p.170 above).

174 Some 300 lines are spent on Lear's original mistake in dividing his kingdom, some 700 lines on his rejection by Goneril and Regan, a further 400 lines or so on his consequent suffering and madness, and about 100 lines on his final moments – a total of about 1,500 lines (nearly half the play) devoted largely to Lear's folly and his finally ineffectual reaction to the hostile forces around him.

175 Norton and Sackville (1562) *Gorboduc (Ferrex and Porrex)*; 1.2.276–7 and 329–30 (*The Minor Elizabethan Drama* (1910/1949) London: Dent (Everyman Library).

176 1.1.129–38.

177   4.2.31–6.
178   3.4.14–16.
179   eg.:

> the most wicked assertion of the unpure Atheiste
> *Machiauel*, who shameth not in most ungodly manner to teach,
> that princes need make no account of godlynesse and true
> religion, but onely to make an outwarde shew of it.

(John Stockwood (1578) *A Sermon preached at Paules Crosse*, p.59)

and:

> *Dissembling* and *Hypocrisy*
> Showes *Wisedome*, and showes *Policy*;
> The world it selfe's turn'd *Macheuill*
> In practising and praysing ill.
> (Thomas Freeman (1614) *Rubbe and a great Cast*, 1st part:
> Epigram 87)

180   *All's Well* 2.3.1–6. I have inserted a comma after 'familiar', without
      which the passage seems self-contradictory.
181   The Dover Cliff trick played on Gloucester by Edgar (4.6) is an
      example (odd, but good Elizabethan 'theatre') of what one might call
      'dramatic metaphor', as when a man 'at the end of his tether' hangs
      himself. It is akin to the knocking at the gate in *Macbeth*, where the
      public, normal world seeks entry into the 'private' world of murder
      both literally and metaphorically.
182   1.1.292–3.
183   1.4.275–89.
184   Lear sees Nature in terms of his own savage and selfish bitterness, just
      as Perdita reveres a Nature as good and simple as herself, despite
      Polixenes's more sophisticated (but equally characteristic) view of
      Nature (see *The Winter's Tale*, 4.4.79–103).
185   2.4.263–6.
186   3.2.59–60.
187   3.2.72–3.
188   3.4.14–22.
189   3.4.28–36.
190   In 3.6 the Fool also leaves the play for good. Putting aside comments
      of the more sentimental kind, one can see that his role as commentator
      is no longer required. Practical considerations of 'doubling' of parts
      may apply here; it is worth noting that the construction of the play
      would allow one young man to take the part of Cordelia in 1.1, then of
      the Fool, then of (say) Old Man (4.1), and then of Cordelia again at
      the end of the play.
191   4.6.75–7.
192   4.6.134–5.

193 See for example, Spenser's (1591) 'The Ruines of Time' (*Complaints*), and Donne's (1611) *The First Anniversary* (An anatomy of the world).

194 4.6.279–84.

195 5.3.8–19, 20–6.

196 His *Daemonologie*, first published in Edinburgh in 1597, had been twice reprinted in London in 1603, the year of his coronation as James I of England.

197 *A Treatise Against Witchcraft* 1590, (F₄)ʳ

198 At least three further editions were published, in 1577, 1588, 1603.

199 Loc.cit. ((n.d.) London: Dent (Everyman Library), p. 280.

200 Richard Edwards: *Damson and Pythias* (J.Q. Adams (1924) *Chief Pre-Shakespearean Dramas*, Boston: Houghton Mifflin, 306–9).

201 *A Wished Reformation of Wicked Rebellion*, 1598, stanza 11. (J.P. Collier (1966) *Illustrations of Early English Popular Literature*. New York: Beom.)

202 1.3.130–42.

203 See OED s.v. 'solicit'.

204 1.3.144–5.

205 1.4.48–53.

206 It is interesting to contrast Lady Macbeth's view of her husband with Albany's view of his wife Goneril in *Lear* (4.2). There Albany starts by saying to her: 'I fear your disposition'; he is speaking for good as against evil, and sees his wife as destroying herself by evil. But Lady Macbeth's values are reversed ('Fair is foul, and foul is fair'); she fears the good in Macbeth as likely to prevent evil (which she does not see as such); her 'I do fear thy nature' is a perversion of Albany's words characteristic of her, and of Macbeth's tragedy.

207 1.7.79–80.

208 1.7.46–7.

209 Many potentially dramatic moments in Shakespeare's plays are not shown on the stage but described (for example, Jaques de Boys's account of Duke Frederick's being 'converted' (*As You Like It*, 5.4) or the description of Leontes's recognition of his long-lost daughter Perdita (*The Winter's Tale*, 5.2)). This is often because of the demands of practical stage-craft or plot-construction, but sometimes, as here, for interpretative purposes; Shakespeare is stressing, not the act of murder (although blood sufficiently emphasises the reality of killing), but the reactions of those concerned, which are far more important for the play as a whole.

210 2.2.31–4.

211 Thomas Hughes *et al.* (1588) *Certaine Devises (etc) (The Misfortunes of Arthur)* 1.4. (W. Hazlitt's (1874) *Dodsley's Old Plays*, vol. IV. London: Reeves & Turner p. 276) (cf. p. 61 above).

212 James Godskall (1604) ('Reader of the word'); *The King's Medicine*, Cʳ

213 3.4.132–40.

214 3.4.141–4.

215 3.5.30–3. Whether Middleton was responsible for 3.5 does not affect the nature of the play, nor the relevance to Macbeth's position that I have indicated.

216 4.3.237–9.

217 1.7.33.

218 5.3.24–6.

219 5.4.19–20.

220 5.5.16–28.

221 Laurence Humphrey (1563) *The Nobles or of Nobility*, S,ᵛ

222 Nicholas Breton (1599) 'The Praise of Virtuous Ladies and Gentlemen' (in *The Wil of Wit, Wits Wil*. A.B. Grosart (ed.) (1879) *Works*, vol.2. Chertsey Worthies' Library, p.58.

223 Christopher Sutton (1600) *Disce Mori. Learne to Die* (at least nine editions between 1600 and 1626); p.289. Cf. the informal burial of Ophelia in *Hamlet* (5.1).

224 Lines 1292–7, 1322–4; 1328–36: G. Bullough, loc.cit., vol.5.

225 Jaques Hurault: (1595) *Politicke, Moral, and Martial Discourses* (trans. Arthur Golding), p.317. Shakespeare knew Golding's translation of Ovid's *Metamorphoses* (1567 and at least six more editions by 1612), a use of Ovid's exciting stories for ostensibly 'moral' purposes (like others' use of Italian tales – Fenton's, for example).

226 2.7.80–3. Menas shows a merely 'practical' reaction to Pompey's foolish scruples, his weakness in allowing moral feelings to overcome political 'reason' ('lower' reason). Enobarbus, at first similarly angry at Antony's folly, ends by learning that emotion and human instinct are more important than this 'lower' reason of political self-seeking.

227 G. Bullough, loc.cit., vol. 5, 11.1014–21. The two lines are underlined in the text.

228 G. Bullough, loc. cit., vol.5, u424–6.

229 Ibid., 11.1748–53.

230 2.2.240.

231 The presence of Cleopatra ensures that the play has a tone quite different from the usual one of Shakespeare's English and Classical 'political' plays, that, for example, of the masculine world of *Julius Caesar*, barely affected by Portia or Calphurnia. Even Lady Macbeth and Volumnia scarcely modify the male quality of their plays; indeed, they take on something of that quality.

232 See G. Bullough, loc. cit. vol. 5, p.290.

233 1.2.130 *et seq.*

234 3.10.35–7.

235 3.13.41–6.

236 3.13.63–5.

237 3.13.195–201.
238 4.9.18–23.
239 *Hamlet* 3.2.366–72.
240 4.14.12–14.
241 Cf. the far less complex but more obviously dramatic effect on Polixeness of the news of Hermione's 'death'.
242 Cf. the general emphasis on this in Daniel's *Cleopatra* and Garnier's (Herbert's) *Antonie*.
243 4.14.50–4.
244 In his *Sonnets* Shakespeare expresses his own 'human' incongruity' rather than that of the many 'fictional' characters of his plays; in doing so, he often needs to create a quality of metaphor and imagery akin to that which I describe all too briefly on this page. Indeed, a book remains to be written on human conflict and the nature of poetry.
245 4.15.9–11.
246 4.15.63–8.
247 Cf. *Hamlet* 5.1.207–08 and *passim*.
248 5.2.76–92.
249 5.2.93–100.
250 Cf. *The Winter's Tale*, 4.4.85 *et seq.*, where a like truth is suggested.
251 5.2.278–96.
252 5.2.306–12.
253 We have seen a similar variation marking the changing nature and emphasis of English drama from its beginnings to Shakespeare (see Part 2).
254 Not always: for example, the figure of Abraham in the *Abraham and Isaac* plays of the fourteenth and fifteenth centuries, where the heart of the dramatic (and moral) effect is Abraham's inner struggle between the desire to obey God and a father's love for his son.
255 *Pericles* (*c* 1608), *Cymbeline* (*c* 1609), *The Winter's Tale* (*c* 1610) and *The Tempest* (*c* 1611).
256 Most critics are agreed that the first two acts are not by Shakespeare, that he reworked an earlier play by another dramatist, and was responsible for the last three acts.
257 *Hamlet* 3.2, in the second section of Hamlet's speech to the Players (11.15–34).
258 4.1.148–58.
259 4.1.156–58.
260 See Nicholas Grimalde (1558) *Marcus Tullius Ciceroes thre Books of duties* (ie. The Offices), 50^{r-v}.
261 See Erasmus: (1549) *The Praise of Folly* (trans Chaloner). C.H. Miller (ed.) (1965) *E.E.T.S.* Oxford: Oxford University Press, E$_3$^{v}.
262 Gervase Babington (later Bishop of Worcester) (1583) *A Brief Conference Betwixt Man's Frailtie and Faith. The Workes*, 1637, p. 254.

263 The effect of Prospero's address to his fellow actors, Ferdinand and Miranda, in this interpretation, is increased if he is seen by the audience as 'master of the play' in the extra sense of being its dramatist-creator, the symbol of all playwrights who furnish 'such stuff/As dreams are made on' for actors to transmit to audiences.

264 The technical skill with which Shakespeare breaks up and keeps interesting a long account so potentially dull, provides (like the ending of the play), a lesson to any dramatist, Elizabethan or modern.

265 *The Tempest*, in one sense, is a 'revenge' play, but not of the usual kind. It is related both to *A Woman Killed with Kindness* and to Chapman's 'Senecan' plays (see Part 2(b)) in showing an alternative to passionate revenge, but its final effect depends on the emphasis on Christian mercy, with which Shakespeare had earlier been concerned in, for example, *The Merchant of Venice* and *Measure for Measure*. Cf. a view contemporary with *The Tempest*:

> Yet, *Christianity* vnhorses euen *Valour* her selfe; and, deposing her, makes new lawes, and proclaimes him the brauest combatant, who can conquer himselfe: that is, who can ascend as high aboue Nature, as to descend belowe himselfe, and to offer seruice where hee owes reuenge.

(Antony Stafford (1612) *Meditations and Resolutions*, pp.14–15.

266 Shakespeare admits Alonso's natural curiosity about what has happened, and yet (because the audience cannot be bored by a recital of what it already knows) postpones telling him until the play is over, while still keeping him, his companions and the audience amused by the reintroduction of Caliban and the minor characters. Cf. p.265–6 above and note 3.264.

Appendix 1

1 See Part 2(a), note 6.

2 Ll. 81–5. All references to *Doctor Faustus* and to *Tamburlaine* are from The World's Classics (Oxford: Oxford University Press) edition of the *Complete Plays of Marlowe* (1939, repr. 1961).

3 *Tamburlaine the Great*, Part 1, 2.7.18–29.

4 11.102–15 and 118–22.

5 11.560–79.

6 See 11.316–26.

7 Cf. Richard Hooker (1594–97) 'Of the lawes of ecclesiasticall politie':

> The reason, why no man can attain belief by the
> bare contemplation of heaven and earth, is for that
> they neither are sufficient to give us as much as

the least spark of light concerning the very
principal mysteries of our faith; and whatsoever
we may learn by them, the same we can only attain
to know according to the manner of natural
sciences, which mere discourse of wit and reason
findeth out, whereas the things which we properly
believe be only such as are received upon the
credit of divine testimony.

(Book V, ch.xxii, 5. John Keble (ed.) 1845 *Works*, 3rd edn, vol. 2, p.
92.) and Francis Bacon:

for if any man shall think by view and
inquiry into these sensible and material things to
attain that light, whereby he may reveal unto
himself the nature or will of God, then indeed he is
spoiled by vain philosophy.

(*On the proficience and advancement of learning*, 1605. W. Aldis
Wright (1885) 3rd edn rev., Book 1.3. Oxford: Clarendon Press, pp.
8–9).

8   See 11.439–41.
9   11.635–52.
10 11.704–6. Faustus's struggle can be seen, in one sense, as a symbol of
    the conflict between the Old Dispensation (God as just) and the New
    Dispensation (Christ as merciful), which has always been (at least for
    ordinary folk) a crucial and disturbing mystery of the Christian's
    human conflict.
11 See 11.706 *et seq*.
12 11.1165–71.
13 11.307–8.
14 1.1342.
15 11.1320–23.
16 1.1327.
17 11.1482–5.
18 11.454–63.
19 Thomas Lupton (*c* 1597) *All for Money*. J.S. Farmer (ed.) (1910)
    Tudor Facsimile Texts Repr. N.Y. AMS: E_{ii}^r. See Part 2(b), pp. 38–9
    above. It is significant that the Prologue to this play recognises that
    there are 'many godly sciences needefull be studied', of which
    medicine, music, cosmography, geometry and astrology are examples,
    but adds:

Yet all other sciences with these before delated [reported]
Shall vanishe as the smoke, and be nothing at length.
Yet heauenlie Theologie, Gods word before declared

Hath bene, is nowe, and euer of such force and strength
That though heauen and earth perishe, as Christes woordes meaneth
Yet his worde shall abyde and remayne for euer.

This suggests part of the theme of *Doctor Faustus*, the temporary
nature and secondary importance of mere earthly knowledge
(cf.p.275 and note App. 1.7.)

INDEXES

(Note numbers refer to pages: references to notes are shown as (e.g.) n.3.123 = Part 3, note 123)

1 Index of Elizabethan (non-dramatic) references

		pp.	notes
Anon.: *The anathomie of sinne*	1603	6	1.10,3.168
Anon. *Cyuile and unciuile life*	1579	23	
Aristotle *The Ethiques* . . . (trans. Wilkinson)	1547	11–12	1.17
Averell, William *A Dyall*	1584	13	1.21
Babington, Gervase *A Brief Conference*	1583	263–4	3.262
Bacon, Francis *On the proficience*	1605	–	App.1.7
Baldwin, William: *A Myrroure*	1559	20–1, 40, 61, 63, 65, 100, 102	1.36,1.37
—— *A Treatise*	1547	8–11	1.35,13.8
Barlow, William. *A Brand*	1607	22	1.40
Boys, John *An Exposition . . . psalmes*	1616	2	1.3
Breton, Nicholas *The Wil of Wit*	1599	7	3.222
Brooke, Arthur, *Romeus and Juliet*	1562	140–2	3.110, 3.112 3.115
Carr, John *The Ruinous fal*	1573	115	3.69
Castiglione, Baldassare: *The Courtyer*	1561	217	3.198,3.199
Cawdrey, Robert. *A Treatise or Storehouse*	1600	191	3.168
Chapman, George *Hymnus in Noctem*	1594	–	2.53
Churchyard, Thomas *Chvrchyards Challenge*	1593	91	3.33
—— *A Wished Reformation*	1598	218	3.201
Cicero *Marcus Ciceroes thre bookes* (Grimalde)	1553	9–10, 263, 264	1.14, 3.260
—— *The thre bookes* (Whytinton)	1553	8–9	1.13,1.17
Clayton, Giles *The Approved order*	1591	178	3.155

		pp.	notes
Davies, Sir John *Nosce Teipsum*	1599	4–5	1.7
Donne, John *The Ectacy*		–	1.15,1.24
—— *The First Anniversary*	1611	–	3.193
Draxe, Thomas *The Worldes Resurrection*	1608	82–3	3.21
Elyot, Sir Thomas *the Gouernour*	1531	19, 19–20	1.29,1.31
Eramus *Enchiridion (trans Tyndale?)*	1534	1–2, 24	1.2
—— *The Praise of Folly (Chaloner)*	1549	16,263,264	1.25,3.261
Fenton, Geoffrey *tragicall discourses*	1567	141, 173–4	3.81,3.107 3.111, 3.145, 3.225
Ferne, Sir John *The Blazon of Gentrie*	1586	80	3.16,3.26
Fletcher, Giles (the Younger) *Christs victorie*	1610	–	2.27
Floyd, Thomas *The Picture*	1600	116	3.76
Freeman, Thomas *Rubbe and a great Cast*	1614	–	3.179
Fulke, William *A Godly and Learned Sermon*	1580	19	1.30
Gascoigne, George *The Droome*	1576	–	1.44
Godskall, James *The King's Medicine*	1604	227	3.212
Googe, Barnabe *Eglogs, Epytaphes*	1563	23	1.42
Greville, Fulke *Mustapha (Tragedy)*	c1595	–	2.36
Guilpin, Everard *Skialethia*	1598	–	1.15
Holland, Henry *A Treatise*	1590	216	3.197
Homilies *Certayne sermons, or homilies*	1547	25–6, 27–8	1.47, 1.48
	1563	240	
Hooker, Richard *Of the lawes*	1594 –7	–	1.28,1.49 App.1.7
Horace: *Epistles*		–	2.17
—— *Epodes*		–	1.41
Howard, Henry *A Defensatiue*	1593	22	1.39
Humphrey, Laurence *The Nobles*	1563	235	3.221
Hurault, Jaques *Politicke, Moral. . . Discourses*	1595	238	3.225
James I (of England) *Daemonologie . . . Edin.*	1597	216	3.196
Jones, John *The Arte and Science*	1579	–	1.19
Leighton, Sir William: *Vertue Triumphant*	1603	151	3.119
L'Espine, Jean de *A Very excellent . . . Discourse*	1592	–	3.80

		pp.	notes
Lloyd, Lodowick *The Consent of Time*	1590	115	3.70
Lok, Henry *Sundry Christian Passions*	1597	2	1.3
Mavericke, Radford *Saint Peters Chaine*	1596	20	1.34
More, Sir George *A Demonstration of God*	1597	4, 17–18, 116	1.6,1.27,3.75
Nashe, Thomas *Christ's Teares*	1593	2–3	1.4
Nenna, Giovanni Battista *Nennio*	1595	–	3.26
Norden, John *Vicissitudo Rerum*	1600	–	1.15
Painter William *The Palace of Pleasure*	1566	7, 115–6 151, 173	1.11, 2.40, 3.34, 3.74, 3.107, 3.118, 3.144
Palmer, Sir Thomas *An Essay of the Meanes*	1606	–	3.135
Perkins, William *A Treatise*	1607	–	3.41
Pettie, George *A pettie Pallace*	1576	14	1.22,1.23 3.107.3.116
Pope Innocent III *De Contemptu: (H. Kerton)*	1576	24	1.44
Rogers, Thomas *The Anatomie*	1576	6, 12, 115	1.9, 1.18, 2.14, 3.71
Sansovino, Francesco *The Quintessence*	1590	160	3.127
Scot, Reginald *The discouerie*	1584	216–17	1.26
Sparke, Thomas *A Sermon . . . at Whaddon*	1593	–	1.51
Spenser, Edmund *Complaints*	1591	–	3.193
Stafford, Antony *Meditations*	1612	–	3.265
Stockwood, John *A Sermon*	1578	–	3.179
Sutton, Christopher *Disce Mori*	1600	236	3.223
Topsell, Edward *Times lamentation*	1599	13	1.20
Tuke, Thomas *The Trve Trial*	1607	10–11	1.16
Vaughan, William *The Golden Grove*	1600 (1608)	191	3.169
Webbe, George *A Posie*	1610	3	1.5
Whetstone, George *The Censure*	1587	115	3.72
Whitney, Geffrey *A Choice of Emblemes*	(1586)	–	3.75

2 *Shakespeare's Plays*

(a) Titles

All's Well that Ends Well, 87, 88–91, 92, 138, 252, 254, 256, n.3.146, n.3.180

Antony and Cleopatra, 127, 138, 142, 147, 170, 172, 215, 232, 235–52, 253, 256, 257, n.3.87

As You Like It, 76–7, 204, 253, 255, 263, n.3.147, n.3.147, n.3.209

Comedy of Errors(The), 73, 74, 100, 253, 258

Coriolanus, 126–38, 240, 251, 253, 268, n.3.66, n.3.101, n.3.134

Cymbeline, 259, 260, 268, 269, n.3.149, n.3.255

Hamlet, 100, 138, 147, 148–72, 172–3, 199, 204, 215, 219, 232, 252, 262, 263, n.3.135, n.3.171, n.3.223, n.3.247, n.3.257

Julius Caesar, 116, 117, 119, 120, 127, 128, 131, 133, 170, 215, 235, 253, n.3.66, n.3.93, n.3.231

King Henry the Fifth, 109, 112, 115, 116, 170, n.3.63

King Henry the Fourth (Part 1), 70, 89, 109, 112

King Henry the Fourth (Part 2), 109, 110

King John, 102, 102–3, 104, 115, 199, 207

King Lear, 93, 138, 147, 198–215, 215, 232, 254, n.3.206

King Richard the Second, 62, 104–9, 110, 113, 115, 215, 235, 253

King Richard the Third, 102, 103, 104, 114, 150

Love's Labour's Lost, 69–73, 86, 253, n.2.41

Macbeth, 53, 74, 108, 127, 138, 145, 172, 199, 201, 215–35, 252, 263, 269, 277, 282, n.3.56, n.3.78

Measure for Measure, Introd. ix, 5, 87, 91–100, 138, 213, 254, 256, 258, n.2.41, n.3.6, n.3.146

Merchant of Venice (The), 70, 79–85, 254, 279

Merry Wives of Windsor (The), 111, 174, 204, 253

Midsummer Night's Dream (A), 75–6, 247, 253

Much Ado About Nothing, 85–7, 144, 254, 256, n.3.6

Othello, 58, 86, 104, 138, 147, 171, 172–98, 199, 201, 202 212, 215, 232, 282, n.3.145, n.3.146, n.3.149, n.3.156, n.3.163

Pericles, 257, 257–8, 259, 260, 261, 262, 268, 269, n.3.255

Romeo and Juliet, 94, 123, 138, 140–8, 148, 149, 150, 152, 172, 232, 256, 257, n.3.87, n.3.163

Taming of the Shrew (The), 75

Tempest (The), 261–7, 269–70,
n.3.255
Timon of Athens, 113–14, 258,
268, 269, n.3.82
Titus Andronicus, 102
Troilus and Cressida, 116, 119–26,
131, 138, 180, 215, 251, 253,
256, n.3.66, n.3.82, n.3.87,
n.3.102, n.3.146
Twelfth Night, 76, 77–9, 80, 204,
254, 255, 262, 269
Two Gentlemen of Verona (The),
73, 74–5, 253, 259

Winter's Tale (The), 188–9, 258,
259–61, 261, 269, n.3.184,
n.3.209, n.3.250, n.3.255

(b) Characters

Achilles, 121, 123, n.3.102
Aegeon, 74
Albany (Duke of), 201, 202, 205,
213, 214, n.3.206
Alcibiades, 113
Alonso (King of Naples), 265, 266
Angelo, 93, 94, 95–7, 98, 99, 213
Antiochus, 258
Antonio (*Mer. of Ven.*), 80, 80–1,
82, 83, 84, 85
Antonio (*Tempest*), 262, 265, 266
Antony (*Ant. & Cl.*), 79, 117, 118,
119, 129, 134, 235–51 (*passim*),
n.3.226
Antony (*Jul. Caesar*), 118, 119, 239,
n.3.93
Apemantus, 113, 114, 126
Ariel, 265, 266
Arthur, 103, 199
Audrey, 76, 77, 133, n.3.147
Aufidius, 129, 133–4, 137, n.3.157
Aumerle, 106, 107

Balthasar, 143
Banquo, 219, 219–20, 221, 227,
232, 233
Barnadine, 99, n.3.47
Bassanio, 80, 81, 82, 85
Bastard (Philip the), 103, 207
Bates, 112
Beatrice, 45, 75, 86, 201, 256

Belch (Sir Toby), 79
Benedick, 75, 85, 86, 201, 256
Berowne, 70, 71, 85
Bertram, 88, 89, 256
Bianca, 197
Bishop of Carlisle, 106, 107
Bolingbroke (Henry), 104, 105,
107, 239
Bottom, 75, 76
Brabantio, 86, 175
Brutus, (*J. Caesar*), 117, 117–18,
119, 133, 235, 236, 239, n.3.78,
(*Cor.*), 133
Burgundy (Duke of), 203
Bushey, 107

Caesar (Julius), 117, 118, 119
Caesar (Octavius), 235–51 (*passim*)
Caliban, 262, 265, 266
Camillo, 260
Canidius, 242–3
Captain (Norwegian), 165
Capulet, 143, 144, 145–6
Capulet (Lady), 143
Cassandra, 122
Cassio, 180, 181, 182, 183, 184,
188, 190, 191, 194, 196
Cassius, 117–18, 119, 235
Celia, n.3.147
Cerimon, 258
Charmian, 250, 250–1
Chorus, 112
Citizen (First), 127, Second Citizen,
127
Claudio (*M. for M.*), 5, 93, 94, 95,
96, 97, 98–9, n.3.47
Claudio (*M. Ado*), 85, 86, n.3.22
Claudius (King), 87, 150–170
(*passim*), n.3.173
Cleon, 258
Cleopatra, 235–51 (*passim*),
n.3.231
Cloten, 259
Clown (*All's Well*), 89
Cominius, 131, 134
Cordelia, 198–214 (*passim*)
Coriolanus, Introd.x, 84, 126–38
(*passim*), 240, n.3.99, n.3.134,
n.3.157
Cornwall (Duke of), 202, 205, 206

Costard, 71, 72
Cressida, 120–6 (*passim*),

de Boys, n.3.209
Demetrius, 237
Desdemona, 69, 75, 143, 166, 175–
    96 (*passim*), 202, 203, n.3.133,
    n.3.162, n.3.163
Diana, 88, 91
Diomedes, 124
Dionyza, 258
Doctor (*Macbeth*), 230
Dogberry, 72, 75, 87, n.3.93
Dolabella, 248–9
Duke and Senators (*Othello*), 175,
    176, 177, 178
Duncan (King of Scotland), 217,
    219, 221, 222, 223, 224, 225,
    227, 231, 232, 233, 234

Edgar, 199, 200, 201, 205, 207,
    211, 214, n.3.181
Edmund, 199, 200, 201, 204–5,
    205, 206, 207, 211, 213, 214, 226
Elbow, 94, 95
Emilia, 167, 188, 192, 193, 196
Enobarbus, 134, 238, 241, 242,
    243, 244, 247, 252, n.3.226
Eros, 244
Escalus, 92, 93, 94, 95
Escalus (Prince), 144

Falstaff, Introd.x, 70, 75, 89, 109,
    110, 110–11, 204, n.3.47
Ferdinand (King of Navarre), 72
Ferdinand. (*Tempest*), 177, 263,
    264, 266
Flavius, 113
Florizel, 261
Fluellen, 112
Fool (The) (*Lear*), 209–10
Ford, 174
Fortinbras, 153, 165, 170
France (King of) (*All's Well*), 88, 89,
    91, (*Lear*), 203
Francis (Friar), 144
Frederick (Duke), n.3.209
Froth, 94

Gardener, 109
Gaunt (John of), 105
Gertrude (Queen), 163, 166, 170
Ghost (of Hamlet's father), 150,
    154, 159, 164
Gloucester (Earl of), 199, 200, 201,
    206, 206–7, 211, 211–12, 212,
    254, n.3.181
Gobbo, 70, 85, 87
Goneril, 201, 203, 205, 206, 207,
    207–8, 208, 211, 213, 214,
    n.3.174, n.3.206
Gower (as Chorus), 258
Grave-diggers, 167
Green, 107
Guildenstern, 156, 168, 169

Hal (Prince), 72, 109, 110, 111, 117
Hamlet, 114, 136, 148–172
    (*passim*), 221, 227, 244, 248,
    251, 263, n.3.173
Hecate, 228
Hector, 122, 123
Helena, 88, 89, 256
Helicanus, 258
Henry the Fourth, 109, 239
Henry the Fifth, 72, 109, 110, 112,
    117
Hermione, 188–9, 260, n.3.241
Hero, 85, 86, n.3.22
Hippolyta, 75
Horatio, 154, 159, 160–1, 164,
    167, 168, 168–9, 169, 170
Hotspur, 89, 122, 238, 244, 256

→ Iago, 65, 147, 167, 177, 178, 178–
    9, 179–80, 181, 182, 184–7, 188,
    189, 190–1, 192, 193, 196, 204,
    205, 206, 226, 232, 255, 274,
    n.3.146, n.3.162
Imogen, 259
Iras, 250
Isabella, 94, 95–7, 98–9, 213, 258

Jaquenetta, 71
Jessica, 81–2, 83
John (Friar), 146
John (King), 103
Juliet, 140–8 (*passim*), 245, 247,
    251, 257, 261

Katherina (*Shrew*), 75
Katherine (Princess), 112
Kent (Earl of), 199, 201, 203, 205, 214

Laertes, 153, 155, 164, 166–7, 167, 170
Lafeu, 89, 206, n.3.28
Launce, 75
Lawrence (Friar), 143, 144, 146
Lear, 83, 125, 198–215 (*passim*), 251, n.3.174, n.3.184
Leonato, 37, 85–6, n.3.22
→Leontes, 260, 261, n.3.209
Lodovico, 191
'Lodowick' (Friar), 95, n.3.47
Lord (Second) (*All's Well*), 90 (*Coriolanus*), 137
Lorenzo, 81–2, 83
Lucio, 93, 94, 99

Macbeth, 108, 125, 137, 207, 213, 215–35 (*passim*), 239, 251, 264, 274, n.3.56, n.3.78, n.3.206
Macbeth (Lady), 53, 219, 222–33 (*passim*), 224, 225, 230, 231, 232, 239, 241, 264, 282, n.3.206, n.3.231
Macduff, 217, 228, 229, 231
Macduff (Lady), 229, 233, 234
Malcolm, 217, 221, 229
Malvolio, 76, 78–9, 204, 256
Marcius (Young), 135
Mardian, 245
Maria, 79
Mariana, 99
Marina, 258
Menas, 239, n.3.226
Menenius, 128, 129, 134, 137
Mercutio, 141, 143
Miranda, 177, 263, 264, 265, 266

Nurse (*Romeo and Juliet*), 94, 123, 143

Oberon, 75
Octavia, 238, 242
Olivia, 76, 77, 78, 79, 204
Ophelia, 153, 156, 157, 159, 166, 167, 170, 201, n.3.223

Orlando, 77, 256, n.3.147
Orsino, 78, 80
Osric, 169
Othello, 69, 75, 125, 137, 143, 172–198 (*passim*), 202, 203, 204, 205, 247, 251, 261, 282, n.3.133, n.3.162, n.3.163
Overdone (Mistress), 93

Pandarus, 123, 125, 126
Paris (*Romeo and Juliet*), 143, 146
Paris (*Troilus and Cressida*), 122
Parolles, Introd.x, 89–91, 97, 136, 256, n.3.28
Patroclus, 121
Paulina, 260
Pedro (Don), n.3.22
Perdita, 260, 261, n.3.184, n.3.209
Pericles, 258,
Petruchio, 75
Philo, 237
Pistol, 112
Players (*Hamlet*), 158, 160, 165
Plebians (*Coriolanus*), 131
Polixenes, 260, n.3.184, n.3.241
Polonius, 72, 150, 153, 159, 163–4, 165, 170, 244
Pompey (*Antony and Cleopatra*), 238, 238–9, 239, n.3.226
Pompey (*Measure for Measure*), 93, 94, 99
Portia (*Julius Caesar*), n.3.231
Portia (*Merchant of Venice*), 81, 82, 83–4
Posthumus, 259, n.3.149
Princess of France (*Love's Labour's Lost*), 70, 71, 72
Proculeius, 248
Prospero, 261–6 (*passim*)
Proteus, 75
Provost (*Measure for Measure*), 99
Puck, 76
Pyramus (and Thisbe), 76

Regan, 201, 203, 205, 206, 207, 207–8, 208, 209, 211, 213, 214, n.3.174
Richard the Second, 104–9 (*passim*), 110, 117, 200, 226

Richard the Third, 102, 201, 205, 226, 239
Roderigo, 178–9, 180, 182, 183, 193, 194, 196
Romeo, 140–8 (*passim*), 245, 247, 251, 257, 261
Rosalind, 77, 81, n.3.147
Rosaline, 71
Rosencrantz, 156, 162, 168, 169

Salerio, 80
Scroop, 107
Sebastian (*Tempest*), 262, 265, 266, (*Twelfth Night*), 77, 78
Second Lord (*All's Well*), 90, (*Coriolanus*), 137
Senator (First), 131
Seyton, 230
Shallow, 111
Shylock, 80, 81, 82–5
Sicinius, 130–1, 133
Siward (Young), 231
Solanio, 80
Stephano, 265

Thaisa, 258
Thersites, 120, 126, 181
Theseus (Duke), 75

Thyreus, 243
Timon, 113, 114
Titania, 75, 76
Touchstone, 76, 77, 256, n.3.147
Tribunes (*Coriolanus*), 129, 130–1, 133, 134, n.3.157
Trinculo, 265
Troilus, Introd.x, 120–6 (*passim*), 129, n.3.99
Tybalt, 141, 143

Ulysses, 121, 122, 123, 130, 134, n.3.102

Valeria, 135
Vincentio (Duke), 92, 93, 96, 97, 98, 99
Viola ('Cesario'), 77, 78, 81
Virgilia, 135
Volumnia, 130, 131–3, 134, 135, 241, n.3.231

Williams, 112
Witches (*Macbeth*), 219, 220, 221, 227, 228, 229, 231, 232
Worcester (Earl of), 238

York (Duke of), 105, 107

3 Non-Shakespearean Plays: Titles

Abraham and Isaac, 31, n.3.254
Albion Knight, 39–40
Alchemist (The), 57, 58
All for Money, 38–9, 279–80, n.Introd.l, App.1, 19
Antonie (The Tragedie of), 236–7, 239, n.3.242
Antonio and Mellida, 50, 55, n.2.38
Antonio's Revenge, 50, 55, 151, n.2.39
Arden of Feversham, 47
Atheist's Tragedy (The), 51, 152

Bussy d'Ambois, 54, 54–5, 64, n.2.44, n.2.45
Bussy d'Ambois (The Revenge of), 55, 64, 152, n.2.44

Caesar and Pompey, 56, 236, n.2.44
Castle of Perseverance (The), 32–3
Cataline His Conspiracy, 65, n.2.50
Certaine Devises and Shewes (see: *The Misfortunes of Arthur*)
Chabot, Admiral of France, 56, 64, n.2.44, n.2.49
Changeling (The), 53
Charles, Duke of Byron (The Conspiracy and Tragedy of), 54, 55, 55–6, 64, n.2.44, n.2.46, n.2.47, n.2.48
Chief Promises of God unto Man (The), 42
Cleopatra (The Tragedie of), 240, n.3.242
Cupid's Revenge, 52

Cynthia's Revenge, 52–3

Damon and Pythias, 218, n.3.200
Disobedient Son (or Child) (The), 37
Duchess of Malfi, 51–2, 114, 152

Edward the Second, 62, 63, 277
Edward the Third, 61–2, 98–9
Endymion, 16
Englishmen for my Money, 44, n.2.28
Everyman, 35, 201
Every Man in His Humour (Eng. version), 57–8, n.2.50, n.2.51, n.2.52
Every Man Out of His Humour, 58

Fair Em, n.3.15
Faithful Shepherdess (The), 46, 78
Faustus (Doctor), 35, 227, Appendix 1, n.3.132
Four P's (The), n.2.23
Friar Bacon and Friar Bungay, 77–8

Gammer Gurton's Needle, 73, 87, n.2.23
Gentleman Usher (The), 54, n.2.44
Godly Queene Hester, 39
Gorboduc (Ferrex and Porrex), 40–1, 198, 202, 217, n. 3.175
Green's Tu Quoque, 45–6, n.2.31

Humorous Day's Mirth (An), n.2.50
Hycke Scorner, 38

Impatient Poverty, 38

Jack Juggler, n.2.23
Jack Straw, 63, n.3.93
James IV, 62
Jew of Malta (The), 49, 82
Johan Johan, 37, n.2.23, n.2.31
Johan the Evangelist, n.2.25
John Baptist's Preaching, 41–2
John (King of England), 102–3
John, King of England (Bale), 42–3, 103, n.Introd.1

Knight of the Burning Pestle (The), n.2.31

Leir (King), 198, 204
Like Will to Like, 38
Locrine, 63–4
Love's Sacrifice, n.3.164
Lusty Juventus, 36–7

Malcontent (The), 114, n.3.156
Mankind, 33
Merry Devil of Edmonton (The), n.2.31
Mind, Will and Understanding (see: *Wisdom*)
Miseries of Inforst Marriage, 48
Misfortunes of Arthur (The), 61, n.2.57, n.2.58, n.3.211
Misogonus, 37–8, n.2.29
Mucedorus, n.3.15

Nature, 34–5, 35, n.2.7
New Way to Pay Old Debts (A), 44–5, n.2.30
Nice Wanton, 37

Old Fortunatus, n.3.63

Pardoner and the Friar (The), 41
Philaster, 46, 56, 258
Poetaster (The), 58
Promos and Cassandra, n.3.35
Ralph Roister Doister, n.2.23

Rare Triumphs of Love and Fortune, n.3.73
Respublica, 40, n. Introd.l, n.2.22
Revenger's Tragedy (The), 50–1, 114, 151
Roaring Girl (The), n.2.31

Scornful Lady (The), 48–9
Sejanus His Fall, 65, 217
Shoemaker's Holiday (The), n.2.31, n.3.93
Sir Thomas More, 60–1, 217, n.2.56, n.3.93
Spanish Tragedy (The), 49, 151, 154, 161

Tamburlaine the Great (Part 1), 271, 272–3
Tamburlaine the Great (Part 2), 271
Temptacyon of our lorde . . . Jesus Christ (The), 42
Thersites, n.2.23
Thre Lawes, 42
Tom Tyler and His Wife, 41, n.2.23
Two Angry Women of Abingdon (The), n.2.31
Two Noble Kinsmen (The), 46–7, n.2.35
Tyde Taryeth No Man, 41

Volpone, or the Fox, 58–9, 114

Wealth and Health, 40
White Devil (The), 51–2, 223
Widow's Tears (The), 48, 114
Wisdom (Mind, Will and Understanding), 33, 33–4, 35, n.2.6
Woman Killed with Kindness (A), 47, 152, 174, n.3.265
Woodstock, 63

Yorkshire Tragedy (A), 47–8, n.2.36, n.2.42
Youth, 36, 38

4 General

Arcadia (The) (Sidney), 16, 258
Aristotle (*Nichomachean Ethics*),
    7–8, 11–12, 21, 59–60, n.2.54
Audiences (Elizabethan), 43–4, 68–
    9, 144, 198–9, 216–17
Audience reaction, Introd.ix, 30–1,
    50, 51, 68–9, 126–7, 171–2

Bias (philosopher), 60
Boccaccio (*Decameron*), n.3.34

'Chain-reaction', Introd.ix, 138–9,
    145, 207
Chapman (G.), *Hymnus in Noctem*,
    n.2.53
Character and plot, 74, 82–4, 85,
    85–6
'Character-in-situation', Introd.ix,
    139, 144–5, 155, 163, 165, 252,
    254, 257
Characters, 84, 135–6
Chaucer (G.), *The Knight's Tale*,
    n.2.35; *The Legend of Good
    Women*, 235; *Troilus and
    Cressida*, 115, 120
Cicero, De Officiis, 7, 8–11, 21
Cinthio (G.G.), *Epitia*, 92, n.3.35;
    Gli Hecatommithi, n.3.148
Claudian, 21
Comedy and tragedy, Introd.ix, 68,
    83, 158, 190, App.2
Comedy (Restoration), n.3.20
Comus (Milton), 56
Conflict (Human), and creative
    writing, Introd.vii–viii; and
    dramatic writing, Introd.viii–ix;
    and early religious drama, 30–1;
    in comedy and tragedy, 68, App.2

Conflict (Human) (forms of):
    Freedom-Fate, 5, 41, 145, ‹
    n.3.100; Greatness-Littleness, 3–
    5, 44–5, 157, 248; Immortal-
    Mortal (Death), 2–3, 35, 71, 79,
    88, 98–9, 101–2, 108, 148, 153,
    157, 167, 172, 237, 245, 248,
    257, 261, n.3.47, Age-Youth,
    Romeo and Juliet (passim), 261;
    Justice-Mercy, 26–8, 42, 83–4,
    94, 95–6, 279, n.3.39, Law(The),
    27–8; Order–Disorder, Introd.x.
    24–6, 42, 60, 63–4, 87–8, 93,
    111–12, 121, 128, 141–2, 205,
    206, 217, 227, n.1.49, n.2.55,
    n.3.48, In the State, 217, 226–7,
    240; Private Man – Public Man,
    Introd.x, 18–24, 42–3, 59–60,
    61–3, 64, 72, 87–8, 93, 96, 101,
    104, 105, 108, 109, 117, 117–18,
    127–8, 131, 155, 157–8, 162,
    174, 182, 191–2, 200, 203, 207,
    217, 226, 233, 240–1, 261, 266,
    n.1.28, n.3.48, Social effects,
    104–5, 217; Reason-Fantasy, 16–
    8, 76, 77, 79, 90, 106, 108, 111,
    126, 141, 192, 195–6, 203, 204,
    207, 209–10, 211, 212, 213,
    220–1, 222, 230, 231, 233, 237,
    237–8, 244, 255–6, 257, 267,
    n.3.17, n.3.147, 'Honour',
    Introd.x, 70, 89–90, 122, 124,
    132, 165, n.3.89, n.3.99; Reason-
    Love (Man-Woman), 12–16, 45–
    6, 48–9, 69–71, 75, 78, 80, 81,
    82, 86, 120, 147, 236, 266–7,
    n.3.15, Jealousy, 15–16, 57–8,
    172–198 *passim*, 185–7, 188,

261; Reason-Unreason, Introd.x,
5–12, 34–5, 35–8, 47–58, 72, 79,
81, 83, 86, 87–8, 94, 96, 118,
119, 120, 122, 130, 131, 133,
141–2, 151, 154, 172, 188, 203,
204, 222, 234, 237, 242, 244,
246, 255, 257, n.3.41, In the
family, 36–8, In society, 9–11, 38,
48, 52, 58–9, In the State (the
ruler), 10–11, 39–41, 93, 109–
110, 133; Soul – Body, 1–2, 33–4,
App.1 (*passim*), n.1.3
Conflict ('social'), Introd.x–xi, 138,
n.Introd.1, n.3.51

Dangerous Corner (Priestley), 184
Death and tragedy, 35, 146, 215
Decameron (Boccaccio), n.3.34
De Contemptu Mundi, 5, 24, 98,
248, 263, n.1.44
De Officiis (Cicero), 7, 8–11, 21
Dispensation (The Old-The New),
27, 52, 84, n.3.46, n.App.1.10
Donne (John), 48, 59, *The Ectacy,*
n.1.15, n.1.24, *The First
Anniversary,* n.3.193
Dostoievsky (F.M.) Raskolnikov
(*Crime and Punishment*), 188
'Doubling' of parts, n.3.190
Drama ('simple'), 73
'Dramatic metaphor', n.3.181
Dunciad (Pope), n.2.53

Ectacy (The) (Donne), n.1.15,
n.1.24
Elizabeth (Queen), 64, 101, 115,
218, 241–2
Elizabethan attitudes, bastards,
207, 'borderline' living, 79,
buffoonery, 274, charity, 211,
class-distinctions, 71–2, 110,
Classical history, 115, Cleopatra,
235–6, cowardice, 89, cynical
'realism', 81–2, 114, 123, death,
2–3, disorder, 25, 26, 60–1, 111–
2, 142, 206, 217, 226, duelling,
141, education, 36, n.2.14,
Elizabeth (Queen), 64, 101, 218,
fantasy, 16, feeling without

reason, 49, 71, 179, Fool (the),
199, free will, 5, gentlemen in
commerce, 80, ghosts, 159, 164,
227, 'great ones', 191, 198, 206–
7, history, 59, human nature, 44,
257, jealousy, 15–6, 173–4, Jews,
82–3, law, 27, life, 44, 79, 264,
love, 13–5, 48, 78, 80, 120, 255,
n.3.20, love 'romance', 76, 87,
lust, 13, Machiavelli, 132, 179,
206, n.1.19, n.3.108, n.3.179,
'malcontent' (the), 178,
melodrama, 170, 199, mob (the),
25, 63, 128, patriotism, 103,
peace, 217; perversion of the
good, 183, 'philosophical'
comments ('sentences'), 8, 152,
n.3.38, political folly, 202,
priests, 114, n.3.115, private and
public life, 22–3, reason without
feeling, 12, 47, 71, 179, 197,
205–6, 255, n.1.19, revenge,
151–2, right living, 9, ruler(the),
162, sexual disease, 125, sin and
repentance, 277, 278, stage
excitement, 170, 170–1, 198,
200, 216, 260, 262, 271, suicide,
236–7, supernatural, 145, 227,
transience of the world, 212,
n.3.193, tyrants, 218,
unnaturalness, 175, 205, 208,
unreason and anarchy, 59,
n.2.53, usury, usurers, 17, n.3.17,
violence, 234, 'wit', 120, 153,
'wit'-'will', 7, 228, witches and
witchcraft, 216–7, 219, 220, 227,
women, 13, 14–15, 71, 236,
worldly success, 23–4
Endymion (John Lyly), 16
Epilogues, 76, 125–6, 258, 262,
267, irony in, 112–13
Epitia (Cinthio), 92, n.3.35
Essex revolt, 101, 239–40
→Evil, 177–8, 179, 183, 201, 214,
222, 233, App.1 (*passim*)

Faerie Queene (Spenser), 16
Fate and chance, 145–6, 170, 221,
n.3.100
First Anniversary (Donne), n.3.193

Gli Hecatommithi (Cinthio),
n.3.148
Goldilocks and the Three Bears, 73–4
Greville (Fulke), 55, n.2.36

'Hammer-blow' sequences, 107,
n.3.57
History in drama, 59–65, 100–2
Homilies, 25–6, 27–8, 42, 63, 217,
240, n.1.47, n.1.48
Horace, Epistles, n.2.17, Epodes,
n.1.41
Hymnus in Noctem (Chapman),
n.2.53

Innocent III (Pope), 24
Irony, 7, 16, 40, 47, 53, 55, 60, 65,
70, 75, 77, 83, 91, 94, 96, 99,
101, 111, 112, 117, 118, 119,
121, 122–3, 124, 126, 128, 129,
130, 131, 133, 136, 137, 139,
144, 145, 146, 153, 162, 163,
164, 167, 169, 170, 180, 182,
189, 192, 193–4, 196, 208, 214,
219, 221, 234, 240, 241, 242,
243–4, 246, 263, 280, n.3.47,
n.3.78, n.3.89, n.3.156, of play-
endings, 112–13, 119, 170, 214,
232, tragic, 169, 176, 184, 224,
230, 274, 275, 278
Irreconcilables, 27, 124–5, 189,
193, 195, 203, 210, 223

James I, 218, 242

Knight's Tale (Chaucer), n.2.35

Legend of Good Women (Chaucer),
235
Life (public and private), 22–3
'Logic of effect' (dramatic), 263
Lyly (John), *Endymion,* 16

Machiavelli, 132, 179, 206, n.l.19,
n.3.108, n.3.179
Macro Plays, n.2.2, n.2.4, n.2.6
Madness, 53, 166, 189, 203, 210,
212, 213
Magic, 266, App.1 (*passim*)
'Man-in-history', 109, 127

Marx Brothers, 77
Metamorphoses (Ovid), n.2.42,
n.3.225
Milton (John), *Comus,* 56, *Samson
Agonistes,* 215
Modern relevances, Introd.xii, 5, 9,
12, 14, 28, 31, 36, 49, 59, 60, 68,
71, 79, 80, 95, 121, 130, 131,
147, 183, 198, 206, 208, 229,
231, 234–5, 257, 267, 275, 280,
n.2.22, n.3.67, n.3.264
Morality plays, 31–5, 36–43, 258
'Morality (social)', 36, 38, 40, 43

Neoptolemus, n.3.124
Nichomachean Ethics (Aristotle),
7–8, 11–12, 21, 59–60, n.2.54

Opening scenes, 92
Ovid (*Metamorphoses*), n.2.42,
n.3.225

Papists, 36, 42, 42–3
Paris, n.3.124
Petrarch, 13, 48
Petronius, 48
Plato, 8, 20
Plautine comedy, 73
Plutarch ('*Lives*'), 116, 126, 136,
237, 238, 241, 242, 244, 246,
n.3.77
Poetry (Shakespeare's), 77, 87, 99,
106, 139–40, 147, 148, 158, 171,
187, 192–3, 195, 199, 200, 208,
213, 223, 224, 224–5, 225, 230–1, 245, 246–7, 248–9, 251, 255,
259, 262, 263, 264, 268
Pope (*The Dunciad*), n.2.53
Power (fitness for), 8, 21–2, 39, 42–3, 93, 100, 110, 115, 226 (see
also: *Lear, Macbeth, Measure for
Measure passim*)
Priam, n.3.124
Priestley (J.B.), *Dangerous Corner,*
184
Prose (Elizabethan), 26, Jonson, 58
Prose (Shakespeare's), 77, 87, 139–40, 148, 171, 199
Proverbs (Elizabethan), n.1.33,
n.1.46, n.1.51, n.2.14, n.3.40
Pyrrhus, 158, n.3.124

Raskolnikov (Dostoievsky), 188
Reason (the 'higher'), 6, 38, 97, 161,
    267, 272, 276, 277–8, n.1.15,
    n.2.6; (the 'lower'), 48, 52, 57,
    65, 88, 90, 102, 111, 130, 161,
    167, 205, 226, 238, 250, 252,
    266, 267, 272, 275, 276, 277,
    278, 279, n.2.6, n.3.9, n.3.147,
    n.3.226
'Reported' scenes, 225, 260,
    n.3.209
Revenge, 151–2, 155–6, 172–3,
    197, n.3.265
'Ruines of Time' (Spenser), n.3.193

Samson Agonistes (Milton), 215
'Semi-soliloquies', 154
'Senecan (Stoic) Man', 55 *et seq.*,
    161
Shakespeare and the critic,
    Introd.xi–xii, 148, dramatic
    language, 139–40, 'growth' of,
    149, 252, 262, and the modern
    theatre, Introd.xii, Sonnets, 246,
    n.3.244
Shaw (G.B.), 71
Sidney (Sir Philip), *The Arcadia*, 16,
    258
Society, Order-Disorder, 24–6,
    Reason-Unreason, 9–11, 38, 48,
    52, 58–9
Spenser (Edmund), *Faerie Queene*,
    16, 'Ruines of Time', n.3.193
Stage-action and character, 163,

191, 209, n.3.133
Supernatural (the), 145, 227, magic,
    App.1 (*passim*)

Tarquin, 225
'Tempi' of plays, 150, 169, 172,
    191, 232
'Three-fold vision', 69
Time, 142–3, 169, 187, 193, 260,
    n.3.163
'Tragedy-in-comedy', 85
Tragedy ('positive' and 'negative'),
    172
'Tragic melodramas', 53
Tragic victims (secondary), 62, 156,
    197, 229, 233
Troilus and Cressida (Chaucer),
    115, 120

'Universal phrase' (the), 246
Usury (usurers), 17, n.3.17

Vice (the), 102, 180, 201
Violence, 60, 108, 110, 194, 217,
    218, 223, 233, 234–5, n.3.172

Wilde (Oscar), 281
Will (the), n.3.41
Wit and humour, 70, App. 2
    (*passim*)
Wit and will, 7, 105, 109, 228
Witches and witchcraft, 17, 49,
    216–17, 219–20, 227, 228,
    n.1.26